British Foreign Policy
since Versailles 1919–1963

British Foreign Policy
since Versailles 1919–1963

W. N. MEDLICOTT

Methuen & Co Ltd

11 NEW FETTER LANE · LONDON EC4

First published 1940
Second edition revised and enlarged 1968

© *1968 by W. N. Medlicott*

Printed in Great Britain by
Richard Clay (The Chaucer Press), Ltd.,
Bungay, Suffolk

SBN hard cover edition 416 10770 2
SBN paperback edition 416 29700 5

Distributed in the U.S.A. by
Barnes and Noble Inc

Contents

Preface

The first edition of this little book was published in the summer of 1940, with the modest aim of setting out briefly the essential facts about British foreign policy before the war. Although no historian can write without assumptions and conclusions my aim was as far as possible to allow the facts to speak for themselves. Now the book has been thoroughly revised in the light of the fuller and more accurate information that has become available since the war; and I have added three further chapters bringing the story down to the early nineteen-sixties. It is possible now to see the period in greater perspective, and my conclusions have been revised accordingly. I have benefited greatly from discussions about the subject with friends and colleagues over the years: in particular I wish to thank Mrs Vivian Saule, who read the whole manuscript and made many useful comments.

London School of Economics   W. N. MEDLICOTT
30 August 1967

British Prime Ministers
1916–60

DAVID LLOYD GEORGE	*appointed* 7 December 1916
ANDREW BONAR LAW	23 October 1922
STANLEY BALDWIN	22 May 1923
J. RAMSAY MACDONALD	22 January 1924
STANLEY BALDWIN	4 November 1924
J. RAMSAY MACDONALD	5 June 1929
STANLEY BALDWIN	7 June 1935
NEVILLE CHAMBERLAIN	28 May 1937
WINSTON S. CHURCHILL	10 May 1940
CLEMENT ATTLEE	5 August 1945
WINSTON S. CHURCHILL	27 October 1951
SIR ANTHONY EDEN	6 April 1955
HAROLD MACMILLAN	10 January 1957

British Foreign Secretaries
1916–60

ARTHUR JAMES BALFOUR	*appointed* 11 December 1916
LORD CURZON	24 October 1919
J. RAMSAY MACDONALD	23 January 1924
AUSTEN CHAMBERLAIN	7 November 1924
ARTHUR HENDERSON	8 June 1929
MARQUESS OF READING	26 August 1931
SIR JOHN SIMON	9 November 1931
SIR SAMUEL HOARE	7 June 1935
ANTHONY EDEN	23 December 1935
VISCOUNT HALIFAX	1 March 1938
ANTHONY EDEN	23 December 1940
ERNEST BEVIN	5 August 1945
HERBERT MORRISON	9 March 1951
ANTHONY EDEN	27 October 1951
HAROLD MACMILLAN	7 April 1955
J. SELWYN LLOYD	22 December 1955
EARL OF HOME	27 July 1960

Introduction

At the beginning of our period it was difficult to define the main principles of British foreign policy except by the use of almost meaningless generalities. It was customary to say that Britain's greatest interest was peace; that she had no territorial ambitions on the continent of Europe; that she would fight, nevertheless, to prevent any power from establishing hegemony over the rest of Europe; that she would also fight to defend the dominions, colonies, dependencies, and communications of the British Empire; that she would – in some circumstances – fight to defend small nations from attack; that she would not fight any power merely because she disliked its domestic policy and methods of internal government. But it was not difficult to find recent exceptions to nearly all these rules. Had her policy before 1914 been one of splendid isolation or had she been the policeman of the world, maintaining the *Pax Britannica*? Theory was suspect; principles were considered of doubtful validity in proportion to their need to be defined. In his memoirs, published in 1925, Viscount Grey warned his countrymen against mistakes in foreign policy 'made by a great thinker calculating far ahead, who thinks or calculates wrongly'.

During the twenty years which followed the Peace of Versailles British Governments had nevertheless to think hard about the increasing threat to the country's traditional interests. There had been challenges even before 1914 to the influential position in the economic and political affairs of the world achieved during the nineteenth century, and none of these challenges can be said to have been removed by the First World War. Great Britain's nineteenth-century position had been due to three favourable circumstances. (1) The Industrial Revolution made her the workshop and bank parlour of the world; her own vast empire, and the absence of serious industrialization elsewhere, enabled her to find ample markets for the export of her manufactured goods and employment for her surplus capital. (2) Various conditions – mainly political – delayed the rise of industrial competitors, or the development of strong naval and military forces, in areas which could seriously challenge her economic and territorial interests. (3) This relative absence of serious competition enabled her in turn to advocate, and sometimes to apply, those doctrines of political and economic liberalism which expressed the highest contemporary conception of progress.

This favourable position could not be indefinitely maintained. The United States after 1865, and Germany after 1879, proceeded to build up powerful industrial systems protected by high tariff walls; this enabled them to exclude many British products from their own internal markets, and to compete against her with increasing success in other countries and in the Asiatic field. A 'scramble' to appropriate fresh colonial empires led after 1880 to vast territorial acquisitions by France, Germany, the United States, Italy, Japan, and even by smaller powers; Britain found her own overseas possessions, markets, and communications threatened by the expanding commerce and territories of her new rivals, and was forced, in imitation and in self-defence, into counter-acquisitions, and into counter-concessions whereby she purchased diplomatic support.

Nevertheless her financial and economic position remained fundamentally unshaken in 1914; her great territorial interests lay outside Europe, and the powers which could threaten these interests had causes of rivalry among themselves which ruled out the possibility of serious military danger to the Empire or to Britain's own shores. In spite of growing Anglo-German tension after 1900 the agreements with France (in 1904) and with Russia (in 1907) did not commit her to military intervention in a continental war. The Hay–Pauncefote Agreement of 1901 and Anglo-Japanese Alliance of 1902 guaranteed her position in the Caribbean and the Far East. Nor did any class desire or believe that it could gain economic advantage from war. The apparent paradoxes of Norman Angell's *Great Illusion* (1909) brought home to the layman beliefs strongly held by the business classes. Looking back in 1937 Professor J. H. Clapham wrote in his *Economic History of Modern Britain*: 'The reasonable expectation of the "capitalist" in 1914 was loss of trade, high taxes and, in his family, death; of the wage-earner, death, taxes and unemployment. . . Industrialists as a class were everywhere pacific, merchants and money-handlers even more so.' Moreover, Germany in 1913 was the best foreign buyer of United Kingdom produce and manufactures, and she was anxiously cultivating good political relations.

Yet Britain fought Germany, from mixed motives of fear and exasperation in which ideological factors played a conspicuous part. Growing distrust of Prussian militarism since Bismarck's day added a strong dash of moral indignation to the mixture of anger and apprehension which greeted the German attack on Belgium and France. Trade rivalry was at best a subordinate factor. England only began to be conscious of Germany as a trade rival in the eighteen-eighties, when her distrust of Germany's political methods was already twenty years old. The United States had proved herself, with the McKinley tariff of 1890, an even more dangerous rival in the economic field, but this had not prevented a steady pursuit of political friendship with her by British Governments after 1895.

The restless and melodramatic policy of the Kaiser before 1914 suggested that the German Government had expansionist plans which probably did not exist. On the other hand, the recent writings of Professor Fritz Fischer and others show that in the name of security Bethmann Hollweg, the German Chancellor, intended in the event of victory to destroy France as a great power, to make Belgium a German vassal state, and push Russia as far away from the German frontier as possible. Everything suggests that if Russia and France had been overwhelmed in 1914 while Britain remained neutral, an Anglo-

German struggle for world supremacy would sooner or later have followed.

Victory in 1918 gave Great Britain self-confidence and a sense of security which lasted until 1929. It was recognized that her commitments had greatly increased as compared with the pre-war years. A secret Foreign Office memorandum in April 1926 placed them under the following thirteen heads, in 'relative order of importance', namely, the Covenant of the League of Nations; the Treaty of Versailles; the Washington Treaties; Egypt and the Sudan; the Straits; Abyssinia (under the Tripartite Agreement of 1906); the Hedjaz, Irak, Transjordan, and Arabia; the Persian Gulf; the Anglo-Portuguese Treaties, 1373–1904; the Mediterranean and East Atlantic Agreement, 1907; the North Sea Agreement, 1908; and the Anglo-Chinese Convention of April 1846. The writer took for granted the obligation to defend every part of the Commonwealth and Empire. He wrote:

> We have got all that we want – perhaps more. Our sole object is to keep what we have and live in peace. Many foreign countries are playing for a definite stake and their policy is shaped accordingly. It is not so in our case. To the casual observer our foreign policy may appear to lack consistency and continuity, but both are there. We keep our hands free in order to throw our weight into the scale and on behalf of peace. The maintenance of the balance of power and the preservation of the *status quo* have been our guiding lights for many decades and will so continue.[1]

This remarkable document reveals the yearning for the relatively free hand of the pre-war days; the lack of expansionist aims; the consciousness of greater commitments in the world; and the willingness to honour them if the need to do so was, albeit reluctantly, accepted.

When Germany's revival after 1932 was seen to have produced, not a mere revival of national self-esteem but a permanent 'revolution of destruction' (in Hermann Rauschning's phrase), the development of effective means of resistance was

[1] B.D., Ser. IA, vol. i, pp. 846–81.

delayed by a continued guilt-complex over the Versailles Treaty. In facing this new danger the Government was ahead of opinion in the middle thirties, but it could not, as in the years after 1907, concentrate its main attention on Europe, or even on the North Sea. After 1935 it had to visualize an ultimate threat by Italy in the Mediterranean and by Japan in the Far East. In some quarters too Soviet Russia, in spite of its League membership, was uneasily regarded as the chief danger or at least the chief troublemaker. And although, under the League Covenant, Britain's obligations to help victims of aggression were certainly more definite and extensive than her commitments (virtually limited in Europe to Belgium) had been before 1914, she was for a time prevented, by the strong currents of pacifist and liberal-socialist opinion, from adequate rearmament or from any compromise or bargains with the dissatisfied and aggressive powers. As late as the spring of 1937 the Parliamentary Opposition voted against rearmament proposals and it rejected conscription in May 1939. It continued, however, to demand Government action to 'build up a strong League' and to resist powerful states who were obviously deaf to any argument other than that of force. Britain had no certainty of armed support from any great power except France, and then only in Europe.

Her temporizing role in foreign affairs after 1931 was also influenced by the bewildering tactics and language of the 'dissatisfied' powers (which really seemed too silly at times to be taken literally), and the preoccupation of the political parties at home with the world economic crisis and its aftermath. In the end the problem of reconciling the ideological and realistic aspects of her foreign policy was solved by Nazi diplomacy; after the summer of 1938 it produced in the British people one of its characteristic moods of implacable exasperation, with a conviction of moral justification enormously strengthened by the almost inhuman patience displayed by its leaders in the face of many past affronts. In a more immediate sense it solved the problem of priorities.

Evidence which is now available makes it clear that the

Cabinet and the Foreign Office in the nineteen-thirties never lost sight of the world-wide vulnerability of British interests, and also of the impossibility of effective military action in more than one sphere.[1] In the twenties Japan had been regarded as the most likely enemy against which to calculate the need for naval strength. In 1934 the Cabinet accepted the view of the Defence Requirements Committee that Germany was the chief potential enemy, and after that Japan, but that it would not be possible to quarrel successfully with both. A quarrel with a third power, such as Italy, was even more to be deprecated. Rearmament commences at this point, with first a phase of modernization of existing ships and weapons, and then a phase of heavy expenditure stretching into 1939 to achieve impregnability of defence at sea and in the air; the striking power of the German Air Force was vastly exaggerated. The four main objectives of the armed forces in order of importance were considered to be home defence, the maintenance of lines of communication to Great Britain, the defence and internal security of imperial territories, and the defence of allied countries. The Army was thought of in pre-1914 terms as a small, élite force which could be used for any of the four purposes, but whether any troops could be spared for the fourth seemed for a time doubtful. Although Government spokesmen continued to argue that it was impossible to defy Germany, Italy, and Japan simultaneously their critics were inclined to demand resistance to all aggressors. The threat to imperial possessions from Japan was almost entirely ignored in public discussions. That Germany had made herself the chief bugbear of both Government and Opposition by March 1939 did not lessen the vulnerability of British interests in the Mediterranean and the Far East.

With war imminent in Europe in 1939 the Government introduced conscription and began to raise a large army; rather too much was hoped for from the blockade and the

[1] The best account of the early rearmament effort is M. M. Postan's *British War Production* (1952), chap. 2, and R. Higham's more hostile *Armed Forces in Peacetime* (1962), chap. 6.

weakening of German morale. It would be an undue simplifying of the story to regard British diplomacy after 1933 as due merely to the attempt to postpone foreign crises while rearmament was hurried on; for indeed there was no great hurry. The constant offers of mediation indeed suggest a genuine belief in the possibility of achieving 'appeasement'. The meaning of this word has been so stretched and distorted since 1939 that it is now used to cover almost every manifestation of British diplomacy in the inter-war years short of an ultimatum, and even that would be described by some as 'appeasement through strength'. At the time it meant simply peace, or the search for peace: those who opposed efforts to this end were liable to denunciation as warmongers, actuated by outmoded wartime animosities, lusting for battle. British ministers, from Lloyd George and Austen Chamberlain to Eden and Neville Chamberlain, used the word 'appeasement' from time to time to protest their devotion to peace rather than to describe any specific policy; and since the purpose of all British policy since 1815 is said to be peace, every manifestation of it could be called a search for appeasement. The later practice of using the word mainly as a synonym for surrender to aggression has so confused the story of pre-war diplomacy that it is best nowadays to avoid its use except in direct quotation. This indeed is not difficult.

The Second World War, unlike the First, did solve many problems for Great Britain, and our story ends with a survey of drastic changes in British foreign relations. It is not paradoxical to say that defeat in France in 1940 was necessary in order to release the forces which made ultimate victory possible. The two potential super-powers, Russia and America, were both emotionally involved in the conflict by this stage, although anxious to keep out of it as long as possible. The value of Britain as the front-line fighter of the liberal-democratic world had been advertised by the French collapse; but what was equally clearly advertised was the fact that England alone could not eliminate the Nazi, Fascist, and Japanese aggressors, even if she could stand alone.

From the new alignment of world forces for the temporary purpose of winning the war there resulted far-reaching changes in the balance of influence and power, and in the process Britain herself ceased to rank as one of the world's strongest states. Communism replaced Naziism as the main ostensible threat to the liberal-democratic world after 1945; the real transformation in the world situation was, however, due to America's willingness, after some hesitation, to throw her full power and weight into world politics, starting with the Marshall Plan and the Atlantic Alliance.

British foreign policy underwent some major changes in consequence. The much-quoted comment of Mr Dean Acheson in 1962, 'Britain has lost an empire and not yet found a role', probably tells us more about the author than about the British, although its purpose was to commend the decision to seek entry into the Common Market. Certainly a very important new role was undertaken in the years 1947–9, with three developments particularly marked. The first was to hasten the full self-government of the remaining dependent portions of the British Commonwealth and Empire, but to maintain and develop the existing economic, political, and strategical links between them. The United States and particularly Mr Acheson never liked this policy. The second was the undertaking of formal commitments to defend Europe, within the NATO Alliance, in peacetime, whereas before 1914 there had been only the guarantee of Belgium, and even in the inter-war years before 1939 only the obligations of the Locarno Agreement. The third development was co-operation with, and acceptance of the predominant role of, the United States in the Atlantic Alliance in what some people call a 'special relationship'.

These three overlapping spheres of activity – the Commonwealth, Europe, and the Atlantic – might involve some conflict of loyalties, but they certainly represented some new departures of substance from the traditional course of British foreign policy. Indeed, owing essentially to the greater security represented by American power, Britain was able to undertake far greater commitments in the world than was the case before

1914 or even before 1939. It may, certainly, be asked whether her busy and on the whole successful concentration of attention on these objectives did not result during the nineteen-fifties in some neglect of newer movements, and particularly of the drive for European economic and political integration. The broad conclusion must nevertheless be that the story of British foreign policy since the beginning of the century should be regarded not as one of shrinking power or a shrinking from the use of power but rather of a long process of adaptation to the realities of the modern world.

I

The Peace Settlement in Europe, 1919–22

The Treaty of Versailles

During the ten years which followed the peace conferences of 1919 Great Britain was primarily concerned in her foreign policy with what we may call the exploitation of victory. She still, as late as 1929, regarded the world through the eyes of a successful, though occasionally conscience-stricken, belligerent; for five years (1919–24) she was concerned with plans for consolidating her gains, and for another five she was able to persuade herself that her new position would be peacefully and indefinitely maintained. The attempt to conduct British policy on these lines brought the Government into frequent difficulties with the French, who found their own attempts to consolidate victory in Europe constantly disappointed. In the Near East, and in the Far Eastern negotiations at the Washington Conference, France in turn displayed open hostility to the British programme.

The history of the peace settlement as it concerned Germany and Austria is in fact largely a record of Anglo-French squabbles.[1] The British ministers were able, indeed, to understand the desire of the French for security, their conviction that

---

[1] This can be followed in P. Mantoux, *Les délibérations du Conseil des Quatre* (1958, 2 vols), and the later chapters of H. I. Nelson, *Land and Power* (1963). Lloyd George's own account is given in *The Truth about the Peace Treaties* (2 vols, 1938).

Germany might again become a powerful and implacable enemy, and their bitter contemplation of their devastated homes, economy, and manpower. In the Cabinet discussions which preceded the peace conference Curzon had described the Kaiser as the 'arch-Criminal of the world', and had supported Clemenceau's proposal that he should be treated 'as a universal outlaw so that there should be no land in which he could set his foot'. But Lloyd George, while determined to make an example of the Kaiser, was already anxious to avoid the permanent alienation of the German people as by the creation of 'German Alsace-Lorraine questions'. The English sense of fair play – or sense of humour – led to the fairly speedy abandonment of the more melodramatic modes of vindictiveness; as pragmatists the British have never been inclined to regard peace settlements as immutable, and their attitude to the Versailles Treaty was no exception. Idealistic and left-wing circles which had fervently embraced Wilsonianism found the treaty inconsistent with their principles and denounced it as immoral even before it was signed. In academic circles a reaction from wartime propaganda soon led to a general wave of scepticism concerning the theory of war guilt, atrocity stories, and the whole anti-German case.

Economic considerations also played their part. The recovery and restoration of her important pre-war markets in Central Europe became increasingly important to Great Britain with the depression which set in in 1921 after the brief post-war boom; France was still sufficiently self-supporting to be able to look with some complacency on the weakening of Germany's military and political strength as a result of internal economic collapse. Moreover, the overstrained nerves of the British Cabinet and country had discovered in Russia a bogy even more horrifying than the defeated enemy. The Cabinet overestimated the ripeness of Germany for communism almost as much as did the Comintern. So it seemed imperative that Germany should not be forced by intolerable treatment to embrace what Winston Churchill called 'the foul baboonery of Bolshevism'.

The personalities of Lloyd George and Curzon helped to embitter their relations with the French. Lloyd George continued until 1922 to take an active part in the international discussions, depressing his French colleagues by his everlasting buoyancy and incalculable sense of humour; Curzon, ruffled on many occasions by what he considered the undue interference of the Prime Minister with foreign affairs, could be alternately tough and tearful, maintaining with increasing difficulty his more normal mood of stately geniality. During the peace negotiations at Paris, Arthur Balfour as Foreign Secretary had supported Lloyd George, while Curzon took charge of the Foreign Office in London. In October, however, Curzon and Balfour exchanged the offices of Lord President and Foreign Secretary, and Balfour's amiable and tactful influence was largely removed from the diplomatic sphere. On the French side Clemenceau resigned office in January 1920, and the British ministers had to deal mainly with Millerand until September, and then with Briand until the latter was driven from office in January 1922 by the Germanophobe irreconcilables under Poincaré.

The severe differences which developed at Paris during the peace negotiations reveal Lloyd George, and not President Wilson, as the sturdy opponent of extreme French demands over the German territorial settlement. In January 1919 Marshal Foch demanded that the Rhine should form 'the western military frontiers of the German countries'; the demand was vigorously pushed by André Tardieu during February and March; Wilson, violently abused in the French press, began to waver. After consultations with his advisers at Fontainebleau Lloyd George massed his objections in a forthright memorandum of 25 March. When France finally gave way she secured in exchange the permanent demilitarization of the area west of the Rhine, an Allied occupation for fifteen years, and a tripartite agreement, signed on 28 June, whereby Great Britain and the United States guaranteed her against any unprovoked German aggression. There was a similar struggle over Germany's eastern frontiers. No one questioned the wisdom of restoring the Polish state. But when the report of the commission on the Polish frontiers was presented to the conference in March, Lloyd George pointed out that it proposed to place 2,132,000 Germans 'under the control of a people which is of a different religion and which has never proved its capacity for stable self-government throughout its history'. A meeting of the British Empire delegates on 1 June went so far as to authorize Lloyd George, in demanding concessions, 'to use the full weight of the entire British Empire even to the point of refusing the services of the British army to advance into Germany, or the services of the British navy to enforce the blockade of Germany'. France and the United States both supported the more extreme Polish claims, and in particular appeared determined that Upper Silesia should go to Poland. In the end, however, after hearing the strong German case on the point, the treaty was modified, on the British proposal, to allow a decision by plebiscite. Danzig also was made a Free City, instead of going outright to Poland.

Although the new frontiers supplied Germany with many grievances it must be admitted that they were generally regarded at the time in the Allied countries as a reasonable enough solution of the extremely intricate problems of land and population involved. Germany had, however, three grievances of a perhaps more legitimate nature. These were the humiliating procedure and insulting tone of the victors; the loss of her colonies, justified by statements concerning her unfitness to govern backward peoples; and the reparations clauses. A good deal of the harshness of the Allied delegates was due to the violence of public opinion at home; the payment of substantial indemnities, and even the cession of colonies, might have been understood by the German people as the exaction of spoils consequent on defeat, but the attitude of moral condemnation, and the excessive size of the reparations demand, proved hard to bear. Many people in Allied countries were nevertheless genuinely convinced that Germany had been guilty of reprehensible conduct which must be denounced at the bar of history. It is probably true, however, that in England the majority in the Coalition who attacked the treaty in April 1919 on the grounds of its undue leniency to Germany no longer mirrored British opinion accurately by July. The vehement attacks on the treaty and on Lloyd George by the Northcliffe press were increasingly regarded in the country as evidence of a personal vendetta.

President Wilson's greatest achievement at the conference was to secure the drafting of the Covenant of the League of Nations and its incorporation in the Versailles Treaty. But the fatal vote of the American Senate on 19 November 1919 meant the virtual rejection of the peace treaty and membership of the League by the United States; it also made the treaties of guarantee of 28 June automatically void. In the British note pledging Britain to conclude a guarantee treaty with France there had been a provision making it dependent on the ratification of the Franco-American Treaty. The Anglo-French ratifications were exchanged on 20 November. Hope lingered for a time that the United States would accept the guarantee and peace treaties even if they rejected the Covenant of the League.[1] But this hope faded early in 1920. The British Government did not refuse formally to defend the French frontiers; but the two powers were becoming increasingly conscious after the end of 1919 of their incompatibility of views on the treatment of Germany, and negotiations for a two-power treaty of mutual defence were not commenced until the end of 1921. France in the meantime preferred to look to Poland and the new Danubian states for support.

After the exchange of ratifications in January 1920 the Ambassadors in Paris were left to supervise the execution of the treaty, but it was felt that the greater political issues must be handled by direct negotiations between the two Governments, and the result was the series of international conferences which were, no doubt, necessary, but which probably created as much friction as they removed.

[1] B.D., Ser. I, vol. v, nos 413, 435, 441.

Assessing Reparations

The Conferences of Paris (8–16 January 1920) and of London (12–23 February), which were concerned mainly with problems of the Mediterranean and Near East, revealed French and Italian suspicion of British designs in the region of the Straits; it was decided that the Sultan should stay in Constantinople, and the drafting of the Turkish Treaty was completed at the San Remo Conference in April (Chapter III). But by this stage German affairs were again in crisis.

Lloyd George's insistent but somewhat ambivalent handling of German problems undoubtedly puzzled the French ministers, although it was broadly consistent with his desire to separate the German people from militaristic influences. The direction of German affairs after the revolution of 9 November 1918 had remained in the hands of the Majority Socialists, but although the new Weimar constitution was successfully proclaimed on 11 August 1919 they were fatally handicapped by the odium of having signed the armistice and peace treaty. The Spartacists, or German Communist Party, had hitherto been the only element to appeal to arms, but trouble now came from the large class of army officers who were faced with dismissal and poverty. However, the Kapp *Putsch* in Berlin on 13 March 1920 failed rather ignominiously; a general strike of Socialists in Berlin brought about its collapse. But the workers, fearing a reaction, refused to return to work and began to form Soviets; when the Government made use of the Reichswehr, most of the movements were suppressed easily enough, but in the demilitarized zone of the Ruhr the organization of the workers into militant armed Soviets met with little effective resistance until the Government sent in troops to deal with them. As this was a technical infringement of the treaty French troops promptly occupied Frankfurt and four other German towns across the Rhine.

Curzon was thoroughly annoyed by this unilateral intervention and on 8 April withdrew the British representative from the ambassadorial conference until the French undertook to refrain from further independent action. The San Remo Conference met immediately after (19–26 April), and it became clear that the personal tension between Curzon and Millerand was merely a sympton of more fundamental differences as to the treatment of Germany. But whereas Lloyd George was prepared to trust the Germans on economic matters and wanted to meet them in order to arrive at a practical and enforceable settlement on reparations, he differed little from the French in his opposition to German rearmament. The Supreme Council on 26 April refused a German request that the Reichswehr should be doubled, and charged Germany with default in respect of disarmament and reparations. Lloyd George did succeed in getting the principle of direct discussions with the Germans accepted. The Ruhr incident was closed when French troops were withdrawn on 17 May, after the German troops had left.

The heads of the Allied Governments met the Germans at the Spa Conference (5–16 July 1920), after settling their programme at preliminary meetings at Hythe, Boulogne, and Brussels. The result was, on the whole, unfavourable to the more liberal tendency represented by British policy. The peace treaty had provided that Germany must give compensation, either in gold or in goods, for all damage to the civilian population of the Allies during the war. She was given the right to make her own proposals, which had to be presented to the Allies within four months of the signing of the treaty; if, after a further two months, agreement was not reached, a reparations commission, appointed by the Allies, was to decide the sum, and to notify Germany of its decision on 1 May 1921. The French regarded with obvious uneasiness the prospect of direct contact with the German leaders, but at Spa they were soon relieved of the fear that insinuating and persuasive German diplomats would succeed in over-persuading the impressionable Lloyd George. The British were stampeded to the French side by the obvious inadequacy of the German reparations scheme put forward by Dr Simons, the Foreign Minister, and by the aggressive tone of the German coal magnate, Herr

Stinnes, who gave evidence as an unofficial expert on 10 July. He insisted on being allowed to stand to make his speech, and started by referring to those who were 'sick beyond recovery with the disease of victory'.[1]

For the rest of the year the discussions made little progress: the idea of meeting the Germans remained distasteful to the French, and a meeting to discuss the question of Germany's total indebtedness was continually postponed. The first real gleam of sense came when Allied and German experts met at Brussels (16–22 December 1920); the German delegation gave on this occasion a frank and detailed description of its country's position, and on the Allied side the problem was examined objectively from the point of view of Germany's capacity to pay.

But after this political considerations once more took control. The growing opposition in France to any settlement modifying the extreme demands of the treaty forced Briand, who had now succeeded to office as Prime Minister, to abandon the more moderate programme. The heads of the Allied Governments made their own proposals at the Paris Conference of 24–30 January 1921. Germany was to pay two series of forty-two annuities; the first series was to produce 226 milliard gold marks between 1 May 1921 and 1 May 1963, the second was to amount to 12 per cent of the annual value of German exports. In case of non-fulfilment the sanctions announced at Spa would be applied. The proposals ignored the Reparations Commission, which in any case had not to decide the matter before 1 May. The figures caused consternation in Germany, and there were powerful demands that they should be rejected, but the German counter-proposals seemed in their turn to be grossly inadequate.

The nature of the German terms, the hostile tone of the London Press, and the fact that the assembling of the conference in London in March 1921 made him the spokesman of the Allies, forced Lloyd George to declare that the German proposals absolutely failed to recognize the needs of the Allies,

[1] B.D., Ser. I, vol. viii, pp. 421–4.

and after further abortive negotiations, sanctions were applied on 8 March 1921.[1] Düsseldorf, Duisberg, and Ruhrort were occupied, customs receipts along the German frontiers within the occupied area were impounded, and a new customs cordon established between the occupied and unoccupied parts of Germany. This action was of very doubtful legality, in view of the treaty provision which postponed executive action until after 1 May.

The German President issued a proclamation denouncing the Allied action, and appeals were made without success to the League of Nations and to the United States. Meanwhile the Reparations Commission had, on 18 April, notified Germany that her total indebtedness was 132 milliard gold marks, and had demanded that in the meantime the whole of the Reichsbank's metallic reserve should be transferred to branches of the bank in the occupied area. An Allied ultimatum on 5 May threatened further sanctions, and on 11 May the new German Government of Dr. Wirth surrendered. Although the Allies had preserved a united front during the crisis, the British reluctance to fall in with the more extreme of the French demands remained.

Poland and Silesia

Meanwhile the Poles, regarded in the Foreign Office as reckless and grasping, and dangerously encouraged by their French friends, seemed likely to confirm Lloyd George's most pessimistic views as to the chances of political stability in Eastern Europe. The Soviet Government had mastered its White opponents by the end of 1919, and in the early summer of 1920 launched a vigorous counter-offensive against the Polish Army, which had recently and rashly advanced to Kiev. There was general alarm at the prospect of a Soviet victory which would spread Bolshevism throughout Central Europe. In July the German Government urged the need for combined action by the forces of the Allies and Germany and even promised that

[1] B.D., Ser. I, vol. xv, pp. 258–61.

Ludendorff would serve under Foch.[1] The French sent experts to Warsaw. On 3 August Curzon called on the Soviet Government to halt its advance; but on the 9th, British Labour set up a Council of Action to prevent the Government's intervention in what it chose to regard as an attempt to start a new war for the destruction of Soviet Russia. In fact the Government did not trust the Poles, and Labour did not want a communized Europe. However, Pilsudski's well-timed counter-stroke and victory on 16 August saved Poland; British munitions, even if they could have been sent, would not have arrived in time. The 350 Councils of Action which had sprung up were not so much demonstrations against Poland, or even against the Government, as against war in any form. In February 1921 France and Poland concluded a military alliance; Britain was confirmed in her desire to avoid all commitments in Eastern Europe.[2]

Shortly after this the plebiscite which Lloyd George's intervention had secured for Upper Silesia was held on 20 March 1921, and to the consternation of the French and Poles resulted in a majority for Germany of over six to four (707,605 votes to 479,359). After the Allied plebiscite commissioners had failed to agree on a new frontier line, the Polish plebiscite commissioner, Korfanty, at the head of an armed force of some 100,000 men, overran a large part of the district in May, defied the authority of the powers, and seemed likely to take over the whole province. After the plebiscite the British troops had been withdrawn; the French troops, which had remained, displayed open sympathy with the insurgents. The complete success of the Poles was prevented, however, first, by the German inhabitants, who organized themselves for resistance under General Hoeffer, then an invalid, and, secondly, by the British troops, which were hurriedly sent back to the province.

The French Government's aim was to prevent the strengthening of Germany by the recovery of the rich coal- and ironfields of Silesia; the British Government, true to the principle

[1] B.D., Ser. I, vol. x, p. 177.
[2] T. Komarnicki, *Rebirth of the Polish Republic* (1957), chaps 7, 8.

of preventing further 'Alsace-Lorraine' problems, and of promoting Germany's return to normal conditions, favoured the return of the industrial district to Germany. The situation was indeed complicated enough without the interruption of these international problems; all the towns in the plebiscite territory, and most of the villages, had returned German majorities, whereas the country parishes were largely Polish. The impossibility of awarding the district outright to either party seemed obvious; but it seemed almost equally impossible to devise a frontier which could make a satisfactory division between the two peoples.

The crisis culminated in a formal French warning to Curzon that the attitude of Great Britain, if adhered to, must lead to a definite rupture between the two countries; his reply on 29 July 'lacked nothing in firmness'. The French, however, agreed at last to another meeting of the Supreme Council, and at the Conference of Paris (8–13 August 1921) it was agreed that the Silesian question should be referred to the League of Nations. The League's decision, arrived at by a committee of four – a Brazilian, a Chinese, a Belgian, and a Spaniard – was adopted on 20 October. It ignored the rule, which had been laid down in the Allied discussions, that closely interdependent districts should not be divided, and Poland, who had had only 40 per cent of votes in the plebiscite, received about half the inhabitants, but only a third of the territory. She received, however, the greater part of the industrial resources, including 53 out of 67 coal-mines, 21 of the 37 blast furnaces, and all the zinc and lead foundries.

Anglo-French Alliance Discussions

No real improvement in Anglo-French relations followed the Conference of Paris. The fundamental difference of opinion over the treatment of Germany remained. British negotiations for an agreement with Russia were an additional source of anger to the French. On 20 October 1921 Franklin–Bouillon signed an agreement with Turkey, which meant France's open abandonment of any pretence at co-operation with Great Britain in the Near East (Chapter III).

The writings of J. M. Keynes, the alarming rise in the British unemployment figures, and the fall of the German mark in November, strengthened Lloyd George's conviction that the existing policies were driving Great Britain and Europe towards economic disaster. The Wiesbaden Agreement of 6 October 1921, signed by M. Loucher and Herr Rathenau, provided for the direct reconstruction of the French devastated areas by means of German plant and materials, but on 20 October the Reparations Commission decided that it was in some respects a departure from the Versailles Treaty. Germany had succeeded in paying a first instalment of a milliard marks by the end of August; as a direct result of this heavy payment the mark slumped in November to 1,020 to the pound, and the possibility of a German default became a matter of immediate concern.

Lloyd George and Briand made a serious attempt in December to find means of removing the outstanding causes of friction. The French did not, however, show much interest in the idea of an Anglo-French Treaty on the lines of the guarantee treaty of 1919. The Comte de St Aulaire told Curzon on 5 December that the treaty had been humiliating to France because it promised France 'assistance', and useless because its provision against German aggression did not satisfactorily cover various forms of indirect aggression. 'It would not cover us against a Polish Sadowa, which, for Germany, would be the best preparation for another Sedan.' He proposed, therefore, a reciprocal undertaking, in which the problem of 'indirect aggression' would be satisfactorily met. During the London Conference, which met (18–22 December 1921) to consider Germany's declaration of inability to meet the payments due on 15 January and 15 February 1922, Briand followed the Ambassador's suggestions by proposing to Lloyd George a comprehensive alliance; Lloyd George at once objected that the British people would be ready to guarantee the soil of France but would not accept responsibility for quarrels which might arise over Poland or Danzig or Upper Silesia.[1]

Lloyd George's offer was due to his desire to keep Briand in office, and to the hope that it would produce French counter-concessions in other spheres, and particularly in the Near East. At home the Coalition Government had its own troubles and was losing ground, although the settlement of the Irish question in December, and the success already achieved by Balfour at the Washington Conference (November 1921–February 1922), gave it a momentary increase of popularity. Lloyd George would have preferred a general election at this stage, but the opposition of Sir George Younger, the head of the Unionist organization, prevented this. He fell back, there-fore, on an alternative plan, which he discussed with Briand at the Cannes Conference (6–13 January 1922), of a great gather-ing at Genoa of all the European powers, including the ex-enemy countries and Russia, to draw up comprehensive plans for the economic reconstruction of Europe. The Anglo-French Agreement was to be the essential basis of this. On 4 January 1922 Lloyd George offered Briand a treaty providing for reci-procal assistance; Great Britain would guarantee French soil against unprovoked German aggression, although she could not contemplate 'participation in military enterprises in Central and Eastern Europe'. The conference also discussed a repara-tions scheme drawn up by Lloyd George and Briand in December, and providing for a partial moratorium for Ger-many in return for increased control by the Allies of her internal finances.

But Briand's days as Prime Minister were numbered. Al-though the reparations proposals had been accepted by the French Government they were attacked by Doumer, the Finance Minister; and although Briand had demanded the ex-tension of the Anglo-French Agreement, and in particular had proposed a military agreement, he was violently attacked by the Right parties for subserviency towards England. He re-signed on 12 January 1922, and was replaced by Poincaré.

[1] Cmd. 2169 (1924), no. 33.

The Genoa Conference

Poincaré's accession to office killed the already faint hope of an Anglo-French Agreement which would settle satisfactorily the outstanding international problems. The Frenchman disliked international conferences; his precise, narrow, legalistic outlook led him to favour the meticulous exploration of the possibilities of agreement by means of notes and conversations through the normal diplomatic channels, and he was in any case predisposed to believe that French interests would be better served by independent action. The League discussions had already convinced the French that little real assistance could be expected from that quarter in the event of war; on the other hand, France had met with considerable success in building up alliances with the smaller powers. A military alliance was concluded with Belgium in September 1920; the alliance with Poland, already almost a great power in size, was signed in February 1921; during the same two years Czechoslovakia, Yugoslavia, and Rumania drew together to form the Little Entente. No political treaties were concluded with France at this stage but it was already clear by the beginning of 1922 that the Little Entente would strongly support France in enforcing the peace settlement.

Great Britain, on the other hand, favoured conciliation with Germany to an extent which almost foreshadowed revision of the treaty, and seemed prepared to give very little in return. Lloyd George was greatly preoccupied with the danger of a Russo-German Agreement.[1] On 23 January Poincaré instructed the French Ambassador to press, in the Anglo-French Treaty, for reciprocal guarantees, the application of the treaty to 'France' (and 'Great Britain') and not merely to the 'soil of France', a military convention, a minimum duration of at least twenty years, and a provision that the two powers were 'to concert together, in case peace were to be menaced'. Curzon was only prepared to agree to the first two of these, and to a duration of fifteen years (to cover the period up to the end of

[1] Cf. B.D., Ser. I, vol. xv, p. 787.

the Allied occupation). On 29 January Poincaré restated the French case in a reasoned memorandum, and Curzon replied on 17 February. These exchanges did little to advance the negotiations, and on 18 March Curzon said that the pact would stand little chance of acceptance by Parliament unless outstanding differences between the two countries had been removed. This was, perhaps, intended as a means of securing an accommodating attitude from the French at the forthcoming Genoa Conference, but it meant the virtual end of the treaty discussions.

Meanwhile the two powers remained fundamentally opposed on the reparations issue; a French memorandum of 15 March, after an elaborate recital of Germany's previous defaults, insisted that 'even now the German Government could, with the help of its nationals, execute in 1922 its entire obligations as laid down in the Schedule of Payments'. An open clash was avoided for the time being only because Germany accepted the severe conditions of supervision of her finances demanded by Poincaré in return for a moratorium.

The Genoa Conference (10 April–19 May 1922) was the last serious effort of the Coalition Government to restore its failing reputation at home by a striking success abroad. Its aim was the restoration of economic prosperity in Europe by a conference of all European powers, including the ex-enemy countries and Russia, and its most important objective was to restore international trade by the resumption of normal economic relations with Russia. Poincaré would not attend in person, and France was represented by Louis Barthou, the Foreign Minister, who was kept severely under Poincaré's thumb. The French reservations excluded the discussion of disarmament and reparations, the revision of the peace treaties, the political recognition of the Soviet Union, or the inclusion of Germany in any form of reconstituted Supreme Council. The Soviet Union, though anxious for the establishment of normal economic and political relations with Europe, found that the Western powers had little to offer in return for the restoration of foreign-owned private property and payment

of Tsarist debts which they demanded. But Lenin was prepared
to send delegates to the conference in order to enjoy the prestige of attendance for his hitherto ostracized Government.
Otherwise Russia preferred to make an agreement with Germany and to frustrate the Western powers. Lloyd George spent
the first week of the conference in secret talks with the Russians; as a result the Germans, fearing desertion by the Russians, signed the draft Soviet–German Treaty of Rapallo of
16 April.

It provided for a mutual renunciation of reparations, Germany's renunciation of compensation for losses to her nationals through Russia's socialization of private property,
mutual facilitation of trade, and the resumption of consular and
diplomatic relations. More important, and unknown to the
other powers, were the secret military discussions which
followed. The Allied powers did not conceal their annoyance
and uneasiness at the treaty, and the failure of their own demands on Russia was more striking by comparison.[1] In spite of
this initial rebuff Lloyd George conducted negotiations with
the utmost ability and tact for six weeks. The private property
question was referred to a conference of experts at The Hague
(June–July 1922), only to be finally dropped with an admission
by all parties that on this question no agreement was possible.
French policy made almost inevitable the failure of the Anglo–
French Alliance negotiations, which finally lapsed in July.

Curzon, probably not sorry to have been kept away from
Genoa by phlebitis, was alarmed lest Lloyd George should, in
a desperate attempt to restore the position upset by the Treaty
of Rapallo, make some disastrous agreement with the Soviet
Government. But the Prime Minister returned empty-handed
from Genoa, and his weakened position was finally destroyed
by the Greek disasters in August and September. After the
revolt of the Unionist Party he resigned on 19 October.

The fall of the Lloyd George administration was due in large
part to problems of domestic policy and economy, and to the
instinctive ingratitude of all democracies in getting rid of their

[1] G. Freund, *Unholy Alliance* (1957), pp. 92–124.

War Lords. Its foreign policy in Europe since the peace conference could not be described as successful, although on the
points that caused the greatest doubt and opposition at the
time – reparations and the desire for understanding with
Russia – it had, following the Prime Minister's lead reluctantly
at times, anticipated the more liberal tendencies of its successors. The open breach between the French and British
Governments was postponed until the Coalition's successors
were in office.

II

The Washington Conference

The Anglo-Japanese Alliance

The British Government appears to have regarded its arrangements with the United States as the most successful aspect of its policy in the post-war settlement. At the Washington Conference, which assembled in November 1921, Great Britain surrendered both her traditional primacy in naval armaments and her alliance with Japan, and in so doing no doubt greatly reduced the possibility of friction on these two questions with the Americans. There was no specific counter-concession or warm response, and both France and Japan were disappointed; nevertheless it was considered wise to seek, even at this cost, the passive friendliness of the United States.

Great Britain had inherited, from the nineteenth century, valuable markets and vast financial interests in China, based on her prosperous concessions and settlement in Tientsin, Shanghai, and other ports and interior towns. The Anglo-Japanese Alliance of January 1902 had been of immediate value to Japan in the Russo-Japanese War of 1904–5, for it had made it virtually impossible for France or Germany to help Russia; later, by guaranteeing the British position in the Far East during the difficult years before the First World War, it had been of equal value to Great Britain. With the collapse of Russia and Germany its value was reduced, and the growth of friction between Japan and the United States had caused the British Government increasing embarrassment. In February 1917, before China or the United States had entered the war, Britain and Japan had agreed to support each other's claims to former German territories in the Far East. During the war Japan pressed the onerous Twenty-One Demands on China and secured Shantung, and although Japanese and American troops made a joint landing at Vladivostok in August 1918 in an ill-defined policy of saving Eastern Asia from bolshevism, mutual hostility steadily increased. At the peace conference in 1919 the Chinese delegation, which showed the ascendency of Chinese Nationalist (Kuomintang) elements, demanded the surrender of Shantung, and were supported by President Wilson, while France and Great Britain supported Japan, in accordance with their war-time pledges. The British were irritated by Chinese intransigence which played into Japanese hands and added to the bitterness and unrest in the Far East. Japan secured the German Pacific islands under a League mandate, but her self-esteem was profoundly wounded when the drafting committee for the League Covenant, under Wilson's chairmanship, re-jected a Japanese proposal recognizing the principle of race equality.

The Anglo-Japanese Alliance would lapse in 1922 unless renewed.[1] The British Government had no illusions about the nature of Japanese ambitions or about the unfavourable effect which renewal would probably have on relations with both the United States and China. When the alliance was renewed in 1911 it had included a provision that it should not be applicable to any power with whom the parties had arbitration treaties. This was meant to exclude the United States. Although the United States Senate rejected the Anglo-American arbitration treaty in the same year after shrill attacks by the German–American and Irish–American Presses, the British were able to conclude in 1914 a 'Peace Commission Treaty' with the United States which the Japanese were told was regarded as the equivalent of a treaty of arbitration. But this does not seem to

[1] The best account of Japanese reactions is I. H. Nish, 'Japan and the Ending of the Anglo-Japanese Alliance' (*Studies in International History*, eds K. Bourne and D. C. Watt, 1967, pp. 369–401).

have made much impression on opinion in the United States and was perhaps unknown there. It was generally accepted in the Foreign Office after the war that the alliance could not be renewed in its old form. Curzon, the War Office, and the Admiralty were nevertheless convinced that, failing a definite promise of American support in the Pacific, it would be dangerous to Britain's weakened position in the Far East to leave the Japanese in disgruntled isolation. As early as February 1919 some form of tripartite Anglo-American–Japanese agreement was seen in the Foreign Office as the ideal solution.

Yet in conservative British circles the tradition of friendship with Japan was still strong and reinforced the tendency to look to the two island empires as natural allies against the still incalculable forces of communism. Great efforts were made by British and Japanese spokesmen to convince the United States that the alliance was not directed against her, and to assure Geneva that it was compatible with the League Covenant. The Japanese military leaders favoured renewal. The visit of the Crown Prince to London in March 1921 was no doubt intended to influence British opinion in the same direction.

But by this stage American inquiries about the alliance had confirmed the British belief that American opinion would not view with equanimity a renewal of the alliance in its old form.[1] The Japanese had put themselves in the worst possible light by lingering in Eastern Asia even after an independent, non-Communist Republic of the Far East had been proclaimed on 6 April 1920, and recognized by the Soviet Government in May. The sentimental interest of the United States in China as a struggling 'sister republic' had been deeply stirred by the cession of Shantung to Japan at the peace conference, and the Chinese retaliation by a boycott of Japanese goods only served to strengthen America's belief in the gravity of her protégé's wrongs. Among the Dominions, Hughes of Australia, Arthur Meighan, Prime Minister of Canada, and Theodore Massey, Prime Minister of New Zealand, were convinced that they

[1] B.D., Ser. I, vol. xiv, nos 24, 40, 261, 323.

must be on the side of the United States in any future Japanese–American dispute. At the Imperial Conference (June–August 1921) Meighan's pressure against renewal, which had been mounting since February, had its effect on Lloyd George and despite the vehement opposition of Hughes it was decided to seek some new arrangement with which America would be associated.

The Government had also become convinced that it must satisfy America's naval ambitions. The Admiralty's plan in 1919 was to maintain thirty capital ships in the post-war era, and after a year of visit and investigation Lord Jellicoe recommended in March 1920 a permanent British Far Eastern fleet based on twenty capital ships. But in April 1921 the Admiralty made it known informally to the Americans through the First Lord that Great Britain would henceforth be content with a navy equal to that of any other power: would accept, in other words, a one-power standard, and be prepared to enter into an agreement with the United States on this point. When the discussions with the Dominions in 1921 had shown the difficulties facing a renewal of the Anglo-Japanese Alliance the British Government decided to propose a conference to regulate Pacific questions; the initiative was, however, left to the American President, Harding, when it was learnt that he was about to make a similar proposal. Invitations were sent in the first instance to Great Britain, France, Italy, and Japan, to discuss the limitation of naval armaments, and as the agenda was to include the consideration of the Far East and the Pacific, additional invitations were sent to Holland, Belgium, Portugal, and China.

Japan alone accepted with reluctance; the expansionist party was deeply suspicious. But the country's isolation, the severe economic depression which had followed the Chinese boycott, the collapse of the post-war boom, and the heavy military expenditure, combined to discredit for a time the militarist and bureaucratic systems; the result was to stimulate the growth of a liberal movement which was later to be led by the Minseito Party, and to derive much of its strength from the heavy industrialists and textile manufacturers. This liberal and pacific tendency was strong enough to enable the Japanese Government to find and accept a basis of compromise with the other powers, although only after a serious struggle over some of the provisions.[1]

The Four-Power Treaty

The main results of the conference were embodied in three treaties. These were: (1) the Four-Power Treaty of 13 December 1921, between Great Britain, France, the United States, and Japan; (2) the Nine-Power Treaty of 6 February 1922 concerning China; and (3) the Five-Power Treaty for the limitation of naval armaments, also of 6 February.

The first provided perhaps the most satisfactory available solution of the problem of the Anglo-Japanese Alliance. The opening stages of the conference were concerned with the American proposals for naval limitation, and there was no reference to the alliance on the agenda, although Balfour opened discussions with the Americans on the point as soon as he reached Washington. The Japanese delegation was, however, already too well aware of the practical difficulties of renewing the alliance in its older form, and was familiar with the idea of a triple alliance (to include the United States) from discussions in the British and American newspapers. *The Times* in particular had swung round against renewal during 1921 after being for long a supporter of the alliance and the Japanese. At the end of November these discussions finally led two of the Japanese delegates to take the initiative by sounding Balfour, who not merely expressed his general approval of a triple or quadruple treaty, but indicated that he had already exchanged draft proposals with the American Secretary of State, Charles Evans Hughes.

The Japanese appear to have been decidedly taken aback at this expeditiousness, and Balfour had to exercise all his tact to overcome their reluctance to open serious negotiations. In the

[1] B.D., ibid., chap. 6.

end they made the best of a bad job, and the treaty provisions were worked out in essentials by the 'Big Three' of the conference, Balfour, Hughes, and Prince Tokugawa, during the first week of December. The French were, on Hughes's suggestion, brought in 'in order to soothe their somewhat ruffled pride', and the smaller powers were excluded in order to satisfy the ruffled pride of the Japanese, who had hinted 'that the treaty would lose much of its sentimental value if it was made the common property of all the powers, great and small'. The Four-Power Treaty was announced to the conference on 10 December. The announcement took the public very much by surprise, for although Press speculation on the terms of a possible alliance had been abundant it had been, for the most part, very wide of the mark.

The problem which faced the three negotiators was to devise an agreement which would be sufficiently innocuous to remove American apprehensions, and at the same time have sufficient meaning to satisfy the Japanese that they were getting anything at all. Balfour's first proposal was believed to have been a three-power agreement in which the United States, Great Britain, and Japan should guarantee their respective interests in the Far East. Such a proposal had little chance of acceptance. The United States Government had informed the other powers before the conference opened that it 'could enter into no alliance or make any commitment to the use of arms which would impose any sort of obligation as to its decisions in future contingencies'. A mutual guarantee would have involved the recognition by the United States of Japan's present and future acquisitions in China and Siberia, and might have compelled her to condone the 'imperialist aggression' which it was the primary aim of her policy to check. The final draft accordingly contained no reference to a general guarantee, but provided that the four powers should respect the rights of each in their 'insular possessions and insular dominions in the region of the Pacific Ocean'. It also provided for joint conferences to discuss any controversy concerning such rights, and pledged the four powers to communicate 'fully and frankly' with one another concerning efficient measures to meet the aggression of outside powers.

The treaty contained therefore two specific advantages for Japan: it enabled her to bring the Anglo-Japanese Alliance to an end without loss of prestige, and it pledged the United States and Great Britain not to attack the Japanese possessions in the Pacific.

Balfour had been anxious that the term 'insular possessions' should include the Japanese mainland in order to avoid giving the impression that Australia and New Zealand were in an inferior position. Baron Shidehara agreed reluctantly, although it was felt to be an affront to Japan's dignity. But in the event charges in the American Press that the provision gave Japan an unfair advantage over the United States led to the reversal of the earlier decision and on Shidehara's request it was agreed on 6 February 1922 that the 'Japanese homeland' should after all be excluded.

The Five-Power Treaty

The guarantee against attack implicit in the Four-Power Treaty was made quite explicit by Article 19 of the Five-Power Treaty for the Limitation of Naval Armament, which virtually prevented the fortification of any Pacific islands within striking distance of the main islands of Japan by the two chief naval powers, Great Britain and the United States. This treaty was not signed until 6 February 1922, and the provisions concerning the non-fortification of the Pacific islands formed part of the bargaining necessary to secure Japan's adhesion to the main principles of limitation.

In 1916 the United States had laid down an ambitious programme of naval building; in 1921 she still had seventeen capital ships, built or building, as compared with the thirty-two British, but by 1924 it was anticipated that the United States would have thirty-three capital ships, while the British programme would remain at the 1921 figure. Three years of neutrality had made the United States financially the strongest state in the world, and an attempt to keep pace with her in an unrestricted naval armaments race would certainly have imposed an excessive strain on the Japanese and British economic systems. The leading American delegate, Hughes, opened the conference on 12 November with a dramatic proposal that 'preparations for offensive war stop now', and suggested an agreed ratio for the five chief naval powers (Great Britain, the United States, Japan, France, and Italy) of 5–5–3–1·7–1·7. This was supposed to correspond generally to the existing ratio before the conference; all building programmes for capital ships, including those under construction, were to be abandoned, there was to be a naval holiday in the construction of capital ships for ten years, and only a limited programme of replacement thereafter until 1936.

The American Press welcomed this programme as a shattering blow to the old diplomacy. Balfour and Beatty were taken aback by the proposals, particularly that of a naval holiday. However, on the urging of Borden of Canada and with the importance of Anglo-American amity in mind, Balfour and the Cabinet felt they must accept the programme, including, to the Admiralty's disgust, the ten-year building holiday. Balfour made this clear in an effective speech at the second session, and the sparring and finesse of the old diplomacy were provided by the Japanese. Admiral Kato demanded a tonnage greater than 60 per cent of that allotted to the other two powers, and this demand had produced, by the end of November, a deadlock which had to be dealt with by the Big Three. The crisis produced great popular excitement in Japan; feelings were particularly outraged by the idea of scrapping the recently launched superdreadnought, *Mutsu*, which had been built by public subscription. The deadlock was ended by a compromise: Japan accepted the 60 per cent ratio, but was allowed to keep the *Mutsu* (and also another superdreadnought, the *Nagato*), and secured the provision that the Pacific islands should not be fortified.

As it happened this arrangement worked, in some respects, to Great Britain's advantage; she and the United States were allowed to complete two battleships each to offset the *Mutsu* and the *Nagato*, and whereas the two Japanese ships were completed and the two American nearly completed, work on the two British ships (of the *Hood* class) had scarcely begun. It did not follow that the British Government welcomed this extra building and expenditure, and it made no attempt to conceal its disappointment at its failure to secure reduction in other categories. The French had been disappointed by Anglo-American readiness to agree when they had hoped to be able to profit from a breach, and they were also intensely resentful over the battleship ratio which put them on a par with the despised Italians. This no doubt stiffened their determination to hold out over submarines.

Briand on 21 November declared that France could not disarm physically until Germany had disarmed morally. Admiral Kato expressed sympathy for the French position. The conference realized that it would have to drop the whole question of land armaments.

Briand had been forced to leave Washington soon after the conference opened, and French naval policy was left in the hands of the uncompromising Admiral de Bon. He said in effect that it was quite impossible to accept the American proposals, which allotted to France a replacement tonnage of five capital ships, equivalent to 175,000 tons; France needed, to guard her communications with her colonies, ten capital ships of 35,000 tons each. The Italians were prepared to agree to the American plan for capital ships providing that they had parity with France. Briand, who did not wish France to bear the blame for a breakdown of the conference, gave way on 18 December on the question of capital ships, but announced that it was quite impossible for him to accept reductions for defensive ships (light cruisers, torpedo boats, and submarines) corresponding to the proposed ratio.

This pronouncement was a great disappointment to the British delegation; Balfour and Lord Lee of Fareham had decided to make a strong bid to secure the total abolition of submarines, but they also felt that if this were not accepted they in return could not accept any restrictions on light classes of ships, nor upon the arming of the mercantile marine. On 22 December Lord Lee stated the British case. The submarine was not an effective offensive weapon save against merchant shipping; during the last war Germany had sunk 12 million tons of shipping and drowned 20,000 non-combatants, but her submarines had done little damage to battleships; 15 million British and 2 million American troops had been transported to France without the loss of a single man except on hospital ships.

The French, Italian, and Japanese representatives replied that the submarine was a legitimate and effective weapon of defence. Hughes read a report of the American naval experts in favour of retaining submarines and against limiting their size, but advocating the outlawry of unlimited submarine warfare. On the following day de Bon declared that 90,000 tons was the absolute minimum that could be laid down for any nation. Even the existing British tonnage was only 82,464; the original American proposal had been that Great Britain and the United States should have 90,000 tons each. The existing French tonnage was estimated at 42,850. On the 24th Balfour said bluntly that a great submarine fleet would be useless to France in case of an attack by Germany, and anyone who looked at the matter from a strictly strategical and tactical standpoint would be forced to say that the French fleet was built mainly against Great Britain. The debate continued on these acrimonious lines for some days, and the final result was that no limitation on the size or number of submarines was found possible. France stuck to her demands for a minimum of 90,000 tons, even when the American delegation proposed a new ratio limiting the British and American maximum to 60,000. This failure also made impossible any limitation of auxiliary craft. American unwillingness to go any further in supporting the British view over submarines seems to have been due in part to the somewhat maladroit way in which Balfour and Lord Lee stated their case: they were thought to have gone too far in appealing to American public opinion on this issue.

The Nine-Power Treaty

The third and last section of the conference's work, embodied in the Nine-Power Treaty of 6 February 1922, concerned China. The Chinese sent a body of able delegates to the conference, and they put their case effectively. Japan, after a good deal of haggling, was persuaded to give up Shantung, and towards the end of the conference made further concessions which amounted to the surrender of seventeen of the Twenty-One Demands of 1915. The Chinese failed, however, to secure the return of Manchuria to China, which would have meant the removal of Japanese troops and the recognition of China's full sovereignty. It could be said that although her right to complete political and economic independence had been fully asserted, the restrictions on her sovereignty remained virtually unaltered. This was not due primarily to the resistance of foreign vested interests, although they had well-grounded fears that their trade and investments would suffer from the abolition of the existing foreign rights in the country. It was due in part to the whole atmosphere of the conference, which had met to remove international friction by the adjustment of the interests of the great powers on a *status quo* basis; in part to the conviction, even on the part of the Americans, that the internal conditions which had led to the nineteenth-century restrictions on China's sovereignty still applied.

There was little real chance at this stage that she could secure the complete abolition of extra-territoriality and the surrender of the international concessions and leased territories, for this was felt to depend on China's legal system reaching an acceptable standard which had not yet been attained. A commission was, however, set up to investigate the situation and to assist the Chinese in legal reform. The Chinese delegation also made a strong effort to secure tariff autonomy – that is, the right of the Chinese Government to have the sole voice in fixing and differentiating tariff rates. Although none of the powers was ready to grant this demand on the spot, it was finally agreed, with some Japanese reluctance, that the existing tariff should be increased to make it an effective 5 per cent, and that the rate should be subsequently raised to 7½ per cent. The conference, by the tariff treaty of 6 February 1922, appointed a committee to meet at Shanghai and establish a revised customs schedule.

The best that China secured from the conference was perhaps the four Root principles, adopted unanimously by the committee on Far Eastern affairs. By these the nine powers[1] promised: (1) to respect the sovereignty, the independence, and the territorial and administrative integrity of China; (2) to provide the fullest and most unembarrassed opportunity for China to develop and maintain for herself an effective and stable government; (3) to use their influence for the purpose of effectually establishing and maintaining the principle of equal opportunity for the commerce and industry of all nations throughout the territory of China; (4) to refrain from taking advantage of the present conditions in order to seek special rights or privileges which would abridge the rights of the subjects or citizens of friendly states, and from countenancing action inimical to the security of such states. This was a statement of principles which it was hoped would save China from the imperialistic struggles which had formed so much of its history for the past hundred years; it also gave the Japanese an opportunity of conciliating American opinion while more specific problems were avoided. There is no reason to think that the British delegation objected to this solution.[2]

The Washington Conference: An Estimate

We may sum up the results of the conference by saying that Great Britain secured a permanent strengthening of her friendship with the United States at the expense of a permanent weakening of her position in the Far East. The United States had taken the initiative in proposing that the naval armaments

[1] These powers were Belgium, China, France, Great Britain, Holland, Italy, Japan, Portugal, and the United States.
[2] For the conference proceedings, see B.D., Ser. I, vol. xiv, chap. 6.

race should be abandoned, and received much praise for the 'magnitude of her renunciation'.

The magnitude of the British renunciation may also be stressed. The maintenance of her position as the world's leading naval power had been a constant aim of Great Britain's policy for over two centuries; it had become one of the most deeply seated of national traditions, and had been secured during the First World War at the cost of tremendous sacrifices of wealth and men. The factors which could be advanced to justify a large British navy – the proximity of potential rivals, and the necessity for adequate forces to defend a world-wide empire – were largely lacking in the case of the United States, where the possibility of naval primacy had scarcely been considered a few years before, and where the desire for a navy equal to the largest in the world was due primarily to reasons of prestige. Great Britain had certainly a stronger case on the grounds both of prestige and of necessity. It cannot even be argued that the British were indifferent to the size of the American Navy; the problem of neutral shipping rights had produced serious tension between the two powers in the early stages of the First World War, and remained a source of some anxiety to the British after 1921, so that a more or less remote possibility of friction continued. Nor does it necessarily follow that the United States Government would have been allowed by technical factors (such as the width of the Panama Canal), or by American public opinion, to embark on a phase of excessively ambitious building. America's chief naval rival was Japan, and there was no desire for war even with her in 1921.

The British position in the Far East was certainly weakened. Article 19 of the naval treaty specifically prohibited the building or extension of fortifications in 'Hong Kong and the insular possessions which the British Empire now holds or may hereafter acquire in the Pacific Ocean, east of the meridian 110° east longitude, except (a) those adjacent to the coast of Canada, (b) the Commonwealth of Australia and its Territories, and (c) New Zealand'. It also prohibited the fortification of similar American islands, such as Guam. The treaty left the

British free to strengthen the naval base at Singapore, but this was too far away to form a base for effective naval operations against Japan. The Jellicoe plan for a Far Eastern fleet had been abandoned, and there was no guarantee that the United States fleet would help in the event of trouble with Japan. In other words, Japan was impregnable against attack either on her mainland possessions, or on her sea communications with Korea, Manchuria, and China; the British settlements in Hong Kong and on the Chinese mainland would, on the other hand, be almost defenceless against Japanese attack. Furthermore the old friendship with Japan, although not formally broken, had been so relaxed that Great Britain could scarcely look to Japan for support in any future trouble with the Chinese Nationalists – a fact which many Britons were to recognize and regret a few years later.

Against this could be set the fact that the concessions to Japan had been sufficient to sway Japanese opinion in favour of the temporary abandonment of her expansionist policy; it appeared at the time that the British Government had been wise to secure this measure of tranquillity in the Far East when her struggle with the Indian Nationalists had already commenced. This consideration also pointed to the expediency of tangible concessions to Chinese Nationalist demands, particularly in view of the strong current of popular sympathy for China in the United States. The British Government showed no undue reluctance to make these concessions during the next few years, but was forced to make them in circumstances which suggested compulsion.

British policy throughout the Washington negotiations, great and positive as the results in many respects were, must be criticized for its willingness to secure the immediate emotional satisfaction of a dramatic act of friendship and temporary pacification at the cost of a permanent weakening of the British position in the Far East.

III

The Peace Settlement in the Near East

The Anglo-French differences over the treaty settlement in Europe were paralleled in the Near East, where the war had in no way modified the fundamental aims of British policy. The protection of the approaches to India called for direct or indirect control over the Moslem areas adjacent to the Persian Gulf and Suez Canal, and the control or closure of the Straits of the Bosphorus and Dardanelles. Britain's hold on Egypt, support of the Arab revolt, and shouldering of almost the entire weight of the fighting against the Turks, enabled her to demand substantially all she wanted in the Arab areas after the war. The ambitions and counter-claims of France and even of Italy could not, however, be ignored.

The broad outlines of the future settlement of the Near East had been indicated in secret treaties between the Allies in 1915, 1916, and 1917. By the Constantinople Agreement of 18 March 1915, England and France had promised Imperial Russia the acquisition of Constantinople, the Bosphorus, and the European shores of the Dardanelles and of the Sea of Marmora. A further agreement between the three powers at Petrograd in March 1916 anticipated the better-known Sykes–Picot Agreement of 16 May 1916, by which France was to receive an administrative zone including Cilicia, a part of central Anatolia, the Lebanon, and the Syrian coastal strip; Great Britain was to receive administrative zones including Mesopotamia, and, on the Syrian coast, Haifa and Acre. There were also to be 'zones of influence', that of France lying south-east of her administrative zone, and including Damascus, Aleppo, Homs and Hama, and Mosul, while the British included the territory between Palestine and Mesopotamia; within these zones of influence an Arab state or confederation, under an Arab chieftain, would be established. Italy was promised in the Treaty of London of 26 April 1915 an 'equitable' share of the Mediterranean region adjacent to the province of Adalia; at the conference at St Jean-de-Maurienne she was promised some 70,000 square miles in Adalia and the Smyrna region.

But the St Jean-de-Maurienne Agreement was dependent on Russia's consent, which was never given; the collapse of Russia and repudiation of the secret treaties by the Soviet Government reopened the question of the future of Constantinople and the Straits; above all, the British pledges to the Arabs, in spirit and probably in letter, were incompatible at some points with what had been promised to the French. There is no reason to think that these contradictions were due to calculated duplicity on the British side. The confusing effect of parallel negotiations in wartime conditions, hasty decisions made to meet immediate crises, and the general sense of unreality inseparable from such large-scale planning for hypothetical victory must be taken into account. Moreover, while each of the continental Allies was consciously planning a territorial encroachment in the area, Britain's primary concern was to fend off interference with her traditional interests as far as possible.[1]

Negotiations with the Arabs were carried on by both the Foreign Office and the India Office, the former through Sir Henry MacMahon with the Emir Hussein of the Hejaz, the latter with Ibn Saud, Sultan of the Nejd. As a result Ibn Saud was promised by the India Office, without Hussein's knowledge, territories in Central and Eastern Arabia. On the other hand, a district later included in the French zone of influence in the Sykes–Picot Agreement had been left to Hussein by MacMahon. Picot was certainly informed on 23 November 1915 of Hussein's demands, although not, apparently, of the complete details: he told Sir Arthur Nicolson that the French

[1] E. Monroe, *Britain's Moment in the Middle East*, 1914–1956 (1963), chap. 1.

Government accepted Arab administration of Damascus, Homs, Hama, and Aleppo, but only under French influence. By 1919 however, with the rapid growth of the idea of national self-determination, the idea of French tutelage was no longer acceptable to Arab opinion. The Balfour Declaration of 2 November 1917, favouring the establishment of a national home in Palestine for the Jewish people, added a further complication, for although the consent of the French and Italian Governments had been secured, the Arabs had not consented and soon showed their resentment and fear of what this policy meant.

The armistice of Mudros with the Turks, of 30 October 1918, left Constantinople and the Straits, as well as Syria, Palestine, and Mesopotamia, in British possession; this meant not merely that France was in no position to take matters into her own hands but also that she was dependent on the British for support in Syria, where she had every reason to anticipate future trouble. The treaty of peace with Turkey was given only a low priority at Paris pending the completion of the more urgent peace negotiations over Germany. An Anglo-French Declaration on Arab policy of 9 November 1918 pledged the two powers to encourage and assist the establishment of native governments in Syria and Mesopotamia; on 15 February 1919 the French Government agreed to the administration of Mosul and Palestine by the British. Meanwhile the situation in the Near East continually deteriorated. As early as 29 April 1919 Italian troops landed at Adalia in furtherance of Italian claims and in spite of British and French objections. Lloyd George forestalled further Italian action by securing on 6 May the agreement of Clemenceau and Wilson to a redistribution of troops in accordance with which Greek troops landed at Smyrna on 14 May.

These moves indicated clearly the British Government's plans and difficulties in respect of Constantinople and the Straits. They were still influenced by the nineteenth-century fear of the possession of this area by a strong and hostile power, and by recent painful memories of the failure of Gallipoli. They were conscious of the difficulty of occupying it themselves in the face of French and Italian opposition. An American mandate would meet these difficulties; unfortunately Wilson's decision on the point was continually postponed, partly because of his illness. Failing this, an international régime, or an occupation by some smaller power such as Greece, or even a reduced and emasculated Turkey, seemed to provide the best alternative. Indian Moslem protests against any excessive slighting of the Sultan and Caliph had also to be considered. By November 1919, when the prospect of an American mandate was fading, the War Office and India Office began to lose interest in the idea of expelling the Turks, although Lloyd George, Curzon, and Balfour remained keenly attached to the idea. In December 1919 they persuaded Clemenceau, who was visiting London, to agree to an international régime. But this solution, in spite of their support, was rejected by the Cabinet on 6 January 1920, in view of its possible effect on Moslem opinion and security in the Middle East. The alternative policy was instead followed of maintaining the Sultan in Constantinople, and of imposing on him terms of peace which would consolidate British influence. Lloyd George commended this policy to the House of Commons on 26 February 1920 as a means, among other things, of ensuring the freedom and safety of the Armenians.

The plan encountered difficulties, not from the cowed and accommodating ministers in Constantinople but from the irreconcilable leader of the new national movement in Anatolia. Mustafa Kemal Pasha, who had landed at Samsun on 19 May 1919 after his appointment as inspector of the third army, had rapidly convinced himself that the old social, religious, and political structure of Turkey needed drastic reform. The Sultan's Government, although initially hostile, remained in touch with the Nationalist movement and were increasingly dominated by it. On 28 January 1920 they adopted the national pact drawn up by the nationalist deputies at Angora. This statesmanlike document proclaimed the independence and the indivisibility of the people of Anatolia and Turkey who were of predominantly Ottoman stock, left the Arabs and the people of western Thrace to choose their own fate, repudiated all restrictions inimical to their political, judicial, and financial development, and undertook to open the Straits to the 'commerce and traffic of the world', providing that the security of the Turks in Constantinople and the Sea of Marmora was maintained. But the massacre of Armenians by the Nationalists in Cilicia confirmed the Allies' hostility to Mustafa Kemal. In an attempt to exert pressure on Kemal's nominal master to prevent further massacres and also to ensure acceptance of the treaty then being drawn up, Allied troops under General Milne extended their occupation of Constantinople on 16 March and the entire Nationalist Government at once removed itself to Angora where on 23 April 1920 Mustafa Kemal was elected President of the Republic.

Meanwhile the Allies went ahead in the hope that their control of Constantinople and the Sultan would enable them to enforce the signature of the treaty. At the San Remo Conference in April most of the important problems remaining from the Conference of London were tied up. The Near Eastern mandates, on which agreement had already been reached, were formally allotted – Palestine and Mesopotamia to Britain, and Syria and the Lebanon to France. By the oil agreement of 24 April 1920 the oil interests of France and England, particularly in Mosul but also in Russia, Rumania, and the British and French colonies, were delimited. French capital was guaranteed 25 per cent of whatever sums might be invested in the oil-fields of Mesopotamia, or alternatively 25 per cent of the output of crude oil in the event of the oil-fields being developed by the British Government. The agreement had subsequently to be modified to meet the demands of the United States, who insisted on an ample share of the spoils of war in this area. The San Remo Conference also considered the problems of Batum and Armenia. The mandate for Armenia had been offered, after the refusal of the United States, to the League of Nations, which on 11 April had also declined the task. At San Remo it was decided to create an Armenian state with access to the sea, but without Trebizond or Erzingan. Allied military advisers asserted that it would take twenty-seven divisions to enforce the treaty. Lloyd George believed that the twenty-one divisions which were at a pinch available would suffice.

By the terms of the Treaty of Sèvres the new Turkish state was to retain Constantinople, the shores of the Sea of Marmora, the Gallipoli peninsula and the interior of Anatolia, but was to lose the mandated and Arab areas; Smyrna was to be administered by Greece for five years, when the local parliament or a plebiscite should decide its fate; the Aegean islands were to be renounced in favour of Italy. Turkey was to renounce to England all rights in Cyprus, Egypt, and the Sudan. A group of representatives of Great Britain, France, and Italy were to supervise the financial, economic, and administrative policy of the country, and the same powers were to take over the functions of the old council of the Ottoman public debt, the German and Austrian members being definitely eliminated. Finally, the Straits were to be open in peace and war to commercial and war vessels of all nations, and Turkey was to delegate control of the Straits and the Sea of Marmora to an international commission which was to be completely independent of the local authority. In spite of bitter protests the Constantinople Government was compelled to sign the treaty on 10 August 1920.

It is the inexpediency rather than the injustice of these terms which calls particularly for comment. The Arabs were successful rebels, and the Turks were willing to let them go; there was certainly a case for the self-determination of the Armenians, and perhaps of the Greeks in western Anatolia. The Straits formed an international waterway in which many powers besides Turkey could claim a legitimate interest; Turkey's rights in Cyprus, Egypt, and the Sudan could never after 1914 have been more than nominal. But the practical result was disaster. An additional agreement between Italy, France, and England provided that Italy should have rights, 'to help Turkey to develop her resources' in southern Anatolia and Adalia, France in

Cilicia and western Kurdistan. But Italy and France soon had the sense to abandon their ambitions; the British Government went ahead.

By the summer of 1920 it seemed probable that another war would be necessary in order to impose the Allied terms. For this the British Government, which had to satisfy the post-war demands for economy and demobilization, was not really prepared; instead of cutting its losses in time it decided to rely on the Greeks. It could at least furnish military supplies. Greece was assigned by the Treaty of Sèvres the islands of Imbros and Tenedos, which controlled the mouth of the Dardanelles. By June, Mustafa Kemal's forces were advancing and at the Hythe Conference the Greeks were authorized to begin an advance against them with their main forces. This was an Anglo-French decision which Count Sforza, the Italian Foreign Minister, accepted with considerable hesitation after further discussions at the Spa Conference in July. The campaign was, however, ultimately carried out successfully, and by the end of 1920 the Greeks were in occupation of large portions of western Anatolia. From the start the Turkish resistance was considerable, and the Greeks suffered some defeats. But by the summer of 1921 their troops reached Afuim-Karahissar and Kutaya, and were able to hold this position for the next twelve months. In the meantime, however, Venizelos's Government had fallen in November 1920 and ex-King Constantine, the Allies' opponent during the war, returned to power. This event rapidly undermined sympathy for Greece in the Allied countries.

The military resistance of Turkey enabled her to conduct a diplomatic campaign which was almost uniformly detrimental to British policy. During 1921 she made settlements with Italy, the Soviet Union, and France which were tacitly or patently hostile to Great Britain. The British and Soviet Governments were declared rivals in the Middle East, and the opening of the Straits under the Sèvres Treaty would place the Russian shore of the Black Sea permanently at the mercy of the British fleet. The Moscow Treaty of 16 March 1921 was essentially therefore a treaty of mutual defence; it disposed of the Russo-Turkish frontier regions to the mutual satisfaction of the two powers, provided for Russia's acceptance of the abolition of the capitulations and of the territorial claims of the national pact, and pledged both powers not to recognize any settlement imposed on either by force. Three days earlier a Turco-Italian Agreement established Italy's right of economic exploitation in south-western Anatolia; Italy withdrew her troops from Adalia in June. Finally, on 20 October 1921, Henri Franklin-Bouillon and Yussuf Kemal Bey signed the Franco-Turkish Agreement which signified France's open abandonment of co-operation with Great Britain in the Near East. By this agreement France gave up her claim to some 18,000 square kilometres of territory, including Cilicia and a section of the Baghdad railway; in return Turkey agreed to the transfer of the section of the railway between Bozanti and Nisibin to a French group, and promised concessions in the Kharshut Valley and elsewhere. Article One provided that the state of war would cease between the high contracting parties.

The justification for France's action is to be found in her consciousness of military and political weakness in Syria, in her conviction that the futile Greek policy must be abandoned, and in her belief that Great Britain had abandoned her in the European settlement. Curzon protested, and the French reply of 17 November was unconvincing in its attempt to prove that the British had had adequate warning, but was on firmer ground in stating that the French Government could not prolong indefinitely the sacrifices of every kind which the occupation of Cilicia involved.

The Greeks were now left virtually alone to face the astute and resolute Turks. In the summer of 1921 the Greek Government had rejected an Allied proposal that Smyrna should be made an autonomous province under Turkey, and had renewed the war; by the autumn, however, they were in a more accommodating mood. After visiting Paris and London, Gounaris, the Prime Minister, whom Lloyd George had described a year earlier as 'a dastardly traitor who would betray the Allies at the first opportunity', placed his country in Curzon's hands. But the fall of Briand in January 1922 and of the Italian Government in February, further delayed matters. On 6 March Curzon was compelled to tell Gounaris that England could not help. The injudicious publication by Edwin Montagu, the Secretary of State for India, of a pro-Moslem communication from the Viceroy, Lord Reading, caused a Cabinet crisis, and Montagu's resignation, and it was not until the end of March that the Allies, represented by Curzon, Poincaré, and Schanzer, could meet in Paris. They proposed an armistice, and a plan for a peace treaty which would have given Turkey the whole of Anatolia, the Straits, and Constantinople, although there was to be a demilitarized zone on the Asiatic shore of the Dardanelles. The Angora Government was not satisfied with these terms. The Greek army, now very near to exhaustion, renewed its advance early in August. When the Turkish army counter-attacked along its entire front on the Sakaria River on 18 August the Greek forces collapsed, and were rapidly driven back towards Smyrna, which the Turks occupied on 9 September. A fire which broke out on the 13th destroyed most of the Christian quarter of the city. By the 20th all the Greek forces had been expelled from Turkish soil.

The Greek advance in August has always been attributed to an injudicious speech by Lloyd George on 4 August, although the Greeks were quite prepared, without any particular encouragement, to continue the adventure. On 4 August he said in effect that the Greeks had been handicapped by the Allies, whereas the Turks were receiving supplies 'from Europe'. 'We cannot allow that sort of thing to go on indefinitely.' The Greeks apparently accepted this as an invitation to advance.

On 11 September the Allied commissioners at Constantinople warned the Turks that they would not allow the violation of the zones which Allied troops were still occupying on the Asiatic shores of the Straits. On the 14th Poincaré agreed to support this attitude at Angora. But when, on the following day, an appeal was addressed by the British Government to Greece, Yugoslavia, Rumania, and the Dominions for help in defending the Straits, Poincaré at once expressed his disapproval; on 19 September he ordered the withdrawal of all French troops from Chanak and the region of the Straits, and advised Great Britain to do the same. The Italian troops were also withdrawn. Curzon left for Paris on the same day to confer with Poincaré and Count Sforza, and some extremely tempestuous and emotional scenes followed. In the end, however, Curzon and Poincaré were able to agree to an invitation being sent to Turkey on 23 September recommending the summoning of a conference on Near Eastern affairs, and proposing as a basis the Maritza frontier in Europe, freedom of the Straits under the auspices of the League of Nations, and demilitarized zones north and south of the Straits. The Allies would evacuate Constantinople, and Turkey was to be invited to join the League. The publicity given to the appeal to the Dominions was evidence of the Government's resolution and had its effect on the Turks. Unfortunately it caused something of a crisis in Commonwealth relations owing to premature publicity and the failure to consult the Dominion Governments in advance.[1]

The crisis was not to end without a direct clash between the British and the Kemalists. French prestige had certainly not been enhanced by the hasty withdrawal from the Straits at the moment of danger. The British stayed, and, when the Turkish cavalry had advanced almost up to the British barbed wire defences at Chanak, Mustafa Kemal in a telegram to General Harington demanded, on 25 September, that the British should evacuate the Asiatic side of the Straits. Harington however, on the 27th, with the approval of the British Government, refused; but he continued negotiations, wisely ignoring what amounted to instructions for an ultimatum by the British Government on the 29th. The Turks finally accepted the armistice conditions, although at the Mudania Conference they made counter-proposals with French support and threatened a further advance if these demands were not immediately granted. It was only after another visit by Curzon to Paris on the 6th that Poincaré agreed to support the British; a

[1] G. M. Carter, *The British Commonwealth and International Security*, 1919–1939 (1947), pp. 84–90.

compromise arrangement was then devised which Turkey accepted on the 10th.

The fall of Lloyd George and the break up of the Coalition Government on 19 October 1922 were the direct result of anxieties engendered or symbolized by the Chanak crisis. Curzon, however, remained at the Foreign Office, and at the Lausanne Conference (November 1922–July 1923) gained successes which showed that in reality the Kemalist victory had not defeated the underlying aims of British diplomacy in the post-war settlement. The British had long since reconciled themselves to Turkish rule in Constantinople, and desired only satisfactory regulations for the future of the Straits. This formed the main subject of discussion in the earlier stages of the conference, and on 20 December Ismet Pasha, the chief Turkish delegate, agreed to the British demands for the de-militarization of the Straits, freedom of passage, and the establishment of an international commission. The Turks had already separated from the Soviet delegation, whose proposal that the Black Sea should be recognized as a *mare clausum* of the littoral powers would have meant its dominance by Russia; on the other hand, Curzon had successfully resisted the political guarantee that Ismet Pasha had demanded. The other outstanding British interest was Mosul; the sympathetic attitude of the *Daily Express* and other English papers encouraged the Turks to believe that Curzon would not be able to persist in his demands on this point, but they agreed to settle the matter by direct negotiation with Great Britain.

By the end of January 1923 the British had, except for Mosul, secured practically all their programme, whereas the French and Italians, in spite of their earlier Turcophil policy, had been unable to make much progress with the Turks on the outstanding financial, economic, and capitulatory clauses on which they were conducting the negotiations. On 31 January the Allies presented their terms in a draft treaty; but any possibility that the Turks would be bluffed into acceptance was ruined by Poincaré's statement through the Havas agency on 30 January that the draft was merely a basis for further discussion. Poincaré's move, which appears to have been due to irritation over British action in the Ruhr crisis, was hastily repudiated on the 31st when it became clear that Britain and Turkey might sign a separate treaty, as Ismet Pasha suggested on 4 February. But Curzon refused to separate himself from his two allies, and the British delegation left Lausanne on 4 February.[1] The Turkish proposal that the economic clauses should be discussed separately was rejected at a short conference in London (21–28 March), and negotiations were then resumed at Lausanne, with Sir Horace Rumbold as the chief British delegate. Prolonged discussions were necessary before mutual Franco-Turkish concessions produced agreement on the financial terms, but the treaty was finally signed on 24 July 1923.

The acceptance of the Kemalists' territorial demands, although delayed until the last moment by the stubborn Greek policy of the Lloyd George Government, supplied in the end as satisfactory a solution of the problem of the Straits as could have been secured by establishing the Sultan or the Greeks in Constantinople. The lukewarm support of British policy by the French and Italians also proved less disastrous than had at first appeared likely; their withdrawal prevented the establishment of larger French or Italian colonies which might have threatened British interests if they had proved hostile, and embarrassing if they had remained friendly and permanently exposed to Kemalist attacks. The success of British policy in the mandatory areas of Palestine and Irak could, of course, be tested only by time.

[1] Harold Nicolson, *Curzon: The Last Phase*, 1919–1925 (1934), pp. 325–50.

IV

Reparations, The Ruhr, Locarno

There could be no mistaking the change that had come over British foreign policy with the fall of the Coalition. In a rather splendid way Lloyd George had offered, for the first and last time in British history, the spectacle of the Gladstonian foreign policy in action. He was a Liberal Prime Minister leading the Concert of Europe, organizing conferences, denouncing wrongdoing by foreigners, coercing the aggressor (the Turk again), and seeking to solve bitter continental disputes by his forceful bonhomie, with a basic reliance on the forces of the home country rather than the Empire; for the little Welshman was, like Gladstone, also a little Englander. But Bonar Law had voiced the country's repudiation of leadership and by implication of the leader. In a famous letter to *The Times* and *Daily Express* on 6 October 1922 he said that Britain could not 'alone act as the policeman of the world' and in view of the French attitude to the peace settlement, might well be driven to imitate the isolationist attitude of the United States. He won the general election in November 1922 with a simple promise of 'tranquillity and freedom from adventures and commitments both at home and abroad'.

The country could not in fact wash its hands of responsibility for the Versailles Treaty as the Americans had done. Although British Governments after 1922 were anxious to disentangle themselves from the Franco-German quarrel and to resume the mediatory role which they had tried to play before 1914, they never succeeded in persuading either British or foreign opinion, or indeed themselves, that Germany was not their concern. But still the escapist urge was strong, and there was a substantial measure of agreement between the parties as to the need for continuing those efforts of the coalition which had been clearly directed towards the tranquillization of Europe.

Curzon's diplomacy, as we have seen, soon extricated the country from its Near Eastern embarrassments, and indeed supplied Bonar Law's Government with its one outstanding success in foreign affairs. The war debt settlement with the United States of February 1923 could hardly be regarded in this light, for the onerous terms created mixed feelings in London. Anglo-Russian relations remained in a state of chilly mutual aversion but did not dominate British foreign policy except towards the end of the Labour Government. The two main developments of the years 1923–5 were the reparations struggle and the attempts of the League to solve the problem of security. In neither case did British policy give full satisfaction to her wartime allies.

Anglo-French Differences: The Balfour Note

Ostensibly the essential difference between the British and French theses on the reparations issue concerned Germany's inability to pay. The French took the view that in Germany the country was richer than the Government, while the great industrialists, with Hugo Stinnes as their leader and model, were building up huge combines in the great industrial centres of Westphalia, modernizing their plants, collecting huge fortunes in their own hands, transferring capital abroad, and evading taxation with the connivance of the Government. The French were not unaware of some measure of impoverishment in Germany in other directions, with a heavy burden of internal debts, the loss of foreign markets, and the transfer of important industrial areas to the succession states. Nevertheless, their psychological approach to the problem of reparations was clearly quite wrong. The Germans were not presented with a heavy but manageable demand which they would have an inducement to meet as speedily as possible. All classes in Germany rightly assumed that the more they paid the more they would have to pay. The opposition of the Nationalists to the policy of fulfilment had therefore the obvious sympathy of the German industrialists; Erzberger, whose financial policy they detested, was assassinated in August 1921, and Rathenau, who had made a serious attempt to meet the Allied demands, in June 1922.

But in practice more was involved in the Anglo-French differences than the fixing of a figure and the devising of inducements to pay it. Incompatibility of political aim and national temperament prevented the rational assessment of Germany's 'ability to pay'. British ministers admitted their failure to sympathize or make friends with Poincaré. Great Britain with her dependence on external markets and a flourishing state of world trade had reason to doubt whether even a large sum in reparations was worth collecting by means of coercion which would once more throw international politics into turmoil. France's economy was so constituted as not to be particularly sensitive to this kind of shock; she felt, too, a grievance on account of her own indebtedness to Great Britain.

The attitude of the British Government towards the question of inter-Allied debts had been made clear towards the end of the Lloyd George ministry. As a result of the war Great Britain found herself with a debt to the United States of £978 million, very much less than the sum owing to her. The American debt had been contracted by Great Britain entirely on behalf of her Allies; she had financed her own war effort from her own resources. The repayment of debts on this scale involved the same practical difficulties as the payment of reparations. The effort to keep up the heavy payments would impoverish the debtor nation, and by reducing its purchasing power, directly hit the exporting industries of the creditor nations; commodities sent as payments would directly compete with the products of the creditor country, and payment by gold was clearly impracticable on the vast scale that these transactions would involve. The essential similarity of the position with regard to both war debts and reparations was not fully realized by the British delegation at the time of the peace conference, although the connexion was more fully grasped by them than by the Americans. President Wilson continued to insist that neither public opinion nor Congress in the United States would consent to the cancellation of any part of the British debt, and in February 1922 Congress set up the 'World War Foreign Debt Commission', with instructions to collect the debts by 1947, and to insist on a rate of interest of not less than $4\frac{1}{4}$ per cent.

Hitherto Great Britain had refrained from any demands on her Allies for repayment, and had thus made clear her desire for all-round cancellation. The British position, which had already been indicated by Lloyd George in a statement on 31 May, was now defined in a note drafted by him and sent on 1 August 1922 by Balfour, as Acting Foreign Secretary, to the European debtor countries. Sir Robert Horne, the Chancellor of the Exchequer, disagreed. The note contained three main points. (1) Great Britain occupied a strongly creditor position, being owed altogether four times as much as she owed the United States. (2) She was prepared to remit all debts due to her by the Allies in respect of loans, and by Germany in respect of reparations, if such a policy formed part of a general international settlement. (3) As this all-round cancellation was impossible through America's insistence on payment, Great Britain would ask from her debtors only as much as was necessary to pay her creditors.

The Note met with an almost universally unfavourable reception. In London the City and the banks were extremely critical; it was clear that in business and some political circles there were still hopes that vast sums could somehow or other be collected from the Continent. The political parties were more interested in their preparations for the overthrow of the Coalition Government. France and the United States were both hostile: both, for different reasons, refused to recognize the connexion established by Great Britain between war debts and reparations. The insistence of the United States Government on the letter of the bond was due partly to the fear of the individual American that the wily and unscrupulous Europeans were cheating him; partly to resentment in official circles over the attempt to pass responsibility for solving the problem to Washington. The French stated the alternative view in its most extreme form: the financial contribution of England and the United States was a form of support to the general cause of which less wealthy nations had supplied an equivalent in flesh and blood. In a very bad-tempered letter on 1 September Poincaré virtually accused the British Government of slackness in her war effort, and of over-charging on her supplies of war material. Germany's reparation debt was the result of her wilful acts of destruction in France, and of the payment of pensions due to losses inflicted by her. Until reparations had been fully paid there could be no question of settling war debts.

His irritation at the British attitude seems to have increased his determination to take 'productive guarantees' from Germany. The German Government had been granted a partial moratorium in May 1922, but after a further fall in the mark in June it proposed to the Reparations Commission on 12 July a total moratorium for the rest of 1922, and for the two following years. From this point Poincaré took the attitude that no further postponement of German payment could be accepted without 'productive guarantees'. On 7 August at the London Conference he defined these as including the exploitation and contingent expropriation of the state mines in the Ruhr Basin, and of state forests; the appropriation of 60 per cent of the capital of German dyestuff factories on the left bank of the Rhine; the collection of customs duties along Germany's western frontier; the appropriation of German customs receipts and of 25 per cent of the value of German exports. The British on 12 August proposed a scheme of alternative and milder guarantees, which Poincaré rejected.

British policy was now in the hands of Bonar Law, who had a good grasp of the technical intricacies of the reparations question, but was in two minds as to the best course to pursue, and inclined to shirk any issues that threatened a breach with the French. A further conference in London on 9 December produced a reiteration by Poincaré of his plans for productive guarantees; he offered to deliver to Great Britain out of the French share of 'C' bonds 'a capital nominally equal to the nominal amount of the French debt'. The 'C' bonds of the 1921 Schedule of Payments were generally accepted as worthless. The conference was adjourned on 11 December. On 26 December, at a further meeting of the Reparations Commission, Barthou moved that Germany should be declared in default on timber deliveries. Sir John Bradbury, the British delegate, characterized the particular default as 'almost microscopic' but the French, Italian, and Belgian delegates voted for the declaration. Bonar Law made it clear that British public opinion would not stand an advance into the Ruhr; Poincaré was determined to go ahead and on 2 January 1923 rejected summarily the British counter-proposals. On 9 January the Reparations Commission declared Germany in default on her coal deliveries, the British delegate again dissenting, and on the 11th the French occupation of the Ruhr basin began.

The Anglo American Debt

The Government was able to offset this crisis in Anglo-French relations with a thoroughly amicable settlement of the debt question with the United States. This arrangement was a further example of the high price that Great Britain was prepared to pay for the removal of possible causes of Anglo-American friction, and as a financial bargain caused consternation in some quarters in London.

The British delegates were Stanley Baldwin and Montagu Norman, the Governor of the Bank of England, whose technical advice was in favour of the acceptance of the best that the United States would consent to offer. Baldwin, who was almost ostentatiously inexperienced, could make little fight against the keen and hard-boiled American negotiators. He did, however, in his opening speech, state clearly the difficulties of payment. 'We intend to pay – but how can international credits be made liquid when the creditor nation is unwilling to permit liquidation through the direct delivery of goods, and is also unwilling to see the current sale of her products to the debtor nation interrupted, and when the debtor nation is unwilling to be put in the position of being unable to buy the products of the creditor nation?' However, there was very little attempt to bargain; and Baldwin agreed to refer the third American offer to London. This provided for the payment of the whole of the principal of the debt, with 3 per cent interest for the first ten years, and $3\frac{1}{2}$ per cent thereafter. As the Cabinet in London was divided on this offer the negotiations were adjourned.

The proposed agreement was backed by Lord Cave, and by Baldwin himself, and strongly supported by the City. Bonar Law in the end gave way, against his better judgement; but he wrote an anonymous letter to *The Times* on 27 January 1923 criticizing the terms. The effect of the settlement was that the British funded debt was fixed at $4,600 million (approximately £980 million at par), to be repaid over sixty-two years with an average rate of interest of 3·3 per cent. France, on whose behalf the debt had been largely contracted, seemed unlikely to pay anything.

The Occupation of the Ruhr

Bonar Law was increasingly unhappy over the state of foreign affairs. At the end of December 1922 Curzon found him 'willing to give up anything and everything rather than have a row'; this attitude did not hamper Curzon in the Near Eastern settlement, but it resulted in a negative and indecisive attitude by the British Government towards European affairs. Nor can it be said that British policy showed any great changes after Baldwin succeeded him as Prime Minister in May. France's activities in the Ruhr were met by a policy of passive resistance on the German side, and by counter-measures from the French and Belgians. A separatist movement in the Rhineland was encouraged. On 24 October 1923 an autonomous state was set up in the Palatinate, and 19,000 of the regular officials deported. The German people were behind their Government in the policy of passive resistance. There were some cases of bloodshed, and the effect on both the French and German financial systems was disastrous. Yet while the two countries seemed determined to ruin each other as speedily as possible Great Britain remained little more than an embarrassed spectator.

Curzon felt keenly the equivocal nature of his position. The Government was not at all inclined to break completely with the French by a wholehearted support and approval of the German resistance, nor could it take any steps to ensure a French success. The special ordinances imposed by the French and Belgian Governments through the Reparations Commission for the carrying out of their sanctions policy remained a dead letter in the British occupied zone. The *non possumus* attitude was partially abandoned in April. On the 20th, Curzon said in the House of Lords that if Germany were to make a statement of her willingness and intention to pay, and to have the amount fixed by authorities properly charged with the duty, he could not help thinking that an advance might be made. Germany thereupon made an offer to the powers (2 May), but France and Belgium rejected it without consulting Great Britain, and the British reply of 13 May was also unfavourable. The Government might at least have commended the German offer to abide by the decision of an expert international commission. A further German note of 7 June went considerably beyond previous offers, but the French continued to insist that Germany must abandon passive resistance in the Ruhr before any negotiations could begin.

A serious crisis over Russian infringements of the Trade Agreement of 1921 somewhat took attention off the Ruhr in May and June. But on 12 July Baldwin told the Commons that the German note of 7 June seemed to contain the germ of a possible settlement, and on 11 August, in a very vigorous note, Curzon did at last speak emphatically to the French and Belgian Governments. He started by refusing to agree to recent claims by the two powers to receive a larger proportion of reparations than those agreed on at Spa, and remarked that sunk ships and cargoes rotting at the bottom of the sea might not shock the eye like the ruined villages of France and Belgium, but they represented equally heavy loses of national wealth. The note upheld the British contentions as to the need for expert inquiry into Germany's capacity to pay and as to the illegality of the Ruhr occupation. It insisted that the British policy was that Germany should be made to pay up to the maximum of her capacity as determined by impartial inquiry, but that as a preliminary to payment her finances should be restored and her currency stabilized. The note certainly encouraged the German Government to face the realities of the situation. On the 8th the mark fell to 1 million to the pound; the Cuno Government fell on the 12th, and a new Cabinet under Gustav Stresemann admitted at last that passive resistance had failed. On 26 September 1923 all ordinances regarding passive resistance were withdrawn, without any assurances being obtained from the other side.

At this point occurred the 'Corfu incident', ominous for the future as an early example of Mussolini's tactics of scoring easy diplomatic triumphs in the Mediterranean when France and England were distracted by German affairs. On 20 August four Italian members of the Frontier Delimitation Commission were murdered by unknown bandits on Greek soil near Janina. When Greece proposed to submit the heavy Italian demands for reparations and apologies to the League, the Italian fleet bombarded and seized Corfu. Mussolini, with the sympathy of France, refused on 5 September to accept the League's intervention, whereupon Curzon gave in and agreed to the 'unofficial' reference of the problem to the Conference of Ambassadors. Greece and apparently Italy both agreed at first to the proposal that 50 million lire should be paid by Greece to a Swiss bank pending a decision by the Permanent Court. But on 26 September the Ambassadors accepted the Italian demand that the money should be paid directly to Italy. Greece complied reluctantly and Corfu was evacuated. Although the movements of the British Mediterranean fleet facilitated the Italian decision not to linger indefinitely it seemed evident that the three Western powers regarded the League with little esteem.

On 20 September Baldwin saw Poincaré in Paris, and when after the meeting a French communiqué (which Baldwin had not seen) announced that 'a common agreement of views' had been established, many people, including Curzon, believed that Baldwin had abandoned the stand made in the note of 11 August. This impression deepened when, after the German announcement of 26 September, day after day went by without any French move. Baldwin, however, on 12 October, invited the United States Government to collaborate in the appointment of an expert committee to inquire into Germany's capacity to pay. The United States agreed on the 15th, and the Belgian and Italian Governments at the end of October. Poincaré at first made reservations which seemed likely to wreck the whole prospect, and did not agree to participate in the expert inquiry until 30 November. The committee, with General Dawes and Mr Owen D. Young as the American representatives, was constituted in December. Great Britain was represented by Sir Josiah Stamp and Sir Robert Kindersley.

Ramsay MacDonald's Foreign Policy

The accession to office of a Labour Government in January 1924 was an important event in the history of British foreign policy. It gave expression to the growing desire of the country for a change in the spirit and the methods followed since the war sufficient to bring Britain and the world to a state of real peace. MacDonald himself had voiced these aspirations at the end of October 1923.

> Our policy has been amateurish, feeble, uncertain. We have, therefore, almost ceased to count except as a hope (a no mean asset, however, if used) . . . Europe is getting sick of Napoleonism. Therefore, my general conclusion is that whilst in Governments there may be no change, whilst vain men gain some reputation

from vociferous sections in their own States for empty triumphs, the general mind turns away from them and looks for other voices and other leaders.

On specific issues nevertheless wide divergences of opinion remained. While there was general support for an improvement in relations with France and Germany, many sections of middle- and even working-class opinion looked with suspicion on the policy of *rapprochement* with the Soviet Union. Labour policy, which included *de jure* recognition (on 1 February), a long-drawn-out conference in London from April to July, and the signature in August of two Anglo-Soviet treaties, accordingly became the basis of attack even by the Liberals. MacDonald gave a lead to the growing body of advocates of pacificism in the country, without convincing those who preferred to rely on the more conventional safeguards of national security. Nevertheless there was common sense as well as idealism in the view that as Great Britain was not in a good position to coerce other powers by arms she might as well appeal to public opinion and place her faith in international goodwill.[1]

The Dawes Report

France was predisposed to listen to such an appeal: the franc had fallen to nearly a quarter of its nominal value, huge deficits were looming ahead, and both governing circles and the masses were forced to realize that settlement by negotiation was inevitable. Yet in a sense French policy had justified itself. German politicians and industrialists had been taught that deliberate evasion of reparations payment was unprofitable; the French had managed to secure 1,392,689,175 francs from Germany during the year; Great Britain and the United States, while looking askance at French methods, were sufficiently

[1] As H. R. Winkler points out in 'The Emergence of a Labor Foreign Policy in Great Britain, 1918–1929' (*Journal of Modern History*, September 1956), the more sober line followed by Labour Governments in 1924 and 1929 may owe more to J. R. Clynes than to Ramsay MacDonald. See also W. P. Maddon, *Foreign Relations in British Labour Politics* (1934), and M. P. McCarran, *Fabianism in the Political Life of Britain, 1919–1931* (1952).

alarmed by the grimness of the struggle to abandon the attitude of disapproving aloofness (itself a matter of prestige).

Poincaré did not at first appear very amenable. On 23 November 1923 the Düsseldorf Agreement was concluded between the French authorities and the Ruhr mine-owners; by assigning certain receipts exclusively to the French it worked to the disadvantage of the other allies, who had not been consulted. On 19 November Poincaré proposed that Allied military control which had been withdrawn during the Ruhr struggle, should immediately be reimposed on Germany, in order to enforce the execution of the military clauses of the treaty, and the surrender of the Crown Prince, who had returned to Germany. A demand was made that the British authorities should allow the Franco-Belgian Railway Régie to run their trains through the British occupied zone in the Rhineland, and finally on 2 January 1924 the Rhineland High Commission, with its Franco-Belgian majority, took certain decisions which amounted to recognition of the self-styled 'Autonomous government' of the Palatinate. Curzon, who had practically a free hand for a few weeks while Baldwin was involved in the election campaign, took a very firm stand on all these points, and secured Poincaré's virtual surrender. On 20 November, after a threat that British representatives would be withdrawn from all inter-Allied bodies, the French agreed that there should be no threat of sanctions or demand for the Crown Prince's surrender. Poincaré did not, after this, make any haste to bring the Düsseldorf Agreement before the Reparations Commission. In the face of strong French protests Mr Clive, the British Consul at Munich, was sent to report on the separatist proceedings in the Palatinate, and his report, which stated that the overwhelming mass of the population in the Palatinate was opposed to autonomous government, was announced in the Commons on 21 January 1924.

Ramsay MacDonald's accession to office on 22 January, after his specific promises of a pacific and conciliatory foreign policy, enabled Poincaré to abandon with a good face the struggle with Great Britain, which Curzon's firmness had, however, already virtually settled. The Clive Report was followed by Poincaré's definite repudiation of the Separatists. On 9 February the French accepted the British proposals of 14 December that the Cologne railways should transport French goods through the British zone. Poincaré's relations with MacDonald were more friendly than with any British minister since his accession to office; in January also the problem of Germany's future had, for the moment, passed into the hands of the Dawes Committee, so that the Foreign Offices were able for some months to postpone direct negotiations on the more important issues. The experts took rather longer to complete their work than had been anticipated. The report, presented on 9 April, insisted on the two essential conditions of a stabilized currency and a balanced budget; a new 'Reichsmark' was to succeed the 'Rentenmark' (introduced as a temporary measure in November 1923), and the bank of issue, although free from Government control, was to be supervised in order to protect foreign interests. German payments were to rise in five years from £50 million to the standard rate of £125 million; they were, however, to be made in German currency, and the recipients were to conduct the transfer operations. A foreign loan of 800 million gold marks would be necessary to tide Germany over her immediate difficulties. The report also insisted that Germany should revert to the position of an economic unit – in other words, that the Ruhr should be evacuated – and the French experts were induced to agree that the report should be regarded as an indivisible whole.

The French Press began, within forty-eight hours of the presentation of the report, to hint at the necessity for additional measures of control; and Poincaré demanded, in return for abandoning his existing position in the Ruhr, a specific British agreement to support France in military and economic 'sanctions' against Germany for any default in executing the Dawes scheme. However, Poincaré's Government resigned on 1 June and he was succeeded, after a considerable political crisis, by M. Herriot, the Radical Socialist leader, supported by the Socialist Party. He promised to accept without *arrière pensée* the report of the experts, but was not prepared to evacuate the Ruhr until the pledges prescribed by the experts had been put into force.

After Anglo-French preparatory talks an Allied conference met on 16 July and made good progress under MacDonald's excellent chairmanship. It was agreed that problems of inter-Allied debts and of security could be dealt with later. The agreement of the United States Government to be represented on the Reparations Commission for the purpose of establishing a default removed the danger of a Franco-Belgian majority on the Commission which would once more force on sanctions. But doubts were thrown on the security for the international loan, and it was also found impossible in practice to avoid the question of the French and Belgian military occupation of the left bank, although this was to have been discussed at a later conference. The first difficulty was met by an American proposal that the German Government should give priority over every other state obligation to the Bondholders' claims in any contingency, including that of a default. In the second case the French and Belgians were to be allowed to continue their military occupation for one year, and to employ their own railwaymen on the strategic railways.

With these points settled, a German delegation was invited to London, and after making strong objections to certain points, finally accepted the Allies' proposals, although under protest, on 16 August. The necessary legislation was passed in the Reichstag by the end of the month. In September MacDonald, with Herriot's approval, proposed Germany's admission to the League. The loan was floated successfully in October, the largest portion being subscribed by the United States. The German Government had also agreed in July to the Allied demand for a final general inspection of German army installations and factories by the Inter-Allied Commission to see that the disarmament clauses were really being carried out. Stresemann was well aware of the secret rearmament measures of the German Army. He took the decision in order to improve Germany's diplomatic standing abroad, and had to face protests and some violence from the army and nationalist groups.

Locarno

Germany and the Allies could now turn to the problem of placing their improved relations on a more permanent footing. This might take the form either of direct understanding between the powers or of a more generalized agreement which would remove both existing and hypothetical causes of war. The second objective was pursued with energy by the League of Nations, although the official British attitude towards these aspirations was cautious and decidedly hesitant, as will be seen in the next chapter.

Germany's attitude depended in some measure on that of the Soviet Union. The Anglo-Soviet Agreement of 7 August 1924 was MacDonald's gesture of goodwill to Moscow, and promised a British loan in return for Soviet negotiations with the British bondholders. Dislike of the agreement and fear of Communist subversion was excited by the so-called Campbell case, and when the Liberals decided to withdraw support on 8 October 1924 a general election followed. It may or may not be the case that the Zinoviev letter, a possible forgery which rang true to many Englishmen, decided the issue.

The general election brought Stanley Baldwin back to office with a decisive majority, and Great Britain entered on five years of Conservative rule, with Austen Chamberlain as Foreign Secretary. The circumstances of the election influenced to some extent the new Government's attitude towards outstanding points in its predecessor's policy, and probably helped to strengthen its hostility to the Geneva Protocol (which the Labour Government had helped to draft) and to the Soviet Union. The quarrel with Russia, and the serious crisis in British relations with Egypt after the murder of Sir Lee Stack on 19 November, compelled it to postpone consideration of the Protocol; this allowed time for full discussion with the Dominions, and largely as a result of their unfavourable comment, Chamberlain in March 1925 informed the Council that his Government had decided not to accept the Protocol. This necessarily meant its general abandonment.

The rejection caused acute disappointment in Belgium and France, where its terms were felt to provide a more definite guarantee of the 1919 settlement than had hitherto seemed possible. They had, however, already been assured, by Chamberlain's important statement in the Commons on 5 March, that the British Government did not propose to revert to a policy of complete isolationism. On 12 March, after announcing to the League Council the British decision, he stated the Government's willingness 'to supplement the Covenant by making special arrangements in order to meet special ends'.[1] Even this cautious statement was too much for some of his colleagues, led by Curzon; but after a threat of resignation this undercurrent of opposition disappeared. He was able to count throughout on the loyal, and almost uncritical, support of Baldwin. The statement of 12 March contained the germ of the Western European pact known later as the Locarno Treaty, and it indicates the extent and limitations of Chamberlain's policy. In rejecting any serious attempt to devise a general system of international security the British Government had in effect declined to participate in regional pacts except where the more immediate interests of the country were involved, although its rejection of complete isolationism meant that an agreement concerning the French frontiers was also visualized.

Two possible forms of this agreement had already been suggested by the British and German Governments in 1922. The British proposal in question was the abortive scheme for an Anglo-French guarantee of each other's territories discussed at Cannes in January 1922. After the rejection of the Protocol the Foreign Office proposed a defensive alliance with France, but the Cabinet, influenced by Balfour, rejected this. The 1922 German proposal was for a pact giving a bilateral guarantee, between Germany and the Allies, of the western frontiers of Germany for a generation. This was rejected by Poincaré as a

[1] B.D., Ser. IA, vol. i, pp. 7–16.

'clumsy manoeuvre'. The offer was repeated in May and September 1923 and again rejected by Poincaré. He cannot perhaps be blamed for regarding it as a tactical move to influence world opinion during the reparations struggle. The German Government had nevertheless shown how a British guarantee of France could be given a form acceptable to British opinion.

Opinion in Germany was again antagonized by the Allied note of 5 January 1925, which announced that the Cologne zone would not be evacuated on 10 January as the inter-Allied Commission of Control had found that Germany was in default in respect of disarmament. There is no doubt that the Commission had good reason for its report. Nevertheless the German Government was sufficiently attracted by the possibility of a Rhineland agreement to persevere. On 20 January a German memorandum proposing a pact of mutual security was forwarded by the British Ambassador, Lord D'Abernon, to London. Chamberlain's response was not at first encouraging; he was so concerned lest discussions between London and Berlin should be interpreted as disloyal to France that he gave an impression of hostility to Germany. During February, however the importance and the possibilities of the German suggestion became clear to him. On 9 February Stresemann made to the French Government the substance of the 1922 German proposal, namely, that the powers interested in the Rhine – 'above all England, France, Italy, and Germany' – should enter into a solemn obligation for a lengthy period not to wage war against a contracting state. Stresemann felt that he could go no farther on his own initiative, but on 24 March Austen Chamberlain gave his provisional support to the proposals, and urged 'that we must work with good faith and goodwill in the hope that we might make them the basis of a real security and a real peace'.

The French and Belgian Governments were willing to negotiate on the basis of the German offer, and during the next few months the essential problem was that of the eastern, rather than the western, frontiers of Germany. France and her two allies, Poland and Czechoslovakia, were naturally apprehensive lest a guarantee of her frontiers in the west should merely concentrate Germany's attention on the east, and the German Government did not even pretend to exclude this possibility. Stresemann's essential aim seems to have been a position of balance for Germany between the Western powers and Russia; each knew enough about German relations with the other to fear the consequences of antagonizing him. He did not intend to do anything that would upset the valuable Soviet–German secret military contacts. But he was prepared to renounce the intention of going to war to alter the eastern frontiers, and to rely on Article 19 of the Covenant, which expressly provided for the modification of treaties by peaceful negotiation.[1]

The dominant opinion in France seemed, at first, to be that this assurance was not enough, and that it would be wiser to reject the German offer altogether if Great Britain were not prepared to extend her guarantee to the east. Herriot's Government resigned on 10 April, and Briand, the new Foreign Minister, continued for the next few weeks to seek a formula which would secure a British guarantee, if not of the eastern frontier, at any rate of the arbitration treaties which Germany offered to Poland and Czechoslovakia. But on 28 May Chamberlain made it finally clear that British participation could only cover the western frontiers, and Briand accepted this in substance on 4 June. This acceptance of the British reservations was facilitated by Chamberlain's obvious devotion to France; his 'honesty coupled with partiality' was, however, to prove a handicap in the later years of the ministry.

Germany also made counter-proposals; she wished to make her entry into the League dependent on the evacuation of the Ruhr, the sanctions area, and the first Rhineland zone; she desired a special status with regard to Article 16 of the Covenant, and wished to stipulate that the security pact must not place Germany in a worse position than she had had under the Versailles Treaty. The reservations were not well received in Paris and London; her first application for membership of the

[1] L. Kochan, *The Struggle for Germany, 1914–45* (1963), pp. 41–53.

League on 14 March 1925 was rejected. But the disputed points were referred to a committee of legal experts, representing Germany, France, Great Britain, Belgium, and Italy. As a result of their deliberations in London during September the five powers were able to assemble at Locarno on 5 October for the final negotiations. Throughout the negotiations Stresemann's difficulties were great. Lord D'Abernon believed that the 'chances of assassination to which he exposed himself were such that no prudent insurance company would have assumed the risk of a life policy'. Apart from the fear of assassination he had to cope with the opposition of von Seeckt, who quite failed to understand the similarity of Stresemann's aims to his own.

His problems were simplified by Soviet Foreign Minister Chicherin, who came to Berlin on the eve of the Locarno meeting and launched a violent Press attack on the League, the Western powers, and Article 16. This alarmed the other signatory powers at Locarno so much that they agreed to address to Germany a collective note expressing the view that each League member was bound to resist aggression 'to an extent which is compatible with its military situation and takes its geographical position into account'. Other difficulties were removed very quickly: Germany agreed to conclude arbitration treaties with Poland and Czechoslovakia simultaneously with the other agreement, and to drop the demand for the immediate evacuation of parts of the Rhineland, although she secured promises on this point which satisfied substantially her immediate requirements. The entire body of documents was initialled on 16 October. By the Treaty of Mutual Guarantee Germany, Belgium, France, Great Britain, and Italy severally and collectively guaranteed the inviolability of Germany's existing western frontier and the observance of the Versailles provisions regarding the demilitarized zone. Article 9 stated that the treaty should impose no obligation upon any of the British Dominions, or upon India, unless the Government concerned should signify its acceptance. The treaties were ratified in all the countries concerned, and the formal signing took place in London on 1 December. Russia was relieved to find that Stresemann had made Article 16 virtually innocuous.

The Locarno settlement, like that of Washington in 1921, purchased a temporary cessation of trouble in certain spheres by arrangements which created conditions of fresh trouble elsewhere. It is clear from the negotiations that neither British nor German opinion would have made possible a similar settlement of the eastern frontiers. The predominant Conservative opinion would not have accepted anything more than the western guarantee; the Liberals were opposed even to this. Thus the Locarno Agreement had provided merely a partial solution of the general problem of security; France retained her distrust of German intentions, and Germany her carefully nourished sense of grievance. The Baldwin Government, however, showed little consciousness of a need to achieve more than the immediate objectives of its European policy in 1925. Germany's election to a permanent seat on the League Council was sadly bungled; in spite of some well-intentioned lobbying by Chamberlain in March 1926 the matter had to be postponed until June.[1] The counter-claims of Poland, Spain, and Brazil were partially met by the creation of three 'semi-permanent' seats, but Brazil ultimately left the League. Against all the evidence Germany was exonerated from accusations of evading disarmament, and the Control Commission was withdrawn on 31 January 1927. Before the end of Austen Chamberlain's term of office, steps were initiated to complete the reparations settlement on the lines laid down in the Dawes plan; this resulted in the Young plan of 1930 (Chapter VI). An air of false security was created by the absolutely punctual payment of reparations instalments, and by the substantial schemes of social welfare which the German Government was able to forward during these years. This partial prosperity was an artificial and transitory product of extensive foreign loans, and the economic crisis of 1930 left German Governments with no adequate answer to those of their opponents who proclaimed the futility of efforts to seek salvation for Germany by conciliating the Western powers.

[1] B.D., op. cit.; cf. no. 378.

V

Great Britain and the League, 1919–29

The League and British Public Opinion

In tracing the main lines of British post-war foreign policy up to this point it has not been necessary to give more than incidental reference to the work of the League of Nations; it was generally agreed that negotiations arising from the peace settlement could best be handled by the existing diplomatic machinery of the states concerned. By 1924, however, the phase of post-war struggle seemed to be passing, and the League, still untried and therefore still a possible source of miracles, was turned to by many sections of European opinion in their search for an international New Deal.

It was already clear by 1924 that there were widespread differences of opinion as to the League's possibilities. In England these differences may possibly have been greater than in other countries, and they certainly led to contradictions in British official policy which justified much criticism and bewilderment abroad. It would, however, be a mistake to assume that this was evidence of some typically British muddle-headedness or hypocrisy. Much the same differences appeared elsewhere. Germany denounced, joined, and later on left it; Italy, one of the original members, flagrantly challenged the jurisdiction of the Council as early as the Corfu incident of 1923; France somehow persuaded herself that her coercion of Germany before 1924 was a suitable preliminary to the system of Peace through Law that she desired; the United States demanded a League, rejected it, denounced war and armaments, and insisted on as fine a navy as money could buy. From the Soviet Union came laborious attempts to open up normal political and economic relations with Western Europe, alternating with flaming denunciations of capitalistic society and all its works; later she too joined the League.

In England the League of Nations was for many classes and individuals a wish-fulfilment, an apparent realization of ideas and aspirations which the emotionalism of the war period had strengthened, but not created. In the recent war England had not fought consciously for the precise political and territorial objectives which had influenced the continental belligerents. She fought neither for the liberation of her own soil, nor for the restoration, acquisition, or emancipation of border provinces; she did not – as in the eighteenth century – fight deliberately for empire, and in spite of her plentiful wartime denunciation of the enemy she had no deep-seated tradition of anti-German sentiment comparable with that of France, or even with the Italian feeling towards Austria. Within the memory of most adults in 1914 France and Russia had, indeed, been greater rivals. After a hundred years of remarkable commercial and industrial prosperity and of immunity from prolonged major wars, Great Britain had no class or group which publicly accepted war as a necessary – if unpleasant – 'instrument of national policy': whereas in the case of at least four continental great powers a powerful war machine was kept in permanent readiness for the war which, though dreaded in many quarters, was regarded as the inevitable solution of various problems of national honour, ambition, or security.

The war was, therefore, to the average Englishman, literally no more and no less than a war to end war. He was not conscious of any objective other than the overthrow of the German 'militarists' who had, he honestly believed, deliberately hurled their military machine against an unsuspecting world. After the successful termination of the war the fundamental aim of the country was to establish a permanent state of peace; it was willing enough to hang the Kaiser, to try 'war criminals', and to destroy the German war machine, but it had no traditional animosity towards Germany itself. It looked for some guarantee that peace would be permanently preserved, but the overwhelming demand for demobilization and the ending of conscription meant that it shrank from the view that world peace or its own security must be maintained by large British armaments.

Instead, there was growing support for the view that a healthy popular self-interest would prevent future wars if only its effective force could be brought to bear; and this necessitated publicity. The Union of Democratic Control, launched early in the war by E. D. Morel, Ramsay Macdonald, Norman Angell, and others, was sceptical about wartime propaganda and made much of the need for open diplomacy, with corresponding criticism of the baleful effects of the professionals whose secret negotiations had so conspicuously failed to keep the peace in 1914.[1] After the war the majority of English men and women accepted the League of Nations as an institution with ready-made machinery for solving peacefully all international problems; its health and vigour were felt, in some rather mystical way, to depend on the zeal of those who believed most ardently in its possibilities. This view was rational in so far as it presupposed a peace-loving majority in each potentially aggressive state responsive to a really authoritative lead from Geneva. But as the League had not eschewed the ultimate use of force, a policy of full loyalty to the League would still necessitate economic and military sanctions against an aggressor government, at least in the last resort. On this point, however, League supporters in the pulpit and the many voluntary societies supporting the peace movement faced but shirked an obvious dilemma. They could not bring themselves to admit that any considerable modification in the existing political and economic situation of Europe was necessary, and on the other hand they could not admit that the maintenance of peace, even by the most orthodox League methods, must in-

---

[1] G. P. Gooch, *Under Six Reigns* (1958), pp. 172–83; H. M. Swanwick, *Builders of Peace* (1924), pp. 23–37.

volve preparedness for a major European war. But it was hoped that the League had provided a happy solution of the problem of making war safe for democracy.

Accordingly it was vaguely accepted that an unequivocal condemnation of any aggressive power would preserve peace, because the aggressor would never dare to involve himself in war with the fifty or so remaining states. But what if the aggressor decided to risk it, and disarmed Britain, as one of the two most prominent League powers, was called on to do most of the fighting? Even discussion of these ultimate realities by professional writers and politicians was condemned as morbid, or as the revelation of an innate lust for fighting which was the first step to war-mongering: rather reversing the spirit of Bernard Shaw's comment that if there were less written about love there would be less love. The Labour Party was strongly influenced by the pacifist urge, although never completely dominated by it;[1] but even the Conservatives talked peace. Balfour, condemning preoccupation with the problem of aggression as pathological, told the League through Austen Chamberlain in March 1925 that just as it was not wholesome for the ordinary man to be continually brooding over the possibility of a severe surgical operation, so it was unwise 'for societies to pursue a similar course'.[2]

The temptation to catch votes with vague and resounding affirmations of faith in the League was almost irresistible. British Cabinets and the Foreign Office were, however, forced to ask themselves precisely what the League was, and what Great Britain could contribute to it. Before the League had come formally into existence on 10 January 1920 American action had done much to make it, in the British Government's eyes, abortive. The United States had not only rejected, at the end of 1919, the idea of herself joining the League, but had also, a year earlier, turned down a British proposal that the wartime inter-Allied economic organization should be widened into a

[1] W. R. Tucker, *The Attitude of the British Labour Party to European and Collective Security Problems, 1920–39* (1950).
[2] Sir C. Petrie, *The Life and Letters of the Rt. Hon. Sir Austen Chamberlain* (1940), ii, pp. 252–64.

general international system, which the ex-enemy countries would be forced, and the neutrals be persuaded, to join. If this plan had succeeded there would have been an international organization of the economic forces of the world, which would, in the words of the Foreign Office, supply 'the inevitable corollary of the whole idea of a League of Nations'.[1]

But the result was a failure to devise means for the control of peacetime capitalistic competition, and this was followed by a general refusal to consider seriously the idea of a world organization in the form of a union of communistic states. The League of Nations thus came into existence without machinery for the control of the international anarchy of economic interests. Even as a political organization the League, without the membership of the United States, Germany, and the Soviet Union, had not the universal authority and clearly defined support of all the world's effective political and military forces, and could not claim that its mere existence automatically extinguished aggression. The non-members provided from the start an extensive neutral element whose non-participation in League action might easily make the imposition of economic sanctions on an aggressor impracticable. Among member states Japan was obviously not prepared to interest herself very closely in resistance to aggression outside the Far East, and Italy, as her action in the Corfu incident in 1923 showed clearly enough, had evolved a 'realistic' attitude towards international politics, which excluded sacrifices for causes beyond the sphere of her more immediate and obvious interests.

And Britain would remain, in Professor Zimmern's terminology, a 'producer' rather than a 'consumer' of security. As a policy of economic sanctions against almost any state would involve a naval blockade, Great Britain as the chief naval power in the League would become the chief producer, and as long as the United States with an approximately equal navy was unwilling to join, or establish a *modus vivendi* with, the League, a conflict over neutral shipping rights with America had to be visualized as the very likely consequence of a sanc-

[1] Alfred Zimmern, *The League of Nations and the Rule of Law* (1936), pp. 151–9.

tionist policy. This would make success difficult even against a European power. In the Far East an economic blockade of Japan would certainly be ineffective without American co-operation, which would probably not be forthcoming. For these and similar reasons British Governments after 1919 felt it necessary to treat the whole guarantee function of the League as, in existing circumstances, unworkable; it was strengthened in this view by the hostility of the Dominions to the sanctions' clauses. On the other hand public feeling in Great Britain made it impossible for the Government to propose leaving the League, or even to propose a formal suspension of the guarantee system; British official policy during the twenties was forced to be satisfied with the alternative of defining and limiting the guarantee obligations, and of demonstrating loyalty to the League by encouraging its less embarrassing activities.

The latter included what became known as the technical functions. Work on these began in 1919, following a tentative plan drawn up by Mr (afterwards Sir) Arthur Salter in the spring. Three organizations – dealing respectively with Communications and Transit, Health, and Finance and Economics – were set up by the League Council at its meeting under Balfour's chairmanship in February 1920. These were all in varying degrees the continuation of the *ad hoc* international co-operation of the peace conference era, and they enabled the League, in spite of its failure to become the effective controller of the world's high politics, to justify some form of existence. A somewhat similar justification was found in the work of the Mandates Commission, and in the settlement under League auspices of specific problems (such as the Aaland isles dispute of 1920–1, and the Upper Silesian frontier problem of 1921) referred to it by League members.

The Draft Treaty of Mutual Assistance

The critical attitude of the British Government towards the guarantee provisions became clear at an early stage. At the first Assembly in November 1920 the Canadian delegates proposed the complete elimination of Article 10, which provided for the maintenance of the territorial integrity of member states. During the next two years proposals from various quarters, which tended to make participation in the application of economic sanctions permissive and not compulsory on member states, received considerable support from British delegates. Nevertheless, the divergences in British opinion were speedily illustrated when the movement towards a complete abandonment of the new guarantees for security was checked by counter-proposals in which individual British representatives at Geneva played an active part.

The French, with their eyes on an apparently irreconcilable Germany, desired to make the League an organization with complete provisions for mutual assistance against aggression; they were supported by Belgium, the Central European succession states, and various non-European states such as China and Haiti, who had similar qualms about their own safety. This system, which was compatible with the maintenance of extensive armed forces as weapons of defence, was directly opposed to that advocated by the Scandinavian states, Holland, and Switzerland. They placed disarmament in the foreground, and, arguing that extensive military forces were both a symbol and a cause of international rivalry, advocated the reduction of armaments to the minimum necessary for the maintenance of internal order. British official circles were in favour of the reduction of armaments, although they could never accept the idea of the sacrifice of naval supremacy in European waters; and they were prepared to consider some limited and localized guarantees of security. It was hard to say what the British public would have agreed to in this respect if it had been presented with more extensive proposals: the Chanak crisis and Bonar Law's letter of 6 October 1922 did not encourage fresh commitments. There was a tendency also to link security with disarmament, partly from a feeling that countries which had disarmed had a greater moral claim to support than those which had not; partly, however, for the more practical reason that extensive disarmament of land forces would make a sanctions policy (imposed by the strong naval powers of the League) correspondingly easier.

At the first meeting of the Assembly in 1920 a proposal by the Norwegian delegate, encouraged by Lord Robert Cecil, led to the appointment by the Assembly of a civilian committee, known as the Temporary Mixed Commission, to study disarmament. An early proposal by one of the members, Lord Esher, was for a scheme of European land armaments based on units of 30,000. France was to have six such units; Italy and Poland, four each; Great Britain and several other powers, three each, and so on. General opposition soon killed this proposal, but Cecil, who at this time represented South Africa in the Assembly, returned to the problem in July 1922 by putting first to the commission, and later to the Assembly, propositions affirming that the reduction of armaments to be successful must be general, and that the provision of guarantees of security, which should also be general, should depend on an undertaking to reduce armaments. From this arose the very ingenious proposals known as the Draft Treaty of Mutual Assistance. Cecil presented his own proposals, which introduced the idea of strengthening the general guarantee of security by regional agreements, to the Temporary Mixed Commission in February 1923; Colonel Requin, the French member of the Permanent Advisory Commission, presented an alternative draft, and an amalgamation of these two schemes was presented to the Assembly in September 1923. In this Assembly Cecil sat as a representative of the Baldwin Government. The draft treaty insisted on the obligation of all members to assist one of their number in a war of aggression, and left it to the Council to allocate their duties; but it also allowed the formation of voluntary regional agreements between states who would be more particularly responsible for the maintenance of peace in their own areas, and limited the obligation to engage in military operations against an aggressor to powers in the same continent.

The Labour Government rejected the draft treaty on 18 July 1924, for reasons very much the same as those of previous

British Governments. Heavy responsibility was again imposed on British naval power, and the scheme of continental agreements cut right across the organization of the British Empire. Moreover, the agreements might foreshadow a return to the pre-war system of alliances. The British Government was not alone in its rejection, for almost all the major powers except France took a similar line. But the tone of the British reply annoyed the large pro-League elements in the Labour and Liberal Parties, who pointed out to MacDonald that he had proclaimed the determination of the Labour Party to strengthen the League. From MacDonald's anxiety to prove his sincerity without involving Britain in a military commitment there sprang the Geneva Protocol.

The Geneva Protocol

The general principles of this new plan were laid down by Ramsay MacDonald and Herriot on 6 September 1924. At a later stage in the debate Arthur Henderson, speaking as a delegate of the British Empire, insisted on reservations which seemed to render the protocol entirely innocuous from the British point of view. The basic idea of the protocol was to maintain the essential connexion between security and disarmament, but to supply a satisfactory test of aggression, and to close the 'gap in Article 15' of the Covenant by means of compulsory arbitration. Article 15 provided that the Council should endeavour to find a solution of any dispute submitted to it by a member, but had left war legitimate if this mediation failed. It had also excluded matters within the domestic jurisdiction of one of the parties. The protocol provided that all disputes of a legal character should be submitted to the Permanent Court of International Justice, whose decision would be binding; other disputes should be dealt with by the Council, but if the Council should fail to arrive at a unanimous decision the matter should be referred to a board of arbitrators, whose decision would be binding. The protocol also provided, as the result of a Japanese proposal, that disputes concerning matters of domestic jurisdiction should be submitted to the conciliation procedure of Article 11. But it also contained reservations which took most of the sting out of it. Great Britain had insisted that she must retain complete juridical liberty to decide what action she would take for the enforcement of sanctions, and Denmark, who was practically disarmed, had asked for a wording which should recognize this fact. It was accordingly provided that each state should co-operate 'in the degree which its geographical position and its particular situation as regards armaments allow'. A further provision was that the protocol should come into force only after a plan for the reduction of armaments had been adopted.

The decision as to whether the protocol should be ratified fell to the Conservatives, among whom opposition to the proposals had been inflated by a somewhat tendentious Press campaign, led as so often by *The Times*. During the winter of 1924-5 the Dominions also expressed their opposition with varying degrees of bluntness, although this was not the main reason for Britain's opposition. They were particularly concerned lest the provisions concerning disputes on matters of domestic jurisdiction should work to their detriment. Canada, Australia, and New Zealand made clear their fear that they might have to submit to arbitration the question of alien immigration. In Great Britain the possibility of difficulties with the United States over sanctions, and with the Dominions over the colour question, were soon raised; the Americans made it clear that in the former case they would insist as neutrals on their full rights of trade. The Foreign Office had, also, long-standing objections to compulsory arbitration. What was wanted, in the words of Sir James Headlam-Morley, was 'a European protocol'. The idea of revising the protocol may have been contemplated, but it was soon abandoned, and as compensation for its rejection in March 1925 the Government offered the suggestion of local agreements, which led to the Locarno settlement. The British objections were embodied in the Balfour memorandum, which was read to the Council by Austen Chamberlain on 12 March. Its main argument was the now familiar one that the League was crippled by the absence of the United States, and that in these circumstances Great Britain and the Dominions could not take the 'strong' view of the Covenant and its obligations; he also pointed out that the framers of the Covenant presumably felt 'that the objections to universal and compulsory arbitration might easily outweigh its theoretical advantages'.

The dismay caused by the British rejection of the protocol was to some extent removed by the success of the Locarno settlement; the 'Locarno spirit' was further exemplified in the close and friendly relationship established between Stresemann, Briand, and Chamberlain.[1] They continued to control the foreign policies of the respective countries until 1929, and by making Geneva their normal meeting-place they automatically raised the prestige of the League and made it for a time the political directorate of international affairs that its founders had intended. Yet the problem of security had not been solved: if anything the new importance of the League made the solution more difficult, for it promoted complacency and a dangerous tendency to regard goodwill as an adequate substitute for specific commitments.

The Disarmament Deadlock, 1925–7

This tendency was well illustrated by the contrast between the halting progress of the disarmament discussions and the easy success of the Kellogg Pact. In December 1925 the Council set up a preparatory committee to prepare material for an international conference on disarmament (which ultimately met in 1932). The only substantial progress hitherto made had been that of naval limitation at Washington in 1921; the new conference was to deal with both land and sea forces. Throughout 1926 the technical experts of the powers struggled to define the nature and value of the armaments in question and the principles on which reduction should be based. The disadvantages of this method of approach were obvious. As the statesmen had failed to discover any system which would give

[1] B.D., Ser. IA, vol. i, pp. 7–8.

general guarantees against aggression the soldiers' conception of security could not easily be challenged.

Each delegation accordingly put forward schemes of disarmament which would increase the relative strength of its own forces. Great Britain, with a small standing army, was interested in preventing the existence of large foreign armies which could win a lightning war before her Territorial forces were mobilized, and new armies raised; her assets were her industrial and financial resources, and her excellent strategical position as a first-rate naval power. France, on the other hand, was determined to maintain a large force which on the outbreak of war would deliver or repel a sudden attack; but she felt inferior in those forces, industrial and otherwise, which constituted 'war-potential' and which could be brought into action after the outbreak of hostilities. She desired, therefore, to maintain her existing ratio of superiority in trained forces to Germany, but to limit war-potential, and budgetary expenditure, and to establish effective international supervision of armaments. Great Britain considered the limitation of budgetary expenditure and war-potential impracticable, but proposed the limitation of war material both in service and in reserve. The Germans strongly supported the British proposal to limit the trained reserves; France and the conscription countries argued strongly against such restrictions. Little real progress towards genuine disarmament could come from such discussions. In March 1927 the British experts deposited a draft convention setting forth their view; the French replied at once with a second draft maintaining their own thesis. In April, after failure to compromise, a draft report was issued setting forth the rival viewpoints. The British and French were also strongly opposed on the question of naval limitation, France demanding a limitation of total tonnage, Great Britain, limitation by separate categories.

The differences concerning naval limitation were illustrated by the abortive naval conference at Geneva in June and July 1927. When the United States Government invited the Washington Conference signatories to a separate conference to

deal with categories of ships not limited in 1921, France and
Italy declined. Great Britain and Japan accepted. The American
proposal was simply that the Washington ratio of 5–5–3 for
capital ships should be extended to cruisers, destroyers, and
submarines, with a total tonnage for each class more or less the
same as those proposed at the Washington Conference. The
British were mainly concerned with securing what was considered an adequate number of cruisers: seventy was fixed by
the British experts, on the basis of experience in the First World
War, as the minimum necessary to protect the number of con-
voys visiting the country, to protect fixed patrol areas, and to
deal with possible attacks of enemy cruisers in massed bodies.
They proposed that cruisers should be divided into two classes,
those of 10,000 tons maximum with 8-inch guns, and those of
7,500 tons maximum with 6-inch guns. Great Britain would
need fifteen cruisers of the larger type and fifty-five of the
smaller, a possible total tonnage of 562,500. The Washington
figure for cruisers had been 300,000. The United States were
not prepared to agree to a total tonnage of more than 400,000,
and they desired twenty-five cruisers of 10,000, which would
allow for only twenty cruisers of 7,500 tons. They were also not
prepared to accept less than 8-inch guns. On this point of
difference no compromise was found to be possible.

The land disarmament discussions remained in a similar state
of deadlock. The preparatory commission resumed its discussions on 30 November 1927. It declined to take seriously a
proposal of the Russian representative, M. Litvinov, for the
immediate and total abolition of all armies, navies, and air
forces, but made little progress with the more conventional
problems. An attempt by Austen Chamberlain and Briand to
expedite matters by separate negotiations led to an agreement,
announced by Chamberlain on 30 July 1928, whereby Britain
withdrew her demand for a limitation of trained reserves, and
France accepted the British preferences in naval limitation. It
was proposed to ban the large cruisers and large submarines
that the United States wished to build. There was much
exasperation in Washington, and the plan had ultimately to be

dropped owing to the refusal of Italy and the United States to accept it.[1]

The Briand–Kellogg Pact

Two attempts to cut a way through all these entanglements were made, but in these Great Britain played only a subordinate part. On 24 September 1927 the Assembly unanimously adopted a Polish resolution 'that all wars of aggression are, and shall always be, prohibited'; and on 27 August 1928 fifteen powers signed the Pact of Paris, or Briand–Kellogg Pact for the Renunciation of War. In the second case the initiative was taken by Briand, who, after a conversation with the American Professor Shotwell, proposed on 6 April 1927 that France and the United States should agree mutually to 'outlaw war' between their two countries. We now know that the plan caused nothing but embarrassment in the State Department as a French attempt to conclude a 'negative military alliance' and the proposal to make the pact universal was an ingenious device to rob it of all practical meaning.[2] The fifteen signatories of the pact agreed to renounce war as an instrument of national policy, and to use only pacific means for the solution of any problem that might arise between them. Other powers joined later; by 1933 no fewer than sixty-five governments had signed.

The pact contained no time limit, but on the other hand it contained no mutual guarantee or machinery of enforcement, and the original authors made it clear that they did not ban wars of self-defence. It is in this sense that the various reservations put forward by the signatories must be understood. Great Britain stated in a dispatch of 19 May 1928 that there were certain regions in the world in which she was vitally interested, and that the protection of these regions against attack was to the British Empire a measure of self-defence. The Suez Canal zone was clearly indicated here. The United States reserved action in defence of the Monroe Doctrine.

[1] R. H. Ferrell, *American Diplomacy in the Great Depression* (1957), pp. 72–3.
[2] R. H. Ferrell, *Peace in Their Time* (1952), pp. 70–83.

Britain's Lost Opportunities

In the last two chapters we have traced – necessarily in summary fashion – the development of British foreign policy between 1922 and 1929 with regard, firstly, to the more immediate and more urgent problems of European politics, and, secondly, to the attempt to construct a better international society, primarily through the medium of the League of Nations. We have seen that in the latter case the effectiveness of British policy was seriously reduced by the fundamental unwillingness of the British public either to accept the risks, or to repudiate the responsibilities, involved in an active League policy, and by the Government's conviction that, with five of the seven great powers openly or virtually neutral, a zealous support of every possible victim of future aggression would involve exertions far beyond the country's military and economic strength.

The British public had fallen into the dangerous habit of assuming that the League, by the mere fact of its existence, had made such exertions unnecessary. It is, of course, difficult to generalize satisfactorily about anything so muddled and so vague as this phase of British opinion. We have seen that the predominant influence was extreme and vivid recollection of the horrors of the previous war, and that the attempt by individuals to formulate a rational policy was a more or less unconscious effort at escapism. It seemed difficult to believe that any national cause was worth an international war: difficult to believe that other people did not, in their heart of hearts, think the same. It was not easy to concentrate attention on those complex problems of foreign politics which still – the fact could not be altogether ignored – seemed to be causing an unnecessary amount of excitement abroad. On the whole it was the conviction of many good people that peace abroad could be adequately guaranteed by sufficient goodwill among Englishmen. No British Government, it would seem, really believed this to be the case. They knew well enough that in certain countries there existed tendencies towards extremes of political and economic nationalism which were fundamentally insusceptible in the sentiments of men of goodwill in Western Europe. These could, in the last resort, be resisted only by force, although not necessarily by the British forces.

But no party had the courage to go before the country with a demand for clear thinking on these unfashionable lines. Successive Governments had made it clear enough to the League and to foreign powers that they would only be prepared to take action in defence of certain specific interests; but no formal refusal was ever made, in language that the British public and world opinion could understand, to adopt economic, and if necessary military, sanctions in other cases. The result was that although a British Government had declined at Locarno in 1925 to guarantee the frontiers of states so near to England as Czechoslovakia and Poland, Great Britain was still thought to be liable in 1931 and 1935 to defend, as a League power, areas so geographically remote as Manchuria and Abyssinia. League action in both cases failed, as it was bound to do, and England, as the strongest League power, was supposed to have suffered defeat. Some might argue that the real delinquents were those British statesmen who, before the first serious test to the League in 1931, had shirked the task of convincing the country that a formal limitation of obligations under Article 16, or even a withdrawal from the League, was necessary.

This was partly because each party had burnt its fingers in attempting to introduce what seemed at the time to be more important innovations in external policy. The Conservatives had failed in 1923 to introduce protection, and Labour had failed in its attempt to come to terms with Russia in 1924. Nevertheless, by 1931 the chance had been lost of retreating from the more impracticable League obligations with a good face. The same is perhaps true of Anglo-German relations; Austen Chamberlain's loyalty to France led him to acquiesce all too readily in their hostility to further concessions. The 'Locarno period' from 1925 to 1929 certainly brought about a noticeable amelioration in Germany's position. But grievances remained which could have been removed at this stage without loss of prestige. Even such steps as the cancellation of reparations, the return of the colonies, the revision by arbitration of Germany's eastern frontiers, might have been carried out before 1930 without any appearance of surrender to German aggression, and the effect would have been to strengthen the more liberal tendencies which were overwhelmed in the débâcle of Germany's economic crisis between 1929 and 1933.

VI

Labour in Office, 1929–31

Labour and Foreign Policy

After the general election in May 1929, Labour, with 288 seats, took office as the largest party in the state; the Conservatives were reduced to 261 seats and the balance was held by 57 Liberals and 9 Independents. The country was probably more tired of the Conservatives than of Conservative policy; it was not convinced by Lloyd George's bold plans to conquer unemployment. The Labour Government's own plans in this direction were neither bold nor successful; the unemployment figure reached over 2,600,000 early in 1931. The ministry's foreign policy, on the other hand, was reasonably successful until its career was cut short by the débâcle of August 1931.

Arthur Henderson did well as Foreign Secretary and Ramsay MacDonald as Prime Minister made one or two notable diplomatic contributions to the Government's record. The Labour Party had had no difficulty since 1919 in enunciating the broader aims of its foreign policy, based on support and extension of the scope of the League and the building of a world society which would eliminate national rivalry by disarmament, arbitration, open diplomacy, the removal of the obnoxious features of the peace treaties, and, ultimately, the abolition of capitalism. The more exigent features of this idealistic programme owed much to E. D. Morel, and MacDonald was closely associated with him for a time. But Morel was not invited to join the Government in 1924, and the more sober

foreign policy followed by MacDonald in 1924 and Henderson
after 1929 may well have owed more to J. R. Clynes. For the
most part the Labour Party's supporters among the English
trade unions and middle classes wanted, not the early achievement of a socialist society after a glorious but probably bloody
revolution, but the tranquillity and relative prosperity which
it was believed might still be attained under the existing social
and economic order.[1] Thus its more immediate objectives did
not differ greatly from those of the Conservative Party; in its
belief that the universal yearning of the masses in all countries
for peace made possible the elimination of the causes of international war it even showed a greater faith in the possibilities
of capitalistic society than its opponents. We have seen that all
British Governments in the nineteen-twenties felt in some
measure that they must use their position of exceptional
influence in world affairs to make the existing position acceptable to other powers. It was realized more quickly in England
than in France that this aim could only be temporarily secured
by an Allied superiority in armaments which made the consequences of war more unpleasant for Germany than the
humiliations of peace: ultimately Germany must be satisfied
by the restoration of her pre-war prosperity, by equality with
other great powers in status, armaments, and other prestige
factors, and by the solution of her frontier problems in Central
and Eastern Europe. Some sort of *modus vivendi* had also to be
established with Soviet Russia, and a solution found of the
continued economic depression. The absence of any decisive
progress in these directions by the Conservatives after the
Locarno settlement in 1925 helped to sway opinion in favour of
the Labour Party, whose programme of 1928, *Labour and the
Nation*, promised a decidedly more constructive policy.
Unhappily the chances of success were already passing when
Labour attained office.

The decisive event was the sensational collapse of the New
York stock market on 29 October 1929, although American
funds had already begun to leave Europe in response to boom

[1] E. Windrich, *British Labour's Foreign Policy* (1952), chap. 6.

conditions at home in 1928. The export of American capital abroad now diminished disastrously, with financial crises in various parts of the world resulting from the calling in of loans or from counter-measures to check the flow of money abroad. This helped to accentuate, or create, widespread industrial depression, with alarming increases in unemployment, and to produce in turn a demand for drastic, or at least dramatic, action in every country concerned. In countries such as France, Britain, and the United States, with more or less stable political systems, it produced an intensification of economic nationalism in the attempt to regain prosperity. In Germany, Italy, and Japan, while giving a powerful stimulus to economic nationalism, it also helped to popularize extremist groups who satisfied the popular craving for decisive leadership and action. The death of Gustav Stresemann on 3 October 1929 removed the one statesman whose ability and personality might have saved Germany from this result.

Thus it may be argued that the Labour programme was already out of date when Henderson took office. This fact did not, however, become really obvious until 1931. In 1929 the main problem of foreign policy still appeared to be the alleviation of the political conditions, including armaments and the Versailles Treaty, which were impeding economic recovery; after 1930 the problem was to solve a world economic crisis which was driving the world towards a fresh era of political strife and international war.

The Anglo-Soviet Agreement

The establishment of normal relations with the Soviet Union was one of the first matters to which the new Government turned. We have noted in earlier chapters the unsatisfactory character of Anglo-Russian relations since 1919, and it will be convenient to give but a brief survey of these differences. The Communist revolution had failed outside Soviet Russia, but it provided a permanent threat to the whole political and social structure in countries such as France and England, and was

resisted there by all the main political parties. The pacific policy
and modified state socialism involved in the New Economic
Policy were evidence, however, that in Russia itself the régime
was on the defensive after 1920. Lenin himself undoubtedly
desired, at this stage, pacific relations, including trade
exchanges and political recognition, with Western Europe. A
Russian trade delegation under M. Krassin visited England as
early as May 1920, and the Anglo-Russian trade agreement of
16 March 1921 was signed by a Conservative minister, Sir
Robert Horne. But many incidents, due partly to the inflam-
matory language of the leaders of the Third International, and
partly to the mere absence of clear purpose among the Russian
leaders, prevented closer economic contacts, or diplomatic
recognition. Die-hard politicians such as Curzon and Churchill
looked with distaste even on the partial recognition of 1921.
Curzon encountered repeated cases of Russian hostility in
1922 and 1923: antagonism in the Near and Middle East;
repeated violation of the Soviet undertaking to refrain from
hostile propaganda; specific problems such as the rights of the
British to fish outside Russian territorial waters near
Murmansk.

When Labour came into office in 1924 the Soviet Union
was granted full recognition in February, but the difference in
attitude between the British parties was more apparent than
complete. The Labour Party was determined to maintain its
own identity and political methods inside the international
labour movement, and showed itself quite capable of defending
British national interests in the trade negotiations that followed
recognition. The conference on this subject which opened on
14 April came to a deadlock at the end of May. The draft Anglo-
Soviet Treaty concluded in August after left-wing pressure on
MacDonald, provided that the British Government would
recommend to Parliament the guaranteeing of a loan only
after the signature of a second treaty defining Russia's liability
to British bondholders, and her method of payment. The fact
that Lloyd George, whose Russian policy between 1920 and
1922 was on the same lines as the Labour Government's, led

the opposition to the treaty, shows how party tactics were exaggerating the differences on the question. The fuss over the Zinoviev letter, which, whether forged or not, repeated typical Comintern pronouncements, illustrated the same tendency. The circumstances made inevitable the refusal of the new Conservative Government to ratify the Anglo-Russian Treaty, but *de jure* recognition of the Soviet Union remained. Conservative hostility was, however, kept alive by the unremitting campaign of the party's right wing, greatly assisted by the financial aid offered to the British workers during the general strike in 1926 and continued Comintern propaganda within the British Empire. After a London police raid on the headquarters of the Russian trade delegation at Arcos House in May 1927 (which, however, seems to have produced nothing very incriminating) the British Government abrogated the trade agreement of 1921, and requested the trade delegation and Soviet diplomatic staff to leave the country.

The Labour leaders took the view that some of the Anglo-Soviet difficulties would disappear automatically if full recognition were accorded. There was, however, still no compromise between British Labour and the Third International. The socialist conference at Berne in 1920 had failed to provide any reconciliation between the Second and Third Internationals, and had even produced an intermediate grouping, the Adler–Longuet, or 'Two-and-a-half' International. The controversy continued after 1924. In August 1925 the Adler–Longuet amalgamated with the Second, with Arthur Henderson as chairman of the executive committee. Discussion produced some spectacular duels between MacDonald and the spokesman of the Third, such as Radek and Bukharin; but compromise proved impossible. Nevertheless the Labour Party still looked optimistically on the case for full recognition. After Lenin's death in 1924 a fight for supremacy among his former associates led to Stalin's triumph and the expulsion of Trotzky and Zinoviev from the Communist Party, in November 1927. The first 'Five Year Plan', aimed at producing the complete socialization of industry and agriculture in Russia,

was launched in October 1928. Stalin's breach with the giants
of the Third International meant that the commercial contacts
with 'capitalistic' countries which were necessary for the success
of the Plan would not in future be upset by the injudicious
thunderbolts of Zinoviev.

Henderson surprised the Commons in his first speech as
Foreign Secretary on 5 July 1929 by informing them that
diplomatic relations with Russia had never been legally
severed. On Henderson's proposal Moscow agreed to send its
Ambassador in Paris, M. Dovgalevsky, to discuss outstanding
questions; he arrived at the end of July, but left almost at once,
since the British Government refused to resume full diplomatic
relations before agreement on outstanding questions had been
reached.[1] Discussions were resumed on 24 September, and a
protocol of procedure was agreed on 5 October: mutual
pledges on propaganda were to be given simultaneously with
the exchange of ambassadors. Russia was not to expect
Parliament's guarantee of a loan. A professional diplomatist,
Sir Esmond Ovey, was, at the Soviet's own request, sent to
Moscow. Negotiations proceeded during the winter with the
new Russian Ambassador, M. Sokolnikov, and a provisional
fisheries and commercial agreement was signed on 16 April
1930. This settled the long-standing disputes concerning the
right of British trawlers to fish up to the three-mile territorial
limit on the Murmansk coast. The commercial agreement was
based on the 'most-favoured-nation' treatment for the citizens,
produce, and manufactures of the two countries. Nevertheless
the British Government was not prepared to sign a permanent
agreement until outstanding questions such as the Russian
debts had been settled.

Sub-committees for this purpose were appointed and
continued at a somewhat leisurely pace until Henderson
announced on 9 November 1930, much to Litvinov's annoyance, that there seemed little prospect of substantial progress

1 D. N. Lammers, 'The Second Labour Government and the Restoration of
Relations with Soviet Russia, 1929' (*Bulletin*, Institute of Historical Research,
May 1964).

over debts and claims. This brought the negotiations to a standstill. Charges of British complicity in counter-revolutionary activities in Russia followed. The fall of the Labour Government in August 1931 did not change British policy. Although the gradual rise in British exports to the Soviet Union from £4,801,000 in 1929 to £9,545,000 in 1930 was useful, the trade balance was still very much in Russia's favour.

The Young Plan and The Hague Conferences

Party differences in England had given relations with Russia a prominence out of proportion to their real importance. A satisfactory solution of Anglo-German differences was the main objective of Labour foreign policy, as it had been of the Conservatives. It was natural enough for British businessmen and Conservative politicians to feel after 1920 that Germany remained, and must remain, an integral part of the world in which they moved, as it was for them to feel that Russia had drifted out of that world completely; distance and the rigours of Soviet censorship made knowledge of Russian life after all somewhat generalized and theoretical. For the British Labourites the position was more complicated; they no doubt felt that they must watch respectfully the application in Russia of the socialist doctrines that underlay their own party programme, but for them too the working conditions, political aspirations, and mental outlook of the German working classes, with their trade unions and social democratic programmes functioning inside a Western European capitalistic structure, appeared decidedly more normal and familiar. Henderson certainly found it easier to establish sympathetic relations with Stresemann and Briand than with the Russians. Their mutual confidence was strengthened by the rescue of the Hague Conference from disaster in August 1929.

The conference had met to discuss the recommendations of the Young committee on German reparations. The Dawes plan of 1924 had not been intended as a final settlement; in

April 1928 Poincaré himself had suggested that a settlement by mutual agreement might be the best guarantee of French security. Stresemann, visiting Paris for the first time in August to sign the Kellogg Pact, had suggested further negotiations. In January 1929 a new committee met, and after very difficult discussions the Germans, headed by Dr Schacht, accepted in May the compromise scheme of the American, Mr Owen D. Young. It fell to the Labour Government to represent Britain at the Hague; the two principal British representatives were Philip Snowden, the Chancellor of the Exchequer, and Henderson.

The aim of the Young report was to provide a final settlement of all economic problems arising from the First World War, and thereby to remove the existing causes of political tension. It reduced and fixed the German reparations debt, arranged for payment by a progressive scale of annuities, and provided, by implication, for the ending of the Allied occupation of German territory and of other means of control and interference in Germany inherited from the Versailles settlement and Dawes plan. It established a Bank for International Settlement which would act as a clearing-house for international payments under reparations, and might later become the directing institution of world finance. The creditor countries had to accept a considerable reduction in the amount that they might have received from the continued working of the Dawes scheme, and they had to surrender their military control of the Rhineland; in return they were to secure the final liquidation of post-war animosities. The crisis at the Hague arose from the fact that in distributing the German payments between the Allies the Spa percentages had been departed from, very much to Great Britain's disadvantage. Moreover, the German annuities were classed as 'conditional' and 'unconditional', and about five-sixths of the latter were assigned to France. It appears that this modification had been introduced in order to give France compensation in cash for the surrender of her military rights in the Rhineland. The Conservatives before going out of office had shown dissatisfaction with this arrangement, and Snowden was convinced that Great Britain was being asked to make inequitable sacrifices to pacify the greedy French and truculent Germans. Henderson, on the other hand, seems to have regarded the financial point as of slight importance in comparison with the positive advantages of removing international friction by the ending of the Allied occupation.

Snowden stated the British grievance bluntly at the beginning of the conference. He referred to earlier British sacrifices; Great Britain had agreed to accept £227 million in settlement of France's war debt of £600 million, and £78 million in settlement of Italy's debt of £560 million; she had already paid £200 million in debt settlement to the United States, and had received nothing from Italy and France. Yet her receipts under the Young plan would come mainly from the less secure 'conditional' payments, and her share had been reduced from 23 per cent (under the Spa Agreements) to 17·5. This seemed a formidable case, but the sum involved, assuming full German payment, was only £2,400,000 per annum. MacDonald at first seemed inclined to restrain Snowden, but sent a telegram on 12 August expressing full support, and adding that Great Britain had 'reached the limit of inequitable burden-bearing'. After this, attempts were made to readjust the figures, although mainly at Germany's expense. On 27 August agreement seemed almost impossible but after pressure from Henderson a meeting of the creditors lasting until 1.30 a.m. on the 28th produced agreement. The Germans gave their consent at 3 a.m. The British claim was largely met from the surplus which would arise from the overlapping of the Dawes and Young plans, and by a rearrangement in the unconditional annuities. The evacuation of the Rhineland was to commence in September, and was to be completed not later than June 1930.

Henderson travelled to Geneva immediately afterwards for the meeting of the League Assembly, and found little sympathy there for the British attitude at the Hague. MacDonald made an excellent speech at the opening of the Assembly, and left soon afterwards; Henderson, however, stayed until the end of the meeting, and by his unaffected sincerity and genial determination did much to strengthen the good atmosphere which he expected the Rhineland and reparations settlement to create. On 5 September Briand broached his project of a 'United States of Europe', and was supported in an impressive speech by the dying Stresemann. It still seemed possible at this stage that the German reparation payments could, and would, continue; The Hague agreements were, in spite of opposition from the German Nationalist Party under Herr Hugenberg, ratified by an overwhelming majority in the Reichstag on 30 November, and by a referendum on 22 December. Further details were arranged in a second Hague conference in January 1930. But before many months had gone by the rapid deterioration in German economic conditions speedily made the schemes of 1929 inoperative.

The League and Disarmament

The Government hoped that the settlement of outstanding differences with Germany and Russia would make possible further progress in disarmament and in the establishment of the League of Nations as the effective director of a peaceful Europe. MacDonald himself took a prominent part in the disarmament discussions, while Henderson's regular attendance at Geneva, and his determination to increase the efficiency and the importance of the League machinery in every possible way, helped to maintain the prestige which it had enjoyed since 1925.

The preparatory commission, which had been appointed in 1925 to prepare material for the disarmament conference, had continued its labours in spite of the failure of the Geneva Conference in 1927. The League Assembly in 1928 presented for the accession of all states a 'General Act for the Pacific Settlement of International Disputes', which provided machinery for conciliation, arbitration of justiciable disputes by the Permanent Court of International Justice, and of other disputes by special machinery. In accordance with its election pledges the Labour Government signed the 'Optional Clause' of the Statute of the Permanent Court in September 1929; after consultation with the Dominions at the Imperial Conference of 1930, Great Britain and all other members of the Commonwealth excepting South Africa acceded to the General Act in the summer of 1931. More specific 'risks for peace' were taken when the Prime Minister announced on 24 July 1929 that the Government had decided to suspend all work on two cruisers, to cancel a submarine depot ship and two contract submarines, and to slow down dockyard work on other naval construction. In a statement on 13 November Mr Alexander announced that for the time being work on the Singapore base would be slowed down, and suspended where possible.

These decisions were justified in their immediate objective of securing a satisfactory naval agreement with the United States and Japan. A new American Ambassador, General Dawes, arrived in England on 14 June 1929 and proposed a fresh attempt to secure naval agreement by avoiding the deadlock which would ensue if the matter were left in the hands of naval experts: the statesmen of the various countries should agree on general principles before the experts were allowed to confer. MacDonald responded warmly. But although the talks continued through August and September and Britain early agreed in principle to a minimum figure of fifty instead of seventy cruisers, divergences of view over cruiser categories and tonnage remained, and the Americans meanwhile delayed the invitation to the States which MacDonald desired. But finally he invited himself, and, unaccompanied by naval advisers, conferred with President Hoover early in October, and addressed both the House of Representatives and the Senate on the 7th. He could regard the visit as a personal triumph, and he successfully resisted further American demands, including Hoover's attempt to curtail Britain's belligerent rights of blockade. Dawes and MacDonald had also been careful to keep in touch with the Japanese so that when the naval conference met in London on 21 January 1930 the ground had been well prepared, although it was evident that there were going to be difficulties over the Japanese claim to 70 per cent of the American tonnage in large cruisers. France and Italy also accepted invitations, but here agreement proved impossible, owing to Italy's claim for parity with France. The French view was that they needed, in addition to a Mediterranean fleet equal to the Italian, further vessels to defend overseas possessions and their two other coastlines. The British Government was not prepared to secure French acquiescence by guaranteeing the French position in the Mediterranean, nor by undertaking more binding obligations under Article 16 of the Covenant. Great Britain, Japan, and the United States did, however, sign a Three-Power pact on 22 April 1930, after Japan had been induced to accept a compromise. Great Britain reduced her demand for cruisers from seventy to fifty, and it was agreed that tonnage might, under certain conditions, be transferred from one category to another. Japan received the right to build up to 70 per cent of the British and American figures. There was to be a five-year holiday in capital ships. The British Government continued for almost a year after the conference to seek Franco-Italian agreement and managed to negotiate 'Bases of Agreement' in March 1931, but these proved abortive.[1]

The naval conference had been a success, but it illustrated the limited possibilities of the Government's methods. A conciliatory manner and a willingness to take the initiative in proposing reduction of armaments might succeed where questions of prestige alone were involved. It made possible friendly transactions with the United States, because neither power had any desire to attack the other. It did nothing to solve the problems of security. The British naval experts still believed that seventy cruisers were necessary to meet the country's war requirements; the French still wanted assurances against German and Italian attack. Japan for the first time had openly asked for parity with Britain and America. Labour had found no means

[1] R. G. O'Connor, *Perilous Equilibrium: The United States and the London Naval Conference of 1930* (1962).

of meeting the French demands, and was no more willing than the Conservatives to undertake military preparations in order to defend other League members under Article 16.

It continued to take seriously the preparations for the great disarmament conference, and the election of Henderson in May 1931 as president was a recognition both of his personal success as a chairman and negotiator at Geneva, and of the role that Great Britain was expected to play in the discussions. MacDonald had his own plans for the presidency; jealousy of Henderson's popularity, and the fact that he had intended to propose General Smuts, caused an embarrassing delay in his approval of Henderson's appointment. But in any case the Labour Government had resigned before the conference met, and the events that ruined the Labour Party had rendered the work of the conference futile before its first meeting took place.

VII

Crisis, Recovery, and Disarmament

Great Britain and the Economic Crisis

The crisis which finally overwhelmed both the Labour Government and the Labour Party in August 1931 was primarily economic. The collapse of the New York stock market in October 1929 was followed by a series of interrelated crises in various parts of the world during the next six years. The profound hostility and distrust between the nations, and the inability of some of the precariously balanced Governments of the post-war world to weather further domestic storms, led to a wave of political crises which in turn prevented the restoration of confidence necessary for economic recovery. Inside the British Empire Australia was the first unit to raise the signal of distress. In 1930 her loss of revenue from external loans and from the sale of foodstuffs and raw materials abroad produced a drastic fall in revenue, and there was a strong demand for the easing of the situation by the repudiation of existing debts. This policy was, however, rejected, in favour of economies and an inevitable lowering of the standard of living.[1]

At home, criticism of the Labour Government rose with the mounting unemployment figures, and it could not really be argued that the ministry was debarred from advocating innovations by its dependence on Liberal support. Sir Oswald

[1] R. Bassett, *1931, Political Crisis* (1958), chaps 1–5, deals fully with the confused relationship of domestic with external financial–diplomatic issues under the Labour Government.

Mosley resigned in May 1930 because it was not prepared to adopt a bold public works policy on Lloyd Georgeite lines. If it had sought a solution on more conservative lines by abandoning its opposition to protective tariffs it might have commanded Tory support. But it remained loyal to a free trade policy in an increasingly protectionist world. Mr William Graham, President of the Board of Trade, had made a striking appeal to the League Assembly in 1929 for the lowering of the economic barriers between nations and for a tariff truce. Stresemann made a similar plea in his last speech. The truce proposal met with a sufficiently favourable response for a tariff truce conference to meet at Geneva in February 1930. Thirty states took part, but the United States sent only an 'observer', and in the meantime, between May 1929 and June 1930, the United States Congress was elaborating the new and excessively high Hawley–Smoot tariff system. Many powers who attended the conference had prepared for it by further increases of tariffs, and the Hawley–Smoot tariff bill was followed by new tariffs in France and Italy, and, in the British Empire, in New Zealand, Australia, and Canada. The conference was a complete failure, and free trade died with it.

Germany was severely hit by the world economic crisis, but in spite of the death of Stresemann in October 1929 the policy of fulfilment which he had represented continued.[1] From 1924 to 1929 Germany had been able to secure all the credit she wanted – mainly in loans from America – and from these resources to pay her reparations debts, to finance further modernization and reorganization of industry, and to execute large programmes of public works. In 1929 her industrial output exceeded that of 1913. But when the world crisis curtailed the flow of foreign money into Germany, and the increasing barriers or decreased buying power of depressed foreign countries curtailed her own earnings in foreign exchange, Germany tended to panic. Her Government made

---

[1] German developments for this period are fully covered in B.D., Ser. II, vols i–iii, with illuminating but occasionally contradictory reports from the Ambassador, Sir Horace Rumbold, and his staff.

heroic efforts to meet the increasing national deficit by drastic economies; in July 1930, however, the Reichstag rejected the budget, and was dissolved, although President Hindenburg instituted a similar financial programme by emergency decree. At the elections of 14 September 1930 the impoverished middle class, terrified by fears of further poverty and deflation, and the smaller shopkeepers and businessmen, fearful of the competition of the great combines and trusts, voted strongly for the programme of Adolf Hitler's National Socialist Party, with its promise of nationalization, dispossession of Jews, and robust foreign policy. The party increased its seats from 12 to 107.

The largest party in the state was still the Social Democrats, who gave their support to the Chancellor Heinrich Brüning, the leader of the Centrists. Nevertheless, the continued necessity for drastic measures of economy made his position increasingly precarious. Further trouble was threatened by the shakiness of Austrian finances, in which the German banks were closely interested. The announcement on 21 March 1931 of an agreement to establish an Austro-German customs union was an attempt to relieve the economic difficulties of the two countries, and a desperate effort to strengthen the Government in Germany by a striking success in foreign policy; unfortunately it had international repercussions which Curtius should have foreseen, and which caused a great strengthening of French hostility during the next few months. Henderson was extremely angry at what seemed a typical example of German tactlessness; he had been doing his best to further the conciliatory tendencies in France represented by Briand's proposal for a European union, and as recently as 3 March, in a debate in the French Chamber on the General Act, Briand had given an assurance that nothing in the nature of an Austro-German *Anschluss* was imminent. Henderson, however, did his best to calm Briand, and the situation was eased when Curtius agreed at the end of March to the British proposal to leave further discussions to the League Council. The failure of the largest Austrian bank, the Credit-Anstalt, on 11 May, made clear the extreme gravity of the Austrian situation, and to that extent justified the Austro-German plan.

The Austrian disaster precipitated a financial catastrophe in Europe which even the British money market could not, for the time, surmount.[1] When the United States and France began after 1928 to reduce and recall their export of capital Great Britain endeavoured to maintain her pre-war function as the world's leading creditor state, and lent extensively in 1928 and 1929, but by 1930 was already beginning to find difficulties in procuring ready money for foreign loans.

On 16 June 1931 the Bank of England advanced £4,300,000 to Austria; this helped to prevent a complete collapse, but was carried out without consulting Henderson, who felt that he had been deprived of a useful bargaining weapon in the negotiations with France over the Austro-German customs union. The Austrian crisis further shook German finances; in the first half of June the Reichsbank lost £36 million. On 5 June the German Government blamed the 'unbearable reparations obligations' for its desperate position. On 20 June President Hoover proposed a moratorium for one year on all inter-governmental payments. This was promptly accepted by Germany and Great Britain; the psychological effect was, however, spoiled by the French Government, which had been given no opportunity to square political opinion. The withdrawals from Germany recommenced. A series of disasters culminated in the failure of the Danat Bank on 13 July; the German Government assumed complete control over the foreign exchange of the country, and in the London Conference (20–23 July) made a final unsuccessful appeal to other powers for aid. The Bank of England was unable to help with a long-term credit; America had nothing to offer; France, with an enormous gold reserve of £486 million, could supply Germany's needs, but demanded political concessions – such as a specific understanding to refrain from treaty revision during the period of the loan – in return. On 21 July the Nazi leaders informed Brüning by telegraph that they would not recognize such

[1] E. W. Bennett, *Germany and the Financial Crisis of 1931* (1963), chaps 7, 8.

terms. Brüning was forced to leave London without the loan. Germany's sole hope now lay in economic and political self-sufficiency.[1]

Britain was herself involved, by this stage, in the most dramatic of this series of national crises. The Macmillan Report on Finance and Industry was published on 13 July 1931, and was followed by heavy withdrawals of gold to France and Belgium; the Bank of England had lost nearly £45 million in gold by the end of the month, and the reserve had fallen to £133 million. On 27 July, MacDonald and Henderson, still apparently worrying as much about Germany as about themselves, arrived in Berlin. Their reception was enthusiastic; there were long conferences, and one of MacDonald's fine speeches at a banquet in the evening. The visit, however, was without result. They returned to London; the House of Commons rose on the 31st, and on 1 August the May Report was published, forecasting a budget deficit of £120 million.

The crisis that followed was more a matter of domestic than of foreign policy, and we can only note the outline of events. There is no doubt that the Government handled the situation badly; no attempt was made to mitigate the effect of the May Report by an accompanying explanation, and it was not, for example, pointed out that the estimated deficit included the provision of £60 million for the Sinking Fund. Henderson was willing to consider a revenue tariff, but Snowden's opposition killed this idea. The Cabinet split on the question of unemployment pay cuts, and resigned on 24 August; a National Government then took office under Ramsay MacDonald.

Recovery

The new Government was so successful in extricating the country from the worst effects of the crisis that it was able to establish itself in office for an indefinite period. On 15 Septem-

[1] B.D., Ser. II, vol. iii, chap. 4; R. H. Ferrell, *American Diplomacy in the Great Depression*, chap. 7.

ber the Commons adopted its supplementary budget, presented by Snowden; the sense of crisis suggested by its drastic economies and heavy taxation was strengthened by the 'mutiny' at Invergordon – a refusal of the ratings to put to sea, as a protest against the 10 per cent cut in their pay. The momentary suggestion that England could be saved only by economies which were driving the country to revolution produced a further financial panic abroad; on the assumption that England was probably 'finished as a great power' vast withdrawals again took place. On 21 September the bank rate was raised to 6 per cent and the gold standard was suspended. After this the overwhelming victory in the General Election of 27 October of the National Government, with 554 seats, made a powerful impression. Confidence in Britain's economic and political strength was restored; this renewed prestige was in itself a factor in the rapid escape of the country from the worst of its embarrassments.

The depreciation of the pound sterling to about 70 per cent of its previous value helped exports, and the rapid collection without any political friction of the increased income tax demonstrated the financial strength of the country. This deepened the conviction of many Labour supporters that the crisis of the previous autumn had been artificially created to discredit them, while convincing the Conservatives that they had saved England by their own efficiency and patriotism. In July 1932 the vast War Loan was successfully converted from 5 to $3\frac{1}{2}$ per cent. The Import Duties Bill of February 1932 imposed protection, and the Ottawa Conference in July established preference for certain British exports in imperial markets. Investment in foreign countries was largely prohibited down to 1929. By adopting the methods of economic nationalism, Britain was utilizing in her emergency a reserve weapon which other powers had already exploited more fully. If it retarded world recovery, it was probably a necessary preliminary to the adoption of a more co-operative international monetary system after the Second World War.

The circumstances of its accession to power dominated the

foreign policy of the new Government during the next few years. For some years the Chancellorship of the Exchequer appeared to be the most responsible post in the Government, and the success in this office of Mr Neville Chamberlain made him the inevitable choice as Prime Minister after Baldwin's retirement in 1937. The last phase of Austen Chamberlain's tenure of the Foreign Office had considerably reduced the popularity which the Locarno settlement had brought him and in any case the Liberals demanded the Foreign Office as one of the two key positions in the Cabinet. Accordingly Lord Reading held the position for a few weeks, and was then, after the election, succeeded by Sir John Simon in November 1931.

An able and conscientious lawyer, Simon mastered with ease the technical problems of current foreign policy; but he was not by temperament a crusader, and his constitutional caution was confirmed by the unwillingness of the new Cabinet to involve itself in crises and fresh responsibilities. France and the United States, to whom Great Britain looked principally for collaboration in foreign affairs, adopted a similarly negative and defensive attitude. Great Britain was not solely to blame for the deterioration in international relations of the early thirties, and it is difficult to see how any isolated action on her part could have secured more satisfactory results in the Manchurian and disarmament questions, the two urgent problems which faced the new Government during its first year of office.

The Disarmament Conference

The Far Eastern crisis will be discussed in the next chapter. It coincided in a most unfortunate manner with the disarmament discussions. The opening session of the disarmament conference had been arranged to commence at 3.30 p.m. on 2 February 1932, but had actually to be postponed for an hour so that an emergency meeting of the Council could discuss the situation at Shanghai. The delay was ominous, and it was soon evident that political conditions in other parts of the world would provide similar obstacles to success. The preparatory commission had reached nominal agreement at the end of 1930, but the draft disarmament convention had only been passed by a majority vote, and in face of the more or less frank disapproval of several powers, particularly Germany, Italy, and the Soviet Union. No complete agreement had been possible on such questions as budgetary limitation, the position of trained reserves and service troops, the definition of offensive weapons, or the outstanding problems of naval disarmament. Above all, no reconciliation had been found between Germany's demand for equality and France's demand for security, which necessarily implied the maintenance of her existing superiority in land armaments.

By the beginning of 1932 the chances of Franco-German agreement were slight; effective mediation by Great Britain, or possibly by the United States, alone supplied hope of a solution. In happier circumstances Arthur Henderson as president might have secured it. But after the fall of the Labour Government relations with Ramsay MacDonald were strained, and an illness in the autumn of 1931 reduced his energy and effectiveness. A different president – Lord Robert Cecil or General Smuts – might have shown greater skill, or received better support, in securing a Franco-German agreement on the one or two occasions when this still seemed possible. Simon's speech at the opening of the conference showed that he had not attempted to secure any such agreement by direct mediation, and was, in fact, content to await events. In any case, Britain's thoroughgoing disarmament of land forces after the war had deprived her of a valuable bargaining weapon. The continental powers were inclined to regard this unilateral disarmament, as they had always regarded her unilateral free trade policy, as a condition forced on the Government by internal politics, and one which they need not meet by corresponding concessions.

The opening discussions (8–24 February 1932) served to expose the now familiar differences between the powers. Simon indicated the difference between 'qualitative' and

'quantitative' disarmament. M. Tardieu emphasized the French
prerequisite of security, which he proposed to reconcile with
disarmament by bringing the guarantee and coercive functions
of the League into effective existence. He circulated a 'Plan'
which was designed to secure this by means of an international
force and the internationalization of civil aviation. Brüning,
who received a warmer reception than any other delegate,
asked for equality of rights for Germany, but did not suggest a
desire or intention to rearm up to the level of other powers,
and did not reject the French plan outright. Litvinov made the
usual Soviet demand for total disarmament, and then joined the
other delegates in laughing heartily at the proposal. He made,
however, some shrewd criticisms of the French plan, asking
what guarantee there was that an international army 'would not
be exploited in the interests of some state which has won for
itself a leading position in the international organization?'
But from all these speeches no agreement on the fundamental
issues seemed likely to emerge, and the reference of the various
points to technical commissions merely led the conference to
mark time for the next six months. A resolution passed on 20
July was intended to consolidate such progress as had been
made, but it did little more than register a ban on chemical
and bacteriological warfare.

The essential problem was, of course, that of German
armaments. The French Government had ample reason to fear
them, and its distrust was increased by the elaborate dossier on
Germany's secret rearmament which it was tempted to publish
on several occasions during the conference. France at the
moment was the strongest military and financial power in
Europe, and her Government was determined to maintain its
superiority over Germany until French security was guaranteed
by Great Britain, the League, or otherwise. Unfortunately the
only effective guarantee of French security would have been a
peaceful and satisfied Germany, and timely concessions might
have confirmed in office the more moderate régime which was
now fighting its last battles with the more irreconcilable
Nationalist and Nazi elements. An opportunity for an agree-

ment occurred in April, when Mr Stimson, the American Secretary of State, visited Geneva, and was followed there by representatives of France, Germany, Italy, and Great Britain. Brüning made proposals which, in the light of subsequent German demands, were surprisingly moderate; he wanted to increase the Reichswehr to 150,000, to reduce the period of service from twelve years to six, and to create a militia army of 50,000 men with three months' service. Stimson and MacDonald were favourably impressed by these proposals; but when Tardieu was invited to visit Geneva on 28 April to discuss them he declined on the ground of ill health. The French Government was facing an election, and concessions would have been particularly embarrassing to it; the British and American Governments should, nevertheless, have done everything in their power to secure France's agreement. Nothing effective was done to follow up the German proposal, and Brüning's cabinet was succeeded in June by von Papen's 'Cabinet of Barons'.

The new German Government almost at once secured a success which might have saved Brüning. A conference under the presidency of MacDonald met at Lausanne on 16 June to consider the situation which would arise when the Hoover moratorium on reparations and war debt payments ended. The result was the abolition of reparations, except for the delivery by Germany of bonds to the value of £150 million. This decision was a proof of the conciliatory disposition of the new French Government under Herriot, and the history of Europe might have been very different if it had been in office at the time of Brüning's offer in April. An agreement on 2 July made the settlement dependent on the satisfactory adjustment of the Allies' war debts with America, and this meant in effect the indefinite suspension, and virtual repudiation, of war debt payments.[1] On 1 December 1932 a British statement of the whole case against war debts was forwarded to the United States; the Government made token payments in June and December 1933, but as America was not prepared to accept

[1] F.D., Ser. I, vol. i, no. 21.

this expedient, or to discuss a scaling of the payments, no further British instalments were sent. In spite of the very weighty technical arguments that could be advanced against continued payments, there was considerable popular irritation in the United States on account of these defaults.

The von Papen Cabinet followed up its success on the reparations issue by withdrawing from the disarmament conference in September in protest against the continued withholding of recognition of Germany's claims to equality. This at last produced a definite step forward, and on 11 December 1932 a five-power conference at Geneva (between France, Germany, Italy, the United States, and Great Britain) produced a declaration recognizing Germany's claim to 'equality of rights in a system which would provide security for all nations'. Although 'equality' was thus reconciled with 'security' the powers were as far as ever from a practical scheme of disarmament, and it was not until the following March 1933 that the British Government, in a desperate effort to save the conference, presented the powers with a precise scheme. This was mainly the work of Mr Anthony Eden, Under-Secretary for Foreign Affairs, and the British technical advisers at Geneva. Its merit was that it presented the conference with a draft convention containing exact proposals and figures; it included the French plan of short service armies, gave suggested figures for the size of armies, limited war material on a qualitative basis, banned military and naval aircraft completely, and proposed a permanent disarmament commission with wide powers of inspection. The plan was presented by MacDonald on 16 March, and the first reactions were decidedly favourable. But in the subsequent discussions point after point was criticized; the Germans in particular were not prepared to give up the long-term army which had been forced on them by the Versailles Treaty, and which they had come to like. In any case the accession to office of Adolf Hitler in January had already placed European politics on a new footing.

VIII

The Far East, 1929-33

Great Britain and The Commonwealth, 1921-31

In two previous chapters (II and III) the post-war settlement has been discussed in its relation to the British Empire. The next ten years provided a period of relative calm between the international storms, and British Governments took advantage of it to attempt to solve the more pressing of the nationalist problems inside the Empire. Some progress was made at the same time in the elaboration of plans for imperial defence. The Imperial Conference of 1923 laid down that each part of the Commonwealth should bear the main responsibility for its own local defence; it provided for adequate facilities to safeguard the maritime communications of the Empire, and noted the vital importance to India, New Zealand, and Australia of a naval base at Singapore. Each of the Dominions tended, however, to object to an active imperial policy which did not directly defend its own interests.

In 1921 South Africa accepted responsibility for the land defences of the naval base at Simonstown, which the Admiralty could use at all times. General Hertzog characterized the Union's relation to the base as an international servitude, similar to the relation of Spain to Gibraltar. The construction of a first-class naval base at Singapore was planned in 1919; it was postponed for some time owing to the Washington Conference, and work had not gone very far when the Labour Government shelved the scheme in 1924. It was restarted by the Baldwin Government in 1925, suspended again by the Labour Government in 1929, and again restarted, this time by the National Government, in 1931. The base did not become really effective until 1938. In any case, it made little sense without a powerful fleet to use it. This had been ruled out by the Washington Conference, which limited the Royal Navy to fifteen capital ships for all purposes.

In Egypt, Great Britain proposed a treaty guaranteeing the independence and integrity of the country in return for the right to defend the imperial communications and other interests, but this was rejected by the Wafd Party in November 1921. The assassination of Sir Lee Stack, the Sirdar and Governor-General of the Sudan, in November 1924, was followed by an ultimatum which had the effect of postponing any further measures of self-government. When another draft treaty was presented in 1928 it was again rejected. In May 1930 an agreement was drafted whereby Great Britain recognized Egypt's independence and limited rights in the Sudan, but negotiations were again broken off by the Wafd. There was a somewhat similar course of events in Irak. The delay in the settlement of the Near East in 1919 caused the wildest suspicion of British intentions, and this was only partly removed when the military occupation ended in October 1920 with the return of Sir Percy Cox as High Commissioner. Feisal, the famous son of the King of the Hejaz, was made king, with overwhelming popular support, in August 1921. Great Britain, as the mandatory power, retained the ultimate word in the Government, and in September 1925, after an acute Anglo-Turkish crisis, a League commission of inquiry recommended that the Mosul vilayet with its valuable oil resources should go to Irak if the mandate were continued for twenty-five years. However, the Labour Government decided to shed its responsibilities and told the Iraki Government in the autumn of 1929 that Great Britain was prepared to support unconditionally its admission to the League. The admission took place on 3 October 1932. Great Britain had thus fulfilled its obligation under the 'A' mandates to prepare the mandated area to 'stand alone'.

In India, as in Irak, nationalist demands for independence tended to cast doubt on the genuineness of the British promise of eventual self-government, and to regard any references to internal dissension or political immaturity as insulting and hypocritical attempts to evade substantial concessions. These developments lie outside the scope of the present work, and it need only be noted that, in accordance with the Montagu–Chelmsford scheme of 1919, a British parliamentary commission with Sir John Simon as chairman presented a report in May 1930 which recommended the establishment of self-government (in place of diarchy) in the provinces, the separation of Burma from India, and a strengthening of the native element on the central legislature. After a series of Round Table Conferences in London (1930–2) and further discussions in India, the Government of India Act of 1935 introduced the Federation of India with provincial autonomy, diarchy at the centre, and British control of foreign affairs and defence. It could not be fully implemented owing to Muslim, Congress (Hindu), and princely rejection.

In China, also, the British had been engaged for some years before 1931 in judicious, though perhaps not very enthusiastic, negotiations concerning the restriction of their privileged position. The Kuomintang, or People's Party, had made its views known to the powers at Washington in 1921, and in 1925, after the death of its leader, Sun Yat-sen, at Peiping (Peking), a split had appeared between the Communist section and the more conservative elements under General Chiang Kai-shek. The two wings held together during the triumphal progress of the Nationalist Army north to the Yangtze Valley in 1926, but before the last remaining opponent, Chang Tso-lin, the war lord of Manchuria, could be dealt with, the struggle within the party came to a head. Chiang Kai-shek was prepared to come to terms with the foreign interests, and in return for financial support to find a way by peaceful negotiations to the revision of the 'unequal treaties'. In December 1926 the British Legation in Peiping announced its sympathy with the aims of the new Nationalist Government, and Mr Miles

Lampson, the able British minister, went to Hankow to negotiate with the Kuomintang. To frustrate this *rapprochement* of Chiang and the right wing with the foreign capitalists, the Communists launched violent anti-foreign campaigns, which produced an attack on the British concession at Hankow on 3 January 1927. The British, however, showed great restraint; they recognized the government set up by Chiang in Nanking, and in February undertook to surrender the concession at Hankow to Chinese control. The Communists also stirred up anti-foreign riots in Nanking and Shanghai. The British forces at Shanghai were strengthened, but the British troops and authorities continued to show restraint; a civil war broke out between the two wings of the Kuomintang, and in July 1927, after Chiang Kai-shek had gained the upper hand, the Russian adviser Borodin was expelled.

After the capture of Peiping in June 1928 by the Nationalists, and the formal recognition of the Nationalist Government under Chiang Kai-shek, there was no repetition of Anglo-Chinese tension comparable with that of the period 1925–7. But there was no certainty that another internal crisis in the Kuomintang might not drive Chiang Kai-shek from office, and his prestige in the party necessitated a somewhat high-handed bearing in his dealings with foreign powers. He was not likely to demand anything so drastic as the surrender of leased territory (such as Hong Kong), but he pressed the treaty powers to relinquish or modify their rights in respect of such matters as extra-territoriality and tariff restrictions. The comparatively slow progress of these negotiations led the Nanking Government on 28 December 1929 to abrogate all extra-territorial privileges of foreigners as from 1 January 1930. Negotiations, however, continued, in spite of further unilateral declarations by the Chinese, and a draft treaty had been drawn up, but not signed, just at the time of the Mukden incident. A report of Mr Justice Feetham on the future of the International Settlement at Shanghai was published in two parts in April and June 1931 and recommended the ultimate rendition of the settlement to Chinese control, although it also laid down that the objections to immediate action were overwhelming.

Thus it is not perhaps surprising that for the British community in Shanghai, and for the Foreign Office in London, the threat to the established position and vested interests of the British in China provided in 1931 a more obvious and immediate source of anxiety than the future policy of Japan. The death of a young Englishman, John Thorburn, who after shooting two Chinese gendarmes was himself shot dead a week later during cross-examination by Colonel Huang Chen-wu, helped considerably at this critical period to increase Anglo-Chinese tension.[1]

Japan and China

Before September 1931 there had been no serious departure by Japan from the pacific foreign policy which she had followed since the Washington Conference. The Minseito Party, whose opposition to financial and foreign adventures attracted both the heavy industrialists and the liberal idealists, had been in office since 1929, and had succeeded for two years in maintaining towards China a 'policy of conciliation' which had something in common with that of Great Britain in the same area in this period. Both Governments saw clearly enough the futility of an uncompromising insistence on the letter of 'unequal' treaties; both had to face some pressure in favour of an unyielding attitude. The Japanese Government found it harder to resist this pressure than the British: the policy of the Chinese Nationalists towards the Japanese was more provocative, Japan's direct interests in Manchuria and North China were greater, and geographical proximity magnified the effects of 'incidents' on Japanese public opinion.

The tendency in some British circles to regard Japanese aggression with complacency was, however, undoubtedly short-sighted. The many difficulties through which Japan had to pass from 1929 to 1931 did not result merely in an isolated outburst of military exasperation in Manchuria; it meant the establishment in power of the military and big business

[1] B.D., Ser. II, vol. viii, chaps 1–7, for events from 1929 to September 1931.

elements favourable to an expansionist policy, and therefore launched Japan on a phase of aggression which made her a much greater and more consistent danger to British interests than the Chinese Nationalists were likely to be. The world economic crisis produced a catastrophic drop in the export trade on which Japan's ill-balanced economic system largely depended; raw silk, her chief export in raw materials, was severely hit in the United States, its best market, and there was a total decline in her export trade from 2,100,000 yen in 1929 to 1,118,000 in 1931. The private soldier and officer classes in the army were largely recruited from the peasantry and small landed gentry, and the agricultural depression supplied a powerful incentive to the discovery of a dramatic solution by military adventure.

Manchuria offered an accessible, and apparently profitable, field. Here Chang Tso-lin's son and successor, the 'young Marshal' Chang Hsueh-liang, after coming to terms with the Nanking Government in December 1928, had hoisted the Kuomintang flag. In 1929 he seized control of the Chinese Eastern Railway, on the ground that the Soviet management had engaged in Communist intrigues; but the Soviet forces replied with substantial military raids into Manchuria, and after heavy defeats Chang gave in completely. In dealing with Japanese interests he was less directly provocative, and the 'conciliatory' policy of the Japanese Foreign Minister, Baron Shidehara, between 1929 and 1931, encouraged the belief that the anti-Japanese programme could be pushed with impunity. The chief expedient was the construction of a Chinese railway system which, properly developed and manipulated, would ruin the South Manchurian Railway Company.

At the end of June a Japanese officer, Captain Nakamura, and his three assistants were murdered in Manchuria by Chinese soldiers; at the beginning of July the Wanpaoshan affair, a riot arising from a dispute between Korean and Chinese farmers in Manchuria, led to anti-Chinese riots in Korea with over five hundred Chinese casualties, and a revival of the anti-Japanese boycott in China. The Japanese claimed that three hundred other incidents remained unsettled, and although Baron Shidehara still clung to the policy of conciliation the Japanese military authorities now decided to seek direct methods of settlement. On the night of 18–19 September, following a further incident in the shape of an explosion on the South Manchurian Railway, the Japanese troops seized without any real fighting the barracks, arsenal, and aerodrome at Mukden; within four days various strategical points in the railway zone and beyond it had been seized, and by the beginning of 1932 Japanese troops were in effective military occupation of the whole of Southern Manchuria. Very little resistance came from Chang Hsueh-liang, who had, a fortnight before the Mukden incident, warned the garrison there against injudicious retaliation to Japanese acts of provocation, and who now withdrew his army south of the Great Wall. There was, however, more resistance in the north and north-west, from both Chinese regulars and guerrillas, and this resistance kept the Japanese forces busy throughout 1932.

The League and the 'Mukden Incident'

The Mukden incident provided the first major crisis in foreign affairs of the new National Government in Great Britain, and its representatives were called upon to play an active part in the international discussions at Geneva before the future of the Government was assured by its election victory on 27 October 1931.[1] Sympathy for Japanese action among the dominant element in the British community in China, the traditional friendship with Japan in political and business circles in England, the irritation caused by Chinese Nationalist activity, and the warnings of military and naval experts, all served to render uncongenial any idea of applying military or economic sanctions against the Japanese. In the country at large Japanese action soon began to have the significance of a blow to the principles of the League, but this also did not produce any

[1] B.D., Ser. II, vols viii and ix, deal with the critical phase of the Manchurian crisis from September 1931 to March 1932.

precise or spontaneous demand for the imposition of sanctions. It was clear that to the majority of Englishmen the maintenance of peace still meant primarily the avoidance of any policy that might lead to war. The economic crisis at home and in Europe also helped to distract attention from the Far East.

The only other League power whose local interests and military resources were strong enough for her to play a useful part in the imposition of sanctions in the Far East was France, but she showed no desire to incur such responsibility. In the spring of 1932 there were indeed rumours of a Franco-Japanese Alliance.[1] The United States Government made it clear as the crisis developed that it would approve any action of the League in restraint of Japan, but for its own part would offer only moral disapproval.[2] The enigmatic policy of the Soviet Government meant much the same. Thus Great Britain would have had to bear the main brunt of the fighting if a sanctions policy had led to war. The British and American renunciation at the Washington Conference of the right to maintain fortifications and naval bases in the western Pacific would have made it difficult for either power to make effective use of the naval superiority over the Japanese which each possessed on paper. Certainly there seemed little hope in this case of restraining the aggressor by the overwhelming concentration of economic and military strength which the authors of Article 16 of the Covenant had depended upon to make war virtually impossible.[3]

On 21 September the Chinese Government appealed to the United States, and to the League under Article 11. A special meeting of the Council debated the matter on the 22nd, and the Japanese delegate deprecated 'premature intervention' by the League. On Lord Robert Cecil's proposal the Council agreed to adopt the procedure followed in the Graeco-Bulgarian dispute of 1925, and to concentrate in the first instance on stopping hostilities. An appeal was therefore made to the two Govern-

[1] Which, however, the French Government continued to deny: F.D., Ser. I, vol. i, no. 211.

[2] R. H. Ferrell, *American Diplomacy in the Great Depression*, pp. 138–60; R. N. Current, *Secretary Stimson, A Study in Statecraft* (1954), p. 81.

[3] See above, pp. 68–71.

ments to refrain from any action which might aggravate the situation, and to find means to withdraw their troops immediately. A further proposal by Lord Robert Cecil was that an account of all the proceedings of the Council relating to the dispute should be submitted to the United States Government. The Secretary of State, Mr Stimson, responded favourably to the extent of announcing that his Government was in wholehearted sympathy with the action taken by the Council in the dispute. But he continued until December to believe that an unsympathetic attitude on the part of his Government might weaken the apparently conciliatory Japanese foreign minister, Baron Shidehara, and encourage the intransigence of the militarists. So he was not prepared to join in the immediate dispatch of a commission of inquiry in accordance with the Graeco-Bulgarian precedent, and in his address to the Council on 25 September Lord Robert retreated from this position. To some observers this early indication of a divergence between America and the League was decisive: it was followed by a hardening of the Japanese position, and the crucial moment, when Japan might possibly have been overawed by world opinion, passed. But it is by no means certain that even in the first week the Japanese Government had the power to control the army. It certainly remained politely unhelpful throughout.

The Council adjourned for a fortnight on 30 September, after recording the Japanese Government's repudiation of territorial ambitions in Manchuria, and its promise to continue, as rapidly as possible, the withdrawal of its troops into the railway zone. During the next fortnight, however, the Japanese continued, equally rapidly, to advance. The Commander-in-Chief, General Honjo, announced that Chiang Hsueh-liang's Government would no longer receive recognition. On 8 October Chinchow, the seat of the provincial government, was bombed from the air. The League found some consolation in the favourable attitude of Washington. On 11 October Stimson sent to Tokyo a strongly worded memorandum concerning Japanese activities; on 16 October, following an invitation from the Council, Mr Prentiss Gilbert, the United States consul at Geneva, took his seat at the Council meeting. But this gesture had little effect except to alarm the isolationists; and meanwhile the Council was getting nowhere. A resolution on 22 October proposed calling on Japan to complete her evacuation by 16 November, after which the two interested powers should begin direct negotiations. But it was lost owing to the adverse vote of Japan, who demanded the reversal of the suggested order of procedure. When the Council again assembled on 16 November there was no sign of the desired evacuation, and the United States observer, General Dawes, warned Briand that his Government would not join in the consideration or enforcement of sanctions. The League, however, was saved from a declaration of complete impotence by the decision, arising from a proposal of the Japanese delegate on 21 November, that the League of Nations should send a commission of inquiry to the spot.

The fact of Japanese aggression was obvious enough by this stage, and it is difficult to regard this decision as anything but the conscious abandonment by the dominant League powers of any real attempt to influence the Manchurian situation. The Commission, which consisted of five members, representing Great Britain, the United States, France, Germany, and Italy, sailed for the Far East early in February 1932, after a protest from Dr W. W. Yen, the new Chinese delegate at Geneva, at the delay in its departure. The chairman was Lord Lytton. The Council's resolution on 10 December reaffirmed the promise of China and Japan 'to adopt all measures necessary to avoid any further aggravation of the situation'; the Japanese operations, however, went rapidly ahead, and Chinchow was occupied on 3 January 1932. The setting up of local, and nominally Chinese, governments in various parts of Manchuria had already indicated before the end of 1931 that the future government of the area would probably be nominally Chinese, but would be completely dominated by Japan. Then on 7 January 1932 Stimson presented to the Japanese and Chinese Governments a note announcing that the United States Government would not admit the legality of any situation *de facto*, nor recognize any treaty or agreement between the two Governments which might impair the treaty rights of the United States or its citizens in China. The effectiveness of this 'doctrine of non-recognition' was momentarily reduced by the muddle which arose between London and Washington in its enunciation. The British Government could not immediately make a similar declaration, as it had to act in concert with the other League powers. A note to this effect was sent to Stimson on 9 January. An official statement, drafted hurriedly over the week-end but initialled by Simon, was published on 11 January and was unfortunately worded, giving the impression of a distinct rebuff. It stated that the British Government stood by the policy of the open door for international trade in Manchuria, but that, as Japan had explicitly stated, as recently as 28 December, that she would adhere to this policy, the British Government had not considered it necessary to address any formal note to the Japanese Government on the lines of the American Government's note.

Simon's failure to follow the American lead at this moment has frequently been criticized, and has helped to propagate the wholly untenable view that Great Britain frustrated an American attempt to take effective action against Japan.[1] The fact is that neither Government was prepared to resort to an economic boycott or military action, and both hoped that the exercise of moral pressure, and the mobilization of world opinion, would provide an adequate substitute. For Great Britain the League supplied the obvious machinery for this type of action. It appeared in London that the State Department had given up the hope that Japan would adopt a more moderate policy, and had decided to make a definite stand in defence of United States' rights on the model of the non-recognition warning addressed to Japan in 1915. It soon became clear that Stimson wished the non-recognition doctrine to be regarded more broadly as a moral force which, if adopted by the civilized world, would supply a substitute for sanctions and

[1] These incidents are placed in their right setting by Sir J. T. Pratt, *War and Politics in China* (1943), pp. 217–29.

effectively check Japanese aggression. It was obviously unwise of him to proceed to enunciate this doctrine publicly in circumstances which made the immediate support of the League powers almost impossible; he was repeating the mistake made when the Hoover moratorium proposal was published without preliminary diplomatic preparation. Isolationist sentiment in the United States no doubt tempted the Government to resist aggression in a style of its own.

This does not alter the fact that Washington was right to argue that mere appeals to Tokyo would henceforth be useless, and the British *communiqué* received a welcome in some parts of the British Press which revealed a latent sympathy for Japanese action in certain quarters in London. But as soon as Stimson's intentions were understood Simon did all he could to support them. The Council assembled on 25 January; on 29 January it drew up a declaration which referred to the American note of 7 January, and stated that it would be impossible for the League to endorse a settlement secured by methods at variance with the treaties referred to by the American Government, or under Article 10 of the Covenant. This declaration was followed, as we shall see below, by further assertions of the doctrine of nonrecognition by the Council on 16 February and by the Assembly on 11 March, and it formed the basis of the League's final condemnation of Japanese action in March 1933.

Shanghai

An extension of the Sino-Japanese dispute now provided a further field for Anglo-American co-operation. After five Japanese had been wounded in Shanghai on 18 January the Japanese Consul-General presented demands for reparations and for the immediate dissolution of all anti-Japanese organizations. Although the Mayor of Shanghai fully accepted these demands on 28 January, Japanese troops were landed, and the Chinese area of Chapei was largely destroyed by incendiary bombs on the 29th. On 1 February Japanese warships bombarded Nanking. Large-scale fighting began when the Japanese attempted to drive the Chinese troops out of the Settlement. Although the Chinese were ultimately dislodged they held their position until 3 March, and their stubborn resistance to the hitherto invincible Japanese had a valuable psychological effect throughout China.

The British and United States Governments protested in Tokyo against Japanese action in Shanghai, and their naval forces and troops in Shanghai were reinforced. These forces were not intended to overawe or fight the Japanese, but rather to defend the Settlement against the local Chinese mob. Indeed, the affair brought home to the British authorities the extreme precariousness of British forces in the Far East, and the impossibility of any effective resistance if Japan chose to attack. As it soon became evident that the Japanese action had probably been taken by their naval command without the approval of the government in Tokyo there seemed a good prospect that by tactful diplomacy the neutral powers could patch up an agreement and bring the affair to an end. The first step was taken when an armistice was concluded under the mediation of Admiral Sir H. Kelly on a British man-of-war. After this the British minister, Sir Miles Lampson, as the representative of the neutral powers, skilfully conducted negotiations for the mutual withdrawal of the rival forces, and an agreement was concluded on 3 May.

The Powers and Manchukuo

But it would be a mistake to assume that a similar display of firmness and energy by the British Government would have secured the withdrawal of the Japanese troops in Manchuria; the willingness of the Japanese to bring the Shanghai incident to a close was due primarily to the fact that it had never been more than a sideshow. On 18 February the North-Eastern Administrative Council, a body of Chinese officials amenable to Japanese control, issued a declaration of Manchurian independence, and during the next three weeks the state of 'Manchukuo', with the ex-Emperor, Mr Henry Pu-yi, as President, was formally established. It was at once apparent that its independence was merely nominal, and that, behind a façade of more or less complaisant Chinese officialdom, real power was in the hands of the Japanese Army. The appointment of Japanese 'advisers' in government departments, industrial enterprises, and public utilities secured to the Japanese the effective control of the political and economic machinery, while the nominal independence of the new state was expected to stifle the criticism of the League, and even of the more timid and more scrupulous in Japan. It also enabled the Japanese to put an end to the operation in Manchuria of such Chinese public services as the Maritime Customs, the Salt Gabelle, and the Post Office.

A further attempt by Stimson to overawe Japan by means of the policy of non-recognition was made in February. His proposal, approved by President Hoover on 8 February, was that the Nine-Power Pact of 1922 should be 'invoked' against Japan. Apparently all this meant was that the remaining eight powers should make diplomatic representations in Tokio on 'non-recognition' lines. The matter was discussed with the British Ambassador on 9 February, and, between the 11th and the 15th, Stimson had several conversations by transatlantic telephone with Sir John Simon in Geneva and London. On receiving the draft of Stimson's proposal the British Government drafted a paragraph containing the non-recognition doctrine, and this was embodied in the declaration issued by the twelve members of the League Council on 16 February; at the same time a written reply to Washington expressed the British Government's anxiety to co-operate with the United States in the matter, and the hope that League powers signatory to the Nine-Power Treaty would also associate themselves with the joint invocation of the treaty. It would seem that the next step should have been a series of approaches by the United States to the other signatories; Stimson appears, however, to have decided not to proceed with his plan, and instead published his proposals in the form of a letter to Senator Borah of 24 February. Later, writing in 1936, he said that his conversations with Simon convinced him 'that the British Government felt reluctant to join in such a *démarche* . . . The British non-joinder obviously killed the possibility of any such *démarche* . . . For several days I was deeply discouraged at my inability to carry out the co-operative plan which we had suggested.'

There seems to have been some confusion in Stimson's mind between Britain's support of the doctrine of non-recognition, and her support of the procedure described as 'invoking the Nine-Power Pact'. The former was given promptly enough; the latter was not excluded, although it was obviously important to avoid any impression in Tokyo that the League procedure had been put aside. The only doubt in the Foreign Office was as to the wisdom of making representations, as Stimson seemed to desire, about both Shanghai and the more intractable Manchurian question; Simon thought that it would be better tactics to deal first with Shanghai. In a speech on 8 August 1932 Stimson did, in fact, express his pleasure at the support of the non-recognition doctrine by the League Assembly in March. 'Never before has international opinion been so organized and mobilized.' The Council of the League on 16 February had warned Japan that it considered that no change in the political independence of any member state brought about by the infringement of Article 10 ought to be recognized as valid by other members of the League, and a Special Assembly, convened on 3 March on China's request, resolved on 11 March that members should not recognize any situation brought about by means contrary to the Covenant or to the Pact of Paris. This resolution was drafted and proposed to the Assembly by Sir John Simon, although British official pronouncements were noticeably more cautious than those of the smaller states who had been able to make their own views known as a result of the meeting of the Assembly, and who could denounce aggression without having to fight it themselves. The Assembly was mainly concerned with the Shanghai question, and after the satisfactory settlement of this in May no further step of importance was taken until the publication of the Lytton report on 1 October.

The Japanese Government, which had hitherto maintained a pretence of reserved judgement towards Manchukuo, granted *de jure* recognition to the new state on 15 September, and at the same time asked for at least six weeks delay in order to send to Geneva its observations, and a special delegate. The delay was granted, and the Council discussed the report from 21 to 28 November. The report, while recognizing the substance of some of the Japanese grievances, rejected the various Japanese pretexts for invading Manchuria, denied that the state of Manchukuo was in any real sense independent, and proposed that an autonomous régime should be set up under Chinese sovereignty. Simon was sharply criticized in left-wing circles in England, and thanked by the chief Japanese delegate for an injudicious attempt at a judicial survey in his speech to the Assembly. He called attention to Chinese provocation.[1] A special Assembly in February 1933 presented a report which followed the recommendation of the Lytton commission, although its condemnation of Japan was not presented in language which would have pointed directly to sanctions. The Japanese Government continued to insist on the maintenance of the new régime, and on the settlement of all differences by direct Sino-Japanese negotiations, and after the voting of the report the Japanese delegate withdrew from the Assembly; on 27 March Japan announced her resignation from the League.

So, for practical purposes, ended the unheroic episode of the League's first attempt to deal with a major aggression. Great Britain was in a position to dictate the course of the League's policy, on the assumption that she would bear the brunt of the consequences. The British Cabinet, convinced that it was powerless to resist Japan without full American co-operation, adopted a resolutely mediatory policy throughout. That Japan now felt little cause for apprehension was shown by her further offensive against Jehol, the mountainous pro-

---

[1] This was the occasion of M. Matsuoka's alleged comment that Simon had said in half an hour what the Japanese delegation had been trying to say in ten days: R. Bassett, *Democracy and Foreign Policy* (1952), pp. 280–301.

vince north of Peiping and the Great Wall; on 12 January 1933
the Japanese War Office claimed Jehol on behalf of Manchukuo, and when Japanese troops entered the province on
25 February resistance collapsed very rapidly. In April the
Japanese troops crossed the Great Wall, and were in a position
to threaten Peiping; the Nanking Government brought temporary relief by signing on 31 May the Tangku Truce, which
provided for the demilitarization, and therefore the Chinese
evacuation, of an area of about 5,000 square miles on the
Chinese side of the Great Wall. For a short period – from
28 February to 13 March 1933 – the British Government imposed an embargo on the shipment of arms to both China and
Japan, but no other state followed its example, and the League's
action petered out with the appointment of an advisory committee to follow the situation and concert action between
member states and with non-members. Of the latter the United
States appointed a non-voting representative; the Soviet Union
declined to participate.

Any criticism of the British Government's role which fails
to take into account the virtual impossibility of effective action
by the League is largely beside the point. Article 16 was not
invoked by China. The imposition of effective economic
sanctions would have been impossible without Russian and
American co-operation. There was little willingness for action
on the part of such interested states as Holland, France, Canada,
and Australia. They did not feel that the faults were entirely on
Japan's side, and in any case her preoccupation with the
assimilation of Manchuria might reduce the danger of aggression against their own interests or possessions. In these circumstances it is hardly possible to blame Great Britain for not
embarking on a policy of coercion in the name of the League.
Such isolated activity could in no sense be described as collective action.

It is easier to criticize the Government's interpretation of the
facts. It steadily put itself forward as a mediator, frequently
citing Lampson's success at Shanghai as evidence of its essential role. It professed satisfaction with Japanese assurances

regarding the maintenance of the 'open door' in Manchuria, and seemed to assume that if it avoided any very serious or open breach with either Government it would be able to get along well enough with them both in the future. A year or two was to elapse before fresh difficulties appeared.

IX

Great Britain and Germany, 1933–5

The Accession of the Führer

On 30 January 1933 Adolf Hitler became Chancellor of the Reich as head of a Coalition Ministry which included nine non-Nazis under the leadership of Papen and Hugenberg, representing the Nationalist Right. During February the bewildered and panicky electorate was bombarded by the Nazis with furious denunciations of the Red Peril, and of Bolshevik plots; all meetings of the Communist Party were banned. On the 27th the Reichstag building was largely destroyed by fire, allegedly by Communists, though even at the time a Nazi 'frame-up' was suspected. Even so the Nazis could secure only 288 seats, representing 43·9 per cent of the total votes cast, at the elections on 5 March. The real extinction of the older parties came when they all, with the exception of the Social Democrats, voted in support of the act of 23 March which conferred dictatorial powers on the Cabinet. The Reichstag and Reichsrat soon became all-Nazi assemblies, and after the death of Hindenburg on 2 August 1934 the offices of Chancellor and President were combined in the person of Adolf Hitler.

The new dictator, as leader of the Germany of 1933, did not control resources more powerful than those at the command of Stalin in the Soviet Union, or display a will to power more grimly persistent than that of Mussolini in Italy. But Soviet foreign policy was now unquestionably pacific, and Italy's limited economic resources made her at most a nuisance rather than a danger to British security. The new German régime combined aggressive intention with powerful war-potential, and Hitler became at once the greatest personal problem in British diplomacy.

Yet the exact nature of this problem was not easy to determine at the time. The writings and speeches of Hitler and his supporters, the party programme adopted in 1920, and the two volumes of Hitler's *Mein Kampf*, published in 1925 and 1927, expounded the political philosophy of the movement in fairly coherent but also incredibly savage and ambitious terms. Should all this be taken at its face value, or was this wild talk in the twenties merely the propaganda of an insignificant revolutionary party trying to attract attention by any means available? Hitler's plans for the future of Germany included the union of all people of German 'race' in a great German state, and the acquisition of control over further territory for the maintenance and future expansion of the German people. This additional territory must be sought at the expense of Russia. 'We put an end to the perpetual Germanic march towards the South and West of Europe and turn our eyes towards the lands of the East.' The Jew had now taken the place of the Germanic nucleus to which Russia owed its livelihood in the past; the Jew is 'a ferment of decomposition', and consequently 'this colossal Empire in the East is ripe for dissolution'. Hitler believed that the only power which would be irreconcilably opposed to this expansion was France: she was and would remain 'the implacable enemy of Germany'. Ultimately a 'final reckoning with France' would have to be sought; for this purpose he hoped to secure the support of France's former allies, Italy and, in particular, England.

In 1921, and for some time after, his public speeches had revealed the violent anti-British feeling of the war years. 'Who now believes that England ever cared about establishing the freedom of small nations, since it has robbed the greatest cultural people of the earth, Germany, of the last remains of its freedom?' he exclaimed in 1921. In the second volume of *Mein Kampf*, however, the possibility of alliance with England was carefully explored. Great Britain would not wish France's position on the continent to be so absolutely assured – owing to the dismemberment of the rest of Europe – that she would be 'not only able to resume a French world-policy on great lines but would even find herself compelled to do so'. The necessary interests of England no longer demanded the destruction of Germany: on the contrary, she tended more and more towards curbing France's unbridled lust after hegemony. In the past 'England did not want Germany to be a world power. France desired that there should be no power called Germany.' Germany was not now fighting for her existence as a world power but only for the existence of the country, for national unity and the daily bread of her children. In another place he admitted that Germany would ultimately have to become a 'world power', but he was evidently prepared to relegate this development to the more or less distant future.

Much of this was alarming, and the Nazi Party was already firmly fixed in the ideas of the British Foreign Office before 1933 as one of the four extremist German groups (along with the Nationalists, the Stahlhelm, and the Communists) who must if possible be prevented from securing power. Moreover, Hitler very quickly showed in his domestic policy that he and his followers intended to be quite as violent and repressive as their programme had promised. The persecution of Jews, Socialists, and Liberals started almost immediately and was fully reported in the British Press, thereby creating a sharp and enduring hostility in left-wing circles where the tendency had hitherto been to commiserate with the Germans on their lot. But this was not incompatible with the view that the party and its leaders might be sobered by office, or – as seemed to be the case now in Italy and Turkey and the Soviet Union – that the revolution might be kept at home. The daemonic element in Hitler's personality was not ignored, but many close British observers believed that he was passionately seeking German equality rather than hegemony in Europe.[1]

[1] In short, they took at its face value propaganda about Germany's sense of grievance under the Versailles Treaty. Cf. D. C. Watt, 'German Influence on

Anthony Eden told Mussolini on 28 February 1934 that Hitler impressed him as sincere in desiring a disarmament convention, 'as he wished to be able to push on with a long programme of internal reconstruction'.[1] It was also evident that Hitler might be biding his time. Looking back with our present-day knowledge we must recognize that he did carry out in the end the broader objectives of the twenties; but not surprisingly he had to modify many of the more specific plans. The Soviet Union did not, after all, obligingly collapse, and the execution of even the first stage of his programme – the restoration of some of the old frontiers and the incorporation of the German-speaking peoples of Central and Eastern Europe – aroused endless alarm and resentment elsewhere, and finally plunged him into war with France and Britain. There is some evidence to suggest that he did not abandon the idea of winning British friendship and alliance until 1937, and he continued to speak of it as one of the primary aims of his diplomacy until 1939.

The policy of the British Government in dealings with Germany was both cautious and ineffective before the spring of 1939. Hovering between threats, concessions, meekness, and rearmament, it certainly gives no impression of dynamism in Downing Street. But until either Hitler or the British public had given a clearer indication of purpose, the Government was almost bound to limit itself to a hand-to-mouth policy. The British public had not lost its memory of Germany as a hostile power before 1919; it was anxious to forget, rather than to love, the Germans. While it was prepared to acquiesce in the abrogation of those parts of the Versailles Treaty which now seemed blatantly unfair or absurd, suspicions were soon aroused by the violence of the German demands on points of less obvious injustice. In such circumstances the British people expected firm language from the Government, although it continued to approve of demands for disarmament and 'sacri-

British Opinion, 1933–38', in *Personalities and Politics*, pp. 117–35; R. B. McCallum, *Public Opinion and the Last Peace* (1944), pp. 62–75; and the similar American reactions discussed in J. V. Compton's illuminating *The Swastika and the Eagle* (1967), especially pp. 58, 128–32.

[1] B.D., Ser. II, vol. vi, no. 307.

fices for peace', and was not, at any rate before 1938, prepared
for permanent commitments beyond the Rhine. On the other
hand, the Führer's policy before the reoccupation of the Rhineland in 1936 consisted in little more than an extremely noisy
glorification of comparatively minor triumphs. Did he aim at a
Bismarckian policy of limited risk and limited objectives, or at
a Napoleonic policy of perpetual expansion? No one knew:
perhaps not even the Führer himself.

The three powers most directly affected by the revival of
German militarism were France, Italy, and the Soviet Union.
Italy, though determined at this stage to prevent the incorporation of Austria in the Reich, was always more inclined than the
other powers to face the inevitability of Germany's return to
the status and conditions of a great power. The French
Government could visualize no type of bargain with Germany
which could benefit France, and hoped, by maintaining its
existing military superiority and its diplomatic instruments –
the League and the Little Entente – to perpetuate its previous
security. The Soviet Union was forced, by the violence of
German hostility, to associate itself with the French system.
The British Government was able to understand both the
French and the Italian theses; it was apprehensive, conscious
of the need for concession, but with little to propose after the
fading of plans for all-round disarmament. One thing, however,
was clear: British public opinion would accept nothing in the
nature of an Anglo-German alliance or axis.

The Four-Power Pact

The need for a timely settlement with Germany formed the
most important element in the proposals for a Four-Power
Pact, which Mussolini presented to MacDonald and Simon on
18 March 1933, after securing Hitler's prior concurrence with
the document in principle on the 15th.[1] The draft proposed

[1] There is ample first-hand information about British policy towards Germany
during the opening years of Hitler's régime in B.D., Ser. II, vols iv–vi, and in
The Eden Memoirs, Facing the Dictators (1962, cited as 'Avon, I'). The German
publication of documents for these years is complete (G.D., Ser. C, vols i–v).

that Britain, France, Germany, and Italy should co-ordinate their policy in European, extra-European, and colonial questions, and should consider a revision of the peace treaties; they should take steps 'to induce, if necessary, third parties to adopt the same policy of peace'. If the Disarmament Conference proved abortive, they should recognize Germany's right to rearm by stages. The proposal appeared to foreshadow the supersession of the League. It virtually invited Germany to frustrate the Disarmament Conference. Revision would clearly affect Poland and the Little Entente states. The pact can be interpreted either as a statesmanlike attempt by Mussolini to conciliate Germany, or as a bid for German friendship, or as an ingenious plan for raising Germany to equality of strength and status with France and England, thereby increasing Italy's relative strength and importance as the mediator between them. The British ministers favoured a policy of mediation between Germany and France, but believed that they, and not the Italians, had the confidence of the two other powers. They did not regard the proposals as acceptable in their original form. Nor did the French. The prompt publication of the Italian text in the Paris Press released a chorus of criticism of concessions to Germany.

The Little Entente states began to show increased interest in the already existing plans for a *rapprochement* with Poland, who objected both to treaty revision and to the fact that her own status as a great power had been ignored by the pact. She alone had taken prompt action in reply to the violent campaign which the Nazis had launched against her as part of the election campaign of February. Since the middle of February Polish Government spokesmen had been talking of the inevitability of a preventive war on Poland's part in reply to Nazi provocations. Although the Poles were increasingly doubtful as to whether the French would join them in a march into Germany there was much sympathy for Poland's attitude. Sir Austen Chamberlain, hitherto the most prominent advocate in England of conciliation towards Germany, spoke strongly in the House of Commons on 13 April 1933 against the savagery, racial pride, and exclusiveness of the new German Nationalism, and exclaimed, 'Are you going to discuss with such a government the Polish Corridor? The Polish Corridor is inhabited by Poles; do you dare to put another Pole under the heel of such a government?'

Germany was not in a position at this stage to conduct a successful war even against the Poles, and her rearmament in its initial stages could not proceed without the acquiescence of foreign governments. Accordingly Hitler's response to Polish pressure was unexpectedly reassuring. Much to the annoyance of the German Foreign Office he agreed to a joint German–Polish communiqué of 4 May 1933 which said that the two powers undertook to treat common interests dispassionately, on the basis of existing treaties. This meant in effect the indefinite postponement of revision as far as Poland was concerned. On 17 May Hitler made to the Reichstag an emphatic and apparently unqualified declaration of peaceful intentions; he asserted Germany's need for equality of rights in armaments, but offered to agree to the realization of these rights over a period of years. Three days later Goering flew to Rome, and the Four-Power Pact was signed on 7 June.

French amendments had removed from the text everything that was directly obnoxious to her; revision was limited to a reference to Article 19 of the League Covenant, and the reference to the colonial question was removed altogether. The Little Entente powers accepted the final text, although with obvious misgivings. The pact certainly helped to sow suspicions between France and her allies, and to emphasize the isolation of the Soviet Union. The British ministers regarded it more hopefully as an innocuous, and possibly constructive, supplement to the Locarno Agreement.

The pact strengthened Soviet suspicions of British hostility. Relations remained chilly.[1] After Henderson had complained to the Soviet Ambassador on 17 February 1931 of the Russian failure to reciprocate British orders in Russia, there was silence for twelve months, after which Simon made an exactly similar

[1] B.D., Ser. II, vol. vii, *passim*.

complaint about the adverse balance of trade. In August 1932 the British Government announced curtly its decision to denounce the Anglo-Soviet trade agreement owing to its incompatibility with Article 21 of the Anglo-Canadian agreement concluded at Ottawa. A violent Press campaign led by *Izvestiya* followed, with some spiteful harassing of the British embassy staff. Negotiations for a new trade agreement began in December, but were broken off in March 1933 by the British Government in the Metro-Vickers crisis. Of the six accused British engineers, two were imprisoned but were released on 1 July 1933, simultaneously with the lifting of the British embargo and Soviet counter-embargo. The British Government insisted that the engineers had never been employed, directly or indirectly, by the British Intelligence Service. The Ambassador, Sir Esmond Ovey, was suddenly recalled on 29 March and did not return. There was some evidence that the Soviet Government feared Japan at this stage more than Germany, and saw Great Britain as a subtle adversary secretly encouraging the hostility of both, replacing France as the spearhead of capitalistic–imperialistic counter-attack. The Soviet Union signed in London on 3 July 1933 during the World Economic Conference a multilateral non-aggression pact with adjacent states (Latvia, Estonia, Poland, Rumania, Turkey, Persia, and Afghanistan), adopting a defini-tion of aggression recently proposed by Litvinov to the dis-armament conference. The Turkish Government regarded this pact with Russia as a counterweight to the Four-Power Pact.

Nevertheless, it could be said that Hitler's advent to power had passed off rather more quietly than had at first been anticipated. For the time being Austria became the main object of Hitler's attention: it probably interested him more than Poland, and in any case was too small and feeble to threaten reprisals. Naziism, backed by violent German pro-paganda, began to make strides in Austria, aided by the split between the Socialists and the Government of Dr Dollfuss, relying on the pro-Fascist Heimwehr. But in August 1933 the British and French Governments failed to persuade Mussolini to join them in representations in Berlin; the Italians were unwilling to go beyond friendly inquiries, and the German Government reply to the other two was that it 'did not regard this interference in German–Austrian differences as permissible'.

Germany Leaves the League

This snub was followed by more dramatic action. France's demand that an adequate guarantee of her own security must precede German rearmament had once more brought the Disarmament Conference to a deadlock in May. It was hoped that the adjournment of the conference on 29 June would allow the essential difficulties to be solved through diplomatic channels. Hitler rejected a French suggestion for a probationary period of international supervision, although on 6 October he expressed to the British and Italian Governments his approval of the original British plan for a five-year period of preliminary disarmament. The Bureau of the Conference met at Geneva on 9 October, and on the 14th Sir John Simon announced British support of the French programme. This involved a preliminary period of four years, during which the continental armies would be transformed into short-service militias, and an adequate system of supervision through a permanent disarmament commission should be set up. In a second four-year period the actual limitation of armaments should be arranged. An essential condition of this programme was 'that the powers now under restriction of the Peace Treaties should not begin to increase their armaments forthwith'. The practical effect of the proposals was that substantial changes in the existing size of armies would be postponed for four years.

On the same day Germany's withdrawal from the conference and from the League was announced, on the ground that the conference could clearly not fulfil its sole object, general disarmament. A plebiscite in Germany on 12 November ratified this decision, giving the Government 92·2 per cent of the votes cast. Hitler had coupled his action with the most emphatic assertions of his desire for peace. A further advertisement of his peaceful intentions was by the German–Polish Agreement of 26 January 1934, in which the two powers renounced the use of force in the settlement of their differences for a period of ten years.

The End of Disarmament

The British Government still hoped to bring France and Germany together on the armaments question, intervening itself as a mediator if a deadlock appeared to be threatened. It seemed better to agree to the comparatively small German increases in question than to run the risk of a repudiation by Germany of all restrictions. By the end of December 1933 Germany had offered terms which included a formal recognition of her complete equality of rights, in return for which she would of her own free will show such moderation in availing herself of equality as to remove any fear of her using it as an offensive menace. Security could be guaranteed by the signature of ten-year pacts of non-aggression. Her specific terms were that the Reichswehr should be gradually transformed into an army of 300,000 men with a twelve-month's period of service, and with defensive weapons including tanks up to 6 tons, and guns up to 155 mm in calibre. Hitler was prepared to accept supervision, so that an international commission could decide whether the 'para-military' forces (the S.A., the S.S., and the Labour Corps) were really innocuous. The proposals in general gave Germany only 20 per cent of the effectives of France and her allies. Yet the French reply on 1 January 1934 took exception to the retention of para-military organizations, argued that the German scheme meant rearmament and not disarmament, and again insisted on the need for a preliminary period of supervision. It did, however, offer substantial reductions, including a 50 per cent decrease in the size of the French Air Force, during the second period. The German Government on 19 January again insisted on the need for equality, and declared that the figure of 300,000 was needed for German security.

France during this period was passing through weeks of serious internal crisis, with the Stavisky scandal in December, and rioting, under Fascist influences, on 6 February 1934. Chautemps fell on 27 January; Edouard Daladier, his successor, on 7 February. There were indications that Daladier desired agreement with Germany, but on the 9th a new and stronger ministry took office, led by Gaston Doumergue, with a capable Foreign Minister in Louis Barthou, who much resembled Poincaré in outlook, and even in appearance. The internal condition of France provided the new Government with a partly genuine excuse for delay, but it too found the idea of legalizing German rearmament extremely distasteful. With the Maginot Line, commenced in 1930, nearly completed, and a strong and well-equipped French Army still in existence, a rupture could be contemplated with considerable confidence. For the mass of Frenchmen their still profound dislike of war struggled with the growing conviction that no pledge of Hitler's could ever be accepted.

The next phase of British policy was therefore without result. A White Paper of 29 January 1934 made further attempts to reconcile the French and German viewpoints. Eden visited in turn Paris, Berlin, and Rome between 16 February and 1 March.[1] The Germans now asked for immediate possession of air defence forces, but were willing for them to be limited to 30 per cent of the combined forces of Germany's neighbours, or 50 per cent of the French military aircraft, whichever was less. The French, in a statement on 19 March, while not entirely rejecting the German proposals, virtually refused acceptance without specific 'guarantees' from Great Britain to meet possible infraction of the disarmament convention. The British Government appears to have been prepared to discuss the extension of the British guarantee, although only in return for substantial French disarmament. Unfortunately the opportunity had already passed. On 28 March the German Government published estimates for the coming year which included an increase of over RM.350 million for defence, and on 17

[1] Avon, I, chaps 5, 6.

April the French Government announced that it considered the negotiations at an end. The French attitude was maintained at a further meeting of the Disarmament Conference on 29 May, when Barthou displayed extreme irritation at the British attitude. A complete breakdown was avoided, but for practical purposes disarmament and the Disarmament Conference were dead: the few diplomatic exchanges between the governments during the second half of 1934 served only to establish this fact.

Dollfuss

The failure of the British disarmament policy made inevitable the search for newer guarantees of security; from this was to emerge almost immediately the scheme of an Eastern Locarno. The gloomiest forebodings as to Hitler's intentions seemed to be confirmed when on 30 June 1934 his 'purge' of the Nazi Party removed at least seventy-seven enemies or suspected enemies of the régime, and a *Putsch* by the Austrian Nazi Party on 25 July led to the murder of Dollfuss. Hitler had indeed as it happened already decided in the previous March (perhaps because he had been taken by surprise at the conclusion of the 'Rome protocols' between Austria, Hungary, and Italy) to abandon the campaign of force and even of official German propaganda against Austria. Instead, the Nazi Party must build up its position inside Austria.[1]

To the British Government the Austrian problem was particularly confusing. Officially Great Britain continued to support Austrian independence. The emphasis laid in the Four-Power Pact of June 1933 on Article 10 of the Covenant, and the representations made to the German Government in August, were followed on 21 December by Sir John Simon's statement in the House of Commons that 'the independence and safety of Austria are an essential object to which British policy is directed'. On 17 February 1934 the British, French, and Italian Governments announced that they took a common

[1] G.D., Ser. C, vol. ii, no. 328

view of the necessity for maintaining Austria's independence. But these declarations did not imply any particular sympathy for the Austrian régime, whose real character had been revealed in the massacre of the Austrian Socialists by the Heimwehr in Vienna between 12 and 15 February, largely it would seem under Mussolini's inspiration. The assassination of Dollfuss was part of a revolution which miscarried; Mussolini moved 100,000 men to the Austrian frontier, Hitler did not intervene, and the Austrian Government, under its new leader Dr Kurt Schuschnigg, was able to suppress the insurrection in the provinces. On 26 July Sir John Simon condemned the murder in the House of Commons, and on 27 September the British, Italian, and French Governments reaffirmed the declaration of 17 February. But to many Englishmen the clerical fascism of Austria, with its machine-guns and concentration camps, was no more attractive than the Nazi fascism of Germany, which at least had the noisy support of large sections of the population.

The Eastern Locarno

The same unenthusiastic acceptance of political realities characterized the British attitude towards the French plans for bringing the Soviet Union into the League and into an 'Eastern Locarno'. Barthou planned in the spring of 1934 a comprehensive scheme of security which would be deprived of any features offensive to the dignity of a peaceful Germany by provision for her participation. The French plan aimed ultimately, however, at agreement between the Soviet Union, Poland, and the Little Entente for joint resistance to Nazi aggression, based on the use of the League machinery of collective security and sanctions. The Little Entente powers (Czechoslovakia, Rumania, and Yugoslavia) had on 16 February 1933 signed a 'Pact of Organization' at Geneva, which established a permanent council of their respective foreign ministers and registered their opposition to revision; on 9 February 1934 Greece, Turkey, Yugoslavia, and Rumania signed at Athens a treaty creating a 'Balkan Entente'. Fear of

Nazi policy played a large part in these two combinations, which promised, therefore, to be drawn without difficulty into Barthou's scheme; Poland was less enthusiastic, but the Soviet Union proved decidedly favourable to the new plans.

To the British Government Soviet internal policy certainly appeared no more attractive than that of Germany; there could be no doubt, however, as to the pacific turn which Soviet foreign policy had taken with the Five-Year Plan. Although the Metropolitan-Vickers trial momentarily revived diplomatic tension between Moscow and London, the British Government was quite ready to encourage Soviet co-operation in measures to neutralize possible German aggression. In pursuance of his plan for an Eastern Locarno, Barthou visited Warsaw and Prague in April, conferred with Litvinov in May, and visited Bucarest for the session of the Little Entente Council on 20 June. The plans were then laid before the British Government by Barthou during a visit to London on 8–9 July. The French and Russian Governments accepted the British view that an Eastern pact which excluded Germany would lead rapidly to the division of Europe into rival camps and so precipitate a repetition of the 1914 situation; on this basis the scheme received the British Government's blessing, an event which was said to have caused 'general and genuine astonishment' in Moscow.[1] It was not prepared to give a military guarantee of the Versailles settlement in Eastern Europe, but reaffirmed the obligations to France under the Locarno Agreement. On 19 July Mr Baldwin announced that the Government had decided on rearmament in the air, and on the 30th remarked, 'When you think of the defence of England, you no longer think of the chalk cliffs of Dover; you think of the Rhine. This is where our frontier lies.'

And in fact British action was not confined to a merely passive acceptance of Barthou's plans. The British ambassadors in Rome, Berlin, and Warsaw were instructed on 12 July to explain and commend the plans to the Governments concerned. The British proposals were based on three draft treaties:

[1] B.D., Ser. II, vol. vii, nos 500, 613.

(1) a pact of mutual assistance between Germany, Poland, Czechoslovakia, the Soviet Union, and the Baltic states; (2) a bilateral agreement between France and Russia, which Germany might join; (3) a convention linking the Eastern Pact with the Locarno Pact and the League Covenant. Italy, which had at first been hostile to Barthou's scheme on the ground that it attempted to isolate Germany, expressed approval of the new arrangements.[1] Poland and Germany, however, held back. Both feared that they might be called on to allow the passage of foreign troops; Poland had territorial claims against Lithuania and Czechoslovakia, and disliked any strengthening of the Soviet Union. Germany had also no desire to abandon indefinitely her revisionist plans, and had a more immediate objective in the fact that the formal recognition of her equality of rights had not been granted. Sir John Simon on 13 July said that Barthou had agreed that equality should accompany the conclusion of the pact, but two days later Barthou denied that any connexion between the two could be established. This provided Germany's ground for refusing her signature on 10 September; Poland virtually rejected the pact on the 27th. On the other hand the Soviet Union was elected on the 17th to a permanent seat on the League Council, opposed only by Ireland, Switzerland, and Portugal. Poland did not oppose, but secured a promise from the Soviet Government not to support any petitions to the League from the Russian minority in Poland; at the same time she announced that she no longer recognized the right of the League to concern itself with Polish minority questions.

After this the British Government could hardly condemn a direct Franco-Soviet agreement, but further negotiations were interrupted by the assassination of Barthou and King Alexander of Yugoslavia at Marseilles on 9 October. The Saar plebiscite in January 1935 caused a further postponement. The Saar had been placed under League administration at Versailles, and it was obvious by this time that there would be a majority in favour of a return to Germany. On 3 December the German

[1] B.D., Ser. II, vol. vi, nos 402, 501.

Government agreed to pay France 900 million francs for the coal-mines, which roughly balanced the amount of French currency available in the Saar. The problem of holding a plebiscite under League supervision was solved by the British Government's offer to the League, to co-operate (with Italy, Holland, and Sweden) in the formation of an international force. This force, under a British general, duly arrived, and in the plebiscite on 13 January 90·35 per cent of the votes were for union with Germany, to Hitler's surprise and relief.

Germany Rearms: the Stresa Front

The final defeat of the attempts to bring Hitler's Germany into satisfactory treaty relations with the rest of Europe came in the spring of 1935. On 7 January 1935 Laval, the new French Foreign Minister, and Mussolini signed the Franco-Italian agreement which, like the Anglo-French agreement of 1904, was designed to settle amicably the colonial differences between the two countries, and so make possible a united front against Germany. To meet the problem of Austria it proposed pacts of non-intervention to be signed between Austria and various 'particularly interested states'. On 31 January Laval and Flandin, the French Prime Minister, visited London, and an Anglo-French communiqué on 3 February expressed the hope that Germany would co-operate in the Eastern and Danubian Pacts, and would also join an air pact as a supplement to the Locarno Agreement. By this each of the signatories would undertake to give support to whichever of them might be a victim of aerial aggression by one of the contracting powers. Germany at once welcomed the air pact, but would only promise 'exhaustive examination' of the other two pacts. She was, in fact, almost ready for her final gesture of self-assertion.

The decision to announce that Germany was rearming had nearly been taken in the autumn of 1934, but had been postponed because of the Saar question, among others. Now she took the final steps. A British White Paper on 4 March 1935, signed by MacDonald but largely the work of Baldwin, referred to the illegal rearmament of Germany as the chief reason for proposed increases in the British estimates. Germany expressed strong resentment; on the following day Hitler made an excuse for postponing a visit by Simon and Eden to discuss the proposals of 3 February. As it was general knowledge that she was already rearming the outburst of anger at the British publication presented a curious psychological problem. On 9 March the German Government announced that the German Air Force had come into existence again on 1 March; on the 16th Hitler, in a proclamation to the German people, announced that Germany would resume complete freedom in providing for her defence; a law at the same time reintroduced conscription and established an army of thirty-six divisions. Simon and Eden depressed Hitler's critics in the Foreign Office and elsewhere by holding the postponed conversations with him on the 25th and 26th. They were told once again of the Führer's objections to the Eastern and Danubian Pacts, and of the large scale of Germany's existing and future armaments, but were given voluminous assurances as to his concern for peace, moral rehabilitation, and even the League. Eden had an almost effusive reception in Moscow on 28th and 29th March, although the Soviet Press had continued its attacks on British foreign policy up to the eve of his visit.[1]

Europe could only accept the accomplished facts. At the Stresa Conference (11–14 April 1935) France, Italy, and Great Britain reaffirmed their approval of the Eastern and Danubian Pacts, and drafted a resolution condemning Germany's repudiation of her obligations under the Versailles Treaty. The resolution was carried unanimously by the League Council next day. A Franco-Soviet pact of mutual assistance was signed on 2 May 1935. And then on 18 June an Anglo-German naval agreement was announced, on lines which had been proposed by Hitler to Simon in March. It limited Germany's aggregate naval tonnage to 35 per cent of that of the British Commonwealth; she had the right to equal submarine tonnage with the

[1] G.D., Ser. C, vol. iii, no. 555; Avon, I, pp. 124–63.

Commonwealth, although she undertook not to exceed 45 per cent without giving notice.[1] To the French protest that the agreement condoned Germany's unilateral rearmament immediately after the League condemnation, the British ministers replied, not very happily, that it was a realist contribution to peace similar to the Franco-Soviet pact.

[1] D. C. Watt, 'The Anglo-German Naval Agreement of 1935: an interim judgement' (*Journal of Modern History*, June 1956).

X

Crises in the Mediterranean, 1935–8

For nearly three years after the early summer of 1935 the international scene was dominated by Mussolini in a manner singularly disconcerting to the British Government, which had every possible reason for desiring to avoid a quarrel with Italy at this stage. The French were even more reluctant to involve themselves in activities which would take their attention off Germany. This Anglo-French aversion to trouble in the Mediterranean was undoubtedly one of the main reasons why the astute and adventurous Duce chose just this moment for action.

The decision was, however, influenced by many other considerations. Italy, like Germany and Japan, was tempted to seek escape or distraction from economic distress by a bold foreign policy. She was very much the weakest of the great powers in natural resources, and the well-publicized and apparently vigorous machinery of the corporate state concealed widespread corruption and inefficiency. Economic considerations came a poor second to national prestige and led to an overvalued currency and attempt at self-sufficiency on disadvantageous terms. The depression hit Italy both as regards exports and other earnings such as emigrant remittances and tourist traffic. After 1931 popular discontent began to voice itself far more openly than had been thought possible in the early years of the régime.

Mussolini had never made any secret of his ambition for Italy as a world power, whose imperialism would dominate the Mediterranean and beyond. Although his foreign policy was, at first, cautious enough, he left the other powers in no doubt as to his belief in the necessity for revision of the peace treaties to rectify what were considered the inadequate gains of Italy after the war. He continued obstinately to demand parity with France in naval armaments, and announced a large naval building programme in April 1930. The increasing economic gloom of the early thirties was countered by robust expressions of contempt for Italy's not very clearly defined enemies: 'harsh to our enemies, we shall march to the end with our friends'. A struggle between two worlds was foreshadowed. 'Either we or they. Either our ideas or theirs. Either our state or theirs.' The response was enthusiastic among the Duce's party followers and in many sections of the public, even if the cowed liberal elements secretly deplored its forceful crudity and ominous promises of bloodshed.

The Italian Invasion of Abyssinia

Abyssinia was for many reasons the predestined victim of Fascist imperialism. Its size, high altitudes, and reputed mineral wealth suggested a profitable field for white settlement and exploitation. It had formed the objective of Italian colonial ambitions in the Treaty of Ucciali of 1889, and the complete defeat of an Italian army at Adowa in 1896 had preserved Abyssinian independence for a generation, but had dealt a humiliating blow to Italy's prestige. Under the provisions of the secret Treaty of London of 1915, Britain had ceded Juba-land in 1924, and France in the agreement of 7 January 1935 had ceded some 44,000 square miles of the Tibesti region in Libya and other areas, as well as some shares in the Jibuti–Addis Ababa railway. Even more important perhaps from the Italian point of view were the various agreements with Britain and France since 1891 which recognized Italy's right to seek economic and other concessions in Abyssinia and which appeared to indicate that Great Britain did not resent Italian influence there. In 1925, after the Jubaland settlement, Angol-

Italian correspondence recognized an exclusive Italian sphere of economic influence in western Abyssinia, although it made Italian concessions specifically dependent on Abyssinian consent. The Franco-Italian agreement of January 1935 recognized Italy's right to seek concessions throughout Abyssinia.[1] Abyssinia had been admitted to the League of Nations in 1923 with Italian support in face of British and French opposition, and in a treaty of August 1928 had allowed Italy to construct and monopolize a motor road through her territory.

The Wal-Wal frontier dispute, from which the war originated, had been brought before the League in January 1935; there was no 'formal' mention of African affairs at the Stresa Conference in April, but France and Great Britain had no desire to encourage aggressive Italian action. When early in May Mussolini invited Great Britain to begin friendly discussions with regard to the Italian proceeding in Abyssinia, the reply was not encouraging. Simon warned Count Grandi, the Italian Ambassador, that a solution of the Abyssinian question by force would have a deplorable effect on British opinion. Nevertheless, there had been no forthright insistence on the British Government's intention to act through the League, and on 14 May Mussolini, in a speech to the Italian Senate, denied that there had been any Anglo-French *démarche* against Italy's proposed action. At the end of May an anti-British campaign was opened in the Italian Press. Throughout the next twelve months the Italians did their best to represent League action in the dispute as an Anglo-Italian quarrel, inspired by British imperialism.

This it was not; Great Britain had no designs on Abyssinia herself, and her interest in it was limited to guaranteeing and improving the water-supply from Lake Tana to the Blue Nile. She had, indeed, grievances against the Abyssinian Government, owing to its continued postponement of permission to undertake irrigation works at Lake Tana, and to the constant

[1] This was suspected at the time, and is now known, to have meant a free hand for Italy in Abyssinia, in return for close Italian co-operation in military affairs with France against Germany: D. C. Watt, 'The Secret Laval–Mussolini Agreement of 1935 on Ethiopia' (*The Middle East Journal*, 1961).

raiding by Abyssinian tribes into British territory. But a Foreign Office commission under Sir John Maffey, appointed in February, reported in June that no local British interests would be involved in an Italian conquest of the country. A copy of this secret report soon fell into Italian hands. British imperial interests strongly favoured, indeed, the avoidance of a breach with Italy. Britain's primary concern in the Mediterranean was to maintain and protect the steamship route to the Far East by the Suez Canal. Since 1878 her Eastern Mediterranean front against Russia had been served by the line of communication from England passing through Gibraltar and Malta; friendly relations with the relatively weak Spanish and Italian states had excluded the possibility of any threat to this route in the western Mediterranean. So habituated was the British Government to the idea of Italian friendship towards the strongest naval power that it was quite at a loss for a policy when an unfriendly Italy threatened to cut the route in two.

But Italian action might necessitate the imposition of sanctions under the League Covenant. A friendly warning as to such complications was given by Sir Robert Vansittart in March 1935. On this point there was evidently grave misgivings among the more senior members of the British Cabinet. Many of the familiar objections to the guarantee function of the League applied with particular force here. A sanctions policy escalating into a Mediterranean war would probably leave France, Italy, and Great Britain too distracted to make effective resistance to future German, or perhaps Japanese, aggression, although there seemed little chance that Italy could win. Moreover, although a rearmament programme had been announced in the spring, it had not been very enthusiastically received, and it was clear that the advocates of 'strong League action' were not facing the conclusion that economic sanctions might produce war. The Peace Ballot,[1] announced on 27 June 1935, gave an overwhelming majority (over 10 million votes) for all-round reduction of armaments, and for economic and non-military sanctions; 6,784,368 votes were cast in favour of

[1] Cf. Lord R. Cecil, *A Great Experiment* (1941), pp. 254–63.

military sanctions and 2,351,891 against, but as many were undecided. There was thus a decided majority in favour even of military sanctions, and it was, of course, certain that in a specific case in which opinion was strongly aroused the support would be greater, although on the other hand the imminence of war might damp the ardour of many. But military sanctions were not equated with war. Nevertheless, it soon became evident that the Italian threat to Abyssinia was arousing much stronger feeling in the country than the Japanese aggression in Manchuria, although there was outspoken opposition to sanctions in certain influential London papers. These considerations led the Government to decide in favour of collective League action, although it was careful to insist that there was no individual quarrel with Italy, and that Great Britain would go only so far as the other League members.

In June, Simon was succeeded as Foreign Secretary by Sir Samuel Hoare, and Eden entered the Cabinet at the age of thirty-eight as Minister for League of Nations Affairs. Baldwin succeeded MacDonald as Prime Minister. Eden had well-grounded objections to the appointment of two ministers for foreign affairs. On 1 August Hoare in the House of Commons gave an indication that Great Britain would, if the occasion arose, support collective League action; this he reaffirmed specifically at Geneva on 11 September.[1] On 3 October the anticipated act of Italian aggression took place, and on the 7th the Council, with the solitary exception of Italy, recorded the fact. Eden played an active part in the League's decision to appoint a 'Committee of Eighteen' to conduct a policy of economic sanctions, and a ban on the export of certain raw materials, and on imports from Italy, came into existence on 18 November. Italy, protesting furiously, went ahead with her military operations.

But the position was disastrously complicated by the existence since September of a 'Committee of Five' with Señor de Madariaga as chairman, and including Eden, Laval, and Polish and Turkish representatives. It approved in principle a

[1] Lord Templewood, *Nine Troubled Years* (1954), chap. 12.

plan which Eden had put to Mussolini in June, and which provided for the cession to Abyssinia of a strip of land in British Somaliland, including the port of Zeila, in order to facilitate territorial and economic concessions by Abyssinia to Italy. Mussolini rejected the plan, although there was no justification for subsequent reports that the two had quarrelled.[1] The British offer involved concessions of territory by Abyssinia, although as the Emperor had promised some compensation in connexion with the Wal-Wal episode, and as Britain had some lingering sense of obligation to Italy under the 1915 treaty, it could be argued that it was not too conspicuously a surrender to Italian aggression. Nevertheless, that element was always present, with a tendency for more sweeping concessions by the weaker party to the stronger to be elaborated as the Italian forces advanced. In October Mr Maurice Peterson, head of the Abyssinian department of the Foreign Office, and a French official, M. St Quentin, continued to discuss these plans in Paris. The talks went on after the League invited Britain and France to seek a settlement early in November. The permanent head of the Foreign Office, Sir Robert Vansittart, was an emphatic supporter of these efforts. Thus the League was sponsoring potentially divergent plans of coercion and conciliation.[2]

France – or her Foreign Minister – must bear the main individual responsibility for the failure of collective action. M. Laval, although he denied that he had given Italy a free hand in Abyssinia in January 1935, except in the economic field, was not prepared to risk a war with Italy and so lose irrevocably an ally against Germany. It has been remarked that it was a curious and unfortunate coincidence that on the one occasion on which France's devotion to the League was put to the test, she was represented by the only French Foreign Minister since the war who did not believe in the League.

[1] M. Toscano, 'Eden's Mission to Rome on the Eve of the Italo-Ethiopian Conflict', *Studies in Diplomatic History*, ed. A. O. Sarkissian (1961), pp. 126–52; Avon, I, p. 226.

[2] M. Peterson, *Both Sides of the Curtain* (1950), pp. 115–16; R. Vansittart, *The Mist Procession* (1958), pp. 536–45.

It soon became clear that the only effective economic sanction would be a ban on the export of oil to Italy; and it was primarily because of French action that the imposition of this ban was delayed until the success of Italy made it ineffectual. It is true that the oil embargo presented many technical difficulties. An embargo would be useless unless American supplies could be cut off; and although President Roosevelt had appealed to the oil industry to limit its exports to the average of the past three years, the export of American controlled oil had trebled by the end of November. Very large stocks, at least ten times the normal quantities, poured into Italian East Africa during the last three months of 1935.[1] Knowing that an oil embargo might stampede Italy into some form of retaliation which would mean war, Laval endeavoured to postpone a decision until a settlement by mediation had been arrived at. The meeting of the relevant League committee was postponed until 12 December, and was then postponed again on French insistence while the Hoare–Laval plan was under discussion.

The basis of this plan was that the Emperor of Abyssinia should cede to Italy the eastern Tigre province, the Danakil country, and a large part of the Ogaden province. Italy would cede a narrow strip of territory in southern Eritrea, giving Abyssinia access to the sea. At this moment there seemed no immediate prospect of Italian victory, and although the plan might be justified on the ground that it would save Abyssinia from losing all her territory later, it was undoubtedly due primarily to the desire to avoid all the disastrous international complications which Laval in particular anticipated. It was not a sudden aberration, but a development of the Peterson–St Quentin discussions. Vansittart, who accompanied Hoare to Paris, approved the plan. It was published prematurely by a deliberate French indiscretion, and it was a vast shock to the British public, which knew nothing about its antecedents. Hoare was ill and overworked, and Laval's eagerness for a settlement seems to have stampeded him to some extent. Nevertheless, the British Cabinet had no more desire than Laval

[1] H. Feis, *Seen From E.A.* (1947), part 3.

to fight, or even quarrel permanently with Italy. After a storm from the British Press, and widespread criticism from the Conservative rank and file under the leadership of Sir Austen Chamberlain, the British Government repudiated the plan, and Hoare resigned.[1] Eden, his successor, informed the Council on 18 December that the Government did not wish to pursue the proposals further.

But Eden, although authorized to support the oil sanction, could make no headway. The League's committee of experts reported on 12 February 1936 that if American supplies were reduced to the normal figure, Italy could continue the war for not more than three and a half months. On 2 March, when the Committee of Eighteen was once more on the point of a decision, M. Flandin, who had succeeded Laval, carried a proposal for a further postponement while a supreme appeal was made to the belligerents. In allowing this proposal to be accepted without a short and specific time limit Eden suffered a diplomatic defeat quite as serious for the British policy as Laval's imposition of his peace plan on Hoare. On 7 March German troops reoccupied the demilitarized zone of the Rhineland, and this new crisis led to the inevitable postponement of the oil sanctions question; within a few weeks, by the judicious use of poison gas, the Italians succeeded in breaking the resistance of their brave, but ill-equipped opponents, and the war was virtually over by the end of April. British irritation at France's recent policy, and a strong undercurrent of popular sympathy for Germany, prevented British support at this decisive moment for the rather half-hearted French plan for a counter-march into the Rhineland. Eden defends this decision in his memoirs.[2] We now know that Hitler had not intended to reoccupy the Rhineland before the spring of 1937, but advanced the date because of the Abyssinian crisis. If oil sanctions had been vigorously imposed in December 1935 the powers would almost certainly have been involved by March 1936 in a

[1] Templewood, pp. 177–82; Peterson, pp. 120–3; Avon, pp. 288–304; A. H. Furnia, *The Diplomacy of Appeasement* (1960), pp. 159–82.
[2] Avon, I, pp. 330–67.

Mediterranean crisis which would have been even more detrimental to the prospect of joint action in other spheres.

The German Government had made the ratification of the Franco-Soviet pact on 27 February 1936 (it had been concluded in May 1935) its excuse for reoccupying the Rhineland and withdrawing from the Locarno system. The British Government affirmed in London on 19 March that its own obligations to France and Belgium had not lapsed. After a plebiscite on 29 March, the German Government published a proposal for a European settlement to include a twenty-five years security pact between Germany and her western neighbours, a Franco-German agreement on 'moral disarmament', and a German re-entry to the League. A questionnaire by the British Government on 6 May was considered, however, to throw doubt on Germany's intentions, and no reply was given. When a proposal was made in July for a meeting of the Locarno powers other than Germany, Italy refused, and thereby gave the first demonstration of the Rome–Berlin axis. It was publicly proclaimed by Mussolini in a speech at Milan on 1 November; on 18 November the two powers issued identical statements recognizing Franco's organization as the government of Spain; the Anti-Comintern pact between Germany and Japan was concluded on 21 November, and joined by Italy a year later (6 November 1937).[1]

The outcome of the Abyssinian dispute was, however one viewed the matter, a serious blow to British prestige. But it was achieved under conditions which created in many quarters abroad and at home an erroneous conception of Great Britain's real attitude to foreign affairs. In 1935 there were still strong and diverse currents of opinion in England hostile to war; there was also a healthy capacity for resentment at the brutality of Italian power politics, and an acquiescence in the Government's vast rearmament programme which would have been inconceivable a few years before. Popular loyalty to the League made it impossible for the British Government to adopt a completely neutral attitude similar to that of the United States;

[1] E. M. Robertson, *Hitler's Pre-War Policy* (1963), pp. 93–9.

on the other hand, the Government's own conception of Britain's strength and weakness forced it to seek means of avoiding war before 1939. It compromised with a policy of limited responsibility, and thus gave Italy an opportunity for a noisy triumph when she represented her Abyssinian adventure as a victory at the expense of British jealousy and imperialism.

These conditions could not, however, continue indefinitely. It was tempting to Hitler and Mussolini to make the British or French look ridiculous by repudiating treaties, defying their representations, and proclaiming the decadence of democracy, but it was also unwise. Its result was to stimulate war feeling in England, hasten British rearmament, and produce ultimately counter-defiance, necessitating a surrender by the totalitarian power in question, or war. Mussolini and Hitler both seem to have believed in their ability to avoid an irrevocable step, and Mussolini did at least fare better than Hitler for a time in this respect. His opportunistic policy kept the Balkan and Mediterranean countries in a state of apprehension for several years, but he found means of accepting the German annexation of Austria, and of remaining neutral in 1939, without loss of face.

The Spanish Civil War

The Spanish civil war involved the powers in a fresh Mediterranean crisis almost immediately after the end of the Abyssinian war. The British Government again showed to considerable disadvantage, although the sensational accusations of pro-Fascist sympathies had little justification. British policy was again a somewhat hand-to-mouth affair, and seems to have been governed by a lack of sympathy for either side. Hoare is supposed to have remarked in the summer of 1936 that he hoped for a war in which the Fascists and Bolsheviks would kill each other off. Or, as A. P. Herbert said on another occasion, 'a plague on both your blouses'. Above all the British Government was dominated by the desire not to allow the war to develop into a European conflict. It does not appear to have made the mistake of overrating Italy's strength, although its anxiety over what might happen in the Far East or in Central Europe seems to have resulted in a somewhat exaggerated deference to Italian naval and air power. But despite the British Government's attitude in urging non-intervention the interference of Italy, Germany, and Russia converted the struggle into a major ideological battle which was reproduced in England, where it produced greater bitterness than had been the case even in 1926 and 1931. It was recognized also, in discussions between what was called the 'Cape' and the 'Mediterranean' schools, that in such a war Great Britain would be unable to use the Mediterranean. But her vital communications with the Far East, and even with the Middle East, could still be served by the Cape route. Meanwhile the Spanish war had led directly to an improvement in British relations with Turkey and Egypt. In June 1936 Turkey secured at the Montreux conference the re-establishment of her sovereignty over the Straits, and the right to remilitarize them; Great Britain's support of this, and the visit of King Edward VIII to Turkey in August, inaugurated an Anglo-Turkish *rapprochement*, greatly stimulated by the unnecessarily large Italian forces at the island of Rhodes. Egypt was similarly alarmed at Italian policy, and at the massing of Italian troops in Libya; nevertheless, the naval and military measures taken by Great Britain in Egypt to meet the possibility of war caused a revival of national resentment against the British occupation. The British Government was at first inclined to consider the moment inopportune for a reduction of its privileges, but some remarks on these lines by Sir Samuel Hoare in November and December 1935 caused so much indignation in Egypt that negotiations for a new treaty were started in March. In July a treaty was signed, based on the draft treaty of 1930. It made provision for Egyptian independence, a close alliance between the two countries, unrestricted immigration (under normal conditions) of Egyptians into the Sudan, and the continuation of a British force in the neighbourhood of Alexandria for eight years.[1]

[1] Avon, I., pp. 390–94.

The Spanish issues were essentially domestic, and this was perhaps the first major European crisis since 1919 that was totally unconnected with the First World War. The abolition of the monarchy in 1931 had been a success for the Radicals but thereafter electoral fortunes had fluctuated. In 1935 the semi-Fascist right wing CEDA was strong in the Cortes and the Radical Government came closer to the right. The brutal repression of the resulting strikes led in its turn to a swing to the left which brought into power a popular-front Government. The Communists were more moderate in their immediate aims than the Socialists under Caballero, but there was no prospect of any early move by the Government to disestablish the Church, divide up the great estates, or socialize industry. There was, however, a certain amount of unorganized violence, with strikes, seizure of estates, and attacks on churches and monasteries. The Conservative elements retaliated; on 18 July 1936, after the murder of a right-wing politician, a military revolt broke out in Spain and Spanish Morocco, and an attempt was made to seize the Government by a *coup d'état*. The blow miscarried, and the Government succeeded in raising forces sufficient to involve the country in a long civil war.[1]

Italian help was received by the rebels under General Franco from the start and had clearly been promised long before the outbreak. Germany responded more reluctantly, but the first German planes reached Morocco on 21 July. The French Prime Minister, Léon Blum, and some of his Cabinet were anxious to aid the Spanish Government but French right-wing opinion was hostile and the danger of a national split grew during July. Blum was also anxious for British support over the sending of arms to Spain, but on a visit to London on 23 July was told by Eden that it was France's own affair. 'I simply ask you one thing. Be prudent.' Eden thoroughly agreed with Baldwin and the rest of the Cabinet that the right course for Britain was to discourage active intervention on

[1] On the war generally: Hugh Thomas, *The Spanish Civil War* (1961); P. A. M. van der Esch, *Prelude to War: the international repercussions of the Spanish Civil War, 1936–1939* (1951), and W. L. Kleine-Ahlbrandt, *The Policy of Simmering* (1962). The fullest account on the British side is in Avon, I, chaps 5–8.

either side. Sympathies in England were in fact divided; there was a certain amount of right-wing support for Franco, while the main upsurge of public feeling was certainly for the Republicans. The Labour Party pledged all practicable support for the Spanish Government on 20 July, but this did not imply a desire for active intervention. Everyone was concerned to prevent the escalation of this civil war. Churchill, a major critic of the Government on so many strategical issues, also favoured a policy of rigid neutrality and continued to do so until 1938. Blum's decision was to send aid unofficially, and to invite all countries to adopt a policy of neutrality; this was supported by the British Government, which henceforth made itself the main exponent of non-intervention. By the end of August the principle of the official closure of the Spanish frontier to arms traffic had been accepted by Germany, Italy, and Russia.

To supervise the operation of the ban an international committee began meetings in London on 9 September 1936, and soon had to consider evidence that its decisions were being flouted by Germany and Italy, who recognized Franco in mid-November on the mistaken belief that the end of the war was in sight. Thus committed, they could not withdraw. Russian supplies saved Madrid from capture at this critical moment. War seemed very near in November and December as the Nationalists announced that they would blockade Republican ports, although their right to do so was not recognized by the British and French. But for all his bluster Mussolini could not fail to realize that this long and doubtful struggle was damaging both to Italy's pocket and her prestige, and his willingness to accept the pretence of non-intervention as long as possible was evidence of considerable concern as to how much the British would stand. In the 'Gentleman's Agreement' of 2 January 1937 England and Italy disclaimed any desire 'to see modified the status quo as regards national sovereignty of territories in the Mediterranean region'. The façade was also maintained by an agreement in March for the withdrawal of 'volunteers' and for the setting up of an international blockade of the Spanish coast to supervise the supply of war materials. Yet during the succeeding months there were repeated attacks on neutral shipping, often it seemed by Italian aeroplanes and submarines in Franco's service, in various parts of the Mediterranean, and vessels attacked even included four British warships. A conference of Mediterranean and Black Sea powers was accordingly convened at Nyon to deal with this further crisis; Germany, who had been invited, and Italy, made the participation of the Soviet Union an excuse for refusing attendance. This was an error in tactics. An agreement was signed on 14 September 1937, by which the participating powers made arrangements for counter-attacks, and for the defence of shipping routes. Italy found it expedient to accept and participate in the arrangements, which led to a rapid improvement in the position; the counter-measures of the British fleet under the agreement showed, indeed, that the democracies were not incapable of conducting a 'white war' to their own advantage.

Germany by this stage had adopted a much more restrained attitude; her warships withdrew from the Mediterranean, and her troops and experts in Spain, which had never been so numerous as the Italian, appear to have received orders to act as unostentatiously as possible. Although the Italian Government finally abandoned any pretence of indifference to the result, and made it clear that it would not withdraw its troops until Franco was victorious, the British Government decided to make the best of a bad job, and to assume that Mussolini would be glad to bring the Anglo-Italian tension to an end if he could do so without loss of prestige at home and abroad. The Anglo-Italian Agreement of April 1938 was the result. The agreement was a comprehensive one; its essential basis was a promise by Great Britain to facilitate the recognition of the Italian position in Abyssinia, and an Italian promise to adhere to the British plan for the withdrawal of 'volunteers' from Spain. Great Britain stipulated that the agreement should not come into force until the Spanish question was settled. Italy disclaimed any intention of seeking a political, economic, or territorial foothold in Spain. Hitler was emboldened by the Munich Agreement to send vital reinforcements which enabled the Nationalists to break the deadlock in central and eastern Spain at the end of 1938. The final victory of Franco was in sight when Britain and France recognized his Government in February 1939. The withdrawal of the Italian troops in 1939 certainly showed that Italy had gained little advantage from all her efforts.

Throughout Great Britain had, in following the policy of non-intervention, based itself on the hope that Spanish national pride would, after the war, prevent any permanent control or occupation of Spanish territory by foreign powers, and that, in the long run, the Spanish people might be most grateful to those who interfered least. If this assumption was sound a victory for either side would have more or less the same result as far as British interests were concerned. But in practice neutrality, or non-intervention, would mean the victory of Franco, who could continue to draw support from Italy and Germany as long as he needed it, and the recognition that its policy of neutrality made Franco's success inevitable undoubtedly influenced the attitude of the Government in its negotiations with Italy after 1937.

XI

The Far East, 1933–40

At this point it will be useful to remind ourselves of the heavy responsibility felt by the British Government for British interests and possessions in the Far East throughout the thirties. In the continuous crisis atmosphere in Europe created by Italian and then German aggression this problem was ignored to a remarkable degree by the public, and, even more surprisingly, by the Press and political writers. And yet it is only possible to understand the Government's handling of the Czech and Polish crises, which will be dealt with in the next two chapters, if we realize that its members were constantly looking over their shoulders to see what was happening at Shanghai and Tientsin, and speculating over the need to send the main fleet at the shortest possible notice to defend Singapore.

Japanese Pretensions in China

After Japan's notification of withdrawal from the League in March 1933 and the Tangku Truce in May there was a temporary relaxation of tension in the Far East. The Japanese were for the moment content with their acquisition of a large and rich province and they began the job of developing and consolidating their gains. The Chinese could do no more than acquiesce, Chiang Kai-shek being more concerned at this time with strengthening his hold on the rest of China, eliminating the Communists, and reorganizing the army and administration. A state of more or less uneasy co-existence was established and a number of practical agreements made, including a through-traffic arrangement with the Peking–Mukden Railway and postal links with the Japanese puppet state of Manchukuo.

This relaxation was, however, only partial and Japanese policy became a source of increasing anxiety and irritation to Britain as it became evident that, despite all statements to the contrary, Japan intended to abolish the 'Open Door' in Manchuria and establish a monopoly of trade and investment there. The only concession to vigorous Anglo-American protests was that the process of discrimination against the foreigner was generally carried on without open declaration, although even this was discarded in the case of the oil monopoly. Though British interests in Manchuria were relatively small the flouting of the principle of equal trade opportunities was disturbing.

The scale and exclusiveness of Japanese claims and the trend of Japanese thought were indicated by Foreign Minister Hirota's statement on 23 January 1934 and by the so-called 'Amau' declaration by a Japanese Government spokesman in April, both asserting Japan's special and exclusive responsibility for the maintenance of peace in East Asia. This was met by a vigorous protest from the British Government, but the Japanese military authorities went ahead with the even more disturbing policy of intrigue and pressure in North China in the name of preserving peace. This culminated in an ultimatum to the Chinese in May 1935 and a further demand in June as a result of which the Kuomintang Party organization and all Chinese Central Government troops were withdrawn from the five Northern Provinces. The Japanese now made attempts to set up a puppet régime with a separatist army exploiting the long-established regionalism of North China.

British policy in the Far East after 1933 continued to be hampered by the conditions which had made it so negative in 1931–2. Economic difficulties and the restrictive effects of the naval disarmament agreements limited expansion of the British fleet even in European waters, while the Japanese began to move ahead. In February 1934 the Defence Requirements Committee, which had no doubt that Germany was the 'ultimate potential enemy', visualized Japan as the greatest immediate problem and favoured the revival of the old friendly co-operation with her. Sir Warren Fisher, the Permanent Head of the Civil Service, strongly supported this policy even at the cost of estranging the United States, which if unwilling to move against Japan might be equally unwilling to be involved in trouble with the British. The United States Government was, indeed, quite unhelpful; during the summer and autumn of 1934 it even advocated a further reduction of naval armaments by one-third, without being able to offer any support to the British in the Far East; the British, with their eyes on Germany and Japan, were now pressing again for seventy cruisers. Neville Chamberlain supported for a time the idea of a *rapprochement* with Japan as a means of concentrating the rearmament effort against Germany. But other members of the Cabinet, including MacDonald and Simon, were not prepared for any course which would strain relations with the Americans. The Japanese were as unyielding as the Americans, and wanted an improvement on the 5–5–3 ratio. In November 1934 the London Press began to oppose the idea of an Anglo-Japanese Agreement, and General Smuts spoke against any policy that would weaken Anglo-American relations.[1] In December the Japanese Government announced its intention to denounce the Washington naval agreements. The London Naval Conference (December 1935–January 1936) was concerned primarily with the Japanese demand for the abolition of the ratio, and for her own absolute parity with Great Britain and the United States. The demand met with an equally absolute refusal from the other two powers, and Japan left the conference.

But the Treasury interest in a Far Eastern solution continued. The Leith-Ross Mission of 1935 was an attempt, both realistic and imaginative, to defend British interests in the Far East

[1] D. C. Watt, 'Britain, the United States and Japan in 1934' (*Personalities and Policies*, pp. 83–99).

and at the same time to bring about some sort of viable settlement. It arose out of a number of circumstances. One was the increasing desire to check Japanese pretensions. British business interests which in 1931 may not have been greatly upset by the Japanese attempt to 'teach the Chinese a lesson' and make them less awkward, were now less happy at the idea of a Japanese monopoly. A Federation of British Industries mission which went to Japan in 1934 with hopes of participating in the development of Manchuria came away with promises but nothing more. At the same time Chinese prestige had increased, and though the British Government and many others in Britain hardly shared the rather uncritical American admiration for Chiang Kai-shek and the Kuomintang, they were interested in the success of his régime, as the only one capable of bringing order and prosperity to a miserably chaotic country. So there was great concern in Whitehall when various factors, among them Japanese attempts to undermine the Chinese currency, the American Silver Purchase Act of 1934, and the general mismanagement of China's economy, combined to threaten the complete collapse of China's currency at the end of 1934.

The Leith-Ross Mission was accordingly sent to China in the autumn of 1935 to assist with the reorganization of the currency and to determine whether a loan was necessary, and it was meant to show the Japanese that Britain had no intention of conceding Japanese claims to the sole guardianship of East Asia. As, however, a clash with Japan was the last thing desired by the British Government the mission had the further object of attempting to restore 'the whole complex of political relationships established at the Washington Conference and by the Nine-Power Treaty as it had existed prior to Japan's seizure of Manchuria', and to persuade Japan to return to the path of collaboration with the Western powers and China.

Although there were signs of interest in financial circles in Tokyo, the civilian and military authorities who wished to establish an exclusive Sino-Japanese relationship disliked British suggestions of an international loan to China. Despite Leith-Ross's efforts this part of his mission failed in Tokyo as it also did in Washington. The other part was triumphantly successful. The Chinese currency, known in Tokyo as Leith-Ross's currency, was reestablished on a sounder basis. In a new wave of confidence the Chinese administration and maritime customs service set about stamping out smuggling at which the Japanese had connived in Northern China; Kuomintang agents even began to filter back into the Northern Provinces.

The result was a considerable increase in Anglo-Japanese friction in 1936. The military in particular were angered and ready to find a scapegoat for the humiliating failure of their puppet régime in Northern China. Their anti-British feeling was reflected in incidents such as the ill-treatment of British sailors at Keelung in Formosa in October, which aroused considerable feeling. Internally, militarism and pro-fascism seemed in the ascendent in Japan, despite the failure of the 'Young Officers' revolt in February. These trends culminated in the Anti-Comintern Pact of November 1936, which though it was aimed, by the Japanese at least, more at coercing China and containing Russia than overtly threatening Britain, nevertheless posed a considerable threat to British imperial security. Japan's repudiation of naval limitations also left no doubt that the future would be one of unlimited naval rivalry. Lastly there was the prospect of unlimited economic rivalry, with the expansion of Japan's energetic selling campaign into traditional British markets. British resentment at Japanese competition and underselling based on low wages and a depreciated yen was matched by Japanese resentment at British measures to protect the Indian and colonial markets by tariffs.

This tension reached a peak in the late autumn of 1936 but subsided early in 1937, though the underlying causes of friction remained. In the spring of 1937 there were signs of a swing among military and civilian leaders in Tokyo towards improving relations with Britain. Some elements of Japanese opinion reacted against the two army-inspired policies of tying Japan to Germany in the Anti-Comintern Pact and of openly coercing the Chinese. The disadvantages of both policies were much more apparent at this stage than the advantages and this was brought home when the Sian Incident in December 1936 made Chinese Nationalist–Communist co-operation against the Japanese probable. The British, like the Chinese, received, therefore, a number of conciliatory overtures from the Japanese, including for instance the settlement in April, with an apology, of the Keelung incident. These overtures were received in the Foreign Office with considerable caution, but they gave food for thought. In the meantime the elaborate manoeuvres at Singapore in February 1937 called attention to the growing strength of this new British base of operations in the Far East.

In the spring of 1937 it was apparent to the British Government that, given the probability that Germany and Italy would pose an increasing threat which would have to be given priority in defensive preparations, there were only two means of averting an Anglo-Japanese clash. One was to exert pressure on Japan sufficient to make clear the disadvantages of an aggressive course; the other was to seek an accommodation with her, taking advantage of the recent overtures. In either case United States co-operation was essential and Chamberlain explained the position and posed these alternatives in a letter to Hull immediately after taking office as Prime Minister in May 1937. Hull, who was inhibited from almost all action by his own caution and by isolationist sentiment in the country and Congress, refused co-operation in either course and re-asserted the opposition of the United States to 'entangling alliances'. In this situation, British policy, with the approval of the Commonwealth expressed at the Commonwealth Conference in 1937, became one of maintaining British interests as firmly as possible but also responding to Japanese overtures for talks to reduce points of friction.

The 'China Incident'

This was the position when the Japanese military in North China, alarmed perhaps by the idea that the more moderate

policies were prevailing, provoked an outbreak of fresh
hostilities with the Lukowkiao Incident of 7 July 1937. The
area of conflict spread rapidly, for the Chinese felt they could
not give in easily this time and the authorities in Tokyo,
though at first genuinely favouring a settlement, were too weak
and irresolute to control their subordinates.

Soon after the outbreak of the 'incident' Eden announced
that the preliminary exchanges for Anglo-Japanese talks would
be discontinued. Anglo-Japanese friction increased rapidly,
particularly after fighting in North China spread in August
down to Shanghai, the great centre of British investments, and
threatened the International Settlement. There were once
again two possibilities before the British Government – they
could either try to organize international diplomatic, economic,
or naval pressure on Japan or they could attempt to bring
about a settlement through mediation. In fact both courses
were pursued, and if they both failed it was hardly through any
lack of effort on Britain's part.

British attempts to bring about negotiations by offering good
offices, either alone or in conjunction with others, began as
soon as news of the conflict came through in July and continued
actively until December, when it became known that Germany
was acting as mediator. Even after this and after Germany's
efforts had failed in January 1938 the British offer of good
offices remained open.

Attempts to organize some form of pressure also continued
until January 1938. Diplomatic pressure was at first favoured,
but the other powers showed little willingness to co-operate
and it had also become apparent by October 1937 that something stronger would be needed to deter the Japanese. Economic pressure was actively considered after China appealed to
the League in September and anger rose at Japanese bombing
of civilians in October. It was evident, however, that both
economic and naval pressure would be ineffectual and risky
without American co-operation. Eden worked hard from
October onwards to obtain this co-operation and to avoid the
danger of Britain's becoming committed to action in isolation

or through the League. Roosevelt's 'Quarantine Speech' on 7 October and American participation in the Brussels Conference of Nine-Power Treaty members in November raised hopes. Eden proposed to Hull on 19 October that aid to China should be combined with pressure on Japan, and on the eve of the conference promised the chief United States delegate, Norman Davis, that Britain would stand shoulder to shoulder with the United States in whatever form of action was necessary, including a substantial force of warships. There was no response from the Americans. The Japanese refused to negotiate or even attend the conference and despite strong British and French pressure Roosevelt felt unable to use the conference to organize international action. Eden in the following weeks offered eight or nine capital ships for a joint demonstration, but if these had been dispatched to the Far East it would have been at the expense of the naval concentration in the Mediterranean at this vital point in the Spanish war.

Flagrant Japanese attacks on 12 December 1937 on the British ship *Ladybird* and the American *Panay* raised Eden's hopes that the United States would participate in the naval demonstration and agree to the staff talks which he had suggested on 26 November. For two weeks this seemed a possibility as Roosevelt's Cabinet was divided and Roosevelt himself appeared keen for action.[1] However, caution and isolationist congressional opinion prevailed, and Japan's note of explanation was accepted on 23 December. Though an American naval officer, Captain Ingersoll, secretly visited and had talks in London in January 1938, and some American ships visited the newly opened base at Singapore, American Far Eastern policy as a whole moved away from co-operation and did not begin to move back again until 1940.

Japan's declaration of 16 January 1938 refusing to negotiate further with Chiang Kai-shek and foreshadowing the establishment of a new régime in China ended hopes for a negotiated settlement. The conflict – indistinguishable from war though

[1] J. M. Blum, *From the Morgenthau Diaries* (1959), pp. 485–93; Avon, I, pp. 535–46.

neither side actually declared it – entered a new phase of long-drawn-out attrition in which, despite their steady advance and control of communications and of most of the major cities, the Japanese found their expectations of quick victory foiled by Chinese tactics of guerrilla warfare and 'trading space for time'.

The following two years brought many minor and some major crises in Anglo-Japanese relations. Apart from the general strategic threat to Britain's position in the Far East involved in Japanese domination of China, Japanese attempts to drive out foreign interests in China fell particularly heavily on the British. Attacks on British interests took many forms but were continual.

The British Government also found that European and Far Eastern problems interacted in a most dangerous manner and their policy in each area was influenced by the other, though after the European crisis flared up again in March 1938 the Far East had perforce to take a secondary place. British Far Eastern policy until 1939, and even more after the outbreak of war, was a holding operation, a policy of refusing to surrender vital interests but not to the point of war, of attempting to support China in an unspectacular way, and of showing readiness to negotiate with Japan over marginal points of friction. The hope all the while was that the United States would emerge from isolation and take a less negative line. The fluctuations of politics in Japan were naturally also kept under close observation by the British Ambassador, particularly movements for and against a military alliance with the Axis. Similarly, the almost equally confusing and obscure fluctuations between co-operation and conflict of the Kuomintang and the Communists in China were observed by the British Ambassador there.[1]

The element of caution in British policy was seen in the spring and summer of 1938 with the reaching of a compromise agreement in May over the administration of the Chinese

[1] B.D., Ser. III, vols viii and ix, deal with negotiations from 4 August 1938 to 5 September 1939.

maritime customs service and the refusal of the Government, announced on 13 July, to guarantee a large loan to China because of the fear that this might provoke retaliatory attacks by the Japanese. The opportunity provided by a more moderate government in Japan was also taken for talks in July, August, and September between the British Ambassador, Sir Robert Craigie, and Ugaki, the Japanese Foreign Minister, for the removal of minor points of friction. The hostility of the militarists brought about Ugaki's resignation and a virtual end to the talks in September.

At the same time a firm attitude was maintained over the Japanese threat in June to Hainan Island and, despite Japanese threats, Britain kept the Hong Kong border open as the major entrepôt for foreign military supplies to the Chinese. Some 75 per cent of war goods for China in 1938 passed through there. This was as valuable a service to China as actually supplying the goods – which Britain's own desperate rearmament needs precluded – and earned the British a major share of hostility in the Japanese Press. The French Government had felt it necessary in October 1937 to prohibit the passage of munitions through French Indo-China by the Yunnan railway. Britain also afforded China support in a valuable but little publicized way through the development of a supply route across the Burma–China border – the celebrated Burma Road – which, begun in 1938, became a major life-line for the Chinese.

The Far East after Munich

Munich and the winter of 1938–9 saw a considerable hardening of the attitudes of both Britain and Japan and the taking of some important steps. The avoidance of a European war at Munich affected the Far East in two ways. The manner in which it was avoided encouraged the Japanese swing towards the Axis, for it was seen by most Japanese as a German victory. The declaration in November of Japan's intention to establish a New Order in East Asia, virtually excluding other powers, symbolized this swing. On the other hand, the fact that a European war had not taken place may well have averted a Far Eastern war on very disadvantageous terms for Britain. The Japanese militarists were certainly spoiling for a fight in the autumn, and had some reason for believing that an attack on British possessions on the Chinese mainland would not bring in the United States.

The temporary relaxation of tension in Europe played some part in British readiness to take the risk involved in a currency loan to China. Anxiety over the serious effect of a currency collapse on Chinese unity – already apparently threatened by the defection of Wang Chin-wei – also played a part, as did Japan's openly stated intention of flouting the 'open door'. United States action in giving China a £5 million loan encouraged the British Government in December to grant China a £500,000 credit for lorries for use on the Burma Road, and, on 24 February 1939, the Chinese were informed that a loan of £5 million for a currency stabilization fund would be guaranteed by the British Government. This decision was announced publicly on 8 March. Neither Britain nor the United States was, however, prepared to go beyond this or to take other than diplomatic action against the Japanese.

It was no mere coincidence that the resurgence of crisis in Europe in the spring and summer of 1939 was accompanied by a major Anglo-Japanese crisis, almost equalling that over Poland in magnitude. Japanese frustration over their inability to defeat the Chinese, to destroy the currency, or to set up a satisfactory puppet régime, and their conviction that British financial and moral support for China was one of the major reasons for this, led to a severe threat to the British Concession at Tientsin in North China, and pressure on the International Settlement at Shanghai. The British Tientsin Concession, which was neutral territory, had been used as a place of deposit for the silver reserves of the Chinese Bank. The Chinese National currency circulated there, and it was used as a place of refuge for Chinese terrorists conducting guerrilla warfare against the Japanese. Britain's refusal in June to hand over the silver and some alleged terrorists to the Chinese puppet authorities, or to recognize the Japanese-controlled currency, led to a complete blockade of the Concession by the Japanese forces. Numerous humiliating measures were imposed on British residents. The British held out and the threat of a full-scale Japanese attack grew during June. However, the British could find little concrete sympathy for their attitude from the Americans or the French, and the Admiralty made it clear that a war in the Far East could not be contemplated. The Cabinet decided therefore, on 19 June, that a tactical retreat must be made. Negotiations were opened and formal talks were announced on 28 June. British policy now devoted itself to the task of walking the tightrope between preventing the break-down of the talks and avoiding any commitment to Japan that would lay Britain open to the charge of abandoning China.

The British Government was soon brought face to face with its dilemma when, as soon as the talks began in July, the Japanese demanded public recognition by Britain of Japan's special position in China. In the Craigie–Arita Formula, signed reluctantly on 25 July, the British were forced to go some way in a compromise and this was something of a blow to British prestige. Japanese triumph was short-lived, however, as it soon became clear that the vaguely worded formula did not imply a change in British policy as Japanese propaganda had claimed; it meant as much or as little as the British wished. The denunciation by the United States of their trade treaty with Japan on 26 July came as a bombshell to the Japanese, and, rather late in the day, altered the position to Britain's advantage. Although it was finally agreed that some of the terrorists would be handed over, the British were able in general to adhere to a rather firmer line in the rest of the negotiations over the silver reserves and the withdrawal of recognition from the Chinese currency. Chinese anxiety over the implications of the Craigie–Arita Formula were softened by the granting of further export credits of £3 million early in August and on 19 August the British felt able to adjourn the talks altogether. Any plans for retaliatory action entertained by the

Japanese military were for the moment overshadowed by news of the Soviet-German Pact of 23 August. Japanese indignation at the cavalier behaviour of their Anti-Comintern partners in concluding a treaty with the common enemy without a word of warning led to the resignation of the Hiranuma Government and a swing back towards neutrality.

With the outbreak of war in Europe the major British objectives in the Far East were to maintain Japanese neutrality and complete the economic blockade of Germany by persuading or preventing Japan from acting as an agent for Germany. During the first winter of the war they had a reasonable measure of success with both projects. The Japanese Government maintained a satisfactory degree of neutrality, albeit unfriendly neutrality, while they waited to see what would happen in Europe. Though their co-operation with the British blockade was only very partial it was sufficient to bring protests from Germany. During the first few months of the war there was some anxiety lest the Japanese should take advantage of Britain's preoccupation and follow up their 'advice to belligerents' of 5 September to withdraw troops from China by attacks on British and French positions there. However, this anxiety faded in the autumn of 1939 and it became evident, over incidents such as the British removal of German reservists from the Japanese ship *Asama Maru*, that the Japanese Government was anxious to reduce Anglo-Japanese friction. Even in June 1940, after German successes in Scandinavia and the Low Countries had raised the ominous possibility of an allied collapse in Europe, the Japanese Government proved ready to conclude a compromise agreement over Tientsin.

It was the fall of France and the final discrediting of the democracies which changed the Far Eastern situation decisively, and we shall have to examine in the context of wartime diplomacy (Chapter XIV) the dire effects of the consequent upsurge of Japanese ambitions on Britain's fortunes.

XII

Great Britain and Germany, 1938

The Problem

Hitler told an audience at Saarbrücken on 9 October 1938 that at the beginning of the year he had decided to bring back to the Reich the 10 million Germans outside it, and the pursuit of this policy landed him in war with Britain, France, and Poland in September 1939. Hitler's intentions had been anticipated by the British Government in 1937, and it had not intended to oppose them if they were pursued by peaceful means. At first he does seem to have favoured a 'peaceful procedure', but by the summer of 1938 was insisting that only the forceful procedure corresponded to the dignity of a great power.

Criticism of British foreign policy towards Germany was for the most part a means of expressing disgust at Hitler's conduct. Whenever anything goes wrong in the world Englishmen ask why the Government doesn't do something about it. The demand in this case was not, in the first instance, for ultimatums or direct threats of war, but for some miracle of manoeuvre or personality that would 'stop Hitler' without them; only after a certain point did both the public and the Government's critics realize that they must be prepared to fight. The Government failed in publicity, rather than in perception or even courage; no doubt there were many things that could not be explained.

Among these was the armaments situation, and the Government's sense of vulnerability in a hostile world. After his accession to office as Prime Minister in May 1937 (with Eden continuing as Foreign Secretary) Neville Chamberlain brought a greater sense of urgency to the execution of foreign policy, but the policy itself was not new. The Defence Requirements Committee, set up in October 1933, had not only recognized Germany and Japan as the essential dangers to the Commonwealth but had laid it down in 1935 that Britain would not have the resources to grapple with Italy for another four years. The Cabinet accepted these views. A heavy programme of rearmament to make the country safe from attack (particularly in the air) but not to equip it for offensive operations, was agreed to in the same year, and authority to rearm was secured in the general election of November 1935, although Baldwin's promise that there would be no very large armaments excluded conscription (but not a large navy and air force). All the Cabinet, including Eden and Baldwin, were willing to conciliate Germany pending rearmament. This was not defeatism; it was due partly to the conviction that Germany really did have some genuine and legitimate grievances, partly to the voluminous Hitlerite assurances of goodwill, partly to the conviction that it was better to strike a bargain such as the naval agreement than to await the inevitable acts of defiance of the Versailles Treaty (as over land armaments). In the early weeks of 1936 Eden proposed to the Cabinet a *modus vivendi* with Germany, including an air pact, while Britain rearmed; he subsequently argued that as economic distress might drive Germany to war it would be good policy to assist her economic recovery, even at the cost of French and Russian resentment. But for a final settlement Germany must reciprocate by arms limitation and return to the League. Baldwin, while sanctioning the big rearmament programme which Chamberlain undertook to finance, told Eden to get nearer to Germany. There was talk in May 1936 of a meeting between Hitler and Baldwin.[1]

Thus the established attitude of the Cabinet towards Germany before Chamberlain took over in May 1937 was a very curious mixture of apprehension and conciliation, and it

[1] Robertson, pp. 72–4; Avon, I, pp. 322–4, 374.

does not appear that he had anything to add to Eden's *modus vivendi* programme of the previous year. On 26 March 1937, in a letter to his opposite number, Mr Henry Morgenthau of the United States Treasury, he defended Britain's policy of re-armament, deprecated further American pressure for world disarmament, described Germany as determined to make herself so strong that no one would resist her demands, and said that only the belief that her efforts would be countered by superior force would deter her.[1] But his subsequent activity shows that he also believed that there was some hope of a bargain with her (even at this stage of British rearmament), and that Eden was missing chances of bringing this about. There is an apparent contradiction between these two positions, and at times Chamberlain took up a third when he said that until rearmament was complete Britain would have to bear patiently with actions which it would like to treat otherwise. In his search for security he at once asked the United States Government for greater co-operation, particularly against Japan, but this was refused (see p. 161). He then asked Neurath to London to discuss the possibility of an Anglo-German agreement; this invitation was accepted and then refused on 20 June (perhaps through the jealousy of Ribbentrop, the German Ambassador in London). After this he turned to Italy, and wrote to Mussolini on 27 July offering to begin negotiations to remove misunderstandings; Mussolini replied favourably.

We must interpret this activity as no more than an attempt to check the drift (as he saw it) of the previous years, and the precise grounds of his later difference with Eden are not altogether easy to define. They do not seem to have differed about Germany. Both accepted the formula of redress of griev-ances in return for German disarmament. In a curious speech at Leamington on 20 November 1936 Eden, after enumerating Britain's world-wide commitments, had even said that she would be prepared to defend Germany against aggression if a new Western European settlement could be reached. In May

[1] Blum, pp. 458–67; Avon I, p. 527.

1937 he told the imperial conference that Britain could not fight Germany, Italy, and Japan simultaneously, and had to seek a *modus vivendi* with them pending the completion of her costly rearmament programme. The consensus of opinion seems to be that he did not oppose the visit of Halifax to Hitler in November, when Halifax hinted at British willingness to recognize Germany's legitimate demands in Central Europe provided that they were developed peacefully. Nor did he dissent when Chamberlain made it clear to the French ministers, Chautemps and Delbos, on 29 and 30 November, that British public opinion would not approve of war to maintain Czechoslovakia in its existing form, or to fight for Austria. In December Eden discussed colonial concessions with the Germans. He and Chamberlain both distrusted Russia. Chamberlain thought that Eden was wasting his time at this stage in trying to secure American co-operation in the Pacific, but it seems that it was only over the approach to Italy that a substantial difference of policy occurred.

Chamberlain had not originally attached great importance to discussions with Italy, who would be but a minor nuisance if agreement with Germany could be secured. When the Germans proved unresponsive in the autumn of 1937 he turned to the idea of a settlement of differences with Italy as a means of isolating Germany, and he believed that Mussolini might welcome an escape from his entanglements back to the position of relative independence that he had enjoyed up to the Stresa Agreement. Facing day by day the wireless propaganda, diplomatic tergiversations, and military aggression of the Fascists in Spain, Eden, on the other hand, clearly hated the idea, and took the view that the moment was inopportune. He resigned on 19 February 1938, after Chamberlain had insisted on opening talks with Grandi on the previous day. There had been an earlier difference between them in January, when Roosevelt had sounded Chamberlain about a plan for a conference of small powers to discuss the general causes of international tension, but not any specific issues. Feeling that this would interfere with his own more urgent plans for dealing with these issues Chamberlain suggested a post-ponement, but agreed rather irritably to the proposal a fortnight later after Eden's horrified protests against any thwarting of the President. Roosevelt soon lost interest in the idea, which the Secretary of State, Cordell Hull, also thought a mistake. It is difficult to see in the breach between the two Englishmen anything more than a difference in timing on the part of two very self-willed men who liked to play the game of politics by ear, although it must be said that in his memoirs, written in 1962, Eden insisted that it was 'neither timing nor temperament nor the gap in years' which had made it impossible for him to work with Chamberlain.[1]

Austria

As soon as he had safely launched the Reich on its rearmament programme in 1935 Hitler began to turn over in his mind plans to complete and use it; as early as May 1935 he thought of the Franco-Soviet pact as an excuse for re-occupying the Rhineland, and the Abyssinian crisis enabled him to carry this out in March 1936, a year ahead of schedule. The re-militarization was vital because it made possible the defence of the great industrial zone on which the full armament effort depended. A four-year plan for the preparation of the country for a major war could then be launched under Goering's direct-ion, in accordance with an unsigned memorandum by Hitler of August 1936 – a document which was probably of more decisive importance in Hitler's policy than the better-known Hossbach memorandum. At the 'Hossbach' meeting in November 1937 Hitler talked at great length about the feasibility of an early offensive, in 1939 or even 1938, providing that certain favourable conditions were present. At this stage he was casting round for means to absorb Austria and

[1] Avon, I, chaps 12–14; K. Feiling, *Life of Neville Chamberlain* (1946), pp. 329–40; I. Macleod, *Neville Chamberlain* (1961), pp. 212–13; W. S. Churchill, *The Gathering Storm* (1948), p. 199; Nancy H. Hooker (ed.), *The Moffat Papers, 1919–1943* (1956), p. 194.

Czechoslovakia without the interference of the Western powers. He no longer counted on British help or connivance. In October 1936 Mussolini had shown him the copy of a paper presented by Eden to the British Cabinet in January 1936, which had spoken of an ultimate challenge to Germany after the completion of British rearmament. Hitler professed to be shocked, and talks to Mussolini in September 1937 seem to have increased his animosity towards England. Ribbentrop, at first an advocate of agreement with England, was now convinced of Britain's basic hostility. However, at the Hossbach meeting Hitler spoke hopefully about the prospect of a French civil war or a war in which Britain and France would fight Italy in the Mediterranean; and although Italy joined the German–Japanese anti-Comintern Pact on 6 November 1937 he was not yet certain of Italian co-operation.[1]

The new course in Germany was heralded by a peaceful purge of German high officers on 4 February 1938; fifteen generals, including General von Fritsch, the Commander-in-Chief, were retired, others were promoted, and von Ribbentrop, the Ambassador to London, replaced the more staid von Neurath as Foreign Minister. The effect of these changes was to remove the chief army and civilian critics of a forward policy; Hitler himself took over the Ministry of War, and Goering was made a Field-Marshal. The arrest in Vienna on 26 January of Dr Tavs, a leading Austrian Nazi, had already indicated the possibility of a fresh German campaign against Austria: but Hitler still wished for an 'evolutionary' solution in the form of a more or less peaceful taking over of power by the Austrian Nazis. The intransigent Austrian N.S.D.A.P. leader, Captain Josef Leopold, was dismissed, after being violently abused by Hitler; all illegal activity was to stop; the peaceful procedure employed so successfully in the Saar in 1935 was to be taken as a model. The fact remained, however, that Austria's hour had come.

The Austrian drama developed rapidly. The Chancellor,

---

[1] G.D., Ser. C, vol. v, no. 489; Ser. D, vol. i, nos 93, etc.; Robertson, pp. 87–97.

Dr Schuschnigg, visited Berchtesgaden on 12 February, and the outcome of stormy scenes with the Führer was his agreement to surrender the Ministry of the Interior to a prominent Austrian Nazi, to an unrestricted amnesty for the Nazis, and to their inclusion in the *Vaterländische Front*. Eight other demands he was said to have refused, on the grounds that they could only be granted by President Miklas. Hitler in return promised that his forthcoming Reichstag speech should give his personal guarantee of Austrian independence, and that the Reich would no longer countenance and support illegal Nazi activities. According to accounts which soon circulated Hitler had treated his visitor to one of his exhibitions of simulated frenzy, had called him 'Jesuit's spawn', spoken with sobs of 'My people – my dear, dear tortured German people', and shouted 'I am the greatest of all Germans – the greatest German who has ever lived, do you hear?' Nevertheless, he was at first satisfied that the peaceful procedure would succeed, and did not attack Schuschnigg in his Reichstag speech. It was Schuschnigg's last-minute attempt to save his country by negotiations with the Austrian socialist leaders, and his decision on 9 March announcing a plebiscite to be held on the 13th, to answer the question, 'Are you for a free and German, independent and social, Christian and united Austria?', which produced the violent phase of German action. Hitler demanded on the 11th that the plebiscite should be called off; Schuschnigg resigned, and his successor, Seyss-Inquart, at once invited Hitler to send German troops into Austria to preserve order. German troops, planes, and tanks at once crossed the frontier; the result was certainly to prevent the bloodshed of a war, but thousands of leaders and followers of the *Vaterländische Front* were imprisoned, shot, thrown into concentration camps, or publicly humiliated in the streets of Vienna.

Still in pursuit of an Anglo-German *modus vivendi* the British Government had instructed the Ambassador, Sir Nevile Henderson, to talk to Hitler on the lines of Halifax's proposals of the previous November. He had a very unproductive interview with Hitler and Ribbentrop on these lines on 3

March.[1] Ribbentrop visited London immediately after, but the discussions also made little progress, and were broken off as a result of the Austrian crisis. On 14 March Chamberlain made in Parliament a strong protest against the German action and denied that the Government had ever given assent or encouragement to the effective absorption of Austria into the Reich. The hard fact was 'that nothing could have arrested this action by Germany unless we and others with us had been prepared to use force to prevent it'. Nevertheless the sense of uncertainty and insecurity in Europe had been intensified, and the Government intended to review their defence programmes in the light of the new developments.

Mussolini on this occasion had given Austria no support, or even a reply to Schuschnigg's last-minute appeals. Hitler sent an effusive telegram of thanks. Nevertheless, Italian alarm at the *Anschluss* could not easily be concealed. In France, Chautemps and his Cabinet resigned on 10 March, and the internal crisis lasted until the 13th, when Blum formed a government of Socialists and Radicals. This crisis did not cause the German invasion, or prevent French intervention, but it obviously increased the practical difficulties of rapid or decisive action. For some months past the abandonment of the former central European policy had been increasingly canvassed even in French official circles, and there were widely differing views as to the value of Soviet co-operation with the Western powers. During a three-day debate in the Chamber, 25–27 February, the Communists had demanded that the Franco-Soviet pact should be strengthened by a military alliance. Flandin, on the other hand, had argued that the sanctions policy had completely upset the Stresa Agreements and their provision for joint Franco-Italian action concerning Austria and the Rhineland, and that France should recognize realities and seek a *rapprochement* with Germany and Italy. The result was really inconclusive; the debate ended in a vote of confidence in the Government, which proposed to steer a middle course.

[1] N. Henderson, *Failure of a Mission* (1940), p. 115; G.D., Ser. D, vol. i, nos 135–46.

The Moscow Press condemned the *Anschluss*, but its most drastic criticisms were hurled at Great Britain, who was stated to have known of, and authorized, the German action. On the other hand, Russia's own capacity for effective action was once more brought into question by the opening on 2 March of sensational fresh trials, involving Bukharin, Rykov, Yagoda, Rakovsky, and seventeen others, the majority being highly placed members of the Political Bureau, Communist Party, or government service. Rakovsky, who negotiated the 1924 agreement in London, said that he had been a member of the British Secret Service from 1924 to 1936. Voluble confessions implicating the accused in wrecking activities and secret intrigues in conjunction with the German, British, and Japanese Secret Services, showed once again that there was either spontaneous and widespread hostility to Stalin's régime, or else a state of persecution mania in Stalin and his immediate supporters which was producing such hostility. Chamberlain, like Eden, had no confidence in Russia's good intentions, and reports from the British embassy in Moscow questioned her ability to conduct war effectively. Moreover, Russian forces could operate in Central Europe only after crossing Polish or Rumanian territory.[1]

Great Britain and Czechoslovakia

The fate of Austria at once turned attention to the problem of Czechoslovakia.[2] The defence of this country against German attack was a treaty obligation of France and the Soviet Union. France's obligations to Czechoslovakia were contained in treaties of 25 January 1924 and 16 October 1925. A Czech–Soviet pact of Mutual Assistance had been signed on 16 May 1935; by this the Soviet Union undertook to defend Czechoslovakia against aggression, providing that France did the same. On 14 March 1938 M. Paul-Boncour, the new French Foreign

[1] B.D., Ser. III, vol. i, nos 148, 202, 210, 270, 355.
[2] The main sources are B.D., Ser. III, vols i and ii, and G.D., Ser. D, vols ii and iii; *Survey of International Affairs 1938* (1951, by R. G. D. Laffan and others), is a good general survey of the crisis.

Minister, assured M. Osusky, the Czechoslovak Minister, that France would honour her engagements towards Czechoslovakia. On the following day the Soviet Government gave similar assurances, subject to the willingness of France to act.

Great Britain had no treaty obligation to defend Czechoslovakia. She had maintained since 1925 that her interests and military strength did not allow her to defend Germany's eastern frontiers by force. Yet she could not remain indifferent to a German threat to Czechoslovakia. Such a threat might affect British policy in three ways. (1) If the German Government acted with its usual screaming propaganda and ostentatious brutality, British public opinion might compel the Government to intervene; (2) if France were invaded as a result of defending Czechoslovakia, Great Britain must come to her support; (3) the annexation of a part, or all, of Czechoslovakia might increase Germany's military and economic strength, stimulate the self-confidence of her 'wild men' and strengthen her for further adventures directly hostile to British interests.

The chief difficulties of the position were suggested by the last point. The annexation of Austria had already turned the flank of the Czech position. If Germany wished for military or economic expansion down the Danube Valley, the way now lay open; Czechoslovakia's chance of conducting a successful war, even of defence, against Germany had passed in 1936 when the remilitarization of the Rhineland made a rapid French advance into Germany impossible. Up to that point Czechoslovakia had adhered to the plan of taking the offensive from the Egerland by an advance west to join hands with the French. Fortifications similar to the Maginot Line had been planned in 1933, but were not pushed rapidly until 1936, and were not completed in March 1938; the fact that they would be completed in 1939 was no doubt one reason for the acceleration of German action in the summer of 1938. In a general European war Czechoslovakia would not be able to defend herself against German attack for more than a limited period, and in a strictly military and economic sense Germany had completed by the annexation of Austria the process of neutralizing Czechoslovakia's capacity to form an effective permanent check on German strength. But while it could be argued that the real strength of an independent Czechoslovakia was over-estimated both in Germany and in Western Europe it was also true that this exaggeration introduced questions of prestige; it led Nazi politicians to over-estimate the increase in German power and the consequent weakening of their opponents.

The view was generally accepted in England that the German minority in Czechoslovakia, 23 per cent of the population in 1919, was better treated than any other in Europe, and that its grievances were due to emotional reactions or economic depression rather than to the oppression or maladministration of Prague. Nevertheless it was not easy to question the existence of a case for secession. The promise of a 'Swiss' régime had not been fulfilled; the Czechs had secured independence in 1919 after three hundred years and meant to maintain their ascendency over the Germans. President Masaryk defined democracy as discussion and this meant a parliamentary state with the Czechs in a permanent majority. All its minorities had come to look abroad for support – the Hungarians to Budapest, the Poles to Warsaw, and the Germans to Vienna or the Reich. With the restored and now powerful Reich as a neighbour it was certain that a refusal of the Sudeten demands could not provide more than a temporary solution. *The Times*, on 22 March 1938, said that if Great Britain were to be involved in war to keep the Sudeten Germans under Czech sovereignty against their wishes she would be fighting against the principle of self-determination. The best remedy would be an international plebiscite. *The Observer* and the Conservative Press in general used similar language.

Chamberlain's important speech to the Commons on 24 March went considerably beyond the immediate terms of the Czech problem.[1] The fundamental basis of British policy was 'the maintenance and preservation of peace and the establishment of a sense of confidence that peace will, in fact, be

[1] Parl. Debates, House of Commons, vol. 333, cols 1405–6.

maintained'. This did not mean that nothing would make them fight; they had treaty obligations to defend France and Belgium (under the Locarno Treaty), Portugal, Irak, and Egypt; they would fight to defend the territory of Great Britain and the Empire, 'and the communications which are vital to our national existence'. He indicated as plainly as possible that the League in its present form could not be regarded as an effective instrument for preserving peace. For collective security it was not necessary to have the co-operation of all the fifty-eight member states, provided that they had the support of enough of the more powerful ones; such combinations, however, which would not really differ from the old alliances of pre-war days, would depend entirely on their strength and size, their military efficiency, and the effective geographical distribution of their forces. Yet there was a hint that the defence of interests in excess of those already indicated was not excluded; there were 'other cases' in which 'we might fight, if we were clear that either we must fight or else abandon, once and for all, the hope of averting the destruction of those things we hold most dear'.

With regard to Czechoslovakia the Government was not, he said, prepared to promise to support France in implementing French obligations under the Franco-Czech treaty, or to give a direct guarantee of Czech independence and integrity. This would involve Great Britain in war, through circumstances over which she had no control; she could not accept this position in relation to an area in which her vital interests were not concerned to the same degree as they were in the case of France and Belgium. Nevertheless, if war broke out 'the inexorable pressure of facts might well prove more powerful than formal pronouncements' and other countries would almost immediately become involved. He had clearly in mind the fact that Great Britain would be compelled, in almost any circumstances, to support France if she were seriously threatened by a German invasion.

In view of later accusations that Chamberlain was stubbornly following a foreign policy of his own it is important to remember how carefully this statement followed official advice and earlier policy statements. His survey of commitments agreed closely with Eden's Leamington speech of 20 November 1936 and the services' list of priorities. The Chiefs of Staff, vastly over-estimating the destructive power of bombing planes in general and of the Luftwaffe in particular, insisted on 10 February 1938 that they would not be in a position to take part in anything but colonial warfare before the spring of 1939; General Ironside, the future C.I.G.S., wrote in his diary on 22 September 1938 that Chamberlain 'is, of course, right' and that exposure to a German attack at this period would be suicidal. But on 22 March the Cabinet decided to abandon the existing financial limit on rearmament expenditure, and on 27 April a big crash programme (Scheme L), to increase to 12,000 planes the already ambitious aircraft figures, was accepted. Chamberlain's speech was also a reply to Churchill, who had called for a 'grand alliance' on 14 March, without being able to point to any major ally apart from a somewhat divided France. The decision to fight for France but not for Czechoslovakia had long been accepted in the Cabinet, but it was publicly revealed for the first time on 24 March, and no doubt damped some ardent spirits. Later, on 14 May, Chamberlain was reported to have told a group of journalists that the Czechs should 'accede to the German demands, if reasonable'. The reservation did in fact mean that while urging the Czechs to do all in their power to reach an agreement, the Government would oppose any German attempt to secure a settlement by force.

April Talks and May Crisis

But this last point was not to become clear until later. At this stage the whole purpose of British policy, in which Chamberlain took an active part but in close accord with Halifax, was anxiously directed to securing a peaceful settlement by mediation. On 22 March Halifax warned the French Government that Great Britain could not go beyond the terms of the London Agreement of 19 March 1936 (p. 149). The parlous state of the

French, with widespread strikes and a flight from the franc, seemed a further reason for avoiding an adventurous policy. Edouard Daladier as Prime Minister and Georges Bonnet as Foreign Minister succeeded Blum and Paul Boncour on 10 April; Daladier brought the strikes to an end with emergency powers, but the franc had to be depreciated to 175 to the pound sterling. Strong pressure from Chamberlain secured Morgenthau's reluctant agreement to this on 3 May. In prolonged talks in London on 28 and 29 April the British ministers refused to go beyond the position taken up by Chamberlain on 24 March, and it was clearly stated that British foreign policy was geared to a rearmament programme which did not allow for a major war before 1939.[1]

Meanwhile Konrad Henlein and the *Sudetendeutsche Partei* (S.D.P.) had opened the Sudeten German propaganda campaign on 16 March. The Prague Government reaffirmed its desire for an understanding. On 24 April Henlein presented to the S.D.P. Congress at Karlsbad an eight-point programme calling for the legal recognition and full self-government of the German areas together with full liberty to profess German nationality and political philosophy (*Volkstum* and *Weltanschauung*). On 7 May the British and French ministers informed M. Krofta that they expected him to go to the utmost limit of possible concession; the Prague Government promised at once to do so, and on the 13th announced that it was prepared to enter into negotiations with the Sudeten Germans. Henlein visited London on 13–14 May; he was not received by any Cabinet minister, but met Sir Robert Vansittart, Winston Churchill, Sir Archibald Sinclair, and others, and seemed to have given an impression of moderation.

During the following week the German Press conducted against Czechoslovakia a campaign of exceptional violence. Sir Nevile Henderson on 11 May told von Ribbentrop of the Franco-British *démarche* at Prague; but on the 19th the German Government complained of the slow progress made by Prague in drawing up the Nationalities Statute, and of its apparently

[1] B.D., Ser. III, vol. 1, no. 164.

unsatisfactory character. On the same day Henlein left for Germany, and Hitler summoned a meeting of his advisers at Munich. Municipal elections which were due in Czechoslovakia led to clashes between the parties, and a more serious riot took place at Brünn, also on the 19th. There were reports of the mobilization of several German divisions. The Czech Government, suspecting that a German invasion was imminent, moved large bodies of troops into the Sudeten area; on the 21st two Sudetens were shot dead on the frontier by Czech guards. Henlein's party announced its refusal to negotiate with the Prime Minister, M. Hodža. Henderson gave Ribbentrop a warning about the British position in terms of the contingent commitment to France set out on 24 March. Bonnet on the 21st assured the Czech and German Governments that France would fulfil its obligations. There was a Soviet warning. Whatever the original German intentions the meeting of Hitler and his advisers at Munich on the 22nd was evidently in favour of peace; and for some weeks after the Nazi Press continued to insist that there had been no mobilization, and that the crisis was due to misrepresentation of the facts by Great Britain.

The most generally accepted explanation outside Germany was that Hitler had been out-bluffed, and the very dangerous view that he had always given way to a display of force began to find favour. Yet for once Hitler may have been innocent of aggressive intent. His indignation expressed itself in the secret directive to the Wehrmacht of 30 May that Czechoslovakia was to be militarily smashed not later than 1 October. On 22 May Halifax reminded Bonnet that Britain would not immediately support France if Czechoslovakia became the victim of a German attack. One result of the May crisis was to place the British Government in the German mind in the forefront of the apparent defenders of Czechoslovakia, a position which should really have been held by France.[1]

On Monday, 23 May, Henlein consented after all to meet

[1] D.G., Ser. D, vol. ii, no. 221; B.D., Ser. III, vol. i, nos 271, 285, 286, 502; vol. ii, no. 855; G. Bonnet, *Quai d'Orsay* (1965), pp. 168–81.

Hodža, and had detailed discussions with the Prime Minister in Prague; Czech concessions increased as the Sudeten demands mounted. Hodža handed the draft of the Nationalities Statute to the S.D.P. on 30 June, but it was not enough. No spirit of compromise was shown by the Sudeten leaders. During July the German Government made it increasingly clear that it supported and encouraged the most extreme demands of Henlein, while the German Press carried on a systematic campaign of abuse and denunciation of the alleged terrorism under which the Sudeten Germans were groaning.

The Runciman Mission

Bonnet had suggested mediation on 10 June, and on 26 July Chamberlain announced that Lord Runciman had accepted an invitation by the Czech Government to act as mediator between themselves and their minorities. He would be quite independent of all governments, and would act in his personal capacity. The British Government's action in proposing the mission, however well-intentioned, was almost bound to confuse the issues both in Central Europe and in Downing Street. For one thing, the mere assertion by the Government of a desire to mediate, and its close personal and political relations with Runciman, made it impossible for him to be accepted as a completely neutral arbiter: if this had been desired, an American or other non-European mission would have been preferable. Then, too, the fact that both sides had agreed to discuss matters with a 'mediator' appears to have given the Government a very exaggerated idea of the possibility of an agreed solution. On 26 July Chamberlain actually told the Commons that throughout the Continent there was a relaxation of the sense of tension present six months before. This optimism may have been genuine. After the somewhat mysterious (or pointless) visit of Hitler's personal friend and aide-de-camp, Captain Fritz Wiedemann, to Halifax on 18 July, it had been announced that Wiedemann had expressed Hitler's desire for a 'non-violent' solution of the Sudeten problem.

If this were so the events of August proved disillusioning. Runciman succeeded in keeping the Czech and Sudeten leaders in contact, but successive offers from Prague were all rejected as unsatisfactory by the other side; the last Czech offer, the 'fourth plan' of 5 September, which introduced a system of cantons, state assistance to industrial areas hit by the depression, and guarantees concerning proportional employment and representation, was almost immediately submerged in the flood of denunciation released by the German Government and Press after Hitler's Nuremberg speech of 12 September. By the middle of August it had become clear that Henlein was receiving and taking his instructions from Berlin, and that he was manoeuvring for the incorporation of the Sudetenland in the German Reich. Herr Kundt, the chairman of the parliamentary Sudeten Party, was believed, on the other hand, to be ready to accept autonomy within the Czechoslovak state, and the German Social Democratic Party in Czechoslovakia emphatically opposed surrender to Germany. Acting on his instructions, Henderson on four occasions between 26 July and 1 September represented to the German Foreign Office that Germany's military preparations might threaten both the Runciman mission and the peace of Europe. Hitler did not reply. The German Press continued to denounce the alleged ill-treatment of the German minority, and the plundering and torturing of the German villagers. In a speech at Lanark on 27 August, Sir John Simon referred to Chamberlain's speech of 24 March and said that a war might be limited at the start, but no one could say how far it would spread. Daladier assured the British Ambassador of France's firmness on 8 September. An official British statement of 11 September again made it clear that the British Government could not remain neutral if a threat to French territory resulted from a Franco-German war over Czechoslovakia.

Meanwhile the various German frontier areas in the Rhineland and elsewhere had been declared prohibited zones, and 200,000 labourers were set to work on the 'Siegfried Line', fortifications similar to the French Maginot Line on the other side of the frontier. The number of these conscript labourers had increased to probably half a million by the end of August. Another million men were under arms in a gigantic 'trial mobilization'. In these circumstances *The Times* leader of 6 September, which suggested that the Czechoslovak Government should consider whether it might not be wise to allow the secession of its 'fringe of alien populations', was thought by many to have been a Foreign Office signal of retreat. The Foreign Office promptly denied knowledge of the leader or approval of the suggestion. In Paris *La République* made a similar suggestion to that of *The Times*, also on the 6th. On the 7th the Trade Union Congress and the Labour Party demanded the defence of Czechoslovak integrity. The Cabinet continued to stand on the formula of 24 March, although the statement of 11 September was a clear intimation that Great Britain would be bound to be drawn in due course into a war over Czechoslovakia.

Hitler's speeches in the opening days of the Nuremberg Conference made frequent reference to Germany's impregnable position in the event of war; Goering spoke in the same strain on the 10th. On the 12th Hitler talked at length of the oppressed Sudetens 'chased and harried like helpless game for every expression of their national life', and demanded that the oppression 'shall cease and be replaced by the free right of self-determination'. At times his voice rose to a scream to denounce 'the liar Beneš', and an audience of 100,000 responded with hysterical applause. This meant the end of negotiations; Henlein immediately after tried to bring about a general rising of the Sudetens which was suppressed without difficulty by Czech troops; his followers fled in thousands to Germany and were received as refugees from Czech terrorism. On 15 September he issued a proclamation demanding union with Germany, and a German advance seemed imminent.

Berchtesgaden

Chamberlain's two visits to Hitler at Berchtesgaden and Godesberg were conceived in a spirit of responsibility for Britain's ally and for European peace, with, it would seem, little anticipation of the discredit which was almost bound to follow any such intervention. A satisfactory outcome was, in the circumstances, almost impossible, for France desperately wished to avoid war, and Hitler was passionately determined to avoid any procedure that might cheat him of the appearance of victory. Chamberlain was thus almost certain to become the scapegoat for an unpopular solution. What did he really hope to do ? Apparently to put himself *en rapport* with an unbalanced man who could no longer be approached through the usual channels; Henderson, for example, had recently said that the delivery of a stern warning from the Foreign Secretary to Hitler on the eve of the Nuremberg Congress would have had disastrous effects, the opposite of that intended. Chamberlain was prepared for signs of insanity, and was quite surprised not to detect any. The real weakness of his position was, however, the insistence of Daladier on 13 September that at all costs something must be done to prevent the entry of German troops, for otherwise France's formal treaty obligations to Czechoslovakia would be involved. Chamberlain's position would have been much stronger as a mediator if he could have given a stern warning that France was ready to fight. But in the circumstances he would have done better to stay at home and leave Daladier to deal directly with Beneš and Hitler.

But after Daladier's desperate appeal Chamberlain telegraphed an offer to visit Hitler immediately, and the meeting took place at Berchtesgaden on 15 and 16 September. Hitler, showing no signs whatever of insanity, succeeded in convincing his visitor that a German invasion of Czechoslovakia was not merely inevitable but also imminent. When Chamberlain asked why, in that case, he had been brought there, Hitler replied that if the Prime Minister 'could give him there and then the assurance that the British Government accepted the principle of self-determination, he was quite ready to discuss ways and means of carrying it out'. He undertook to refrain from active hostilities until Chamberlain had had time to consult his colleagues on the question. On the following day Chamberlain returned to London to consult Runciman and the Cabinet; there were Cabinet meetings on the 17th, and on Sunday the 18th. After prolonged argument all the Cabinet, including Duff Cooper, accepted the Berchtesgaden terms.[1] Daladier and Bonnet flew to London for further discussions. They were opposed to plebiscites, but pressed hard for a British guarantee of the Czech state. The final result was the Anglo-French proposals presented to the Czechoslovak Government on 19 September. The essential points were four. (1) The two powers were now convinced that the further maintenance within the boundaries of the Czechoslovak state of districts inhabited by Sudeten Deutsch could not continue without imperilling the interests of Czechoslovakia herself and of European peace. (2) Areas containing over 50 per cent of German inhabitants would probably have to be transferred. (3) 'Some international body', including a Czech representative, should arrange for adjustment of frontiers, and of possible exchange of populations on the basis of the right to opt. (4) The British Government would be prepared to join in an international guarantee of the new boundaries of the Czechoslovak state against unprovoked aggression. The earliest possible reply was asked for, as the Prime Minister had to resume conversations with Hitler not later than the 21st.

Runciman on the evening of the 16th had recommended the cession of the Sudeten districts but no one in the Cabinet appears to have liked this solution. The Government was left in no doubt that many sections of public opinion strongly opposed cession; crowds in Whitehall shouted against concessions to Hitler, and a deputation from the National Council of Labour announced opposition to a Sudeten plebiscite. The

[1] Duff Cooper, *Old Men Forget* (1954), p. 229; he wrote later: 'much confusion of thought was caused by people asking whether we should or should not fight for Czecho-Slovakia. But that was not the issue. Nobody wanted to fight for Czecho-Slovakia' (p. 225).

final word, however, was with France, and Bonnet appears throughout the summer to have favoured cession as a last resource. He seems mainly responsible for the fact that several assurances given by the Soviet Government in August and September were virtually ignored, and reported only sketchily to London. Certainly the view of Flandin, that France's obligation to Czechoslovakia had ceased with the collapse of the Locarno system, found growing support in influential French papers including *Le Matin*, and throughout the summer the section of the Press responsive to Bonnet's influence appeared to take seriously the view that there was at least some justification for the stories of Czech atrocities. The French Cabinet only endorsed the Plan on the understanding that no pressure should be exercised on Prague, and that, if Prague refused, the Franco-Czech treaty should remain valid. This face-saving provision put the responsibility on Bonnet, who in turn hinted to the Press that his hands had been forced by the British. However, the French Minister in Prague, de Lacroix, was instructed to say that France would not support Czechoslovakia if she refused the terms. The British minister gave a similar warning. After agonized debate the Czech Government accepted the proposals on 21 September.

Godesberg

The final stage of renewed crisis was due to a typical German display of unnecessary heavy-handedness of the type which had ruined so many German diplomatic adventures since Versailles; having secured substantial victory by the Czech surrender everything pointed to the expediency of a tactful and cautious handling of the final transactions. Instead, when Chamberlain met the Führer again at the Rhineland spa of Godesberg on the afternoon of 22 September he was presented with a memorandum detailing plans for German occupation of the ceded areas which certainly removed completely any pretence of the 'self-determination' which Hitler had promised on the 15th. Chamberlain said he was outraged. No agreement was reached on the 22nd, and after correspondence between the hotels on the 23rd the Prime Minister brought back to London a memorandum which he undertook to submit to Prague, without identifying himself with it.

The memorandum announced a time limit, 1 October, for the first time; in the discussions Hitler had originally demanded 26 September. By this date all Czech armed forces, police, customs officials, and so on were to be removed; German troops would occupy areas designated on an attached map 'without taking account as to whether in the plebiscite there may prove to be in this or that part of the area a Czech majority'; the territory was to be handed over intact, i.e. all military, commercial, or traffic establishments, wireless stations, railway rolling stock, gas-works, power stations, and all foodstuffs, goods, cattle, and raw materials were to be handed over undamaged. Further areas, beyond those occupied, were to have, under an international commission, plebiscites in which a simple majority would be decisive. The Czech Government was to liberate all political prisoners of German race. No German or international guarantee of the remaining Czechoslovak state was included. 'I expected,' said Mr Chamberlain later, 'that when I got back to Godesberg I had only to discuss quietly with him the proposals that I had brought with me; and it was a profound shock to me when I was told at the beginning of the conversation that these proposals were not acceptable, and that they were to be replaced by other proposals of a kind which I had not contemplated at all.' Hitler repeated what he had said at Berchtesgaden: that this was the last of his territorial ambitions in Europe.

The document meant war, for it involved a demonstration of force on Germany's part which would bring the Franco-Czech military alliance into action. The purpose of Chamberlain's diplomacy was, in accordance with French wishes, to restore the appearance of an agreed solution, and the Cabinet had also to decide whether to change the ultimate guarantee of France, as set out on 24 March, into a promise of immediate support in war. Chamberlain appears to have favoured the first alternative, but Halifax, after a sleepless night, supported the second on the morning of the 25th, to the extent of insisting that Hitler's terms must be rejected.[1] On the evening of the 25th Daladier and Bonnet were questioned closely as to France's military plans, and their replies were not reassuring. But it was evident that they could not accept the Godesberg terms; and Chamberlain after the meeting gave Daladier an assurance that Britain would go to war with France. The Czech reply to the German terms stated that the new proposals went far beyond what had been agreed to in the Anglo-French memorandum; it was 'a *de facto* ultimatum of the sort usually presented to a vanquished nation' and was absolutely and unconditionally unacceptable. The French Cabinet on the same day unanimously rejected the German memorandum.

Chamberlain's aim was now to save the peace by making it clear to Hitler that Britain would fight alongside France, but also to do so in a way which would avoid driving Hitler over the edge. The first aim was achieved by messages which Sir Horace Wilson was instructed to deliver to Hitler on the 26th, proposing a German–Czech conference and warning him that if France fought Britain would be brought in. A statement from Downing Street later on the 26th, made on Churchill's urging, announced that if Germany should attack Czechoslovakia France would come to her assistance and Great Britain and Russia would certainly stand by France. At 5 p.m. Wilson delivered the first part of Chamberlain's message to Hitler. In the evening in a speech at the Berlin *Sportpalast*, Hitler denounced Beneš as a liar and a scoundrel and again demanded the surrender of the Sudetenland by 1 October. He was grateful to Mr Chamberlain, but German patience was at an end. But Wilson delivered the second part of Chamberlain's message at 12.15 p.m. on the 27th, and a reply to it was received at the Foreign Office at 8.40 p.m. on the same evening. It was after this, at 11.30 p.m., that the mobilization of the British fleet was announced. In France mobilization papers had been sent out on the 24th. Hitler's letter was in almost conciliatory terms, and protested his willingness to agree with the Czechs on

[1] Lord Birkenhead, *Halifax* (1965), quoting Sir Alexander Cadogan's diary.

details and to abide by fairly conducted plebiscites. Everything goes to suggest that this was the decisive turn in German policy which enabled France to acquiesce.[1]

There were moments when it seemed that President Roosevelt might give a helping hand; there was little doubt that he would have enjoyed giving a rebuff to Naziism if this could have been done without risk or cost to the United States. He thought of offering himself as a mediator, but, more *rusé* is such matters than Chamberlain, dropped the idea when his ambassadors warned him that it would be bound to lead to some American guarantee of the settlement. He sent messages to the parties on 26 and 27 September urging the need for a fair and peaceful settlement, and was much annoyed when his Ambassador in Rome failed to be first in recommending the Munich Conference. Essentially, however, the policy of the United States was still that of the 'eternal question mark'.[2]

Munich

The ridiculous lengths to which Hitler's astonishing diplomatic methods had dragged the crisis produced corresponding though momentary relief when it was at last announced on the 28th that, after appeals by Chamberlain to Hitler and Mussolini, an invitation had been sent by the Führer to a meeting between these three and Daladier at Munich on the 29th. Bonnet had supported the British proposal for an orderly taking over process in the Sudetenland by a five-point plan of his own, which went farther than the British. The German people, who had given the clearest indication by their uneasy silence of lack of anything approaching enthusiasm for the threatened war, showed by a repetition of the demonstrative welcome given to Chamberlain on the 15th that they regarded him as a possible saviour from unnecessary disaster. The Munich discussions proceeded smoothly enough, and the final paper

[1] B.D., Ser. III, vol. ii, 1093, 1096, 1097, 1118–29; I. Kirkpatrick, *The Inner Circle* (1959), pp. 110–26.

[2] E. L. Henson, 'Britain, America, and the month of Munich' (*International Relations*, April 1962); Moffat Papers, p. 211.

compromise certainly modified the more extreme German requirements, although it did not prevent the cession of the Sudeten districts, which had never been in doubt. Relief at the news was widespread, vocal, and transient. Many who shared it were later to express surprise at the self-satisfaction with which the Prime Minister himself seemed to regard the settlement. This was, of course, in part an attempt to put the best possible face on a transaction of very questionable expediency, in part perhaps an exaggeration of the significance of the recent Anglo-French stand. There had certainly been a definite threat of war, and a partial retreat by the Führer afterwards. To Governments as anxious to avoid war as the British and French this stand probably appeared very much more dramatic and momentous than it did to the rest of the Continent.

But, in fact, Chamberlain believed that Hitler's last-minute retreat from complete intransigence had a wider significance; he had shown that he wished to avoid war even at the point at which German strength was greatest. He believed (as he said so rashly in April 1940) that Hitler had missed the bus in 1938, when his military superiority over the Western powers was greatest. This was a misreading of the armaments position, but the same view was held by Duff Cooper and the Chiefs of Staff. He accepted the view that the incorporation of the German-speaking areas in the Reich was in itself necessary in order to remove a permanent source of crisis; the real problem, as he told the House of Commons on 3 October was 'to find an orderly instead of a violent method of carrying out an agreed solution', and he claimed that the difference between the two documents proved that this had been achieved. He evidently hoped that the Anglo-French stand had been sufficiently forceful to persuade Hitler that Germany would not be allowed to proceed by force in future, and that the most serious causes of friction between Germany and other powers had been removed. 'I have always had in mind,' he said immediately after the Munich discussions, 'that if we could find peace in Czechoslovakia it might open the way to appeasement in Europe.'

The obvious criticism that we must pass on British policy is, in the first place, that the developments since March did represent the triumph of German force at the expense of Austria and Czechoslovakia: Hitler regarded his last-minute concessions as innocuous face-saving devices contemptuously thrown to the British and French Prime Ministers to ease their relations with public opinion. The Anglo-French acceptance of the principle of cession did not appear as a spontaneous and voluntary attempt to solve a local frontier dispute, but as a deliberate and reluctant choice of this solution only after one of the parties had repudiated any other procedure than that of violence: for this reason, and with a man of his temperament, their action was bound to invite rather than discourage the employment of threatened violence as a diplomatic bargaining weapon in future.

It could further be argued that British diplomacy in the crisis had shown a depressing lack of accurate timing, menace, and quick thinking. Chamberlain could be forgiven for not displaying the bounding egoism, fits of screaming rage, and boastful assertiveness which had distinguished the Führer during the previous six months. But the British Government seemed to have a curious knack of waiting until it had been manoeuvred into humiliating positions from which it was forced to extricate itself by decidedly clumsy expedients. If it is argued that the responsibility for this situation lay primarily with France, this merely emphasizes the fact that Great Britain had been manoeuvred into the position of accepting most of the blame. They had the worst of both worlds with Russia: they were probably right in assuming that Stalin had neither the power nor the intention to risk involvement in war with Germany, but the matter was not put to the test. The contacts were rightly left to Bonnet in view of the Franco-Soviet and Soviet–Czech Treaties. But the British seem to have shown no curiosity about the position. Although the Soviet Government probably had no desire to go to Munich the omission to invite it there was speedily proclaimed in Moscow to be a snub and manifestation of anti-Soviet feeling. The latter sentiment was probably not absent, but the real reason – as far as Munich was concerned – was no doubt that Hitler would have regarded the presence of a Soviet delegate as in itself a diplomatic defeat, and almost certainly have accepted the alternative of war.

But in defence of British policy it must be said that a European war to keep the Sudetenland under Czech rule would not have commanded the unqualified support of British and neutral opinion; the attempt to solve the legitimate grievances of the German people was honourable and statesmanlike; and many of the difficulties in which the British Government found itself were due to the French Government's perplexities, and to the almost impossible position created by Hitler's inability to realize that his thirst for a dramatic victory was effectively and rapidly destroying the last hope of that Anglo-German co-operation which he still seemed to desire. Moreover, while British opinion was healthily angry at Hitler's behaviour it would not yet take seriously the thought of a major war. The Dominions were kept informed, and did not dissent from British policy throughout the crisis.

The next few weeks showed clearly Hitler's belief that a continuance of the tactics of mingled threats and promises would complete the demoralization and immobilization of the British Government and British opinion. After the Munich conversations he and Chamberlain signed an agreement that they were resolved that the method of consultation should be the method adopted to deal with other questions that might concern the two countries, and which referred to the 'desire of our two peoples never to go to war with one another again'. But on 9 October, in his speech at Saarbrücken, after remarking that if an Eden, a Duff Cooper, or a Churchill came into power they would unleash immediately a world war against Germany, he said that it would be well 'if England would free herself from certain arrogances left over from the Versailles epoch', for 'this tutelage of foreign governesses is something that Germany cannot and will not stand'. This outburst was partly a proof that Chamberlain's intervention in September rankled, partly a veiled threat occasioned by the British rearmament plans. On Ribbentrop's instructions and against the advice of the German Ambassador in London a Press campaign was launched to discredit those in England who might resist Germany's future demands. There was little hope left by the end of October that the Reich considered itself genuinely 'appeased'. Moreover, the execution of the Munich Agreement proceeded during these weeks on even more brutal lines than the terms had indicated, and further territorial demands, in excess of what had been accepted in September, were made. Poland and Hungary secured their share of the spoils; Poland occupied Bohumin on 9 October, and ultimately annexed about 400 square miles of Czechoslovak territory. She was anxious for Hungary to annex Ruthenia in order to prevent the creation of an independent Ukrainian state which might, under Nazi inspiration, lead to unrest among her own Ukrainian minority. Magyar claims on Prague were settled in the 'Vienna award' of 2 November, the result of 'arbitration' by Ribbentrop and Ciano[1] which Czechoslovakia and Hungary were bound to accept. Hungary received parts of Slovakia and the lowlands of Ruthenia, but the mountainous strip of northern Ruthenia was left to Prague, and therefore provided a possible future channel of Nazi expansion eastward. These events were witnessed with increasing indignation in England; on top of them came the murder of Herr vom Rath in Paris, followed by the terrible anti-Jewish pogrom of November, with its wholesale burning and looting of shops and synagogues, its organized mob violence, and its astonishing fine of £86 million levied on the Jewish community. The pogrom finally destroyed the possibility of any Anglo-German agreement based on the rectification of surviving German grievances.

[1] Count Galeazzo Ciano had been Italian Foreign Minister since June 1936.

XIII

The Coming of War

After Munich

In the spring of 1939 Great Britain and France laid the foundations of a new system of collective security by giving specific guarantees of support to certain states which were directly threatened by German and Italian hostility. The preference for this method rather than for the full Geneva system of collective security meant that the guarantees were intended to be taken seriously. The new policy was enunciated sufficiently promptly to suggest that the British Government had made up its mind during the previous months that it must be prepared to abandon the older position of non-intervention east of the Rhine; this was, indeed, implicit in the promise on 26 September 1938 to guarantee the diminished Czechoslovakia.

This transition was largely concealed from the public by the fact that members of the Government continued until the eve of the new German *coup* in March 1939 to talk hopefully of Hitler's peaceful intentions. No doubt this was due to an ill-judged effort to avoid increasing existing tensions and there had in practice been several indications since November that official bonhomie was wearing thin. Chamberlain told Parliament on 14 November that no British mandates would be returned to the Reich. On 7 December Malcolm MacDonald finally rejected any idea of returning the German colonies. 'It is not now an issue in practical politics.' In his speech to the Press Association on 13 December the Prime Minister said he 'must deplore the present attitude of the German Press'; he condemned a recent attack on Earl Baldwin, denied that he favoured the system of Naziism or Fascism, and repeated a remark he had made on other occasions, that 'history teaches us that no form of government ever remains the same'.

Hitler's usual speech on 30 January 1939 did not appear to foreshadow any new territorial claims, and gave considerable space to the necessity for increasing German exports. The process of German unification was now practically ended: 'all the streams of German blood now flow together in this Reich'. Colonies were 'in no sense a problem which could cause a war'. Taken at its face value the speech was not alarming to Great Britain. An increase in Anglo-German trade would be only too welcome to the English business world, and on 3 February, in a speech at Hull, Halifax denied that Britain had fought the last war to destroy German trade. But Hitler boasted of the 9,000 million marks spent on rearmament (possibly a ten-fold exaggeration of the amount actually spent), and on 10 December the German Government had announced its intention to build up to 100 per cent of the British submarine tonnage; on the following day the Foreign Office had had apparently authentic information that Hitler had ordered preparations for a bombing attack on London in peacetime from Dutch bases.[1] So behind the façade of official optimism France and Britain had plenty of reason for alarm and they arrived early in February 1939 at an agreement for joint military action against a German attack. As a result of subsequent military conversations during February the British Cabinet agreed to increase the Regular Army to ten divisions and with corresponding Territorial reserves.

Italian policy too was equivocal and not particularly reassuring. Mussolini seemed anxious to avoid a breach with England; after the withdrawal of 10,000 Italian troops from Spain in October 1938 the British Government agreed to bring the Anglo-Italian agreement of 16 April into force, and the

[1] Ivone Kirkpatrick, *The Inner Circle*, pp. 136–9; B.D. Ser. IV, vol. iv, nos 40–5, 98, etc.

British Ambassador was actually applauded in the Italian Chamber on 30 November. On the other hand, there were noisy demands for French colonial concessions which were emphatically rejected by the French Government. The Italian Press stormed, but the Italian Government did not present its demands in a more official manner. Chamberlain's visit to Rome (11–14 January 1939) marked a further step towards an Anglo-Italian *détente*. We now know that Mussolini had no intention of following Hitler into an early war. One plausible assumption was that Hitler intended to move eastward, and expected that the Western powers would be only too pleased to leave him alone. The Franco-German declaration of 6 December 1938 had recognized that there was no territorial question outstanding between the two countries. The mounting exasperation against Hitlerism in both the governing classes and the masses of France and England was something that Hitler never properly understood; he continued to believe that they were without spirit, lacking zest for an unnecessary quarrel. Mussolini, it seems, was, for a time, less confident.

The New Adventure: British Reactions (March, April 1939)

After the Vienna award of 2 November 1938, the German Press had described the solution of the Magyar claims as definitive, and had apparently accepted, for at least the time being, the view that Germany had no further demands to make on the three docile and helpless fragments of the former Czechoslovak state. This praise of the superior qualities of Axis state-building ceased suddenly in December, and it began to be conjectured abroad that new plans were afoot.[1] Hitler, in fact, issued instructions for the preparation of plans to extinguish the 'rump Czech state' on 17 December 1938. Ribbentrop opened discussions in October 1938 with the Poles over Danzig and the Corridor but they reaffirmed their non-aggression pact with Russia in November, and in January 1939 rejected categorically

---

[1] Subsequent references to German diplomacy in this chapter are from G.D., Ser. D, vols iv–vii.

German proposals that they should join the Anti-Comintern Pact and establish a 'corridor across the Corridor' in the form of a railway line or autostrada under German sovereignty. In mid-January the new Hungarian Foreign Minister, Count Csaky, was given to understand that the Reich would no longer object to Hungarian annexation of the rest of Ruthenia. On Chamberlain's initiative, inquiries as to the guarantee of Czechoslovakia, envisaged by the Munich Agreement, were addressed to the German Government by Britain, France, and Italy early in February 1939. After reports that Germany would make further demands in exchange for the guarantee, a German note of 28 February refused altogether to give it, on the ground that as there were, after all, still Czech–Magyar differences, the conditions visualized in the Munich Agreement had not been fulfilled. It also said bluntly that it considered that the intervention of the Western powers in Central Europe, under the form of the guarantee, would be harmful rather than beneficial. A fortnight later the Czechoslovak republic came to an end.

After Munich a new Government under the Germanophil Rudolf Beran had been formed in Prague, and had done its best to satisfy the Nazi demands; Slovakia had also been linked with the Czech state by a federal tie which satisfied all the essential demands of the Slovak autonomists. In spite of this, Prague was attacked by every means under Nazi control, with anti-Czech propaganda from the Vienna radio station inciting the Slovaks to secede, and with repeated official demands to the Czech Government for concessions. On 14 March President Hacha was summoned to meet Hitler in Berlin; after a ceremonious reception he was subjected to five hours' pressure during the night by Hitler and his advisers, during which the sixty-seven-year-old President had a heart attack and fainted repeatedly. He was said finally to have agreed to the destruction of the republic at 4.30 a.m. on the 15th after a threat that otherwise Prague and other large centres would be bombed at five o'clock. The German troops occupied Prague on the same day. On the 14th Hungarian troops invaded Ruthenia (Carpatho-Ukraine) and the Slovak state proclaimed its independence. On the 15th Father Tiso telegraphed to Hitler that the Slovak state placed itself under his protection, and he replied from Prague on the 16th, taking over the protectorate. On the same day Hungary annexed Ruthenia. In Prague the German troops were followed promptly by the Gestapo, which at once took over local key positions and interned Jews, Communists, and other political undesirables in concentration camps at Milovice and Saaz. The gold reserves of the National Bank were taken over, and, after the Bank of International Settlement and the National Bank of Switzerland had surrendered in May Czechoslovak gold reserves deposited abroad, the Reich gained control of nearly 400 million marks in gold and foreign exchange.

Thus the principle of self-determination was thrown overboard, and the new policy provided the occasion for Hitler's official adoption of the principle of *Lebensraum*. 'Bohemia and Moravia have for thousands of years belonged to the living space of the German people,' he said in his proclamation on 16 March. The Nazi conception of *Lebensraum* was well enough understood abroad: it implied absolute control – political, military, and economic – of an area, in Europe or overseas, sufficiently extensive to furnish the resources which would give her the complete freedom of action typical of a 'world power'. The execution of the complete scheme – which in *Mein Kampf* had involved German control of a large part of European Russia – had, however, been widely considered to be too impracticable to be taken seriously. Many people who feared and distrusted Hitler still saw in his foreign policy little more than the impulsive outbursts of a brutal, unbalanced man. Chamberlain, who preferred the theory of a Nazi foreign policy activated by brainstorms to one of planned, Napoleonic aggression, was one of those who thought of the maintenance of peace too exclusively in terms of controlling Hitler's moods. But he was not alone.

The British Government's first pronouncements on the new situation, although critical, were in somewhat anodyne terms of condemnation.[1] But on 17 March the British

[1] B.D., Ser. III, vols iv–vii, cover the last months of peace.

Ambassador was called from Berlin to report, and the indignation of Parliament and the Press convinced Chamberlain and Halifax that the new course of German policy must be resisted. On the same day, in an address to the Birmingham Unionist Association, Chamberlain enumerated Hitler's specific assurances in September against any further territorial aggression, condemned the recent treatment of the Czech and Slovak states, pointed out that in the 'unpleasant surprises' hitherto sprung by the German régime there was at least 'something to be said, whether on account of racial affinity or of just claims too long resisted' for the 'necessity of a change in the existing situation', and demanded, 'is this the end of an old adventure, or is it the beginning of a new'? On 18 March the British and French Governments presented notes protesting sharply against the German action and refusing to recognize the situation thereby created; the German Government in turn declined to accept the notes, and recalled its Ambassadors in London and Paris 'to report'. The abrupt transition in Chamberlain's attitude, following some ill-judged optimism about the prospects of peace during the previous weeks, seemed unconvincing to many: had he previously been very gullible, was he now genuinely alerted? He was; the show of optimism had been a calculated, and as usual with this Government, inept publicity gesture aimed vaguely at relaxing European tensions, and the real trend of its policy had been seen (but hardly appreciated) in the acceleration of the Anglo-French preparation for war in Europe since January. Chamberlain had long been told by the Chiefs of Staff that a bolder policy could not be undertaken before the spring of 1939, and he was greatly reassured by the welcome increase at this point in aircraft production. His aim, however, was still to save the peace, this time by a demonstration of strength. But he was ready for the war which must follow if this attempt failed.

Accordingly the second half of March, when the British Government makes the decisive moves on these lines, is the real turning-point in British policy, and probably for that of France and Germany. None of the three felt able to draw back if the other two stood firm. Among the other great powers, the United States and Japan were determined not to be involved in the European struggle, while Italy and Soviet Russia meant to stay out if they could. There was a further shock on 17 March with the announcement of what appeared to be a German ultimatum to Rumania, and although this turned out to be something of a mare's nest it provided the occasion for the new phase of British policy. Halifax had at once invited Russia to join the Western powers in helping Rumania, and on the 20th the Cabinet agreed to a plan whereby Britain, France, Soviet Russia, and Poland would consult together in the event of a threat to the security of independence of any European state.

The launching of this guarantee system is a classic example of the pitfalls of open diplomacy. There was a strong demand in the British Press, among the Labour members, and a little less publicly among Government supporters, for strong, immediate, but ill-defined action to 'stop Hitler'; on the other hand, the Labour Party felt none of the vague ideological enthusiasm for the Poles that it had felt for the Czechs, and the leaders of the party, when it came to the point, were frightened at the commitment to a war in Eastern Europe. The British plan immediately ran into the obstacle of Soviet–Polish animosity, which the Government could hardly proclaim in public (although the Opposition leaders knew all about it); while this barrier was being anxiously reconnoitred in Anglo-French discussions, there were renewed cries for drastic action. On the assumption that Chamberlain was holding back, thirty Conservative M.P.s, including Eden and Churchill, put down a resolution in the Commons on 28 March favouring the 'foreign policy of the Foreign Secretary'. Hitler meanwhile was conducting his own war of nerves. It was effective in persuading the Lithuanian Government on 21 March, in response to a German ultimatum, to agree to return the Memel Territory to the Reich. The emphasis was more on persuasion than on threats when Ribbentrop urged a settlement over Danzig and the Corridor on the Poles on the 21st, with a hint of compensation in Slovakia. But Beck made counter-proposals on the 26th which would have partly nullified Germany's advantage if accepted. Finally the London Press found a mouthpiece in the young *News Chronicle* correspondent in Berlin, who in a personal interview on 29 March persuaded Chamberlain that a German attack on Poland was imminent.[1] On the same day it was announced that the Territorial Army was to be increased to twenty-six divisions. On the 31st Chamberlain gave the Commons the news that the British and French Governments intended to give Poland immediate support if attacked.

Undoubtedly the Government had been hurried into this decision by the belief that both its own position at home and the prevention of immediate German aggression abroad called for an impressive gesture. Its willingness to give the guarantee might have proved a decisive bargaining weapon in bringing the Polish and Soviet Governments together if its implementation had been part of a comprehensive understanding. As it was the British and French were committed to Poland without any promise of reciprocal support, and the Soviet Government could sit back and leave the capitalist world to fight and die by self-destruction. France it is true already had treaties with Poland and the Soviet Union, but she had never consolidated her position with Russia by a military agreement. The Labour Party's hesitations were removed by the Russian Ambassador, Maisky, who told a group of Labour M.P.s on the 30th that his Government would welcome the British guarantee to Poland.[2] Hitler did not react publicly for some time; but in a secret directive on 3 April he instructed the Wehrmacht to be ready to destroy Poland at any time after 31 August.

There is no doubt that Hitler meant to solve in Germany's favour the problems of Danzig and the Corridor, an issue in German eyes comparable to the Alsace-Lorraine problems of pre-war days. There is no doubt too that he wanted a dominating position for Germany in Europe, and that he wanted to demonstrate to himself and to the world the might of the

---

[1] Ian Colvin, *Vansittart in Office*, pp. 298–311.
[2] Hugh Dalton, *The Fateful Years* (1957), pp. 236–9; and private information But cf. I. Maisky, *Who Helped Hitler?* (1964).

German armed forces. There seems no reason to think that he had not thought out the shape and character of the new, triumphant Germany – after all, the alternatives were few and he had been brooding over them since 1920. Certain problems remain, however, in assessing his intentions. Evidence available since 1945 shows that he understood the advantages of striking quickly (not later than 1940) before his opponents were fully rearmed; this meant of necessity that Germany must make do with a rapid output of existing types of machines and equipment rather than follow the slower process of expanding her armed forces on an extended industrial base and with newer types. But this lightning campaigning was not quite compatible with the great conquests and military glory for which he also seems to have hankered. It may be that he reserved this consummation of his military genius for a future date when he could strike down Russia after a second phase of rearmament. In the meantime there was really nothing foolish in the British Government's persistent search for a peaceful settlement. Hitler had displayed sufficient guile and sense of manoeuvre to suggest that he might know how to draw back from the brink of catastrophe; his proclaimed aims, however ferociously expressed, were all in the ambit of the Versailles grievances; and there seemed no doubt that his rages when thwarted were not always simulated to impress peace-loving Englishmen.

The period of surprises was not over. Italian troops occupied Albanian ports on 6 and 7 April, and had overcome resistance throughout the state by the 10th; King Zog fled from Tirana. The new aggression directly threatened both Yugoslavia and Greece; and it threatened almost as directly Rumania's communications with Salonika by the railway route through the Morava and Vardar Valleys. The Italian occupation arose from differences of policy which had for some time separated King Zog and Mussolini. It could not be ignored by France and England, although they had no desire at this moment to drive Mussolini into complete co-operation with Hitler. The Duce's recent utterances had shown no great enthusiasm for German policy; in a speech on 26 March he had said that 'although professional pacifists are particularly detestable individuals' Italy considered that 'a long period of peace is necessary to safeguard the development of European civilization'. On the 9th he sent fresh assurances to both Halifax and Perth that Italian troops, aeroplanes, and pilots would leave Spain immediately after the victory parade. Accordingly the Anglo-Italian Agreement was not denounced, although it was announced on 13 April that Anglo-French guarantees against aggression had been offered and accepted by Rumania and Greece.

France and England had thus laid the foundations of a 'peace front' which would, it was hoped, allow the building-up of an adequate scheme of collective security. This meant, above all, the establishment of a satisfactory agreement with the Soviet Union. Germany on her side, disconcerted for the moment by the Anglo-French assurances to Poland, postponed her campaign for Danzig, and set to work to discover means of destroying or immobilizing the coalition against her. These two lines of activity occupied the main attention of the powers for the next three months.

The Anglo-Soviet Negotiations (April–August)

The British Government's first move in the building of the 'peace front' had been its inquiry on 18 March as to what the Soviet Government would do if Rumania were subjected to an unprovoked attack. The Soviet Government evaded a direct reply by proposing an international conference to consider the question of German aggression; the British in turn declined this proposal on the ground that it was premature. The unwillingness of Poland and Rumania to accept Russian aid probably influenced both the Soviet proposal and the British reply. Litvinov showed great annoyance at the unilateral guarantee to Poland, in spite of an assurance by the Prime Minister that there were no 'ideological impediments' between the Western powers and Russia. The Russian Press continued its attacks on the two Western powers, arguing that their policy was still to entangle the Soviet Union in a war with Germany.

The Anglo-French–Soviet discussions commenced on 15 April and were only broken off after the announcement of the German–Soviet non-aggression pact on 21 August. The British negotiators had two serious handicaps from the start. The first was the ingrained Soviet suspicion of the British Government which may have been deepened by the events of 1938, but which had its origin in remoter causes. The second was the tactical disadvantage of seeking Soviet support after, and not before, the British Government had pledged itself irrevocably to the support of Poland and Rumania. The Soviet and British Governments were mutually distrustful; each suspected that the other's interest in any form of collective security was a device to evade personal responsibility for resisting German aggression. Each was privately convinced of the fundamental immorality and inherent inefficiency of the social and economic system of the other. Each doubted the other's military strength, internal stability, and loyalty to public commitments. The British ministers still appear to have taken seriously the possibility of Communist revolutions in Western European countries. There is no certainty that the Communists recognized any difference in principle between bourgeois parliamentary democracy and the Nazi–Fascist dictatorships.[1]

Litvinov, as the official sponsor of the League and pro-French orientation since 1934, had achieved a good personal standing at Geneva, and had given many close observers the conviction that he was a sincere believer in the League system. But he was obviously less influential in Russia than outside: he was not a member of the *Politburo*, and did not even become a member of the central committee of the Communist Party until 1934. One effect of the various purges of high civil and military officials between 1936 and 1938 had been to remove from Stalin's immediate circle practically everyone who had lived in, or even had knowledge of, any foreign country. Wild suspicion of foreign intrigue had played, indeed, an important part in the accusations at the trials. In his speech to the Eighteenth

[1] Cf. W. Laqueur, *Russia and Germany* (1965), pp. 196–9.

Congress of the Soviet Communist Party on 10 March 1939
Stalin had spoken in a detached way of the rivalry between the
Anti-Comintern Pact signatories and the Western democracies:
among the latter Britain and France had rejected collective
security and taken up an attitude of non-intervention, not
wishing to hinder Germany from embroiling herself in war
with the Soviet Union. To this he added a broad reference to
the willingness of the Soviet Union to maintain peaceful relations with its neighbours, which could be interpreted in Berlin
as a tentative offer of a Soviet–German agreement.

The Anglo-Soviet discussions opened with a British proposal on 15 April that the Soviet Union should give a promise
of assistance to certain East European states similar to that
given by Great Britain. The French made a separate proposal on
somewhat different lines. Litvinov replied promptly with a
counter-proposal of a pact of mutual assistance between the
three powers against aggression. Before the British reply was
received Litvinov was released on 3 May from the office of
Foreign Commissar 'at his own request', and his duties were
temporarily assumed by M. Molotov. On the following day the
Moscow wireless announced that Molotov would carry on the
policy of Western security which had for years been Litvinov's
expressed aim. In spite of this assurance there was considerable
uneasiness in Western Europe at the change: as a Jew and the
spearhead of the anti-German policy, Litvinov was evidently
not the best person to strike a bargain with Hitler, if that was
what Stalin now desired.

Halifax told the British Ambassador, Sir William Seeds, on
8 May, that 'the time is not yet ripe for the comprehensive
counter-proposal which the Soviet Government have made to
us', and he suggested a Soviet statement that if the two powers
were involved in war as a result of their guarantees to certain
Eastern European countries, Soviet assistance should be available, if desired. While avoiding a commitment to a full alliance
this appeared to remove Russia's complaint that she might be
left to fight alone. The ostensible reason for this coy diplomacy
was the reluctance of Poland to be politically associated with

the Soviet Union: Halifax felt that he must reject the Soviet proposal of 18 April because under it the Soviet Union would be bound automatically to render military assistance to Poland and Rumania. But there are scattered references in the British Foreign Office documents to other reasons. It was remarked that the British Government did not want 'to forfeit the sympathy of the world at large by giving a handle to Germany's anti-Comintern propaganda', and that Soviet military help was likely to be of limited value (a view supported on the whole by the British service attachés in Moscow and elsewhere). The theory evidently was that Hitler might behave himself after a warning (which had been given in the guarantee system) but might go mad if provoked too far. The French thought these hesitations unwise. It was not until 20 May, as a result of French and British pressure from a variety of sources, that Halifax, after discussion with Maisky at Geneva, agreed to negotiations for a full alliance.[1]

Meanwhile the announcement on 12 May of a provisional Anglo-Turkish Agreement was expected to have a beneficial effect on the Moscow negotiations. The growth of friendly relations between England and Turkey since 1935 had been primarily the result of Turkish apprehension at Italy's aggressive policy, but Germany's policy had more recently been viewed with alarm by the Turks. There had been a marked increase in hostility towards German businessmen and mercantile shipping in Turkish ports since Munich, and that event had, on the other hand, finally convinced Turkey of Britain's peaceful intentions. German and Italian penetration of the Balkans was increasingly feared, and Turkey's control of the Straits would enable her to decide whether Britain and French aid could reach Rumania. On 8 April after a visit by M. Gafencu, the Rumanian Foreign Minister, to Istanbul an official statement announced that the two powers intended to maintain the policy of the Balkan Entente and Salonika Pact with resolution. By the agreement of 12 May Great Britain and Turkey undertook to co-operate effectively in the event of war

[1] Cf. B.D., Ser. III, vol. iv, no. 489.

in the Mediterranean area, and they recognized that it was 'also necessary to ensure the establishment of security in the Balkans'. A definite long-term agreement was to be concluded in due course.

With the Anglo-French acceptance of the substance of the Soviet proposals on 24 May a second phase of Molotov's diplomacy began, characterized by a flat refusal to accept any significant modification of the Soviet programme. This could only mean that he was seeking to exploit Russia's favourable bargaining position to the full; it also meant that agreement was postponed while Germany made up her mind. He told the German Ambassador on 20 May that a basis for Russo-German agreement could be found, but left it to the Germans to make concrete proposals.[1] On 31 May, in a speech to the Supreme Council of the Soviet Union, he said that the Anglo-French proposals were hedged in by reservations, and were more favourable to the Western powers than to the Soviet Union, as they contained no provision for the defence of Estonia, Latvia, and Lithuania, which might not be able to defend themselves against aggression. He did not remark that the Russian proposals had contained no provision for the defence of Holland and Belgium. In the light of subsequent events the reference which immediately followed to the progress of commercial negotiations with Germany may be regarded as a further attempt to force the hands of the British and French.

Throughout June the negotiations continued to be held up over the question of the Baltic states. There was undoubtedly real ground for the Russian apprehension that these states might be forced to accept German political or military control and might not dare to appeal for help. But, like Poland and Rumania, they were as much afraid of the Soviet Union as of Germany, and had no desire to give either power any excuse for marching in. The British Government now proposed that Britain, France, and the Soviet Union should 'consult together' over threats to the neutrality or independence of any European state. On 12 June, Mr William Strang, head of the central de-

[1] G.D., Ser. D, vol. vi, no. 424.

partment of the Foreign Office, left for Moscow with these new proposals. Molotov rejected them almost offensively on the 16th. Finally, Halifax gave in on this vital issue: he agreed on 27 June to abandon the demand for the prior agreement of threatened states that it was proposed to help. In return he wanted this provision extended to Holland and Switzerland: France added Luxemburg. Molotov refused this addition. By the beginning of July all the Soviet demands had been met, but Molotov then demanded a satisfactory formula for 'indirect aggression' and it was on this point alone that disagreement remained. Molotov wanted it to be extended even to cases where no threat of force existed.

But it seemed very probable now that the Soviet Government was deliberately quibbling over this point as a means of marking time, and would easily agree about a form of words when it was convenient to do so. A more formidable obstacle was its insistence, which had indeed been mentioned as early as 2 June, that a military agreement must precede the signing of the political agreement. By the end of July it was known in London that Russo-German conversations had been taking place, but it was hoped that they had failed. The British and French Governments clearly had to accept any proposal that would keep the negotiations going. Strang left Moscow on 7 August, and French and British military missions arrived there on the 10th. The sending of the British military mission had necessitated the personal intervention of the Prime Minister, who had overridden the objections of the service departments. It was argued later that better results would have been achieved if, instead of Strang, some important political personage, such as Halifax, had been sent to Moscow. It is true that Ribbentrop went to Moscow in August to sign the German–Soviet Pact. But he went to sign after negotiations had been conducted by the German Ambassador, and the British had a representative there of equal standing in the person of the British Ambassador, Sir William Seeds. There was, indeed, no obstacle to a Russian agreement with the Western powers if the will to sign had existed in Moscow.

Germany and the Peace Front (April–June)

The German Government's reaction to the Anglo-French 'peace front' negotiations expressed irritation rather than alarm; although a temporary halt was called to the advance into Eastern Europe there seemed no inclination to abandon it. After the end of March official and Press pronouncements in Germany angrily condemned the critics of Germany's recent foreign policy. The attacks were directed mainly against Great Britain. This 'war of nerves' was merely a continuation of the Press war of the previous winter. The possibility that it would strengthen and consolidate anti-German feeling instead of terrorizing it into silence never seems to have been grasped in Berchtesgaden or Berlin.

In a speech at Wilhelmshaven on 1 April Hitler claimed that he had made numerous attempts to solve every problem by discussion, and that all his offers had been rejected. The recent anger abroad at German action in Czechoslovakia was perhaps 'rage over the lack of success of a carefully evolved plan aimed at creating a tactical State for the new policy of encirclement'. The Axis was the most natural political influence in the world, based on reason, justice, and idealism. He poured scorn on the 'transitory ties of heterogeneous bodies on the other side'. German Press comment and official speeches continued on these lines throughout April. The Italian occupation of Albania was warmly approved. Some papers suggested that King Zog was in the pay of the British intelligence service.

On 15 April Roosevelt was misguided enough to address to Hitler and Mussolini a 'peace' appeal, the essential point of which was an inquiry as to whether each would guarantee not to attack certain states (all the European and Near Eastern states were named) for a period sufficiently long (ten years at least) to give every opportunity to work by peaceful methods for a more permanent peace. As the President was determined not to involve himself in any way he could not follow up his appeal by even the mildest of threats, or even indulge in a prolonged slanging match with Hitler, who replied in a long and sardonic speech in the Reichstag on 28 April. He also had a lot to say about England's attitude and was possibly aiming at a bargain with her. Nevile Henderson had been sent back to Berlin three days before, and had announced the British Government's decision to introduce conscription. Hitler's references to England in the speech emphasized his desire for Anglo-German friendship and his sincere admiration for the 'immeasurable colonizing work' of the Anglo-Saxon people. As he did not interfere with British policy in Palestine and else-where she should not interfere with Germany's policy in her sphere of interest. He then announced his denunciation of the Naval Agreement of 1935. 'Should the British Government, however, wish to enter once more into negotiations with Germany on this problem, no one would be happier than I at the prospect of still being able to come to a clear and straight-forward understanding.' With regard to Poland he described the 'offer' of 21 March, and the Polish reply of 26 March which he treated (quite correctly) as a rejection. This attitude was 'incomprehensible'. Worse still was the fact that Poland, like Czechoslovakia a year ago, believed 'under the pressure of a lying international campaign that it must call up troops'. This led to the 'so-called guarantee offer'; Poland would now, in some circumstances, be compelled to take military action against Germany. This conflicted with the German–Polish Non-Aggression Pact, which he therefore denounced. He replied to Roosevelt by saying that he was prepared to give assurances to each of the states named, on condition of absolute reciprocity. Already, however, 'all states bordering on Ger-many have received much more binding assurances . . . than Mr Roosevelt asked from me in his curious telegram'.

Early in May Ribbentrop met Ciano at Lake Como, and it was announced that their two countries would conclude a comprehensive military and economic pact. This treaty, the 'pact of steel', was duly signed by the two Foreign Ministers at Berlin on 22 May. It made formal provision for the military co-operation which had been implicit in their previous 'Axis' policy, but with the vital reservation, which soon began to be hinted at in the Italian Press, that Italy was not to be called on to go to war for two or three years, or to fight against Poland. Japan refused to join a triple military alliance directed against any power except Russia, whereas Hitler wanted to avoid a quarrel with Russia and use Japan to overawe the French and British. Non-aggression pacts were offered by Germany to Finland, Estonia, Latvia, and the Scandinavian states. Norway, Sweden, and Finland refused, but pacts were signed with Denmark, on 31 May, and with Estonia and Latvia on 7 June. On 15 May Hitler commenced a tour of the western fortifications. On 6 June he addressed the Kondor Legion of Germans who had fought for General Franco in Spain, and admitted that he had decided to help Franco as early as July 1936. The speech, like that of 28 April, made no attack on Communism or Bolshevism. Goebbels during June conducted an anti-British campaign throughout the country; Dr Ley described British defensive measures as 'childish bluff', a mixture of conscription and football; all the German leaders continued to denounce the British encirclement policy, war-mongering, and hypocrisy.

This campaign did not produce any signs of failing nerve in London; the Government was, however, convinced that Hitler had not realized that the British and French pledge to Poland must be taken seriously, and that he was therefore deliberately preparing a Polish crisis. On 5 May Beck replied in the Polish Parliament to Hitler's action in repudiating the German–Polish Agreement, and on this and other occasions indicated his willingness for discussions, but without response from Germany. The German Ambassador, Herr von Moltke, returned to Warsaw on 5 May, but had no official meeting with Beck during the next two months. Ill-feeling between the two countries grew steadily. The German papers repeatedly contained stories of Germans ill-treated and beaten to death. There appears to have been no foundation for these stories, and indeed the German minority in Poland was probably the most anti-Nazi group of non-Reich Germans in the world.

The publication since 1945 of the essential documents on pre-war German policy clears up a number of problems concerning Hitler's intentions. His talk to a number of senior officers (recorded in the 'Schmundt minutes' of 23 May), shows his conviction at this point that Britain would probably fight alongside France, and also his determination to get what he wanted from the Poles. He hoped to isolate Poland, that is, to buy off or frighten off the Western powers, but was prepared to fight a two-front war against the three if necessary. It is significant that this exposition did not include plans for war with Russia. It has to be remembered that an agreement with Russia was necessary, even if the Western powers were not prepared to fight: it would be impossible otherwise to destroy Poland without Soviet interference. Yet after Molotov's hint on 20 May the German Foreign Office was not instructed to try to negotiate a Soviet–German Agreement for at least another two months, apparently because of fear of a rebuff, a mere 'peal of Tartar laughter'.[1] So the policy was to use the time before the Wehrmacht was due to strike on 1 September to overawe Poland by a war of nerves, to induce the Western powers to back out of their guarantee obligations if possible, to secure an agreement with Russia at the critical moment, and, if war with all three potential great-power rivals could be avoided, to use the year 1939 to strengthen his psychological ascendency and military-economic base for a decisive blow at any remaining opposition, perhaps in 1940. The only possibility that seemed to have been clearly ruled out was a war against the combined strength of Britain, France, and the Soviet Union in 1939.

The British Government's anxious efforts to assure Hitler that their intentions were entirely serious conflicted somewhat with their cautious inclination to avoid language that would drive him over the edge. The State Department had much the same idea and feared that the British decision on conscription would goad him into desperation.[2] On 23 June a memorandum, replying to the German note of 27 April denouncing the Naval Agreement, reaffirmed the British Government's intention to support certain countries if attacked by Germany, but went to

[1] G.D., Ser. D, vol. vi, no. 598.
[2] *The Moffat Papers*, p. 240.

such pains to deny the justice of the German charges of encirclement, trade hostility, and so forth that its tone must have seemed to the Germans defensive, and almost apologetic. The blockade of Tientsin (p. 166), which began on 14 June, was triumphantly proclaimed by Goebbels to be a further proof of British impotence.

Tension over Danzig mounted during June; the Gestapo arrested a Polish customs inspector, M. Lipinski, on 11 June and beat him up; other arrests were made, and no Polish representative was allowed to see Lipinski. On 17 June Goebbels spoke in Danzig, and after accusing Poland of demanding East Prussia and Silesia from Germany repeated Hitler's statement that 'Danzig is a German city and will come to Germany'. Herr Forster, the *Gauleiter* of Danzig, returned from Berlin on 23 June, and started to organize a 'Free Corps' of about 4,000 young men sent from East Prussia.

At this point a full and unequivocal statement of British policy was made by Halifax on 29 June, at the annual dinner of the Royal Institute of International Affairs, after the French Foreign Minister had urged him to give a clear warning to the Reich that France and Great Britain intended to fulfil their obligations to assist Poland. The speech was considered to have provided a reasoned and much needed statement of the case for Great Britain's present phase of foreign policy, and a challenge to totalitarian theories and criticism.

> Today we are bound by new agreements for mutual defence with Poland and Turkey: we have guaranteed assistance to Greece and Rumania against aggression . . . We know that, if the security and independence of other countries are to disappear, our own security and our own independence will be gravely threatened. We know that if international law and order are to be preserved, we must be prepared to fight in its defence.

The country had made an immense effort, unparalleled in time of peace, to equip itself for this task: none of this formidable array of strength would be used except in defence against aggression. 'No blow will be struck, no shot fired.' Great Britain's first resolve was to stop aggression: no more and no less. Germany was not being encircled, but was isolating herself. All outstanding international problems could find a solution 'once everybody has got the will to settle', but 'it is impossible to negotiate with a country the leaders of which brand a friendly country as thieves and blackmailers and indulge in daily monstrous slanders on British policy in all parts of the world'.

The speech made a considerable impact because of its timing, and it offered something of a challenge to the incessant enunciation of totalitarian theories and claims. On the following day (30 June) Halifax suggested to the Polish Government that a *fait accompli* was being prepared, and that the moment had come for consultation between the Polish, French, and British Governments in order that their plans might be co-ordinated in time. Beck in his reply on 1 July advised against any joint *démarche* at this stage, although he accepted the British view as to Germany's intentions. He was, however, 'determined not to be scared by any psychological terrorism into imprudent action'. This decision turned out to be wise; during the next few days the situation in Danzig eased sufficiently to show that Germany was not yet ready for action. On 1 July Bonnet presented to the German Ambassador a note saying that France would immediately come to Poland's assistance if an alteration in the *status quo* in Danzig occurred. On 10 July Chamberlain in the House of Commons reaffirmed the intention of the British Government to support Poland in resisting a 'unilateral solution' of the Danzig question imposed by Germany.

The Last Phase (*July–August*)

In spite of a superficial improvement in the Danzig situation in July there was no evidence that Germany intended to drop the question, and a renewal of the controversy early in August ushered in a final stage of furious polemics on lines strikingly similar to the German anti-Czech campaign of 1938. But it seems evident from the German documents that Hitler had now become more confident than he had been in the early summer that Britain and France would not fight, or that they would offer at the most only a token defence of Poland. There were probably several reasons for this change of view. Throughout the summer the Germans were surprisingly well informed, from a 'reliable source' in London, as to the British alliance negotiations with Russia, and the Italian Government also succeeded in purloining documents from the British embassy in Rome with information about the negotiations. Mussolini arranged for one British document, critical of Stalin, to be placed in Stalin's hands, and he believed that this had materially affected Stalin's attitude. Apart from this it was easy to see that the chance of Soviet aid to the Western powers was receding by mid-July, and the defection of Russia was expected to cool Anglo-French ardour. The anxiety of the British Cabinet for a peaceful solution is in reality proof of their acceptance of the likelihood of a war which Britain and France must fight, but it was easily misunderstood in Berlin as evidence of cold feet. From British sources came a number of hints, through various intermediaries, of the Government's continued willingness for a 'comprehensive settlement' which strengthened this German view, although it was also hinted, however delicately, that Germany must abandon future expansion and must disarm in return for any colonial or economic concessions. There were talks with two well-meaning Swedish gentlemen, Axel Wenner-Gren and Birger Dahlerus, whose value lay in their links with Goering, but Goering had nothing to concede, and in fact Dahlerus warned him early in July that Britain would fight if Danzig were attacked. Dr Helmuth Wohlthat was a German official who came to London for a whaling conference from 17 to 20 July, and was sounded by R. H. Hudson and Horace Wilson, but he had no authority to negotiate and nothing came of the conversations.

So by the beginning of August there remained little for the British and French to do except wait for Hitler and Stalin to declare themselves. The possibility that Molotov was manoeuvring to secure a Soviet–German Agreement had been obvious enough since his speech of 31 May. He quoted Stalin's precept, 'to be cautious and not let our country be drawn into conflict by war-mongers who are accustomed to allow others to pull the chestnuts out of the fire for them', as a comment on the Anglo-French proposals. Later in the speech he said that while carrying on negotiations with England and France, the Soviet Government did not in the least consider it necessary to renounce business ties with such countries as Germany and Italy. Trade negotiations had been initiated by the German Government at the beginning of 1938, with the German offer of a credit of 200 million marks. They had been interrupted, but 'there were signs that the resumption of these negotiations is not excluded'. Early in July there were rumours, which were emphatically denied in Germany, that von Papen had gone on a special mission to Moscow; unofficial trade talk in Moscow could be assumed from the fact that on 21 July it was announced that official negotiations had begun there. The decisive step was taken by Germany at a private dinner on 26 July when Schnurre, a German official acting under instructions, broached the idea of a comprehensive Soviet–German Agreement to Astakov, the Soviet Chargé d'Affaires in Berlin. Parallel discussions were conducted in Moscow by the German Ambassador, and it appears that Hitler had accepted the probable Soviet conditions in principle by 4 August. On 19 August the trade and credit agreement was signed in Berlin; on the evening of 21 August it was announced to the world that the two countries had negotiated a non-aggression pact, and that von Ribbentrop would fly to Moscow on the 23rd to sign it.

The Italians viewed these developments uneasily. There was much bravado, concealing great irresolution. Mussolini was almost offensively haughty in receiving a new British Ambassador, Sir Percy Loraine, on 27 May. Ciano, the Foreign Minister, described it, with apparent approval, as 'the most frigid reception the Duce has ever accorded a diplomat'. But Ciano was alarmed to find in conversations with Hitler and Ribbentrop at Ober Salzburg (11–13 August) that the German decision to fight Poland was implacable; Hitler 'rejects any

solution which might give satisfaction to Germany and avoid
the struggle'. He told Ciano that he was 'absolutely convinced
that the Western democracies would, in the last resort, recoil
from unleasing a general war'. Ciano was even more alarmed to
find that Mussolini, who had been anxious on the 9th to prove
to Hitler that war would be folly at this time, had decided on
the 13th that honour compelled him to march with Germany.
But after further shifting, and evidence that the Italian people
were anti-German and anti-war, Mussolini finally decided for
peace, on the ground of Italy's shortage of supplies.

Hitler had now to bring the Polish issue to the point of crisis
justifying war, and with a Soviet–German Agreement in sight
he took exception to a Polish ultimatum of 4 August demanding that customs officials should be allowed to function without
molestation and threatening reprisals. On 8 August a *note
verbale* from the German Government expressed 'lively surprise' at the Polish ultimatum, and its threat of reprisals on the
basis of 'incorrect rumours', and the Polish reply expressed in
turn 'liveliest surprise' at the German action. Beck told the
British Ambassador on the 10th that it was the first time the
Reich had directly intervened in the dispute between Poland
and the Danzig Senate.

On 13 August two more Polish customs officials were
arrested. Dr Burckhardt, the League High Commissioner,
visited Berchtesgaden on 11 August; Hitler did most of the
talking, violently denouncing Polish conduct. Later Burckhardt said that a settlement had become impossible by this
stage, but might have been achieved if Hitler had attempted it
earlier.

The British Government, which had the best of reasons for
desiring Polish restraint, appears to have been satisfied that the
Polish Government and Press had done their best to avoid
language which could be construed as provocative. The German Press was conducting a campaign of mounting violence
against both Great Britain and Poland, its general line of argument being that the British 'blank cheque' had emboldened
Poland to refuse reasonable demands, to inaugurate a reign of

terror against the German minority, and to plan a military attack on Danzig and even on the Reich itself. On 18 August it was stated that 76,000 refugees had fled from Poland into Germany up to the middle of August.

The self-confidence which Hitler had shown in the talks with Ciano was now at its height. General Halder records him as saying on the 14th: '*The men of Munich will not take the risk. Utmost possibilities*: Recall of ambassadors. Embargo on commerce with Germany, promotion of trade with Poland. League of Nations.'[1] Hitler addressed the commanding officers on the 22nd at a meeting which was recorded; one version had secretly reached the British embassy by the 25th. He was still convinced that the British and French, deprived of Russian support, would not fight, and that, for this year at any rate, he would have to deal only with Poland. He made disparaging remarks about all his opponents, urging the generals to act brutally, to close their hearts to pity, to use the greatest harshness. Goering congratulated him enthusiastically, 'and made bloodthirsty promises'. But then came a setback: the British did not cave in after all.

The announcement, late in the evening of 21 August, that a Soviet–German non-aggression pact was about to be signed left the British Government in little doubt that a German attack on Poland was imminent. Information reached Nevile Henderson on the same day that German military preparations for this purpose would be completed by 24 August. The Cabinet met on 22 August, and decided to summon Parliament for the 24th, when the Houses would be asked to pass the Emergency Powers (Defence) Bill in all its stages. Preliminary measures of mobilization were decided upon. At 9 p.m. on the same evening Henderson was instructed to convey without delay a personal letter to Hitler. He flew to Salzburg on the morning of the 23rd, and had an interview with Hitler at Berchtesgaden at one o'clock in the afternoon. The letter referred to the British measures which had been taken on the 22nd, and the announcement in Berlin that after the Soviet–German Pact intervention

[1] G.D., Ser. D, vol. vii, pp. 560–70.

by Great Britain on behalf of Poland need no longer be reckoned with. 'No greater mistake could be made.' The letter then observed that the difficulties of the Polish–German situation could be mitigated, if not removed, if there could be for an initial period 'a truce of both sides – and indeed on all sides – to press polemics and to all incitement'.

Henderson had a stormy conversation with Hitler, who made no long speeches but whose language 'was violent and exaggerated both as regards England and Poland'. The Ambassador 'contested every point and kept calling his statements inaccurate but the only effect was to launch him on some fresh tirade'. Hitler asserted that the Polish question would have been settled on the most generous terms (those of 21 March) if it had not been for England's unwarranted support: when the Ambassador replied that the Polish answer had been given on 26 March, while the British guarantee was only offered on 31 March, Hitler retorted that the Polish reply had been inspired by a British Press campaign. He violently attacked the Poles. The British proposal of a truce evidently did not interest him. But the British attitude was clearly an unpleasant shock.

Later in the afternoon, when he handed the Ambassador his reply, he had recovered his calm. 'Though he spoke of his artistic tastes and his longing to satisfy them, I derived the impression that the corporal of the last war was even more anxious to prove what he could do as a conquering Generalissimo in the next.' The reply was harsh and unyielding. Germany had never sought conflict with England and for years had endeavoured – although unfortunately in vain – to win England's friendship. The Reich possessed certain definite interests which it was impossible to renounce, such as the German city of Danzig, and the connected problem of the Corridor. The reported British and French measures of mobilization could only be directed against Germany: if they were carried into effect, he would order the immediate mobilization of the German forces.

His decision was, in fact, the reverse of this. The British and French attitudes, together with the completion of the Anglo-Polish Agreement (under discussion all the summer) on the

25th and the evidence, confirmed on the same day, that Italy would not come in, were felt to justify a postponement of the attack on Poland for about a week. As there would be little point in this if the British and French were going to war, anyway, we must assume that the essential point of the delay was to give them a plausible excuse for retreat: in short, that he still doubted their resolution.

At 1.30 p.m. on the afternoon of 25 August he received Henderson at the Chancellery in Berlin and made proposals which would, he hoped, lead to a settlement with England as decisive as his recent agreement with Russia. With regard to Poland there must be the settlement that Germany desired: the 'Macedonian' conditions on her eastern frontier must end, the problem of Danzig and the Corridor must be solved. After that he was prepared and determined to approach England with a large, comprehensive offer. 'He is a man of great decisions, and in this case also he will be capable of being great in his action.'

The offer amounted to very little: he accepted the British Empire and was ready 'to pledge himself personally for its continued existence', but only on condition that his colonial demands were fulfilled; all that could be regarded as an 'offer' was his vague promise 'to fix the longest time-limit' for a settlement of the colonial question. Henderson made it quite clear that there was no chance that the offer would be considered by the British Government unless it meant a negotiated settlement of the Polish question; nevertheless, in accordance with Hitler's own proposal, he flew to London on the morning of 26 August in a plane placed at his disposal by the German Government. At 5.30 on the afternoon of the 25th, Hitler gave the French Ambassador a message assuring Daladier that he had no hostility towards France. On the afternoon of 28 August Henderson flew back with the British reply.

In London there was a sense of inevitability which was shared by the Government, Parliament, and the general public; there was really nothing to do now except to say no to further manifestations of the German technique of aggression. The

Anglo-Polish Agreement, signed on the 25th in London, provided that each party should furnish the other full support and assistance in the event of aggression by a third power. Rudolf Hess in a broadcast on the same day described Chamberlain as 'a blind old idiot bound to an impossible policy and led by the nose by Jewish financiers'. The British continued, in co-operation with the French, to urge the Polish Government to avoid provocation and fresh incidents, and late on the 25th proposed the formation of a corps of neutral observers; on the 26th they suggested that the Polish Government should offer Germany an exchange of populations as a means of meeting the more permanent problem. The latter proposal would be a pledge that the Polish Government was genuinely seeking to overcome the difficulty, and would give them some definite and new point of departure on which to open up negotiations. Beck professed interest in both proposals on the 27th, but the situation was now developing too rapidly for them to be carried any farther.

The British reply to Hitler's verbal proposals was handed to him late on 28 August; he appeared to be not unfavourably impressed, and was 'again friendly and reasonable' in manner towards the Ambassador. The reply echoed his desire for complete and lasting friendship, and agreed that there must first be a settlement of the differences between Poland and Germany. Great Britain could not acquiesce in any settlement which would jeopardize Poland's independence. Hence any settlement arrived at would have to be guaranteed by other powers, and the Government suggested the initiation of direct discussions between the German and Polish Governments, on a basis which would include the safeguarding of Poland's essential interests and the securing of the settlement by an international guarantee. The Polish Government had already agreed to enter discussions on this basis. Hitler promised to give his reply next day.

The object of the British reply was to distinguish clearly between the method of negotiating a solution and the nature of the solution itself: it was felt that if the former problem could be satisfactorily solved the real difficulties would be found to be comparatively slight. This, however, involved the whole question of Germany's honesty of purpose: had she a real case against Poland, claims which would stand examination in the light of day? 'Self-determination,' decided by a plebiscite, would give her Danzig but not the Corridor; exchanges of population would remove the possibility of the persecution of minorities but would not give her increased territory. The German midday press on the 29th reported the alleged murder of six Germans in Poland; when Sir Nevile Henderson visited the Chancellery again at 7.15 in the evening he found Hitler in 'a far less reasonable mood'. Henderson naturally suspected that the story of the six murders had been fabricated by the Nazi extremists to prevent any weakening on the Führer's part. It also supplied a last-minute excuse for insisting on an immediate settlement. The German reply accepted the mediation of Great Britain with a view to the visit to Berlin of some Polish plenipotentiary, but counted on the arrival of such a plenipotentiary the next day, 30 August. Proposals for a solution would be drawn up at once and if possible placed at the disposal of the British Government before the arrival of the Polish emissary. The Ambassador said that the demand for a plenipotentiary next day sounded very much like an ultimatum: this drew prompt and angry denials from Hitler and Ribbentrop, who said that Henderson 'did not care how many Germans were being slaughtered in Poland'. The remainder of the interview was stormy.

The German proposals left little hope of a peaceful settlement. A message from Halifax at 4 a.m. on 30 August described the demand for a Polish representative within twenty-four hours as unreasonable; Henderson nevertheless recommended that the Polish Government should take advantage of this eleventh-hour effort to establish direct contact with Hitler if only to convince the world that they were prepared to make their own sacrifice for the preservation of peace. But Sir Howard Kennard telegraphed in the morning that it would be, in his opinion, impossible to induce the Polish Government to send a representative immediately to Berlin on the basis proposed by Hitler, and the British Government did not even ask the Poles to consider the proposal. Instead they sent a reply which was handed by Henderson to Ribbentrop at midnight of 30 August, that is, at the end of the day on which the Polish representative was to arrive, if the German demand were taken literally. The British note stated that they were informing the Polish Government of the German proposals of the 29th, but that in their view it would be impracticable to establish contact as early as the 30th. The Government noted the German willingness to enter into discussions with the Poles, agreed that the method of contact and arrangements for discussion should be arranged with all urgency, strongly urged a German–Polish agreement to refrain from aggressive military movements, and suggested the arrangement of a temporary *modus vivendi* for Danzig. Ribbentrop made it clear that the German Government regarded the failure of a Polish plenipotentiary to appear as the final end of the negotiations.

Hitler's mood at this decisive moment can hardly have been amiable, and this was reflected in Ribbentrop, whose reception of the Ambassador was 'one of intense hostility', which increased in violence as the interview progressed. 'He kept leaping from his chair in a state of great excitement, and asking if I had anything more to say.' To the suggestion that he should open discussions with Warsaw through the Polish Ambassador he replied that such a course would be 'utterly unthinkable and intolerable'. Finally he 'produced a lengthy document which he read out to me in German, or rather gabbled through to me as fast as he could, in a tone of the utmost annoyance'. The Ambassador was only able to gather the gist of six or seven of the sixteen articles of the proposals for a German–Polish settlement. Ribbentrop refused categorically to give a copy of the text, saying that the document was now out of date since no Polish emissary had arrived at Berlin by midnight. Henderson was handed a copy of the proposals next day at 9.15 in the evening; at nine o'clock the proposals had been broadcast with a statement that the German Government regarded them as having been rejected. They had, of course, never been communicated to the Polish Government. The proposals would certainly have formed an excellent basis for negotiation, assuming a genuine spirit of compromise on both sides: although they provided that Danzig should return to the Reich, they also proposed a plebiscite under international supervision in the Corridor, left Gdynia to Poland, provided for an international committee of inquiry to hear complaints by German and Polish minorities, and stipulated that the two countries should give the most binding guarantees of the rights of their respective minorities.

The appearance of reasonableness, combined with the completely unreasonable procedure proposed, indicate that the Poles were not to have a chance of accepting terms which would have given Germany far less than she intended to gain by conquest. Halder noted Hitler's intention to fabricate a plausible incident at the right moment. The British Government continued on the 31st its efforts to procure the opening of negotiations through the Polish Ambassador in Berlin, but the German news agency published a message stating that the wireless station at Gleiwitz had been attacked that evening by Poles, and that this had apparently been the signal for a general attack by armed Poles at two further points on the German frontier. These reports, which were absolutely denied by the Polish Government, formed the excuse for the opening of hostilities by the Germans on 1 September at 5.30 a.m.

In Rome the Council of Ministers announced that Italy would 'take no initiative in military operations'; the enigmatic policy of Moscow was discovered to mean that Soviet troops would not move for at least the time being. Chamberlain's critics appeared to expect an instant declaration of war, and were disconcerted by mysterious signs that some talks were still going on. The essential cause of the slight delay was the insistence of the French General Staff that there must be a forty-eight hours period after the presentation of a French ultimatum so that mobilization could proceed without the risk of German air attack. Italy also confused the issue. There was a strange panic in Rome on the evening of 31 August when the British authorities, more or less accidentally, cut off telephonic

communication with Italy; this followed Mussolini's proposal
earlier in the day for a conference to review the clauses of the
Treaty of Versailles. Ciano thought it necessary to make an
emotional appeal to Loraine against war between their two
countries: Loraine was 'on the verge of tears'. But he promptly
took steps to forestall any hostile move by the British Mediterranean fleet. Mussolini made further proposals for discussions, but these fell through when Halifax insisted on prior
withdrawal of German troops from Poland. On Sunday,
3 September, at nine in the morning, the British Ambassador
informed the German Government that unless satisfactory
assurances were received by 11 a.m. Great Britain would be at
war with Germany. The coming of war was announced by the
Prime Minister at 11.15. In the afternoon similar action was
taken by France.

War Guilt in 1939

The British people entered the Second World War in a sober
mood, widely convinced, however, that it was unavoidable. A
frame of mind had been created by German action in the Czech
crisis, and they had come to regard it as a challenge to their own
courage and standards of international conduct; the challenge
appeared to have been deliberately repeated in the German
attack on Poland. This growing tendency to regard every
German show of force, physical or oratorical, as a direct threat
to themselves was powerfully sustained by the press and by the
assumptions of politicians (including those of the Government
parties). There is no doubt that if Hitler had wanted to pursue
his objectives in Central and Eastern Europe without interference he would have been well advised to adopt more subtle
and persuasive methods.

Accordingly there seemed at the time to be no possibility of
another debate on war guilt. It was nevertheless pointed out in
the first edition of this work, published in 1940, that there had
been equally little doubt about German guilt in 1914, and that
this had not prevented the enunciation of very elaborate

theories of Allied war guilt by European and transatlantic scholars after 1919. While it seemed useless to discuss the possibility of a 1939 war-guilt question at that time it was suggested that the historian of the future would have to ask himself certain questions. Was war inevitable? Was there a German danger to England – immediate or delayed? Had Great Britain any greater obligation than other powers to defend smaller countries, such as Poland, against German attack? Could England be blamed for the peculiarly ferocious methods of Nazi foreign policy? Were German aims as far-reaching as the violence of her methods appeared to suggest?

To each of these five questions, left unanswered in 1940, an affirmative answer might be given today, but with important qualifications in each case. It is perhaps significant that none of the five mentioned the Versailles Treaty. There does not appear to be any reason to alter the conclusion that was put forward tentatively at the time, which was that German policy could not be adequately explained as a reaction to historical conditions. Germany's more obvious, and more legitimate, grievances under the Versailles Treaty had been removed before the Nazi Party secured power in 1933. Reparation demands had been scaled down, and then virtually cancelled, between 1925 and 1932. Her status and independence as a great power had been recognized by the withdrawal of Allied troops, the right to rearm (recognized in principle in 1932), and admission to the League. After 1933 she recovered the Saar, and completed her rearmament. The loss of colonies was a grievance which neither the German people nor the German Government wished to make a cause of war. The immediate cause of war was the line of events associated with her successive attacks on Austria, Czechoslovakia, and Poland in 1938 and 1939, but here her case against the Versailles Treaty was more questionable; she lost no territory in 1919 to the first two states, and there were strong arguments, on historical and linguistic grounds, for the new Polish–German frontiers, although it was never denied in England that Germany had counterclaims of considerable strength in the same areas. Defeat, the Versailles settlement, and the dark years that followed it, had called into being the irreconcilable right-wing groups, and ruined the chance of a general acceptance of Weimar republicanism; nevertheless it was the economic distress of 1928–32, much more than the events of the early twenties, which brought the Nazis to power. The development of Fascist parties in other countries also suggested that it was at least an over-simplification of the German problem to attribute Nazism merely to the Versailles settlement.

The post-war publication of British Foreign Office documents abundantly illustrates the British Government's desire to avoid a fresh conflagration. From the time of the Versailles Treaty it had doubts about the wisdom of the Polish settlement, and at Locarno it was not prepared to guarantee any German frontiers east of the Rhine; in November 1937 the French ministers were told that it did not feel called on to maintain the Austrian and Sudeten clauses to the point of war, because it was not believed that war on these issues alone would commend itself to British opinion. In 1939 Danzig and the Corridor were regarded in London as genuine irritants to Germany, but it was no longer believed that they were the genuine causes of Hitler's action. On the outbreak of war Ribbentrop's defence of German policy, in the introduction to a White Book of German diplomatic documents, maintained that Great Britain had instigated the war in order to prevent Germany's recovery of her legitimate position as a great power, and this theme was taken up by Alfred von Wegerer in a short book which circulated in an English translation in the United States, but not in England, in 1940. Many years later, in 1964, a very elaborate study of war origins by Professor David L. Hoggan, *Der erzwungene Krieg*, published in Tübingen, presented Halifax as the real author of the war, plotting, like Grey before him, to encircle Germany and to persuade Poland to reject reasonable German demands. This is an isolated work which has not been taken very seriously in any quarter. The opposite view, which blames the British and French leaders for timidity and connivance and credulity in the face of outrageous Nazi forcefulness, has had a much greater vogue, conveniently and misleadingly summarized by equating 'appeasement' with 'surrender'.

But in fact the British aim was neither the encirclement nor the encouragement of Germany. To begin with it was appeasement in its original, constructive sense of promoting those peaceful conditions which were assumed to be the basic aspiration of all peoples and governments, but it was assumed even in the twenties that the German sense of grievance after defeat was a complex emotion which could be at one and the same time genuinely felt and coolly exploited for political advantage. Appeasement in turn became a sophisticated policy of concession and economic aid with the aim of satisfying popular German feeling sufficiently to take the wind out of the sails of the militarists; it was on these lines that the search for a *modus vivendi* was justified to the British Cabinet by Eden early in 1936. There was never any doubt among Cabinet ministers and the Chiefs of Staff after 1933 that a rearmed Germany would either make war or threaten war; British rearmament planning and a sense of responsibility for the amelioration of European conditions were continuous from this point onward. The change in policy after 17 March 1939 is thus more apparent than real. It was still believed that Hitler was exploiting genuinely felt grievances and there still seemed a likelihood that he would stop if threatened. The Government now felt strong enough to enter a war if he did not, without believing that issues such as the German claim to Danzig were by themselves worth a general war.

Chamberlain's judgement of Hitler's personality (not on the whole it would seem differing from that of Halifax and his Cabinet colleagues) favoured the 'brain-storm' theory that he was a brutal, fanatical man, basically shrewd, but liable to be pushed into violence by his own gusts of passion rather than by long-term plans of gain or aggression. It accordingly seemed necessary to take care not to 'drive him over the edge', and to try to separate him from the wilder and more fanatical followers who worked on his feelings. Nevile Henderson shared this view. Chamberlain had looked for signs of madness at Berchtesgaden in 1938. A week after the outbreak of war on 10 September 1939, he noted his opinion that Hitler had been wavering up to a late date, half inclined to accept a 'peaceful and reasonable solution of the Polish question', but that 'at the last moment some brainstorm took possession of him – maybe Ribbentrop stirred him up'. There was some support for this view at the time among historians, who had been interpreting German policy in 1914 on rather similar lines, and it was remarked in the first edition of this work that 'whatever the ultimate aims and vaguer dreams of Hitler there seems no evidence to support the view that he had any precise objective after March 1939 except the destruction of Poland'.

Today there is ample evidence from German sources of a severely practical programme of rearmament, carefully planned to produce victory when Germany's relative superiority was greatest (in 1939 or 1940), and not when full re-equipment was complete (some time between 1943 and 1945, when her opponents' rearmament would be complete too). The basic political assumptions seem to have taken their final shape by 1937. By this stage Hitler had abandoned hope of an agreement with Britain and France, was reasonably sure of Italian co-operation, was convinced that the Reich's need for food supplies and raw material sources called for territorial expansion 'in the East', and was apprehensive about Russia's growing power, which he had affected to despise in *Mein Kampf*. The element of careful calculation in his plans is emphasized by his indifference to the restoration of the 1914 frontiers except over Poland, and even here his main purpose in 1939 seems to have been to mobilize German opinion; he had maintained amicable relations with Poland readily enough between 1934 and 1938. Similarly he could not bother himself about colonies, which would be cut off in war by blockade. In fact he was uninterested in any overseas expansion. His ultimate plan was concrete, grandiose, and not original: it was the creation of a great European land empire, comparable in size and resources with the United States, incorporating the fertile agricultural land of Poland and the

Soviet Ukraine. The enslavement or extermination of a great many Slavs was implicit in the programme; the hegemony of Europe a natural consequence.

Chamberlain had never doubted that a rearmed Nazi Germany would throw its weight about, and from 1934 onward his steady support of rearmament up to the limits of security shows his belief that only the certainty of effective resistance would check German heavy-handedness by showing Hitler that it would be unprofitable. He also banked on the anti-war sentiments of the German masses. If he failed to penetrate the deeper intentions of Hitler he was not so gullible as not to suspect that they might exist. He knew that England's huge responsibilities throughout the world vastly exceeded her resources. He had no gifts for warlike oratory, and if he had he would not have used them: his aim was to bring all Europe to a reasonable state of peace. 'When war was still averted, I felt I was indispensable, for no one could carry out my policy,' he wrote on 10 September 1939. 'Today the position has changed.'[1]

[1] Feiling, *Neville Chamberlain*, p. 417.

XIV

Diplomacy at War

The Phoney War

The war did not diminish the responsibilities of the Foreign Office, but there was a change of purpose: the aim of diplomacy was no longer to persuade others to keep the peace but to arrange with allies and neutrals the most favourable conditions for waging war.[1] An indispensable preliminary, in view of Hitler's evident doubts on the point, was to insist on French and British zest for the battle. After the rapid German victory in Poland in September 1939 the Führer, seeking a cheap escape with the spoils, proposed in an address to the Reichstag on 6 October a conference to discuss the reorganization of 'the space recognized as a sphere of German interests'. He had, he said, no demands (apart from colonies) on France and Britain. The War Cabinet ignored this peace offer, and Chamberlain's comment on the 12th was intended merely to affirm Allied resolution. 'The plain truth is that, after our past experience, it is no longer possible to rely upon the unsupported word of the

[1] The systematic publication of British diplomatic documents stops with the outbreak of war, but there is a detailed and authoritative account of wartime foreign policy in Sir E. Llewellyn Woodward's *British Foreign Policy in the Second World War* (1962), an 'official' history based on a full study of the official documentation. Also based throughout on full access to the cabinet papers and other official material are Sir Winston Churchill's six volumes of wartime memoirs, *The Second World War* (1948–54), and Lord Avon, *The Eden Memoirs: The Reckoning* (1965). These three works offer authoritative first-hand accounts of most of the major transactions with foreign Governments during the war, although ketschy on economic aspects.

present German Government . . . the proposals in the German Chancellor's speech are vague and uncertain, and contain no suggestion for righting the wrongs done to Czechoslovakia and Poland.'

This amounted to a refusal to negotiate with Hitler on any terms which he could conceivably accept, and this unyielding stand against Germany was not to be modified at any stage during the war. Hitler's violent speech at Munich on 8 November may be taken to mark the end of the first Nazi peace offensive, although peace feelers from allegedly unofficial German sources, never easy to evaluate, continued to reach London throughout the war.

The Government had been reinforced on the outbreak of war by the return of some of the Tory dissidents. Labour stayed out, rather indiscriminately grumbling. Winston Churchill went to the Admiralty and the ringing warrior tones began to be heard again in the land. But conditions did not yet favour the initiative in boldness, either on the fighting fronts or in diplomacy. Although Chamberlain believed that Hitler's greatest chance of victory had passed in September 1938, he doubted whether the Anglo-French forces could win a decisive victory even in a long war. He thought that the best hope lay in a collapse of the German home front, accelerated by propaganda and the Allied blockade. In any case, there was every advantage in postponing the heavy fighting in France while British rearmament was rushed along. Moreover, the balance of strength would be disastrously tilted against the Allies if the four greater neutrals – Italy, the Soviet Union, Japan, and the United States – became actively hostile or seriously obstructive. All this called for careful and rather circumspect diplomacy. The conditions suited Lord Halifax, who continued in office as Foreign Secretary until December 1940.

So in Europe, in the absence of serious fighting during the winter of 1939–40, blockade (directed by the Ministry of Economic Warfare) became the Allies' chief weapon, and was the subject of much diplomatic activity. But it was a weapon that had to be used with a certain caution.[1] Forcible rationing of neutrals was considered impracticable. The aim was to prevent the re-export to Germany of any goods which had reached the adjacent neutral countries after passing through seas under British control, and to limit the export of home produced goods from these countries to normal pre-war quantities. The enforcement of these conditions was made possible by the exercise of the belligerent right of contraband control. Any neutral Government which disliked the cost and inconvenience of having its shipping intercepted and cargoes seized was invited to negotiate a war-trade agreement, by which uninterrupted passage could be secured in return for an undertaking to limit exports to Germany to the required figures. By the spring of 1940 war-trade agreements had been concluded with Norway, Sweden, Holland, Belgium, Iceland, Denmark, Greece, and Spain.

Even Italy proved acquiescent for a time. While her irascible dictator balanced the risks of unwanted war against the safety of inglorious peace, she accepted some economic restrictions, although with much fuss and protest. The Allies had their dilemma too: was it possible to conciliate her without building up her economic strength as a potential ally of Germany? Would economic pressure revive the sanctions mentality of 1936? Her conduct in 1914 and the hope of an Anglo-Italian Agreement since 1937 probably made the Foreign Office a little too optimistic, but they felt justified in taking some risks. Normal imports for Italy's own use were therefore allowed through the blockade, although goods in transit to Germany were seized. Italy responded for a time; early in February she even seemed on the point of concluding a comprehensive trade agreement including the sale of aircraft and ammunition to England. But something swayed the Duce to the side of war: perhaps no more than Hitler's ominous silence for some weeks. The deal was abruptly cancelled on Mussolini's order, and the British then banned German exports of coal to Italy by sea. Italy protested strongly on 3 March. Duce and Führer met on

[1] W. N. Medlicott, *The Economic Blockade* (1952), i, pp. 43–58.

the Brenner on 18 March, and the decision to fight was taken. Britain began to withdraw shipping from the Mediterranean at the end of April.

The shadow of German and Italian power hung too ominously over the Balkan states for them to make any decisive move into the Allied camp, although as Britain and French capital controlled over 50 per cent of the Rumanian oil industry it was possible for a time to resist German pressure in that field on equal terms. But the guarantees given to Rumania and Greece were becoming an embarrassment to all the parties. Turkey was more forthcoming; she probably feared Italy and Russia more than Germany, but took her stand against all three. The final agreements of the Anglo-French–Turkish Pact, which had been provided for in the declaration of 12 May, were signed on 19 October 1939, and in the economic field she decided not to renew the Turco-German clearing agreement, but instead to move towards a free-exchange policy in association with France and England. They signed a valuable, but expensive, chrome agreement with her in Paris in January 1940.

But there was an undoubted fragility about the Allies' position in the Mediterranean which was reflected in the circumspect reactions of Britain's other ally, Portugal, to proposals for a war-trade agreement. Moreover, the attempt to ease relations with Italy caused irritation in the United States. The war had thrown American opinion into considerable confusion, and Englishmen, who had become accustomed to listening respectfully to trenchant American appeals for resistance to aggression, were not a little disconcerted when the same voices now called urgently on America to keep out of war. But it seemed that there was at least passive goodwill. The arms embargo was repealed on 3 November. Then came the first of many reminders that the United States did not intend her goodwill to be taken for granted.

For two months, until the end of January 1940, there were repeated protests over alleged discrimination against American shipping, the seizure of German exports, and the interception of American mails, all reminiscent of Lansing's protests in 1915 and 1916. The British Treasury's attempt to husband the dollar resources needed for the purchase of war material in the States, by cutting down on the purchase of American citrus fruit and tobacco, met with further official protests. These criticisms soon found their way into the American Press. But there was not much public response, and this may explain why the State Department's phase of ill-humour began to be replaced by a more co-operative attitude in the spring of 1940.

Altogether then the first winter of the war passed without any notable successes – or disasters – for British foreign policy. The neutrals were mainly concerned to keep themselves out of trouble. Wartime foreign policy required the building up of a happy relationship with available allies; all the Dominions entered the war except Eire, and with France a good working partnership was speedily achieved. Unity of command and a Supreme War Council were established on the outbreak of war, and five inter-Allied meetings between 12 September and 5 February 1940 made detailed arrangements for the co-ordination of action in the supply of munitions and war material, economic warfare, financial policy, and wartime trade. Six allied executive committees were set up, and others were added later. There was an agreement in the spring not to make a separate peace. And yet the anti-British feeling in France which German propaganda sought so industriously to fan was never entirely absent, and it was to secure a powerful stimulus with France's defeat in the following summer.

It was fed, too, by Communist propaganda. 'Revolutionary defeatism' was one of the many trials of the French Government and did nothing to ease relations with Moscow. The British, however, clung to the faint hope that after all Russia might, somehow or other, be brought into the fight against Germany. A barter agreement for the exchange of Russian timber for rubber and tin was concluded in London on 11 October 1939, and there were great hopes of a more far-reaching economic bargain, which Maisky seemed to favour but did nothing to advance. It was the Soviet attack on Finland on 30 November, far more than the Soviet–German pact of

August, which marks Stalin's real breach with British opinion; doubtless there was some element of delayed shock in this, and no disposition this time to explain away the aggression as a self-defensive gesture against Germany. Soviet Communism was angrily denounced as the predatory twin of Naziism. Russia's expulsion on 14 December 1939 from the League of Nations, following her rejection of a British proposal that she and Finland should accept the League's mediation, was undoubtedly popular.

But this was no justification for the reckless moves in the Finnish crisis which made war with the Soviet Union possible for a time. The military implications of these plans lie outside the story of foreign policy, and it is only necessary to recall the fact that aid to Finland was visualized as part of a complicated scheme whereby the opening of communications through northern Norway and Sweden would enable the Anglo-French forced to control and cut off Swedish iron-ore supplies to Germany. The plan pleased the French, who wanted to deflect the German armies from the French frontier, and preferred a front in Scandinavia to one in the Balkans. It was strongly supported by Churchill. The Opposition called emotionally for help to Finland. The folly of a strategy which promised to add the Soviet armies to those of the Allies' existing enemies does not seem to have bothered either the Government or the Opposition. The plan failed through the inability of the Foreign Office to persuade Norway and Sweden to permit the passage of Allied troops, formally requested at the beginning of March 1940; shortly afterwards, Finland made peace. Molotov at any rate had no desire to widen the war, and he eased relations with Great Britain a little by an offer through Maisky on 27 March to resume the trade talks which had been suspended since November.

Planning for Survival

The military disasters from April to June 1940 transformed the purpose and spirit of British foreign policy quite as powerfully as they did the conduct of the war. For this there were three principal reasons. The first was that the dictates of prudence seemed no longer relevant: just as all resources, including the full strength of the Navy, would be expended in resisting an invasion, so too British diplomats had to use whatever language of threats or persuasion was needed to ensure survival, without too much regard for long-term impressions. The second was that Germany's victory greatly simplified international relations: every state in the world had now to ask whether it wished to mount the Axis band-wagon or pray for its overthrow. Issues were suddenly and sharply defined; it was reasonable to hope that a great many nations might be persuaded in due course to help or share the British cause. The third was the impact abroad of the new leadership.

Winston Churchill, who succeeded Chamberlain as Prime Minister on 10 May 1940, was not only a powerful and immensely dominant leader. He was also a highly experienced, resourceful, and persistent politician, a first-rate administrator who understood the capacities of modern official machinery, and a formidable and persuasive negotiator. In December 1940, when Halifax went to Washington to succeed Lord Lothian as Ambassador, Eden became Foreign Secretary and virtually the second figure in the Government until July 1945. In the field of foreign policy this was a potent partnership, with Eden supplying a professional balance and the consolidation of many bold and rapid Churchillian gestures. It was essentially an attacking diplomacy in place of the circumspection of recent years. Their personal relationship and habits of intimate consultation were free of all serious friction, even if Churchill's methods of work were as trying to Eden as they were to the Chiefs of Staff. Eden in any case could not resign a second time. He was not an innovator by nature, and it was undoubtedly the Prime Minister's unflagging drive that created the opportunities.

While it was true that many of Hitler's potential victims had a new and urgent interest in Britain's survival it was not to be expected that the more vulnerable would take risks in defying the Axis powers. For that matter, Britain herself made propitiatory moves as Italy and Japan became bolder. British attempts to meet Italian complaints about the blockade, which for a time had made good progress, were abruptly ended by Mussolini on 31 May. The search by Reynaud, the French Prime Minister, for a basis of agreement with Italy, and Roosevelt's attempt at mediation, were equally ineffective. The Duce explained from his balcony that Italy had only one watchword – to conquer. Italy declared war on France and Britain on 10 June.

The Anglo-Japanese Agreement of 19 June settling the Tientsin question (see p. 167) after long negotiation was regarded as a fair arrangement before the fall of France, but the Japanese were soon claiming that it was too favourable to Britain in the new situation. In spite of threats and some nasty incidents the Japanese did not attack the largely undefended British or Dutch possessions, but it was considered expedient in London to agree to the closing of the Burma Road for three months. Cordell Hull publicly condemned the decision, without showing any desire to confront Japan himself.

Indeed, the first tendency in the United States and Latin America was to write off Britain as doomed. Rumours, many of Swedish origin, circulated in June and July as to the Cabinet's willingness for negotiation. They seem to have had no foundation, and were partly countered by the dramatic offer on 16 June of an Anglo-French union (first proposed to the War Cabinet it would seem by Chamberlain) and by the attempts to persuade the French Government to send the French fleet to British ports and to continue the war from overseas bases. These evidences of Britain's continued determination were strengthened by the crippling of the French fleet at Oran on 3 July. New Ambassadors of high political standing – Sir Stafford Cripps and Sir Samuel Hoare – were appointed to the two vital capitals, Moscow and Madrid. Hitler's peace 'offer' – which offered singularly little – in his speech of 19 July was totally rejected by the English Press on the 20th and by Halifax in a broadcast speech on the 22nd. The Battle of Britain ended successfully in September.

But these events, although finally proving the country's will to survive, gave no recipe for victory. The main task of British diplomacy for the next twelve months was to develop latent goodwill among the neutrals into the greatest possible measure of practical assistance, which often meant no more than a not uncourageous decision on their part not to recede from previous engagements. Again, as in the first period of 'phoney war', it suited Britain's desperate rearmament plans that major fighting was suspended in Europe, although Wavell's victorious offensive in North Africa (December 1940–March 1941) and the honourable but disastrous intervention in Greece (March–April 1941) involved military effort and anxiety. The broad aim was, however, to weaken Germany by air attack and the maximum economic pressure, while building up strength for an ultimate major offensive, which could hardly be won, however, on British resources alone.

In these plans the increasing participation of the United States was vital. Her co-operation made possible the introduction in July 1940 of a drastic change in economic–warfare strategy to 'control at source'. This meant that the examination of neutral cargoes for contraband would normally take place in the ports of the exporting country and not on the high seas. Interception at sea remained, but only as an occasional check and ultimate sanction. Thus the navicert system, an invention of the First World War which had been applied voluntarily in the United States and elsewhere in 1939, was made compulsory. At the same time, the imports of the remaining neutral states of Europe were rationed to the amounts needed to maintain their own economic life, and arrangements were made under which the many facilities available in British ports throughout the world would be withheld from the ships of neutral companies carrying on trade injurious to the Allied cause. The tacit agreement of the United States authorities to allow these arrangements to be operated in American ports was vital to their success, and facilitated their introduction into Latin American countries. There was more positive help from some private American sources. Insurance companies soon began to withhold the comfort of insurance from neutrals who were being refused it by British companies. In turn, the United States Treasury under Mr Morgenthau relied heavily on British expert information in the development of plans for freezing Axis assets.[1]

Otherwise the United States authorities were more generous in advice and exhortation than in practical help until Roosevelt had been safely re-elected in November 1940. At the highest level, nevertheless, the intimate correspondence between Churchill and Roosevelt, which had started in September 1939, served splendidly the needs of the crisis weeks. Its first major achievement was the successful formulation of the destroyer-bases deal. On Churchill's suggestion this was presented in August as a voluntary surrender of British bases in the Caribbean islands to which the United States could reply as it liked; he did not wish it to be linked with the transfer of the fifty destroyers, but the constitutional position in the United States required that there should be a *quid pro quo* for the transfer of the ships. At the end of August American officers had secret discussions with their British equivalents in London, and the beginnings were laid of the joint military plans that came to fruition in 1942. The British Government also appreciated the continued flow of supplies, for which it had, however, to pay, from factories which it had also, in large measure, to finance, and although everything was paid for until November it became necessary for Churchill to appeal frankly to the President on this point in a famous letter which reached him on a Caribbean cruise. The idea of leasing material to Great Britain was first mentioned by Roosevelt on 17 December 1940, and in March 1941 Congress passed the necessary legislation.

But in Europe it was evident that while none of the neutrals felt secure for a moment against German–Italian attack each hoped that if he fed the crocodile enough the crocodile, as Churchill had said so baldly in January 1940, would eat him last. Each accordingly worked to a definition of neutrality which in practice gave the Germans all they asked for in the

[1] Medlicott, *The Economic Blockade*, i, chap. 14.

economic field; they gained some military and political advantages too in certain cases. There was also, however, some encouragement for the British.

M. Molotov's offer on 27 March 1940 to resume negotiations for an Anglo-Soviet barter agreement may have been no more than a sign of his alarm at the deteriorating relations of the two countries over Finland. His talks with Sir Stafford Cripps in Moscow in February probably had the same purpose. But he did not recede from his offer when Anglo-French fortunes deteriorated during the following weeks. The Churchill Government accordingly decided to send Cripps to Moscow on an 'exploratory' mission, and when the Soviet Government objected to this makeshift arrangement, appointed him as Ambassador in place of Sir William Seeds (who had been in England since January). The British Cabinet hoped that the barter agreement (rubber and tin from England, timber from Russia) would be valuable for political reasons; and Molotov on 21 May anticipated and scotched these hopes in a broadcast (no doubt for German consumption) in which he said that Soviet–German trade could not be discussed. But he promised that imports from Britain would not be re-exported.

Cripps was not entirely disappointed by his reception in June. He had a long interview with Stalin on 1 July, the importance of which has probably been underrated (as by Churchill in his memoirs). Stalin reminded Cripps that Germany could not win as long as Britain commanded the seas; he was not so gullible as to accept what Hitler said at its face value, but did not believe that it was physically possible for him to dominate Europe or the world. This was, after all, Stalin's first interview with a foreign Ambassador since his reception of Ribbentrop in August 1939, and Britain's forces were at their lowest ebb; it seems reasonable to assume that it was a calculated gesture of encouragement. This view is strengthened rather than otherwise by the fact that, in spite of Cripps's increasing exasperation, the commercial negotiations made no progress.

The plain fact was, of course, that Britain had nothing to

offer the Soviet Union in adequate compensation for a breach with Germany. Stalin had decided to feed the crocodile, and to impress himself on Hitler as a worthwhile but not subservient collaborator. The Soviet–German Agreement of 11 February 1940 gave Germany a six-months advantage in agreed commercial exchanges, although with provision for periodic balancing-up of the account which the German negotiators found highly annoying. Although the possibility of a barter agreement with England may have been kept alive in order to strengthen the Soviet bargaining position with Germany, Cripps was unrealistic in his strongly expressed belief in August that with 'some sacrifice and a thoroughness equal to that of Germany' Britain could substantially improve Anglo-Soviet relations. He was even prepared to hand over the gold reserves of the Baltic states, which had been blocked in London after the Soviet occupation of the states in June. Owing partly to American objections there were no concessions over Baltic gold, but he was authorized in October to propose a comprehensive agreement, including, on the part of the Soviet Union, a neutrality as benevolent to Great Britain as that applied to Germany, in return for an economic agreement and *de facto* recognition by Great Britain of Russia's position in recently occupied territories from the Baltic States to Bessarabia. But the Russians were completely unresponsive, and in some remarkably disillusioned language Cripps advised the British Government in December 1940 to abandon the negotiations. Eden could not bring himself to do this until the following February 1941. Anglo-Soviet relations were cool and inactive for the next few months.

The smaller European neutrals also moved with extreme caution. But they were prepared to accept, and even extend, their economic dependence on Britain. Sir Samuel Hoare, as Ambassador to Spain, acted quickly and decisively in urging a generous policy of remedying Spanish shortages (but without harm to the blockade) as the best means of preventing her active support of the Axis. Franco declared his country's non-belligerency on 13 June 1940, and the Spanish Press let itself go against Great Britain; but Spain did not enter the war, in spite of German and Italian blandishments. Turkey did not feel bound under her treaty with Britain and France to declare war on Italy, and the German victories were a severe shock; but the battles of Oran and of Britain modified this pessimism, and as in Spain a programme of economic and military assistance was designed to keep her out of Axis control. A Turco-German commercial agreement was signed on 25 July 1940, but this was partly countered by an Anglo-Turkish financial agreement on 22 November and by plans for extensive purchases and supplies. So too Sweden, Switzerland, and Portugal fed the crocodile but continued to do business with the outer world, and at this stage it was satisfactory to the British Government that they were determined to keep out of the Axis camp.

For a time the Balkan situation looked a little more hopeful. The British Government offered help after the unexpected success of the Greeks in throwing back the Italian attack, which began on 28 October 1940; fearing that Germany would be drawn into the Balkans, the Greeks did not seem over eager to accept, but later changed their minds. Late in February 1941 Eden with General Dill visited Athens and Ankara, and they spent most of March in Cairo. Their influence was decisive in persuading the British and Dominion Governments, in spite of some apparent doubts on Churchill's part, to send military help to Greece, and after the Yugoslav Government had first signed the Tripartite pact on 25 March and then repudiated it on the 27th, there were efforts to concert action between Yugoslavia and Greece. But the new Yugoslav Government also showed well-founded doubts as to the wisdom of bringing the Germans into the Balkans. Hitler solved the problem for them by his attack without warning on both Yugoslavia and Greece on 6 April. The British forces were withdrawn, following the Greek Government's chivalrous advice, on 21 April. Turkey continued prudently to maintain her neutrality.

Diplomacy could have done little more in a situation dependent on the severest realities of military weakness, but it may well be asked whether it should have done less: the fear of a loss of chances or of reputation through overcaution certainly encouraged the plunge into this futile repetition of the Norwegian adventure.

The Soviet–American Reinforcement

The widening of the ring of major belligerents promised bigger and more immediate rewards than the attempt to join hands with Hitler's smaller victims in Europe. It is true that Sir Stafford Cripps could make no headway with the Soviet Government during the first half of 1941. On 19 April he passed on a warning as to German preparations for attack which Churchill decided to send to Stalin; Eden gave a similar message to Maisky on the 16th. There was no response, and Churchill's sense of timing led him to observe to Cripps on the 22nd that 'frantic efforts to assure them of your love . . . only looks like weakness' and that the right course should be 'a sober restraint on our part, and let them do the worrying'. The flight of Rudolf Hess to Scotland in May no doubt strengthened fears in Moscow of an Anglo-German bargain. Stalin sought to mollify Hitler with desperate gestures of friendliness, and ended by rudely and publicly denouncing poor Cripps as a mischief-maker on 14 June. But none of this lessened the British Government's conviction that the opportunity for collaboration might soon arise. When the German invasion took place on 22 June 1941 Churchill broadcast an assurance of British assistance to Russia on the same evening.

The German attack transformed the character of the war, even although it was Hitlerite strategy rather than British diplomacy that forged the Anglo-Soviet Alliance. The military situation was in any case too desperate for either Government to waste time in recriminations. As soon as Stalin had convinced himself that the British did not intend to follow the German invasion by making a bargain with Hitler he proposed a short agreement providing for mutual assistance and support and excluding the conclusion of peace except by mutual agreement. This was signed in Moscow on 12 July. On 19 July he asked for a 'second front', either in France or northern Norway. The somewhat apologetic tone of the first three paragraphs of this message is curious and was perhaps an attempt to explain his earlier collaboration with Hitler on the grounds of military necessity.

Churchill was forced to reply that these proposals, as well as further suggestions in early September for a campaign in France and the Balkans and in mid-September for the sending of twenty-five or thirty British divisions to the Caucasus, were all impracticable, and Stalin spoke bluntly of his disappointment.[1] He may have failed to grasp the true nature of the problems of limited manpower, logistics, and shipping which governed British strategy; he certainly acted from the start on the assumption that the survival of Soviet Russia was the supreme war aim to which all other plans and ideals should be subordinated. He never seems to have believed that Britain and the United States, as the representative capitalistic powers of the Western world, would welcome or assist this victory except in so far as it contributed to their own survival. Nevertheless, the basis of the grand alliance had been rapidly constructed; and the United States, still neutral, was not aloof.

The complexities of her position were due to the ambiguities, in Roosevelt's eyes, of both American public opinion and Japanese intentions. It had been decided in November 1940, in high-level strategical discussions in Washington, that if the United States ever found herself at war with both Germany and Japan she would concentrate first on winning the war in Europe. But to both Roosevelt and Churchill, and doubtless to Stalin as well, it was apparent that the annihilation of Hitler might well be delayed by an American breach with Japan, although it might also be the case that only such a breach would bring America completely and officially into the world struggle.

As it happened the Japanese themselves gave the next decisive turn to developments, and we must now look briefly at the course of events in the Far East. Bogged down in China, they could hardly expect to survive a German defeat; on the

[1] G. M. A. Gwyer, *Grand Strategy*, III (i), pp. 95–8, 146–50.

other hand, they did not wish to involve themselves gratuitously in war with the United States and Great Britain. They wanted time and a free hand to crush China and build the Greater Japanese prosperity sphere in Eastern Asia. Japan's accession to the Axis on 27 September 1940 was rightly interpreted as a warning to the United States and of course Great Britain not to interfere with these plans; it did not foreshadow an early entry into the war. The Burma Road was reopened on 28 October 1940, without incident.

The British Cabinet's aim was to discourage Japan from entering the war by limiting her stocks of imported raw materials, relying on the fact that she was the most vulnerable of the great powers to economic pressure. A Far Eastern committee under Mr R. A. Butler was appointed to keep policy under review, and it did its best to encourage the stout resistance of the resourceful Netherlands officials in Batavia to Japan's economic demands. In these economic proposals the British were bolder than the Americans for the next six months. The United States preferred total embargoes on a few commodities to any comprehensive programme of restrictions, partly in order to avoid Japanese accusations of encirclement. When rumours of a fresh Japanese advance in South-east Asia circulated in February 1941, Roosevelt had to tell Halifax that public opinion would not allow the United States to declare war on Japan unless American territory were attacked. Mr Eden's strong warning to the Japanese Ambassador on 7 February may, however, have had an effect. When Matsuoka, the Japanese Foreign Minister, visited Europe in March and April, Churchill sent him a warning through Stafford Cripps to mend his ways; the Soviet–Japanese neutrality pact of 13 April was the somewhat cryptic reply.

Instead of the joint warning by Britain, the United States, and the Netherlands desired by Churchill in April 1941, Hull began talks in May with Admiral Nomura, a new Japanese Ambassador, for a settlement based on the independence of China, and the Foreign Office watched somewhat apprehensively. But the Japanese could concede little, and the decisive moves came in July; they preferred to profit from the Soviet–German struggle to seize, not the Russian Far Eastern territories but southern French Indo-China. The United States Government, which had decided to wait for an 'overt act', froze all Japanese assets in the United States on 26 July, and with admirable promptitude and no knowledge of America's precise intentions the British Government announced a similar decision on the B.B.C. at 7 a.m. on the same day.

The intransigence of Japanese policy from this point was sustained by a conviction of spiritual dominance over the irresolute democracies. There was no doubt about the ultimate superiority of American resources and the impregnability of the United States to attack. But many in Tokyo believed seriously that after the anticipated triumph of the Axis over Russia and Britain in Europe, and after Japan had seized an unassailable position in China and the south Pacific, the Americans would lose heart and come to terms. The British view throughout 1941 was that the Japanese leaders had their own forms of irresolution, and that bold warnings of dire consequences might deter them; from this point of view the American gestures came too late. There now seems little doubt that the Japanese move into southern Indo-China in July 1941 was based on the belief that the Americans would not react. However, in the freezing arrangements the United States administration had discovered an extremely drastic weapon, and in September Roosevelt agreed that the pressure should not be relaxed. Hull continued to negotiate, partly in the hope of encouraging the peace party in Tokyo; but it was never possible to accept the minimum Japanese terms even for a temporary *modus vivendi*. On 4 December Roosevelt assured Halifax of the armed support of the United States in the event of a Japanese offensive in Malaya. The Japanese attack on the United States fleet at Pearl Harbor on 7 December 1941 took place before Roosevelt's warning to this effect had been dispatched to the Emperor of Japan.[1]

[1] W. L. Langer and S. E. Gleason, *The Undeclared War* (1953), chap. 28; R. J. C. Butow, *Tojo and the Coming of the War* (1961), pp. 234–61.

Churchill had no doubt that the entry of Soviet Russia and the United States into the war had made possible a victory for Great Britain which had hitherto been little more than a matter of faith and hope. 'So we had won after all!' he wrote later. Subsequent events confirm this view, although they also reveal the precarious military position of the alliance in its opening months. Sir Robert Craigie, the British Ambassador in Tokyo, regretted, indeed, the decision not to press Hull's counter-proposals in the last stage, and believed that a valuable breathing space might have been secured. Hitler and Mussolini, although promptly supporting their ally Japan, were evidently in two minds as to whether the Japanese alliance balanced American belligerency, and consoled themselves with the hope that the war would be won before the United States could mobilize effectively. They had feared a Japanese–American bargain. It is possible that the breathing space might have been prolonged, for Japan would then have had time to realize (following the successful Soviet counter-offensive in December) that Russian power was still uncrushed.

The immediate problem for the three allies was now to devise working arrangements to fight the war; but these soon led to wider discussions on wartime strategy and the architecture of the post-war world. Once committed to the world struggle there could be no return by the two potential super-powers to the cautious neutralism with which they had sought to evade their destinies in 1939 and 1940. Although she had a lead in wartime experience Britain could not, in the long run, match their resources. Nor could she easily reconcile herself to the ideological positions from which each of the two, robustly convinced of the uniqueness of its mission, viewed the future. This was clear enough from the start in the case of Soviet policy. It underlay the Anglo-American partnership, although hidden for a time by personal affection, dedication to immediate ends, and the common heritage and cross-fertilization of ideals and programmes between the two countries.

The Atlantic Charter, which emerged from the meeting of Churchill and Roosevelt at Placentia Bay in August 1941, was the fullest statement of British war aims that had yet appeared. The eight points of the Charter affirmed that the two countries, Britain and the United States, sought no aggrandizement; they desired to see no territorial changes that did not accord with the freely expressed wishes of the peoples concerned; they respected the right of all peoples to choose the form of government under which they would live; they would, 'with due respect for their existing obligations', further access on equal terms by all states to the trade and raw materials of the world, and they desired the fullest collaboration between all nations in the economic field; they wished to see established a peace which would afford safety to all nations to live within their own boundaries in freedom from fear and want, and to travel the high seas without hindrance; finally, the disarmament of nations which threatened, or might threaten, aggression was essential, pending the establishment of a wider and permanent system of general security. The vagueness of some of the phraseology helped to conceal the latent differences between the two Governments on certain matters, such as post-war economic and colonial policy, but was really due to the fact that as the United States was not yet a belligerent she had to state wishes rather than intentions.

The Charter was coolly received in Moscow; it contained nothing of immediate value or ideological significance to Russia, even though it committed still-neutral America to a desire for 'the final destruction of the Nazi tyranny'. With no confidence as yet in British or American goodwill, Stalin and Molotov appear to have decided that their only diplomatic asset was Anglo-American fear of a German victory. The note of harsh urgency which was thus added to the normal surly combativeness of Soviet diplomacy was no doubt intended to frighten the Western powers by the fear of Soviet defeat (or even a separate peace) but was also a means of rallying public opinion abroad to the Soviet cause. At the same time, as a German defeat must produce a renewal of the struggle between Communism and the West, it seemed desirable to use the occasion to tie down the two Western powers as speedily as possible to an acceptance of Soviet plans in Eastern Europe. On 12 August 1941, a message from Churchill and Roosevelt proposed a conference to allocate joint resources. This three-power conference took place in Moscow at the end of September with Beaverbrook representing the United Kingdom. It quickly reached agreement. Britain undertook to send to Russia ample supplies, including large quantities of American products already earmarked for Great Britain. But Mr Eden's attempt to reassure the Soviet Government that Russian interests would not be ignored in the peace settlement merely invited Molotov to give his peculiar negotiating technique an airing. In December 1941 Stalin and Molotov, in talks with Eden, rejected the idea of a general declaration of post-war intention and demanded a military alliance and complete agreement as to post-war frontiers in Europe.[1]

Although the United States Government, now at war, disliked many features of the Russian plans, which included the absorption of the Baltic states, Bessarabia, and parts of Poland and Finland, the British Government decided late in March 1942 to sign a treaty recognizing the Soviet claims to their 1940 frontiers other than those of Poland. If they expected that this substantial gesture would induce counter-concessions they were soon disappointed. When Molotov came to London in May 1942 it was found that he had raised his demands, and now the British drew back, offering instead a twenty-year post-war alliance without mention of frontiers. Rather unexpectedly, Molotov signed this document on 26 May 1942, for more urgent and immediate issues were afoot.

In spite of the reluctance of the State Department to be stampeded into territorial concessions to Russia, Roosevelt believed that he could win the confidence of the Soviet leaders, if necessary at Britain's expense. This was one aspect of a general tendency on the American side to try to improve on British methods or to take the lead where these had proved unpopular. In blockade issues with the European neutrals the Americans usually favoured a tougher line; but in certain areas, such as

[1] Avon, II, pp. 287–303.

Latin America at the beginning of 1942 and French North Africa at the end, they thought they could prove more tactful. In the case of Russia the problem of a 'second front' (in the form of a British invasion of France with token American backing) tended to monopolize all political discussion during 1942.

Although the technical objections to it were unanswerable, the United States and Soviet Governments continued to act as if they were not. In Washington in May 1942, Roosevelt and Molotov agreed to a communiqué stating that 'in the course of conversations full understanding was reached with regard to the urgent tasks of creating a second front in Europe in 1942'. Eden did not oppose its publication as a means of confusing the enemy, but he and Churchill, both before and after Molotov's visit to Washington, had made clear the impossibility of a successful invasion in 1942, and this was reiterated by the new British Ambassador, Sir Archibald Clark Kerr, in conversation with Molotov on 4 July. But Molotov now insisted on treating the communiqué as a firm promise. The purely practical difficulties were essentially matters for military decision, but diplomacy at the highest level was involved in the efforts of both Roosevelt and Churchill to retain Stalin's goodwill over these issues. Roosevelt had neatly left to Churchill the onus of refusal. It was high time for him and Stalin to meet face to face.

Tensions in the Grand Alliance

From this point until the end of the war the triumvirate of Heads of State, completely dominating their own Governments, led the grand alliance in wary collaboration, writing to each other freely and bluntly if not always quite frankly, and meeting from time to time. But whereas Roosevelt and Stalin met only twice (at Teheran and Yalta), Churchill met Stalin five times (Moscow, August 1942; Teheran, November–December 1943; Moscow, September–October 1944; Yalta, February 1945; and Potsdam, July 1945), and Roosevelt ten times (Teheran and Yalta again, and also Placentia Bay, August

1941; Washington, December 1941 and June 1942; Casablanca, January 1943; Washington, May 1943; Quebec, August 1943 and September 1944; and Malta, January 1945). Thus Churchill, although the eldest of the three, was the most peripatetic; and as he survived both, he was presumably the best fitted to stand the strain of constant travel. But the strain was heavy and the results not always commensurate with the physical effort.

Churchill's tremendous stubborn enthusiasms and commanding oratory led to some ganging up of the other two against him, but this development was not without its useful side. For the time being Britain, with her resources fully deployed and with three years of active warfare behind her, had to lead and shepherd the entry of the United States forces into Europe, and to determine the degree of aid that Russia could be given. This was certainly the position during Churchill's first visit to Moscow (12–16 August 1942). Having secured in July Roosevelt's agreement to the invasion of North-west Africa he presented this plan and a massive bombing programme to Stalin, after announcing that a landing in northern France was impossible in 1942: the reception was a mixture of gloom, some rudeness, and then a qualified approval which led in turn to a day of harsh complaint by the Soviet spokesmen. Churchill fought back, telling Stalin that he could find no ring of comradeship in his attitude. But the visit ended with a long convivial party in Stalin's family circle, and each of the great men seemed satisfied that he had impressed the other.

Relations continued on these lines during much of 1943.[1] The battle of El Alamein in November 1942 gave the British Government and people the fillip of a major victory. British land, sea, and air forces played the major part in the subsequent complete destruction of the Axis position in Africa. For political reasons a United States general, Dwight D. Eisenhower, was thought to be the most suitable leader of the allied forces in North-west Africa, and after the successful landings there on 8 November 1942 he and his American advisers were involved in some devious negotiations with both General

[1] H. Feis, *Churchill, Roosevelt, Stalin* (1957), pp. 105–279.

Darlan and the Free French; but with the appointment of Mr Harold Macmillan as Minister Resident in late December 1942 the British had more say in the political discussions. They were present in force and got what they wanted in January 1943 at the Casablanca meeting, helped by the absence of certain possible critics.

Roosevelt had been anxious to persuade Stalin to attend and he was determined that Cordell Hull should not do so. Stalin replied that the military situation was too hot for him to leave Russia even for a single day, and in any case he did not understand what there was to talk about: the British and Americans had only to complete their plans for the promised invasion of Western Europe in the spring of 1943. While the non-attendance of the Russians facilitated the acceptance of the British plans to complete the clearing of the Mediterranean along with the build-up of forces in Britain for an invasion of France, the non-attendance of Hull and therefore of Eden precluded the broader political discussions which Churchill appears to have desired.

For some weeks after the Casablanca Conference the British and American Governments looked not unhopefully on their future relations with Soviet Russia. With El Alamein and the German surrender at Stalingrad early in February 1943 the chance of an ultimate German victory had passed. The German surrender in Tunis in May 1943 was an allied victory second only to that of Stalingrad. The naval victory of Midway in June 1942 had put a similar limit to Japanese hopes. Allied defeat was now unlikely, victory probable if still far ahead. In March 1943 Eden visited Washington for talks about the shape of the post-war world. The Americans were thinking of a world security organization in which for many years executive power would be in the hands of Great Britain, the United States, Russia, and China, and although Eden doubted the capacity of China for this role he accepted the prospect of Russian collaboration. Stalin did not fail to grumble (on 15 March) at the decision to postpone the invasion of France after the spring of 1943, and he warned Churchill that any further delay would be 'dangerous' to 'our common cause'. But it was not until the Anglo-American decision, taken at the Trident Conference in May, to knock Italy out of the war and to fix 1 May 1944 for the cross-Channel invasion, that the full strength of Stalin's exasperation with his allies was revealed.

If this failed to destroy hopes of eventual collaboration with Soviet Russia it was no doubt because the British and American Governments were feeling a little guilty about their decision. They had undoubtedly spoken hopefully about an invasion in 1943. The truth of the matter was that Russian publicity had identified northern France as the only adequate field for a 'second' front, whereas the true second front of the Allies was in the Pacific. Stalin had rejected out of hand all American suggestions that he should come into the war against Japan, but Anglo-American–Chinese resistance to the Japanese forces spared him the embarrassment of a Japanese attack on the Soviet position in the Far East. He was careful to avoid trouble with the Japanese; some contraband was even allowed to flow from Germany to Japan via neutral Turkey and the Trans-Siberian railway. But he seemed unimpressed by the argument that the cross-Channel attack was being held up by the demands of the Pacific war for landing-craft, among other things. His reference to the dangerous possibilities of the situation may have meant only that Russia's military position was in danger without a substantial diversion in the West. It may also have been a warning as to the possibility of a separate Soviet–German armistice, rumours of which circulated at the time.

Certainly there was an angry exchange of letters between Stalin and Churchill in June, after which the Prime Minister discontinued the correspondence for a time. The successful Soviet counter-offensive against the Germans at Kursk in July was a further guarantee that the Soviet forces were well established on the path of ultimate victory, but the knowledge does not seem to have mellowed Stalin's judgement of his allies. One grievance was that Hess had not been brought to trial as a war criminal; perhaps Stalin genuinely believed that he was being kept ready to negotiate a separate peace with

Germany. He also complained that he was not being fully informed about Anglo-American diplomacy in Italy.

The British plans for the invasion of Italy had been accepted mainly because they provided for a continuance of the momentum of victory in the Mediterranean, whereas the concentration of available forces for the invasion of France, strongly urged in some American quarters, would have kept them idle in England throughout the autumn and winter. Approaches from Fascist quarters since December 1942 had shown the Foreign Office that defeat was likely to topple the Mussolini régime, and Marshal Badoglio himself had made overtures before the invasion of Sicily, which began on 9 July 1943. The King of Italy dismissed Mussolini on 25 July, and appointed Badoglio head of a new Government; but his problem was to extricate Italy from the alliance with Germany without becoming her victim. Badoglio at first hoped that Hitler would release Italy from the alliance, but recognizing the impossibility of this decided on 31 July to seek an armistice with the Allies. Roosevelt and Churchill were willing enough to facilitate future collaboration with the Italians by lenient treatment, but required first their unconditional surrender; and while the Italians wished to delay surrender until the Anglo-American forces were on Italian soil, Eisenhower, as the Allies Supreme Commander in the Mediterranean area, was anxious to be assured of their acquiescence or, if possible, active support as soon as possible. Throughout August there were accordingly some involved negotiations, with a series of progressively more important secret Italian agents visiting Sir Ronald Campbell in Lisbon and Sir Samuel Hoare in Madrid. But finally the Anglo-American terms for an armistice were accepted by Badoglio on 1 September. They were to be announced by the Italian Government on the eve of the invasion; and when Badoglio tried to back out, Eisenhower publicly announced on 8 September 1943 that Italy had agreed to surrender unconditionally. Badoglio confirmed this shortly afterwards.

The success of the landing at Salerno that followed was merely the prelude to a long and stubborn campaign in which

the United Nations forces had to fight their way up the peninsula in face of the reinforced German troops, and there was
continuous argument between the three Allies both as to the
usefulness of the campaign and the treatment of the Italians. It
may never be possible to say that the Prime Minister's aims
were primarily political, for he professed to see no incompatibility between the strategical programme and political objectives that he thought suitable for the Anglo-American effort
to end the war. In August, at the Quebec Conference, the
Americans were still inclined to underrate the difficulties of the
cross-Channel invasion, and to interpret the British insistence
on these difficulties as half-heartedness. The zest with which
Churchill expounded the rewards of an Italian victory similarly
led to dark suspicions as to the political ends, of a not very well-
defined character, that he was supposed to be seeking for
Britain's advantage in the Mediterranean area after the war.
All that we can say is that the tying down of large German
forces in Italy and the Balkans was regarded by Alan Brooke as
a practicable means of diverting German divisions from
northern France, and that there is no evidence that Churchill
planned major operations in the Balkans. The point is relevant
to an account of wartime foreign policy only in so far as it
affected the relations, present and future, between the three
great powers.

Stalin was not prepared to accept invitations to Scapa Flow
or Alaska in the summer, but on 25 August he proposed a
meeting of Foreign Ministers, which took place at Moscow,
19–30 October 1943. This was notable for the presence of
Cordell Hull; he and Eden agreed on most points and they had
to face some more questions about the second front, but it was
considered an encouraging sign that Molotov was prepared to
discuss post-war collaboration. He even agreed to sign a four-
power declaration providing for co-operation in the maintenance of world peace after the war, although he boggled at
first at the proposal to include China among the four. His subsequent agreement was associated with a secret assurance that
the Soviet Union would join in the war against Japan as soon

as Germany was beaten. The conference accepted Eden's proposal for the setting up of a European Advisory Commission to deal with questions connected with the termination of hostilities, although he was less successful in securing agreement as to its terms of reference. Stalin, and even Molotov, were genial, but hardly enough to justify Churchill's claim of a 'prodigious' achievement.[1]

The meeting between the three leaders themselves finally took place at Teheran, from 28 November to 1 December 1943. The site offered the maximum degree of inconvenience for the other two delegations, but Stalin was evidently determined not to go far from Russia, or to forgo the security of a Russian embassy. Consequently, the meeting was short. But it lasted long enough to show Roosevelt's determination to gain Stalin's confidence, and his belief that the chief obstacle to this was Soviet suspicion to prior Anglo-American agreement. His separate talks with Stalin were justified as a means of establishing the *rapport* which Churchill was believed to have achieved in 1942, but close observers doubted whether any real friendship existed behind the expansive affability of plenary meetings and dinner parties. Russians and Americans were agreed in deprecating the British enthusiasm for the Italian campaign and its logical continuance into the Balkans; but the single-minded devotion of the Americans to the second front in France appeared less convincing when Roosevelt proposed the diversion of precious resources for BUCCANEER, a campaign in Burma.

This plan had emerged from a meeting with Chiang Kai-shek and his wife in Cairo before the Teheran Conference began; and the promise was given without the consent of his British allies, who would have had to find the men and the material. But there was also a declaration, comforting no doubt to the Chinese leaders, that Japan would be forced to disgorge all her conquests since 1914, and this served to introduce talk at Teheran in which Stalin reaffirmed his country's ultimate entry into the Far Eastern war, and also her interest in the spoils. On

[1] Avon, II, pp. 407–20.

30 November in a private talk with Stalin, Churchill explained once again that the real problem of strategy in the West was not manpower or material but landing-craft, and he perhaps corrected some misunderstandings. Subsequently the Anglo-American staff discussions, which had been frustrated before the conference by the President's concern for Russian and Chinese susceptibilities, were completed in Cairo. Firm plans were made for the OVERLORD operation in May 1944, and on 5 December Roosevelt announced that BUCCANEER was abandoned.

The Diplomatic Road to Victory

From this point onward wartime diplomacy was less a matter of planning campaigns than of co-ordinating resources and effecting the transition to a peace of security. All the war aims that lay beyond mere victory were increasingly debated. The Atlantic Charter of August 1941 had been followed by the United Nations Declaration of 1 January 1942. The signatories in Washington included Russia and China; they reaffirmed the 'purpose and principles' of the Charter, and undertook to employ their full resources for victory. The term 'United Nations' was conveniently comprehensive and avoided the use of such contentious words as 'ally' and 'alliance'. The principles appeared meaningful and inspiring until they were measured against the needs and appetites of national governments.

The Foreign Office during 1942 drew up some tentative plans for post-war security based on the American four-power programme, but it was not until Eden's visit to Washington in March 1943 that ideas began to crystallize. Churchill desired a Council of Europe, with American backing. The State Department felt that it would be difficult to commend this plan to the American people, although they might accept responsibility for the general policing of the world. Eden had to point out that the virtual disarming of all states of the world except the big four would be difficult to commend to France and the Dominions. And what was to be done with Germany and Japan?

The will of the victors to oppose their rearmament might weaken, and the partition of Germany be followed by a new, passionate campaign for unification. Roosevelt had plans for an Anglo-American declaration about trusteeship which on the one hand would fix an early date for the independence of all colonies (including particularly the British) and on the other hand would give respectability to United States' own plans to annex certain Japanese islands in the Pacific. The setting-up of a new world organization free from the defects of the League was axiomatic. At the Moscow meeting in October 1943 Molotov, as we have seen, accepted post-war collaboration in principle, but was much more concerned with the replanning of Eastern Europe. In London, plans for the new world order continued to occupy the attention of a Cabinet committee under Mr Attlee. But it was not until the Dumbarton Oaks Conference in August–September 1944 that they took their final shape.

When they did so it was to reveal a stubborn objection on Russia's part to any degree of dependence on the untried world organization; this dissolved some of the optimism with which Russia's intentions had hitherto been viewed by Hull and perhaps by Churchill at the time of the Moscow and Teheran meetings. The difficult course of Soviet negotiations with the Poles had already supplied ample warning that Stalin did not intend to allow any interference with his dominance of Russia's satellite neighbours. In spite of the events of 1939 and 1940 the Polish Government in London had, although with difficulty, accepted the Soviet Union as an ally in 1941. But it asked for the restoration of the frontiers of 1 September 1939 and followed up inquiries about Polish officers and men unaccounted for in Russia by asking for an investigation by the International Red Cross into the German allegation that the officers had been massacred by their Soviet guards at Katyn. After a further Polish inquiry about the missing officers on 20 April 1943 the Soviet Government angrily broke off diplomatic relations with Poland.

Britain was thus faced with one of the awful dilemmas of

diplomacy: she had entered the war as Poland's ally, but she did not wish to end it as Russia's enemy. If the aims of her two allies were irreconcilable, how should she meet the conflicting challenges of expediency and goodwill? The answer could only be that after every effort at mediation had failed she must accept whatever Soviet terms seemed least harmful to Poland's future. For a time the main issue was that of citizenship: since December 1941 the Soviet Government had claimed all Polish citizens in the annexed provinces as Russian. But this was bound up with the definition of frontiers. By August 1943 the British Cabinet had come tentatively to the view that Poland must accept the Curzon Line of 1920 with compensation in Eastern Prussia and elsewhere at German expense, and Roosevelt was already converted to this view. At Teheran Stalin mentioned the Curzon Line and the Oder as Poland's future frontiers. Russia also wanted Königsberg, and agreed to Churchill's suggestion that Poland should have East Prussia and Oppeln. But Stalin showed no disposition to help the Polish underground, who were, he said, killing 'partisans' (Russian agents) rather than Germans. During the first half of 1944 Churchill's efforts to ensure friendly working relations between Russia and the Polish Government in London were harshly rejected by Stalin, who made it plain that he would recognize the Polish Government only if it were purged of its allegedly anti-Soviet elements.

D-day came on 6 June 1944, and as the Russian and Anglo-American forces advanced on Germany from east and west the politics of liberation became increasingly dominant. With the disappearance of German power Great Britain and the Soviet Union would stand face to face as the only two major European powers. There was no doubt in the Cabinet that the Soviet Government would seek to dominate the newly liberated countries in the Baltic area, Eastern Europe, and the Balkans, with the double purpose of establishing a strong defensive glacis round its frontiers and of spreading Communism; its aim might be somewhat tentative in the second case, but would not be in the first. By the early summer of 1944 Churchill and Eden were agreed as to the need for plain speaking to Stalin as to the permitted limits of Communist advance. They were determined that Britain should maintain her position in Turkey and Greece, and equally so in Italy. On 18 May the Soviet Ambassador reported his Government's agreement to Eden's proposal that the British should take the lead in Greece and the Russians in Rumania. But this proposal was greeted with something like consternation in the State Department. Yet its readiness to acquiesce in Russian plans to dominate Poland while dismissing as power politics the British efforts to keep Communism away from the Mediterranean countries was not due to mere perversity. It was rather that, while distrusting in some measure the independent political activity of all foreign states, it considered Great Britain to be more amenable to American pressure.

Anglo-American relations were moving into the condition of partnership in which the United States Government called the tune, satisfied on the one hand that Britain would usually acquiesce and on the other that it was unlikely that certain aspects of British policy would commend themselves to American opinion. It was not easy in London to decide how far the administration shared or sheltered behind these popular conceptions or misconceptions. As 1944 was a presidential-election year, there was an added incentive to pass the buck to the European partner. Thus on 9 April 1944 Hull committed himself to a public demand for the immediate cessation of supplies to Germany by the five European neutrals; but when this proved impracticable it was announced in Washington that a compromise settlement had been accepted on the urgent request of the British Government.[1] Again, a prolonged campaign in Congress for the sending of relief supplies to civilians in countries under Axis occupation had been based on an exaggerated estimate of shortages and ignored the practical difficulties of supply, but by supporting the demand the State Department placed the onus of refusal on the British Government. Internal political considerations were also presumably

[1] W. N. Medlicott, *The Economic Blockade* (1958), ii, pp. 412–6.

involved in the decision in March 1944 to reduce lease–lend supplies to Britain and to limit the British dollar balances to a billion dollars. There was a good case even from the point of view of American self-interest for a more imaginative financial policy; but the eloquent appeals of Churchill, Keynes, and others had little apparent effect on American politicians and financiers, who were wont to refer to the lack of understanding of the 'farmer from Kansas'. In the case of the Greek proposal Roosevelt at first suggested a three-power consultative machinery, much to Churchill's annoyance, but on 12 July he finally accepted the British lead in Greece for a three-months' trial period.

Altogether the semi-paralysis of American initiative during the second half of 1944 came at an embarrassing point in British wartime foreign policy. Roosevelt clearly did not intend to commit himself over Poland or other major issues, and his reported statements to Stalin and to the Poles about the frontiers were seriously conflicting until after the election in November. Churchill believed that a bargain, if a tough one, could be reached with Stalin, but he wished to bring in the new world to redress the balance of the old, and the new world was reticent. Roosevelt tried without success in July to persuade Stalin to come to a tripartite meeting in Scotland, saying frankly that it would help his election prospects. After this Britain and the United States had to watch impotently the tragedy of the Warsaw rising against the Germans in August and September, and the refusal or inability of the Soviet forces to intervene. An Anglo-American Conference in Quebec in September agreed readily on outstanding strategical issues, and too readily perhaps to a plan for the 'pastoralization' of Germany, drafted by Morgenthau and Lord Cherwell. Churchill, who had at first objected violently, agreed in order to please Roosevelt, who soon, however, came to see the absurdities of such vindictiveness, even in an election year.

With the United States holding back, it thus fell to Churchill and Eden to make the essential arrangements with Stalin and Molotov for the deployment of forces in post-war Europe.

Roosevelt agreed somewhat reluctantly to Anglo-Russian discussions in October, which would, however, be preliminary to a later tripartite meeting. A British proposal in January 1944, accepted by the Soviet Government in February, had already fixed the Soviet zone of occupation of Germany southward from Lübeck some 200 miles west of Berlin, but it was not until after the Quebec meeting that Roosevelt agreed that British forces should occupy the north-western and American the south-western zone: he had been holding out since the Teheran meeting for the reverse. At the Moscow meeting (9–18 October 1944) Churchill and Stalin agreed to some strangely precise percentages as to their respective influence in the liberated states: the practical effect was that Soviet Russia took the lead in Rumania and Bulgaria, and the British (in accord with the Americans) in Greece; there was to be a fifty-fifty division in Hungary and Yugoslavia. Molotov later secured an 80 per cent share in Hungary. Meanwhile Churchill and Eden strove desperately to bring the London group of Poles to agree with Stalin on the Curzon Line and to agree with the Russian-sponsored Lublin group about the future government of their country. British forces, directed at one point by Churchill himself, prevented a Communist seizure of power in recently liberated Greece in December, and for this action and its intervention in Italian politics the Government earned the public disapproval of Mr Stettinius, the newly appointed Secretary of State.

The Yalta meeting of the three leaders in February 1945 was of decisive importance in determining the terms of Russia's entry into the Far Eastern war, and Roosevelt promised her substantial advantages at China's expense without consulting either Churchill or Chiang Kai-shek. Churchill signed the agreement to these terms against Eden's advice.[1] Nevertheless it was the Moscow meeting of October 1944 which had really decided the balance of forces and influences in post-war Europe.

Churchill tells us that at the moment of victory 'apprehension for the future and many perplexities had filled my mind as I

[1] Avon, II, p. 513.

moved about among the cheering crowds'.[1] His concern was for the future of his country in a world threatened, as he thought, by an implacable Soviet power in Europe and an unrealistic government in Washington; the death of Roosevelt on 12 April 1945 had but added to the current uncertainties. The new President, Harry S. Truman, seemed for a time to share Roosevelt's view that Britain and Churchill represented a resurgence of old power politics of which the United States was innocent and from which the Soviet Government could be restrained within the new United Nations Organization. At the Potsdam Conference in July, called primarily to dispose of the ruins of German power, Truman seemed sympathetic towards some of the British problems, but the doubt remained. Meanwhile the United Nations Organization was set up at the San Francisco Conference (26 April–26 June 1945) with Eden, supported by Attlee and Halifax, as leaders of the British delegation. It was satisfactory that both the United States and the Soviet Union were members; it was hoped that in this, as in other matters, the victors would co-operate more readily than they had done twenty-five years before. Shortly afterwards the atom bomb, the existence of which had been quietly mentioned by Truman to Stalin at Potsdam, ended the Far Eastern war and inaugurated an entirely new era of great-power politics.

[1] W. S. Churchill, *The Second World War*, vi, p. 495.

XV

Bevin

Victory in the Second World War as in the First was achieved at a heavy cost in men and wealth. It soon became all too clear that the country would not be able to maintain the onerous position as one of the world's 'big three' that it had held at the moment of victory. In some respects the position was similar to that of the nineteen-twenties, but there were notable differences. There was again competitiveness among the victors, but whereas Britain and France, the two dominant powers, had a rough equality in strength and influence in the twenties, now the Soviet Union and United States pulled far ahead of the next grade of states in both military power and economic resources. The British imperial system, based on a world network of strategical bases, co-operative Dominions and dependent territories, on sterling and on sea-power, had survived, under strain, in the twenties; it was now to lose vital power. Of less significance, perhaps, was the fact that a new party had come to power which rather prided itself on its readiness for change.[1]

A Socialist Foreign Policy?

It may well be that the actual response of a Conservative Government to the external crises of the later nineteen-forties

[1] For the post-war period there are two useful surveys of British foreign policy of medium length: C. M. Woodhouse, *British Foreign Policy since the Second World War* (1961) and F. S. Northedge, *British Foreign Policy* (1962). The Chatham House *Survey of International Affairs*, more or less annual volumes under various editors, give a consecutive detailed account from 1946.

would have been little different from that of Mr Attlee's Government, and it is certainly the case that the main emphasis was on domestic reformism, with a circumspect approach to welfare economics and state control of the 'commanding heights' in the Labour Party's election programme. In his first statement in the Commons the new Foreign Secretary, Mr Ernest Bevin, left no doubt as to the new Government's intention to continue the foreign policy to which its leaders had adhered in the wartime coalition, and he specifically referred to its intention to do so in the case of Greece.

Nevertheless the party's propagandists and publicists had for years been claiming, in rather general terms it is true, that they stood for a socialist foreign policy which would give a lead to democratic forces throughout the world, and be in contrast with what was called the 'shameful record' of pre-war Toryism, dedicated to the defence, at whatever the cost, of capitalism and all the reactionaries of the old order. In *Let Us Face the Future*, virtually an election manifesto, the National Executive of the Labour Party had claimed for itself 'a common bond with the working peoples of all countries', and continuity in foreign policy was deprecated from the start by Michael Foot and other Labour back-benchers in the new parliament. The result was that the main critics of the conceptual framework of Attlee–Bevinite diplomacy during the next five years were found mainly on the left of the Labour Party, while the Tory opposition tended to be more critical of tactics than of the programme.[1]

In fact the leaders of the Labour Party had by no means repudiated the party's traditional slogans and heady aspirations. Disarmament, the rule of law, collective security (through the United Nations now), the abjuration of power politics, colonial emancipation, and the achievement of a socialist civilization as the only foundation of a lasting peace, all continued to be referred to at suitable intervals. Bevin, while following a very realistic policy, justified it as a practical approach to such goals.

[1] M. A. Fitzsimons, 'British Labour in search of a Socialist foreign policy' (*Review of Politics*, April 1950).

Those who advocated the rule of law must be prepared to enforce the rule of law; the international police force must be supplied with policemen. At many points he had merely to back the more relevant among the contradictory plans of the leftists. However, the essential basis and justification of his policy was not the pursuit of ideals but the handling of immediate post-war difficulties as they arose, by the best means at his disposal.

In so doing (closely in agreement throughout with Attlee and their leading Cabinet colleagues) he effected some major changes in the basic aims of British foreign policy, thereby reversing or in some cases completing the tendencies of the inter-war years. The first and probably the least controversial of these was to make collective security (in the framework of British interests) a reality by an adequate British contribution and by ensuring the co-operation of powerful like-minded friends. This involved not only the continuance of conscription but also the willing acceptance of United States political and military leadership, now that she seemed ready to play a role in world affairs commensurate with her strength. It also involved the realization of Churchill's efforts (rather unenthusiastically accepted by the United States at the time) to restore France's position in Europe as the basis of a Western European grouping which would be some counter weight to Soviet and also American preponderance. A second development was to accept responsibility for the defence of Western interests wherever they were threatened, and not only in the restricted areas (west of the Rhine and so on) of the pre-war years. As late as January 1947 Bevin professed to have doubts as to whether Russia or Germany was the greater danger,[1] but as the preoccupation with Communism became decisive the problem of security became world-wide, and the tendency to give priority to empire defence disappeared. The third major development was the acceptance of the need for major changes in the Commonwealth, including in particular the abandonment of political and strategical control over India,

[1] Duff Cooper, *Old Men Forget*, p. 371.

Burma, and Ceylon, but without in any sense destroying the Commonwealth; he stood for the growing belief in the Labour Party that in its free-association form the Commonwealth would be a more viable entity than in the past.

These were the broader trends of Bevin's five years of office, and they went a long way towards adjusting British policy to the changed conditions of the post-war world. The process of adjustment was not complete by 1950, and it was fiercely challenged in some quarters. It had yet to be seen whether Britain could play a major role in all three fields – Commonwealth, Anglo-American, and Western European – nor was it at all certain that other powers interested in each field would welcome her contribution in the terms that she herself had chosen. The first eighteen months were particularly frustrating. Not only was the United States seemingly anxious to withdraw from Europe but she was also harshly critical of the continuing Commonwealth links, and not at all anxious to regard the Anglo-American relationship as one involving peculiar obligations on her part. Bevin's problem was increasingly that of bringing the United States and the Western European powers into a system of regional defence. But more immediate than any of these problems was that of the country's financial viability, the indispensable basis of any successful foreign policy.

America and the Sterling Problem

For the first time in history sterling became daily news: earlier monetary crises, not excluding those of 1914 and 1931, had been by comparison transitory and esoteric. Now, with the decline of empire, the defence of the pound got more publicity than the defence of the frontiers; and if the man in the street could not yet quite understand the dollar problem, he at least knew now that it existed. The new Government's first major crisis was due to the abrupt attempt of the United States Treasury to impose its own financial authority on the world. Before very long this was replaced by a more co-operative attitude, but sterling was still fighting for its life twenty years later.

The Government, in accordance with the wartime plans, hoped to regain and improve on the country's pre-war economic standing. Britain had lost during the war 28 per cent of her merchant shipping tonnage, exports had dropped to about one-third of the pre-war level, and debts of over £3,500 million, mainly in the sterling area, had been incurred. The income from overseas investments, insurance, shipping, and other sources on which she had relied to cover her annual excess of imports over exports was greatly diminished and it was planned to increase exports to at least 175 per cent of the pre-war volume to cover the gap. Accordingly she looked to the United States for help in financing imports and meeting other external charges during the early post-war years while the economy reconverted itself from its heavy wartime tasks.

It seemed, however, that the new administration in Washington did not propose to be the arsenal or banker of democracy in peacetime. The war with Japan ended quickly on 14 August 1945, and the first shock was the prompt discontinuance of lease–lend supplies on 21 August.[1] Negotiations for a loan conducted by Lord Keynes followed in Washington in September. After refusing to grant either a credit of $6,000 million as a free gift or an interest-free loan, the United States Treasury agreed to a loan of $3,750 million at a 2 per cent interest, repayment to start in 1951. The British experts hoped, far too optimistically as it turned out, that this, together with a Canadian loan of $1,250 million, would be just sufficient to cover the total adverse balance which Britain was expected to have accumulated by 1951. But the Americans also insisted on the full application of the Bretton Woods system, which implied the ending of Empire preferences and full convertibility of sterling by 1947, and a settlement with the sterling creditors before 1951.[2]

[1] Harry S. Truman, *Year of Decisions* (1955), pp. 145–52, 409–11.
[2] R. W. Gardner, *Sterling–Dollar Diplomacy* (1956); cf D. C. Watt, 'American Aid to Britain and the Problem of Socialism' (*Personalities and Policies*, pp. 53–80).

This was dollar diplomacy with a vengeance. The arrangements would be heavily in America's favour, for they would enable Britain's sterling creditors to buy if they chose in the dollar market without there being any liberalizing of the United States system from which British exports might benefit in compensation. There was a convenient American theory that economic co-operation within the Commonwealth in the form of preferences was morally indefensible, whereas protection, as exemplified in the high American tariffs, was a natural and legitimate expression of a healthy national life. When the United States signed a treaty of alliance with Nationalist China in November 1946 there were confident prophesies in the American Press as to the vast gains that would result for American exporters, mainly at Britain's expense, in the Far East and India, soon to be independent. The British occupation forces were withdrawn from Indo-China and Indonesia, but Washington disapproved of the decision not to retire from Hong Kong, Singapore, and Malaya. The large-scale measures to combat Communist terrorism in Malaya were, for a time at least, misunderstood. The moralistic current in American foreign policy, which had raged so powerfully against Nazi, Fascist, and Nipponese wickedness in recent years, now dashed itself for a time against residual imperial barriers, mainly British. The unnecessary violence of this attack was due to something much more concrete than the vague humanitarian sentiments of American liberals. Powerful interests undoubtedly hoped to profit at Britain's expense.

Since the two powers remained in close alliance the moves and pronouncements of Britain's critics in the United States were more akin to the attacks of a parliamentary opposition at home than to the more fundamental enmity that was being shown so nakedly in Moscow. For the same reason Attlee and Bevin persevered in their efforts to make Anglo-American co-operation the basis of British foreign policy. But for at least twelve months after VJ-day the American mood was puzzling. American leadership in world affairs was now taken for granted, but it was evidently hoped that this would be confined to the

negotiations of reasonable settlements through the United
Nations. Accordingly, many American political writers and
even politicians were clearly anxious to persuade themselves
that the Soviet Government aimed at nothing more than a
somewhat rapacious garnering of the fruits of victory, similar
to the 'power politics' that the British were supposed to be
industriously pursuing in Greece and Turkey and the Middle
East. For this reason Churchill's speech at Fulton in Missouri
in March 1946 was unpalatable when he asserted that the Soviet
leaders desired 'the indefinite expansion of their power and
doctrines', although his call for a revival of the Anglo-
American front as a means of resisting Soviet pretensions found
quiet approval in some American quarters. In April and May
the debate on the ratification of the loan agreement recalled the
battle in Congress over lease–lend in 1941. The shadow of
Communism was over the discussion and isolationist opposition was defeated by a majority which had heard Senator
Vandenberg and others justify the agreement as a matter of
'intelligent American self-interest'.

During the autumn and winter of 1945–6 the Council of
Foreign Ministers, set up at the Potsdam Conference, held a
series of meetings mainly to discuss the European peace
treaties. The Soviet diplomatic technique of calculated stubbornness was for a time exploited. The London meeting (11
September–2 October 1945) produced Soviet demands for a
share of the former Italian colonies, the cession of Trieste to
Yugoslavia, what amounted to a free hand in the Balkans, and a
final abrupt demand for the exclusion of the French and Chinese
foreign ministers. The meeting broke up at this point. Some
conciliatory gestures by the American Secretary of State, J. F.
Byrnes, followed, and it began to appear that Molotov's
intransigence was really due to the exclusion of Russia from
the administration of defeated Japan. The State Department
probably had a guilty conscience about this (the British
Government was also uneasy at being virtually excluded) and
offered concessions at the Moscow meeting (16–27 December)
which were followed by a rather more accommodating attitude

on Molotov's part. After this, experts got to work in London on the drafting of the peace treaties, which were examined at a further Foreign Ministers' meeting in Paris (April–June 1946), and then by twenty-one states (including the major powers) from July to October. Treaties with Italy, Rumania, Bulgaria, Hungary, and Finland were eventually signed in Paris on 10 February 1947.

In the course of these negotiations the virtual control of the Balkan states was secured by Russia, while Italy was kept in the American orbit. Molotov abandoned his earlier demand for a colony in North Africa. Although a crisis was rapidly approaching over German affairs Byrnes seems to have retained some optimism about future Soviet intentions until the summer of 1946. Truman had been increasingly sceptical on the point since January but he was probably anxious to avoid an open breach with Russia before the mid-term elections in November. While the American attitude remained doubtful the British ministers felt that any faint chance of an understanding with Russia ought not to be thrown away. In December 1945 Bevin had offered (unsuccessfully as it proved) to extend the Anglo-Soviet Treaty of 1942 from twenty to fifty years, and a year later he was still protesting his desire for understanding with Russia. Apart from the tactical need to keep the door a little ajar there was much diffused pro-Soviet feeling in the Labour Party to be considered.

The Palestine Question

Meanwhile the Palestine question was placing a noticeable strain on Anglo-American relations. Bevin had promised to solve it and he could do so only by reconciling the would-be irresistible force of Zionism with the would-be immovable body of Arabism – something which baffled Conservative ministers had conspicuously failed to do before the war. The Peel Commission had recommended partition in July 1937; the Arabs had rejected this solution angrily, and continued to insist that Palestine must remain an Arab state, and preserve

its Arab majority. The White Paper of May 1939 had then
limited Jewish immigration to a total of 75,000 over the next
five years, but this seemed to shock everyone except the
Arabs; in 1942 a congress of the Zionist Organization in the
United States adopted in the Biltmore programme an uncompromising plan for the setting up of a Jewish state after
the war. Faced with these extreme demands on both sides the
British Government felt that it could only look for a compromise solution, or work to maintain the existing balance by
force, or return the mandate. The chances of the first were
never bright, but might have had some success with resolute
American backing. Truman, however, accepted the Biltmore
programme, backed the Zionist demand for the immediate
entry of 100,000 Jewish refugees, and evaded any commitment
to help in enforcing the decision on the Arabs.

Although Truman's memoirs are silent on the point it is
usually accepted that his attitude was not uninfluenced by the
usefulness of 5 million Jewish votes in the forthcoming elections. This may well be the case, and with the complete
absence of an Arab lobby in Washington and of any word of
recognition of the Arab point of view in the American Press
there was no counter-inducement. But many other arguments
supported the Zionist case. The endemic habit of deploring
British imperialism, with school textbook recollections of
George III and the more or less complete ignoring of the
evolution of the free-association Commonwealth under George
V and George VI, had recently manifested itself in a fresh
phase of grumbling about British policy in India, stimulated
as usual by the skilled publicists of the Hindu Congress Party.
The sole purpose of the Labour Government was to bring the
Indian groups, as bitterly divided as the American states in
1861, to a peaceful agreement on the constitution of an independent India. But it was widely proclaimed that the Labour
politicians were slightly disguised old-time imperialists,
determined to preserve the empire by the old divide-and-rule
tactics; and all this reinforced Zionist propaganda. A really
violent Press and propaganda campaign in the United States

attributed every hesitation to agree to the complete Biltmore programme to British chicanery and power politics. The essential strength of the Zionist position lay, however, in the goodwill and sympathy created by Nazi persecution, and in a widespread emotional response to the yearning for immigration to the 'national Home'. In England the Labour Party in 1944 had itself advocated immigration sufficient to give a Jewish majority in Palestine, and had airily dismissed the problem of Arab resistance with the comment that the Arabs should be encouraged to move out as the Jews moved in.

Attlee, however, after coming to office, followed Churchill in treating the problem as one for inter-Allied, and particularly Anglo-American, handling, and did his best to counter the assumption that the reluctant Arabs, or even the embarrassed British, should be expected to solve it alone. Bevin managed to secure the appointment of an Anglo-American committee of inquiry in November 1945; it reported in April 1946. It condemned violence and rejected partition, but recommended the issue of 100,000 immigration certificates pending the elaboration of new trusteeship arrangements which would in due course replace the mandate. Truman agreed promptly to the proposal for 100,000 visas, but showed great reluctance to take part in discussions as to the working out of detailed plans. After much delay a small Anglo-American committee was appointed for this purpose in July 1946, and it reported in favour of provincial autonomy for several years, after which, if conditions were suitable, partition or a federal state would be introduced. British proposals for provincial autonomy had already been put before Parliament in July 1946; they included provision for substantial external aid from United States, German, and Jewish sources, and a continuance of overall British responsibility through the High Commissioner for foreign affairs, customs and excise, and defence. Truman rejected the plan, and the Jewish Agency did likewise. In the meantime, violence was increasing, as organized Jewish terrorist groups assassinated British, Arabs, and dissident Jews; the King David Hotel in Jerusalem was blown up, with 152 casualties, in July 1946. On 18 February 1947 Bevin told the House of Commons that as Jewish demands for, and Arab opposition to, the creation of a sovereign Jewish state were irreconcilable, and as the British Government had no authority under the mandate to impose either solution or partition the country, it must refer the problem to the United Nations.

Although the unpleasant incidents of the terrorist campaign and the heavy cost of £100 million a year to maintain the British forces may have created some mood of escapism in London, there was no intention on the Government's part to surrender the British position in the Middle East; on the contrary, if a choice had to be made the Government was prepared to lose the goodwill of the Zionists in order to retain that of the Arabs. But the tossing of this hot potato to New York can only be understood in the wider context of British diplomacy. Just at this point the mounting threat from Communism was producing signs of a major reorientation of United States policy for which Bevin had been anxiously waiting. The reference to the United Nations, foreshadowing a surrender of the mandate, did not end the peculiar Anglo-American tendency to bicker over Middle Eastern issues, but it probably eased the course of negotiation elsewhere.

Western Defence and Marshall Aid

The original plan for the administration of defeated Germany by unanimous agreement in the Control Council between the four commanders of the zones of occupation (Soviet, American, British, and French) had broken down over the question of reparations. The British zone was an industrialized food-deficiency area which depended on the agricultural surplus of the Soviet zone. In defiance, as the Western powers argued, of the Potsdam provision that Germany should be treated as an economic unit, all such surpluses flowed east and not west, together with reparations in the form of a proportion of the current output and capital equipment of the British and

American zones. The practical effect of this was that the British Government had to allocate £80 million, partly from its meagre dollar resources, to supply the British zone during 1946. When in April 1946 Molotov rejected Byrnes's proposal for a twenty-five-year treaty to ensure the demilitarization of Germany he cited the refusal of the other powers to agree to an unconditional figure of $10,000 million for Russian reparations from Germany as a whole. It was suspected that the provision for joint inspection and intervention was an equally important consideration. On 3 May the United States Commander, General Clay, suspended reparations deliveries from the United States zone, and this was followed by the fusing of the British and American zones into a single economic and political unit, Bizonia. It was evident that the iron curtain which Churchill had denounced at Fulton had descended round the Soviet zone; economic information was withheld and all contacts with the other zones and with officials of the Western powers were excluded as far as possible. In July Molotov not only denounced Clay's decision but by accusing the Western powers of hostility to German unity and a desire to stifle Germany's economic development made a bid for wider influence. Byrnes countered in a speech at Stuttgart on 6 September which held out the prospect of a provisional government for an economically self-supporting Germany. He also said that American forces would remain in occupation.

All this meant that the United States Government, although still hesitant about precise commitments, was moving towards a more thoroughgoing and open support of a Western defence system than had seemed necessary to Truman hitherto. From this point until the completion of the Atlantic alliance in 1949 Bevin displayed first-rate diplomatic skill in seizing opportunities which might not recur to bring both the United States and the Western European Governments firmly into such a system, and his tactical ability was as remarkable as his broad grasp of the ultimate objectives. There were three points in particular during the next twelve months at which he acted with great assurance and success on rather general American hints of a growing concern for Europe.[1]

Soundings in New York in December 1946 had drawn from Byrnes a promise that the United States would ease the economic burden of the British Government in Greece and Turkey, although it could not undertake at this stage to provide military equipment. It would appear that Bevin agreed with Churchill as to the danger of hurrying on a Western European grouping which might induce isolationist reactions in Washington, either because of the survival of wartime coolness towards de Gaulle, or more generally through a fear that Europe was ganging-up against the new world. But by the beginning of 1947 American interest in the idea was obviously growing. De Gaulle had retired from the French leadership in January 1946. After a succession of weak governments the friendly Léon Blum was in office for a few weeks, and in January 1947 Bevin swiftly completed the negotiations for an Anglo-French treaty of alliance, valid for fifty years, on ground prepared by the British Ambassador, Duff Cooper. This was accepted by Blum's successor, and ratified on 4 March, being appropriately known henceforth as the Dunkirk Treaty. Accompanying it was a remarkable series of official pronouncements as to Britain's devolution of world responsibilities. Agreement on the future constitution of an independent Burma was announced in London on 28 January (on the same night the temperature was the lowest since January 1940). On 14 February the decision to refer the Palestine problem to the United Nations became known. On 20 February Mr Attlee announced that power would be transferred into Indian hands not later than June 1948. And on the 21st the State Department received advance notice that British assistance to Greece and Turkey must cease entirely on 31 March.

The severe cold and the fuel crisis perhaps added some irrelevant drama to these fundamental decisions; Bevin was nearer to the truth, but was perhaps not stating the whole

[1] Cf. Roy E. Jones, 'Reflections upon an eventful period in Britain's foreign relations' (*International Relations*, October 1963).

truth, when he attributed the precipitate British action over Greece and Turkey to financial stringency. The dollar loan was certainly running out more quickly than had been anticipated, but the Attlee Government seems if anything to have been over-optimistic about its financial position at this stage, and it continued to shoulder heavier commitments elsewhere. It looks as if this was a well-judged psychological challenge on Bevin's part. The State Department certainly reacted splendidly; the Under-Secretary of State, Mr Dean Acheson, and his colleagues immediately decided that Great Britain 'had within the hour handed the job of world leadership, with all its burdens and all its glory, to the United States'. Truman and George Marshall, a new Secretary of State, agreed. On 12 March the President enunciated the Truman Doctrine: a promise of economic support to 'assist free peoples to work out their own destinies in their own way'. Greece and Turkey were mentioned, but the application was general. Acheson recognized that 'Bevin had thrown me the ball' and he threw it back with an advance notice to Bevin of the speech of George Marshall at Harvard on 5 June. This said that there must be some agreement among the countries of Europe as to their requirements from the United States before anything further could be done. 'I seized the offer with both hands,' said Bevin later, and he took the initiative at once in a meeting in Paris which led to the presentation of definite plans for Marshall aid.

It is said that Marshall made his offer only after an assurance from George Kennan that the Soviet Government would reject it. But he denied in his speech that the new policy was directed against any country or doctrine. The American leaders had to face many critics who disliked the idea of foreign aid as much as they feared foreign entanglements which would involve them in another war. So it was certain that they could act only on a strong lead from Europe; this gave Bevin freedom to manoeuvre, and, still seeking to keep the door ajar for Russia, he arranged with Bidault to invite Molotov to come to Paris on 27 June to discuss the possibilities. Molotov's dilemma is

obvious enough: massive economic aid flowing into Europe
and in particular into the Soviet satellite countries would not
only advertise capitalism (supposed to be on the verge of
collapse) but would also strengthen American political
influence; on the other hand, the dollars had a certain attraction
and could not be lightly rejected. He proposed in effect that the
European countries should be left to state their own requirements without outside scrutiny, and he objected to aid to
ex-enemy countries until the needs of the rest of Europe were
satisfied. Bevin and Bidault insisted on the need for a comprehensive European plan. When the Soviet Government refused
to go further, invitations were sent out for a meeting of
interested states which met promptly on 12 July. The Czechoslovak Government, after accepting, was forced to withdraw
through Soviet pressure. The Committee of European Economic Co-operation was set up without Soviet participation on 15
July 1947, less than six weeks after the Harvard speech.

From this point the technical discussions as to Europe's
economic needs went rapidly ahead, and led in due course to
the programme of substantial aid which was still in 1947 the
essential contribution of the United States to victory in the
Cold War. Although the ultimate deterrent was her atomic
ascendency the immediate need seemed to be to counter
subversive activity by restoring the confidence of the European
peoples in the economic future of their own countries. Bevin
and his advisers on the T.U.C. were convinced that the Soviet
Union hoped to engineer mounting civil strife in various West
European countries, using strikes, political action, and ultimately, if opportunity offered, force. In the meantime there was
no compromise over Germany; the reparations deadlock continued. At the London Conference of the Foreign Ministers
(25 November–15 December 1947), Molotov again insisted on
the handing over of $10,000 million worth of reparations
before the taking of any steps to secure Germany's economic
viability, although he also demanded that a central German
Government should be set up as speedily as possible and be in
existence before the convening of a peace conference. He

refused any statement of accounts, and replied to the British and American complaints as to the cost ($700 million a year) of feeding Germany that they were using Germany as a base for the development of war industries. His aim was evidently to retain four-power control of Germany in the hope that the setting up of a central government would in some way or other facilitate 'democratic' (Soviet-dominated) predominance. In the meantime no agreement could be reached on German frontiers or an Austrian settlement, and the British, United States, and French ministers broke off the conference on 15 December.

In the discussions which immediately followed the breakdown Bevin received a third indication, again in rather general terms, as to Marshall's willingness for closer ties with Europe. The London Conference and the virulence of Molotov's language had almost killed the lingering hopes of both Marshall and Bidault that a *modus vivendi* with the Soviet Union could be arrived at by tough but even-tempered negotiation – although Bidault had seemed until very recently to be following the earlier American tendency to stand aside from the Anglo-Soviet confrontation. The Dunkirk Treaty had not led to military discussions, and the Foreign Office was still speaking of these as 'premature' in November 1947. While convinced that the closer political and military co-operation between the West European states and America was necessary, Bevin had hitherto confined himself to economic discussions, partly because of their urgency, partly because no more could be achieved at the moment. For this reason perhaps he appears to have spoken about economic integration to the French with an enthusiasm which hardly squares with his subsequent cautious attitude to the subject. Duff Cooper tells us that during the Paris conferences in the summer Bevin had been entirely in favour of 'the Western bloc, of customs union with France, common currency, etc.' which Duff Cooper himself had been advocating since 1944.[1] The convertibility crisis may also have genuinely, although temporarily, increased the attractiveness

[1] Duff Cooper, *Old Men Forget*, p. 376.

of close economic links with France. However, Commonwealth representatives in September promised to back sterling,
Marshall aid was assured, and Cripps succeeded Dalton in
November. Then in December, when Bevin broached the
idea of Western union, Marshall promised to do what he
could to help in Washington, subject to the approval of Congress.

Bevin publicly launched his plan in a speech in the Commons
on 22 January 1948. He had already discussed it with Bidault,
and set in motion negotiations with the Benelux countries
(Holland, Belgium, and Luxembourg). In explanations to
Field-Marshal Montgomery, the C.I.G.S., on 23 December of
the strategical implications of the programme he had made it
clear that the concerting of an Anglo-French treaty with the
Benelux countries was only a beginning, and that he hoped to
bring in other non-Communist countries, including the
Scandinavian and Italy, and above all the United States. In his
speech he justified his programme by emphatic criticism of
Soviet policy, which was aimed at disrupting production at
home and nullifying American aid; there was a ruthless effort to
bring Greece into the Russian orbit. He looked beyond Europe
to the Commonwealth and the colonial possessions of the
Western European states to ensure co-operation on a grand
scale. The reaction of Parliament and the Benelux countries
was favourable, and Communist manifestations drove the
point home. At the turn of the year the offensive of Greek rebel
bands against the town of Konitza and the constitution of a
People's Republic in Rumania foreshadowed the seizure of
power by the Communist minority in Czechoslovakia in the
last week of February. *Pravda* angrily denounced Bevin's
programme as an attempt to rebuild Germany's war-potential
for use against the Soviet Union, but the opposite was the case:
knowing that Germany was to remain disunited, Bevin felt he
could risk her economic rehabilitation. France now agreed to
merge her occupation zone with those of the other two powers,
and a conference in Brussels in March speedily completed
discussions on a West European treaty of union, which was

signed on 17 March. It provided for economic, social, and cultural co-operation as well as for defence.

Bevin's achievement is notable not only for the vigour and good judgement with which he used his opportunities but also for the robust way in which he survived disappointments and criticism. On the other hand, it must be recognized that some of the talk about Britain's decline was unwarranted and was probably a help on balance – fear of the loss of the British shield certainly did much to create some crusading zeal in Congress and the triumph of Marshall's economic aid programme. In the form of E.R.P. (European Recovery Programme) this passed the Senate on 14 March 1948 and the House of Representatives on 2 April, by substantial majorities. The fears and criticisms as to the danger of bolstering the British socialist régime expressed in the Congressional Hearings and elsewhere were thought by some observers to be even more offensive and direct than those accompanying the loan discussions of 1946. If some of the American leaders had private misgivings on the same lines they were, however, prepared to avoid public offence, and to leave the British to work out their socialist experiment for themselves.[1] Bevin and Attlee had also to deal with the grumblings of their own left-wingers, but they probably gained support both abroad and at home from those who felt no confidence in the alternative.

The Government's subservience to the United States, with its corollary, hostility to the Soviet Union, was the basic complaint of these dissidents; a hundred Labour M.P.s criticized the official policy on these lines in an amendment to the Address in November 1946. Their views were crystallized in a pamphlet, *Keep Left*, published in May 1947 and signed by their chief spokesman, Mr R. H. S. Crossman, and fourteen supporters. The large Labour majority clearly allowed the luxury of back-bench dissent. In the Government's first year Franco's régime in Spain and Bevin's failure to do anything in particular to 'liberate the Spanish people from their Fascist

[1] E. Watkins, *The Cautious Revolution* (1950), pp. 366–7; W. E. Mallalieu, *British Reconstruction and American Policy* (1956), p. 188.

prison' (as the party chairman, Harold Laski, had promised in 1945), was the most prominent theme. But the *Keep Left* group complained more comprehensively of an absence of unifying purpose in both home and foreign policy. Views ranged from the advocacy, by a diminishing group, of wholehearted co-operation with the Soviet Government to plans for the creation of a socialist 'Third Force' which would keep the balance between Soviet and American power blocs. It was hoped that the radically inclined Congress Party in India, with which Labour had close links, and the socialist Governments of Australia and New Zealand, together with a general leftish trend in some other parts of the Commonwealth, might make possible a linking of European democratic socialism and the emergent members of the Commonwealth. Bevin wanted all this and the powerful Anglo-American link too. It has been pointed out that there were other possibilities of Anglo-American tension in the Labour preference for long-term bilateral commodity and bulk-buying agreements abroad, which offended against American zeal for multilateralism; but in fact this did not become a major issue. Many party critics, however, such as Mr Zilliacus, deplored the regional agreements culminating in the Atlantic Alliance as a retreat from the United Nations back to power politics.[1]

The years 1948 and 1949 put the new policies to the test, with satisfactory results on the whole. The Palestine question was in the hands of the United Nations from April 1947 onward, and a partition plan was put before the General Assembly in September and continued to be debated until its adoption on 29 November; as it was known to be unacceptable to both Jews and Arabs the British Government did not support it and was not prepared to join in imposing it by force. Instead, it was announced that the mandate would be terminated on 15 May 1948, and that British troops would be withdrawn by 1 August. No longer able to leave the enforcement of their impracticable schemes to the British, the United

[1] M. A. Fitzsimons, *The Foreign Policy of the British Labour Government*, 1945–1951 (1953), pp. 50–4.

States and other Governments were obviously disconcerted by this move; there were some routine condemnations of British policy, on the ground now that it was a sell-out to the Arabs, but the Soviet Government proposed that the Security Council should take steps if necessary to enforce the partition plan, and this was quite sufficient to lead the United States to abandon partition and propose a temporary trusteeship on 19 March 1948. The practical result was that the state of Israel was proclaimed on 15 May and hastily recognized by the United States; the British forces drew out as smoothly as possible, and the converging attacks of the surrounding Arab forces were decisively defeated by the tough Israeli Army. Britain was the scapegoat of everyone, and particularly of the Arab states.

From this situation were to flow many of the essential difficulties of Britain's Middle Eastern policy in the fifties, complicated by the continued American reluctance to support British policy wholeheartedly there. This was in marked contrast to the situation in Europe, although in the Pacific too it was becoming evident that the State Department preferred to go its own way. Bevin's firmness and good timing were seen at their best as the German crisis mounted during 1948, and here the power of the Anglo-American bloc was fully demonstrated.

After the Brussels treaty of 17 March 1948 had been warmly approved by both the United States and Canadian Governments, the Vandenberg resolution, carried in the United States Senate by 64 votes to 4 on 11 June, proposed United States support for collective security measures within the terms of the Charter. Talks in Washington and London between representatives of the Brussels powers and the Canadian and United States Governments for a wider security system continued successfully during the second half of the year. Their trend was sufficiently obvious and well-publicized to call forth the strenuous opposition of the Soviet authorities, who chose Berlin as the duelling ground. The main lines of a constitution for a federal West German republic and its full association with the West European economy were set out in the London agreement of 1 June 1948, published on the 7th. The new plans included currency reform for Germany, and when the introduction of the new Deutsche Mark was announced for the three Western zones on the 18th, Marshal Sokolovsky announced a currency reform for the Soviet zone and the whole of Berlin, whereupon the three other occupying powers introduced the new West German mark into their sectors of the city. Since April the Russians had been progressively limiting traffic into and out of Berlin; now, on the excuse of repairs, it was completely severed. The Russians were not asking for war. They were gambling on what seemed a reasonable technical assumption that the other powers had no means of breaking the blockade of this island in the Soviet seas. Bevin's answer in the Commons on 30 June was uncompromising. 'A grave situation might arise', but 'none of us can accept surrender'. Nevertheless he opposed reference of the issue to the Security Council as long as possible, believing that direct negotiation would be more likely in the end to provide a compromise.

The Berlin blockade continued until 11 May 1949. The problem of supplying two and a half million people was solved by a vast use of transport aircraft; Great Britain contributed a third of the flights, a quarter of the tonnage of supplies, and the bulk of the ground organization. The United States was otherwise the main contributor, sending in planes from other theatres, and adding a strong force, based on British airfields, of B-29 Super-fortresses carrying the nuclear deterrent. If anything was needed to consolidate the Atlantic community it was this crisis, and the North Atlantic Treaty was duly signed in Washington on 4 April 1949, with Bevin representing Great Britain. In addition to France and the Benelux countries the other signatories were the United States, Canada, Iceland, Italy, Norway, and Portugal. Cutting his moral and psychological losses, Stalin dropped the currency question, and agreed to lift the blockade on the sole condition that the Council of Foreign Ministers should be called to discuss the future of Germany.

The problem now was to complete as far as possible the institutional readjustments of British diplomacy necessitated by the continuous extension of commitments since March 1939, and to deal at the same time with a series of individual crises which put these new arrangements to the test. When Bevin died on 14 April 1951 at the age of 70, a few weeks after relinquishing the Foreign Secretaryship through ill-health, defence arrangements had still to be elaborated in Europe, and the Middle and Far East were in crisis. There was little improvement during the short and uncomfortable tenure of the office by his successor Herbert Morrison.

Containing Communism in Asia

The establishment of the multi-racial Commonwealth gave the Labour Government a sense of achievement which the United States could neither understand nor share. The more constructive side of the new relationship was seen in the Colombo Conference of January 1950, a further example of Bevin's imagination and initiative. It was the first conference ever held of Commonwealth Foreign Ministers, and its meeting in an Asiatic Dominion under the chairmanship of Mr Senanayake, the Prime Minister of Ceylon, was at once a reminder of the gravity of Asian problems and of the equality of status of all the Commonwealth members.

By this stage the United States administration had come to value the major British campaign against Communism in Malaya, but it remained lukewarm about such developments as the Colombo programme. The conference, which was attended by Pandit Nehru and the Ministers of External Affairs of Canada, Australia, and New Zealand in addition to Bevin and Philip Noel-Baker from the United Kingdom, specifically affirmed that there was no incompatibility between the maintenance of Britain's traditional links with the Commonwealth and her development of newer and closer links with Western Europe. The sessions dealt mainly with the problems of South-east Asia, and as a result very largely of the initiative of Mr P. C. Spender of Australia a consultative committee was established on a basis of mutual self-help to plan a detailed programme of economic and social aid to underdeveloped areas. The committee met in Sydney in May and set up a Commonwealth Committee for technical assistance which was working at headquarters in Colombo by the end of the year. Plans to spend over £1,000 million over the next six years were drawn up. These developments certainly gave the Commonwealth a new role, even if the newer Dominions distinguished themselves by their insistence on political neutralism and the heavy Colombo programme was dependent on contributions from non-Commonwealth sources, including the United States.

With the Communist forces in eastern Asia making the running for the next few years British policy was to support the United States in efforts at containment, but to be on the alert to prevent the irrevocable step which might make it impossible to draw back from a major war. Bevin had combined firmness with the attempt to keep open the normal diplomatic channels with Moscow even during the Berlin airlift crisis, and with a hostage to fortune in the shape of Hong Kong there was no disposition to hurry into a breach with the Communist régime in China. Besides, in Labour circles in England there was little enthusiasm for Chiang Kai-shek's régime and some tendency to regard Mao Tse-tung's followers as progressive nationalist patriots rather than true Communists. Britain recognized the new régime on 6 January 1950. When the Soviet delegate proposed on 10 January that the Communist Chinese representative should replace the Nationalist on the Security Council Britain favoured the change, although she refrained from voting as the defeat of the proposal was a foregone conclusion. But it proved impossible to establish diplomatic relations, for the Chinese Government seemed determined to avoid contamination and demanded, among other things, that Britain should break off all relations with the Nationalists. She was also accused of hostility towards Chinese residents in Hong Kong and on 11 April the military compound of the British embassy in Peking was seized. Yet the British, although willing and anxious to support American resistance to the Communist challenge throughout Asia, remained fearful lest an uncompromising American attitude, particularly towards China, should perpetuate divisions which might otherwise at least find in time some working basis of surly mutual forebearance. For this reason, and also because of their desire to give meaning to the new Commonwealth relationship, they listened more patiently than the Americans to non-committed Nehru's admonitions to both sides.

When, after its invasion by North Korean forces on 25 June 1950, Truman ordered the United States forces to help South Korea, Attlee at once placed at his disposal the British naval forces in the Far East, which at the time were about equal in strength to those of the United States. In due course Commonwealth land forces equivalent to about a division took part with other U.N. troops. Anxious to prevent the escalation of the war, Attlee visited Washington early in December 1950 to urge the President to refrain from using the atom bomb against the Chinese, who had come to North Korea's assistance against General MacArthur's brilliant counter-offensive. Truman, who probably did not need advice from anyone, removed MacArthur from his command in April 1951, and armistice talks began in July; but some difference in outlook remained. The British Government also felt some misgivings over American policy towards Japan. To strengthen the bulwarks against Communism, Japan was to be recruited as an ally, as was West Germany in Europe; under the peace treaty of September 1951 she was to be rearmed, and she undertook to accept Chiang Kai-shek's Government in Formosa and not the Communist régime in Peking as the legitimate Government of China. Australian and New Zealand uneasiness at Japan's restoration to great power status were met by the signature at the same time of the A.N.Z.U.S. pact between the two powers and the United States; Great Britain signed the treaty with Japan but was not offered even observer status in the pact.

Middle Eastern Problems

And in the meantime Herbert Morrison struggled unhappily with new problems in the Middle East. Britain and the United States had, although for different reasons, put themselves in the wrong with both parties in the Arab–Jewish conflict. They had repaired their own differences in the tripartite agreement on 25 May 1950. In the declaration embodying this agreement they joined with France in deprecating an arms race between Israel and the Arab states, although legitimate defence requirements were to be met. They also pledged themselves to maintain the existing armistice lines. American and British views as to what was desirable in this area hardly differed, but each had doubts as to the expediency of the other's tactics, particularly towards the Arab states. Not that the Arabs were satisfied with either.

When the remarkable exhibitionist, Dr Musaddiq, nationalized the Persian oil industry on 20 March 1951 and proposed to dispossess the Anglo-Iranian Oil Company with inadequate compensation and in violation of the basic Oil Convention of 1933, American reactions were confused. Perhaps there were some who really believed Dr Musaddiq's assertion that he was opening 'a hidden treasure upon which lies a dragon', and not the British view that the dragon was but a goose laying golden eggs to Persia's advantage. There was the usual inclination in some quarters to accept at their face value the Doctor's excited complaints about imperialism, and a few American critics even compared the situation with 1783, although another and more sophisticated commentator pointed out that to establish a true parallel it would have been necessary for the A.I.O.C. to turn the whole of Persia into a concentration camp and shoot its leaders. The United States Ambassador to Teheran, Dr Grady, became a severe critic of the company after resigning in September 1951; on the other hand, it was admitted that the British had been good employers and that the financial arrangements were comparable with those of American oil companies in other Middle Eastern countries. Relying on the conviction that Musaddiq could not make his nationalized enterprise a success or persuade the American companies to take over, the British Government decided to await events, but he continued to bite off his own nose with remarkable agility until his overthrow in a counter-revolution in August 1953.

Apart from the Anglo-Iranian dispute it was the Anglo-Egyptian relationship which frustrated hopes of a regional defence system for the Middle East. The Anglo-Egyptian Treaty of 1936 had been attacked in Egypt as soon as the war ended in 1945, although it still had eleven years to run. Bevin had done his best to find a 'new basis of approach' which would meet the strategical interests of Britain and the Commonwealth by the negotiations of a treaty of mutual defence. But this formula could never be stretched to cover all the nationalist Egyptian demands. A draft agreement concluded by Bevin and Sidky Pasha, the Egyptian Prime Minister, in October 1946 provided for a staged withdrawal of British troops to the Canal Zone and then from the Canal Zone itself, but it was repudiated and Sidky was dismissed by King Farouk when the British refused to interpret it as including Egyptian sovereignty over the Sudan. The Egyptian Government failed in July 1947 to get any satisfaction from the Security Council over the Sudan, and chose to regard its failure against Israel in the fighting of 1948–9 as proof that the Israelis were the spearhead of Anglo-American imperialism in the Middle East. The anxious American efforts to disprove this charge by sympathizing with some of the Egyptian grievances against the British merely delayed agreement without popularizing American policy. Further negotiations over the withdrawal of British troops from the Canal Zone made no progress, and a supreme effort in October 1951 by Great Britain to satisfy Egyptian honour and interests by the formation of a Middle East defence organization was immediately rejected. Under this plan Egypt would have been a founder member along with France, Turkey, the United States, and Great Britain. It was to have included British withdrawal and the shared defence of the Zone. Almost immediately after this major rebuff a new Government took office in England under Mr Churchill.

Bevin emerges as one of the great figures in the history of British diplomacy. He had plenty of courage and manly character, but in this his predecessors were not lacking, even if their virtues were not always immediately obvious. His more individual characteristics are less easy to define. Lord Strang has compared him to Castlereagh, arguing that Castlereagh was the founder of a tradition of firm but conciliatory diplomacy of which the true heirs were Salisbury, Grey, Eden, and Bevin, in comparison with the challenging or hectoring or merely nagging diplomacy of a Canning, Palmerston, or Lord John Russell.[1] It may be conceded that there are many interesting parallels between post-war problems after 1815 and 1945; in both cases the glory soon departed while the obligations of victory remained, and the Foreign Secretary had to supplement shrunken resources, military and economic, by European collaboration. But Bevin in a new age of crisis was also a tough and forthright negotiator more reminiscent of Palmerston or Churchill than of Castlereagh, and his tactical sense – the precious gift of judging accurately and almost intuitively when to move boldly forward, when resistance had hardened, when to cut losses – was combined with a capacity for action of a high order as soon as the need became clear. He believed that he understood the working-man better than the Tories, and could safely apply the brinkmanship of trade union negotiation in foreign affairs; a surprisingly wide range of difficult foreign potentates, from Hitler to Stalin, came into his list of ex-working-men. Much more was involved, however, than skill in manoeuvre. He and his advisers had also thought out the broad objectives of policy in a difficult age of transition, and by the time of his retirement in March 1951 some at least of these had been achieved.

[1] Lord Strang, *Britain in World Politics* (1961), pp. 110, 344; cf. the same author's appreciation in *Home and Abroad* (1956), pp. 287–98.

XVI

Eden, Interdependence, and the Future

Eden and Dulles

The Bevinite revolution in British policy was acceptable to, and sometimes warmly welcomed by, the Tories, and fulfilled many of the broader anticipations of the two leading parties during the war. Churchill came back to power with a small but decisive majority on 26 October 1951. Eden, now almost an elder statesman at the age of fifty-four, returned to the Foreign Office with a great reputation and the powerful support of his illustrious chief, who gave him a remarkably free hand. Finally he succeeded to the Premiership on 6 April 1955.

Thus the handling of British diplomacy by the Tories during the crises of the early fifties carried further the adjustments in general policy of the Attlee-Bevin era: there was, in a real sense, continuity of policy in foreign affairs. The results were not, however, completely satisfactory: certain in-built disadvantages of the Bevinite arrangements soon appeared. The British Government was prepared to play a leading role in a number of spheres but with a consequent withholding of exclusive attention from any one, and with persistent criticism of her loyalty to each. The problem was partly one of resources, economic and military; with a wide dispersal of troops and armaments from the Rhineland to Malaya her contribution in a crisis in any one field or in a new one – such as Korea in 1950 – was bound to appear relatively ungenerous as compared with that of the United States, or even of a state of lesser magnitude which was prepared to put all its political and military eggs in one basket. In the economic field the interests of the Commonwealth and the sterling area were difficult to reconcile with the European Community. All this produced rebuffs. On the other hand she was too useful to everyone not to be able to command a good deal of grudging support in every field, and she preserved her freedom of thought and a sense (perhaps deceptive) of pervading influence in excess of her natural strength.

This pursuit of partly overlapping policies in distinct but closely related fields became known as a policy of inter-dependence, a word which had no particular derogatory significance in itself, but which was coming by the early nineteen-sixties to involve some notion of irresoluteness. Mr Dean Acheson's much quoted reprimand of 5 December 1962, 'Great Britain has lost an empire and has not yet found a role' meant exactly this: interdependence was not a policy or even a group of policies but a failure to rethink. The remark is so staggeringly inadequate as a description of the hard work and solid aspirations of Bevin and his successors that we must continually remind ourselves of the sense of achievement, in both Labour and Conservative circles, represented by the new arrangements.

To the United States Government, increasingly dedicated to the conception of a life and death struggle with Communism, the British ministers' busy preoccupation with the Common-wealth in its new form seemed tiresome and perhaps a little sinister. This was due in part to the assumption that the empire had been a disguised tyranny which could continue only as a form of neo-colonialism, in part to the conviction that Britain could use her time and resources to better advantage elsewhere. Thus it was easy to dismiss the Englishmen's pride in the attain-ment of the free-association Commonwealth as an attempt to put a good face on a long political retreat. American com-mentators persisted on speaking of the changes in the empire since 1945 as due solely to weakness. On the other hand, if retreat seemed too slow – if the Foreign Office resisted seemingly unreasonable demands – accusations of 'old-fashioned imperialism' soon appeared. The efforts to win and retain the goodwill of the self-governing Dominions had, however, been continuous since the nineteenth century and were redoubled in the case of the new and more choosy members after 1947. This was certainly not mere drift. It was the end-product of an evolutionary process of which the rest of the world seemed largely ignorant. The Labour Party believed that it had a natural affinity to the radical politics and social reformism of the new states. Among the Conservatives, generations of family contacts, a tradition of careerism and service, responsibility as one of the two older parties for every facet of empire policy since the eighteenth century, and the intricate financial relations of the sterling area (the only bulwark against the almighty dollar) could more easily be regarded as an inducement to cling to outmoded forms of power and influence, but the Conservatives too were discovering new possibilities in the new Commonwealth every day.

Neither Bevin nor Eden regarded these Commonwealth developments as in any way incompatible with the creation of the Western Alliance and the fostering of an intimate special relationship with the United States. The State Department had no substitute for this relationship at the moment. The Big Four of 1945 had soon disintegrated; Truman had lost all hope of working with Soviet Russia by 1947, if not before, and the other potential ally, Nationalist China, had succumbed to the Communists in 1949. Britain was to remain throughout the fifties America's only active and relatively powerful friend among the major powers. The attempt to build up Japan, West Germany, and France was a necessary consequence, but was not received with undiluted enthusiasm even by these states themselves. So useful was Britain as the chief supporter of the strongest power that the Foreign Office could afford to stand up to the State Department on points of difference if it did so with good judgement and without rocking the boat too much, as it did indeed tend to do at times.

Eden had marked skill as a negotiator; he had much

experience of the peculiar routines of modern diplomacy, and a certain dynamism which gave some vigour to his talk and proposals, and also seems to have led him rather readily to impatience at rebuffs. The frustrations of a British Foreign Secretary were many, but they were not all due to the obtuseness or calculations of his foreign colleagues. The variety of British commitments partly concealed the new limits of national power, and the task of diplomacy was to steer a course between the lurking disasters of over-boldness and self-effacement. He had a number of successes during the next three years, but usually in the form of persuading allies to accept somewhat unpalatable decisions.

The immediate issue which faced Eden on his accession to office was to decide whether Europe could be defended without adding a third treaty relationship to those of the Commonwealth and the Anglo-American partnership embodied in NATO. European unity had been much talked about since the war, and deceptively encouraged by both Tory and Labour spokesmen. Continental advocates of economic and political unity had welcomed Churchill's speech at Zürich on 19 September 1946 although he had spoken of European union as, by implication, something that Britain would aid and befriend, but would not join. The creation of the Council of Europe after so much consultation in 1947–8 was a valuable adjunct to the Brussels Treaty, and the Labour leaders were glad to see any development that would rally opinion in support of the Marshall Aid programme and military co-operation. But they did not think that political opinion in Western European countries was ready for a genuine pooling of power and surrender of sovereignty, and they were certainly not ready for it themselves. In 1949 a Council of Ministers and a Consultative Assembly, consisting of delegates of the participating countries appointed as their governments saw fit, were set up, but they were restricted, owing largely to British influence, to general discussion and debate. Bevin, perhaps through ill-health, did not respond imaginatively to the movement as he had done to Marshall's programme, and would only concede that progress towards European integration might be made piecemeal by functional co-operation, particularly in the economic field.

Even so he regarded the Schuman Plan of May 1950, with its provision for the control and development of the French and German coal and steel industries by a single higher authority, as a challenge to his own policy, and (with the full support of the Labour Cabinet) was unresponsive to the invitation to Britain to join. There was a flurry of Labour criticisms of the plan and its right-wing sponsors during the following weeks, and Aneurin Bevan announced that he was not prepared to entrust the workers to international capitalists. All this caused great exasperation on the Continent, but there were hopes that the Conservatives would be more forthcoming.

The Conservative Opposition had criticized the bald neo-isolationist form of some of the Labour pronouncements, and no doubt was not greatly bothered by the accusation that it favoured the internationalization of steel and coal as an antidote to nationalization. The majority of Mr Churchill's colleagues were in fact as opposed as the Labour Party to the handing of control of Britain's vital resources to a supranational body. The immediate issue that faced Eden arose from the proposal of M. Pleven, the French Prime Minister, in October 1950 for a European army, including a German contingent, made up of contributions from its own national forces by each of the member states. Units were to be merged, there was to be a European Defence Council and a European Minister of War, and membership was to be conditional on the acceptance of the Schuman Plan. Although Dr Konrad Adenauer, the new Federal German Chancellor, was not easy at the relatively large share that Germany was thus expected to play in the defence screen against the Red Army, he made a strong plea for Franco-German reconciliation and for the Pleven Plan in a speech at Stuttgart on 4 November. The Labour ministers had regarded the plan in its original form as impracticable, and although modifications were introduced during the following year and German rearmament was agreed on, a partial deadlock was reached by the summer of 1951. France would only agree to West German rearmament within the framework of a European Defence Community. While agreeing to this, the British and United States Governments were not prepared to join the European army themselves. There is some evidence that the new Churchill Cabinet intended to move cautiously for a time; Sir David Maxwell Fyfe (later Lord Kilmuir) suggested in his memoirs that an agreed Cabinet statement, which he was authorized to make to the Consultative Assembly of the Council of Europe on 28 November 1951, promising 'thorough examination' of proposals for a European army, was meant to be non-committal. He felt himself 'humiliated' when Eden a few hours later bluntly told a Press conference in Rome that British forces would not participate.[1]

This was not a very happy start, and in a visit to Paris in December 1951 Churchill and Eden softened the blow a little with a promise that Britain would not reduce her forces on the Continent and would associate herself as far as possible with E.D.C. More formally the British and United States foreign ministers, in a joint declaration in February 1952, reaffirmed their agreement to maintain forces in Europe. The elements of a solution existed – the acceptance in principle of some German rearmament, the willingness of Britain, France, Italy, and the Benelux countries to supply forces for European defence, United States co-operation, and the willingness of all to serve under the supreme NATO command. The difficulties – French distrust of Germany, her professed doubts as to British intentions, the possibility of some isolationist move in Washington – were a challenge to the negotiating skills which Eden had to offer. In the end, a satisfactory arrangement owed much to him. The first landmark was the signature on 26 May 1952 by the Federal German Chancellor and the foreign ministers of the United Kingdom, France, and the United States of the Bonn Conventions (Cmd. 8571), ending the occupation and granting sovereignty to the German Federal

---

[1] Lord Kilmuir, *Political Adventure* (1964), p. 187.

Republic. On the following day a treaty was signed in Paris by France, Italy, the three Benelux countries, and West Germany establishing E.D.C., and Eden signed three supplementary documents. One established mutual security guarantees between the United Kingdom and the E.D.C. members; a second was a protocol to the North Atlantic Treaty by which its members undertook to regard an attack on any E.D.C. member as an attack on themselves; the third was an Anglo-French–American declaration affirming their abiding interest in the effectiveness of the E.D.C. Treaty and in the maintenance of their position in Berlin. But these agreements had to be ratified, and another two years went by before a final decision was reached.

In the meantime Eden was busily concerned with the liquidation of threatening situations in the Middle East and Far East; something of a conflict with the State Department over means rather than ends developed in both fields and was to be accentuated while Dean Acheson was succeeded as Secretary of State by John Foster Dulles. A dedicated, obstinate, and somewhat insensitive man, Dulles was pleased at times to label his own brand of peacemaking 'brinkmanship': the threat of force was implicit in all his major initiatives, although he generally deplored it when it was made by other powers – Britain, Russia, China, or Guatamala. With Eden and Dulles each uneasy at the tactical stubbornness of the other, and each on the other hand irritated by the other's corresponding phases of lukewarmness, a curious tension developed. Even before Eisenhower took office, Churchill and Eden had urged him not to appoint Dulles as his Secretary of State.[1]

The Egyptian rejection of the Middle East Defence Organization and unilateral abrogation on 15 October 1951 of the 1936 treaty and 1899 *condominium* agreement was followed by a demand to the new Churchill Government on 27 October for the evacuation of both the Canal Zone and the Sudan. The British Government saw no reason for abandoning its position

[1] Lord Avon, *The Eden Memoirs, Full Circle* (1960), cited as Avon III: pp. 66–4.

before the expiry date of the treaty in 1956 unless Egypt were prepared to agree to some constructive alternative; nor was it prepared to hand over the Sudanese to Egyptian rule against their wishes. It was believed that the Wafd Party, in office under the now rather senile Prime Minister, Nahas Pasha, had staged this crisis and the accompanying anti-foreign riots to distract attention from its corrupt and unpopular domestic rule. Egypt's action was no doubt also influenced by the apparently successful Persian defiance of the oil company, and the conviction, following the Tripartite Pact of 1950, that the Middle East Defence Organization as an anti-Communist front implied the indefinite postponement of action against Israel. But Britain remained on terms of close alliance with Irak, dominated by the resourceful Nuri es-Said, and with Transjordan (independent since 1946, renamed Jordan in 1949); Turkey was ready to enter the Middle Eastern defensive system, and vast British and international interests were involved in the safety of the Suez Canal. An alternative to the great British base in the Canal Zone would also have to be found if evacuation took place. While the State Department agreed with the Foreign Office as to the need for a Middle Eastern defence system it sought to win the confidence of the Egyptians with gestures of friendship which merely advertised Anglo-American differences: the American Ambassador, Mr J. Caffrey, made no pretence of supporting the British position, and even advocated recognition of King Farouk's claims to the Sudan. The Egyptians saw that they could play off the Americans against the British, but they had no intention of accepting the American lead.

The State Department was, no doubt, anxious to live down the memory among the Arabs of its indiscriminate championing of the Zionist cause, and with the important exception of its support (in return for oil concessions and an air base) of the Saudi Arabian régime its aim was to stand well with revolutionary régimes such as that of Egypt and Iran, which made some appeal to American liberal ideology. Moreover, its broader strategical objective was a modernized version of the traditional British policy of barring Russian expansion south, and it was desperately afraid of opening the door to Communism. With the independence of India, on the other hand, the British Government had become less concerned with the protection of the route to the Far East, and much more concerned with the defence of its oil and other interests throughout the Middle East from local disturbances. This concern for stability gave it a greater interest than the Americans in the maintenance of the Persian Gulf sheikhdoms and of the monarchical régimes in Jordan, Irak, and Iran, and a keen interest, which the Americans did not share, in the unimpeded passage of oil from the Gulf through the Suez Canal.

Eden was active during 1952 and 1953 in continued search for an Anglo-Egyptian settlement, and gradually the gap narrowed. The declining prestige of King Farouk and the old gang of professional politicians had been accompanied by further waves of anti-foreign rioting. At the end of January 1952 these had become so serious that the intervention of British troops to protect British lives in Cairo and Alexandria was contemplated. This was averted when the Egyptian Army was called in to restore order, and in July 1952 the army itself seized power under General Neguib. Farouk abdicated. Neguib promised well, and with his junta of officers seemed ready for genuine domestic reforms and a more rational tone in diplomatic negotiations; nevertheless Eden found his speeches 'a constant irritant' and in any case he was gradually losing ground to Colonel Nasser (who finally replaced him as Head of the State and President of the Revolutionary Council on 17 November 1954). Neguib seemed, however, genuinely anxious to leave the Sudan to make its own choice, and an Anglo-Egyptian Agreement to this effect was announced simultaneously in London, Cairo, and Khartoum on 12 February 1953. In spite of subsequent Egyptian accusations of British bad faith it was by a genuinely independent decision that the Sudan opted for complete independence in November 1953.

The year 1953 also witnesses a decisive development in

British ideas about Middle Eastern defence.[1] Early in December 1952 the Cabinet decided in principle to transfer its military headquarters in the Middle East to Cyprus, and this brought nearer the possibility of a new Middle Eastern grouping. Negotiations with Neguib progressed slowly on the basis of a withdrawal of British forces from the Canal Zone, with very circumscribed provisions for the British maintenance of the base and return in an emergency. At last on 27 July 1954 an Anglo-Egyptian Agreement provided for the British evacuation of the base within twenty months, but for its maintenance by British civilian staffs for seven years. Meanwhile in Persia Musaddiq's adventure had drawn to a close; unable to sell oil, he tried in May 1953 to secure aid from the United States, but Eisenhower nerved himself to refuse in spite of the usual fears of a Communist swing. Musaddiq was tumbled from power on 19 August 1953 by General Zahedi and the army, acting under the Shah's orders. A year later, on 5 August 1954, after prolonged negotiations in which the United States Ambassador to Teheran played a helpful part, a satisfactory settlement of the Anglo-Iranian oil dispute was concluded.

But in the meantime the international limelight had been concentrated mainly on South-east Asia, where the decisive voice was that of the United States. Few of the factors inhibiting Dulles's boldness in the Middle East operated in the Pacific. The restoration of French rule in Indo-China in 1946 had come just too late to prevent the establishment of a veteran Communist, Ho Chi Minh, as the head of the provisional Government of Vietnam; the Vietminh Party which he led provided the only effective outlet for nationalist feeling, and his Government was soon recognized by the Communist bloc. In 1950 the French placed the ex-emperor, Bao Dai, at the head of a new Associated State of Vietnam, nominally independent within the French Union; this was the Government that Great Britain and the United States chose to recognize, and in defending it the French received American encouragement, advice, and arms. But in spite of brilliant political and military

[1] Woodhouse, op. cit., pp. 130–5.

initiatives by General de Lattre de Tassigny in 1951 the French position deteriorated, and pessimism grew in Paris; after de Lattre's death it seemed that increasing international support would be needed if the French forces were to continue the struggle against mounting guerrilla and sabotage attacks by the Vietminh, reinforced from China. Eden appears at first to have accepted the American contention that the French effort in Indo-China was in the general interest. But when in 1954 the French decided to fight out the issue in a pitched battle at Dien Bien Phu, beginning on 13 March, Eden drew back. It speedily became evident that the French had underestimated their opponents' strength, and Dulles discussed various forms of American intervention with the French Government. But on 25 April the British Cabinet declined to approve an American proposal that United States naval aircraft should go into action at Dien Bien Phu on the 28th.

The decision was due essentially to Eden's reading of the situation in Europe. He doubted both the resolution of the French and the continued intransigence of the Russians. On the first point it was significant that France alone of the six partners in the E.D.C. had still not agreed to ratify the treaty of 27 May 1952, and she seemed to be making heavy weather of her military effort in Indo-China, with continued complaints that her allies were not doing enough. To the argument that the demands of Indo-China made it impossible for her to strengthen her forces in Europe Eden had pointed out to Pleven at the end of May 1952 that Britain had a larger army in Europe than France, two-year National Service which the French had not adopted, seventy thousand men in the Canal Zone, and strong forces in Malaya. Dulles, much exasperated, told a Press conference in December 1953 that there might be an 'agonizing reappraisal' of American policy if France failed to ratify E.D.C. By April 1954 there seemed no doubt that French morale over Indo-China was crumbling, and that even the offer of American help was not sufficient to arouse much enthusiasm.[1]

[1] Avon, III, chap. 5.

The Soviet Government, on the other hand, was showing a certain calculated reasonableness. With the death of Stalin on 5 March 1953 something of the tension seemed to have departed from Soviet relations with the West, although the slight easing of atmosphere might mean nothing more than that the new leaders, Malenkov, Molotov, and Khrushchev, were feeling their way. They at last showed themselves willing to discuss the future of Central Europe, evidently seeking a means to frustrate the ratification of E.D.C. and the inclusion in it of the Federal German Republic. The French Government needed final proof of Russian hostility in order to secure parliamentary approval of E.D.C. Accordingly, the Berlin Conference of the Foreign Ministers of Britain, France, the United States, and Russia (25 January–18 February 1954) had discussed alternatives with unusual politeness, although it was impossible for Molotov to accept the proposal of the remaining ministers for German reunification preceded by free elections. It was evident that he was also gunning against NATO, and he made the deadlock over Germany a reason for holding up a peace settlement with Austria. But he also proposed a further conference of five powers including China, and this the other three were quite willing to accept. The prospect of Russian backing for peace in Asia redoubled Eden's efforts to prevent a widening of the Vietnam struggle.

In the ensuing conference at Geneva (26 April–21 July 1954) Eden threw his prestige and patient negotiating gifts into the search for settlements in Asia which were bound to involve some element of accommodation and consequent American distaste. His task was facilitated and American suspicions no doubt increased by Molotov's co-operation. They agreed to share the chairmanship of the conference, and Molotov seemed as uncertain as to the intentions of the Chinese Foreign Minister, Chou En-lai, as were the delegates of the other three powers. Dulles saw no merit in conciliatory gestures in dealing with opponents who seemed to him incapable of compromise. During his stay in Geneva for the first week of the conference it was noted that he ignored Chou En-lai's existence; he then departed, and in his place W. Bedell Smith, the Assistant Secretary of State for Far Eastern Affairs, was certainly more cheerful and co-operative. There were reports from time to time during the remainder of the conference of American impatience and disinclination to accept the anticipated results. Probably this did no harm; it gave some encouragement to the French, and was a warning to the Chinese, who in any case probably wanted to consolidate their position at home and were without the means of fighting American nuclear power. Eden and Churchill flew to Washington on 24 June for a three-day visit which led to Dulles's agreement to leave the French a free hand for the next few weeks in seeking agreement at Geneva. This meant that plans for a South-east Asia security organization could be elaborated by the experts, but not publicly launched until the conference was over.[1]

The practical result was a qualified peace settlement on the basis of the partition of both Korea and Vietnam. In mid-June the conference had to abandon the discussion of plans for the unification of Korea owing to the refusal of the Communist delegates to recognize the authority of the United Nations or to accept the proposals of the United Nations' delegates for 'free, impartially supervised elections'. But the two Koreas henceforth refrained from interfering too blatantly with each other, and in due course Chinese and United Nations troops were withdrawn. In Indo-China, agreement for a cease-fire was concluded at last on 20 July. The main provisions were for a dividing line in Vietnam at approximately the 17th parallel, for the withdrawal of French forces from the Red River delta and Viet Minh forces from the south, for the withdrawal of Viet Minh troops from Laos, and for the holding of general elections during 1955 in Cambodia and Laos, and on 20 July 1956 throughout Vietnam. The United States Government did not endorse the settlement. It did not trust the Chinese Government, it did not wish to afford Chinese Communism any involuntary recognition. Moreover, it was the French who had surrendered in Vietnam. Time was to show that the pessimistic

[1] Avon, III, chap. 6.

views of Dulles were more realistic than the optimism of Eden. America's future objectives in the area were plainly indicated in the joint communication to the French Government agreed to by Eden and Dulles on 29 June: this stated that the armistice must not impose on Laos, Cambodia, or South Vietnam any restrictions materially impairing their capacity to maintain stable non-Communist régimes. The general election provision threatened to do this in view of the larger population of Communist North Vietnam.

The agreements with Egypt and Iran and the Geneva settlement meant the temporary placating of many restless forces which had been threatening the security and peace of mind of the Western powers throughout the world. The Soviet Union was believed to have reached parity with America in nuclear weapons by about this time. The next stage was to strengthen the defences, and Eden's energies were mainly concerned during the remainder of his term of office as Foreign Secretary with the completion of pacts for regional defence in the three widely separated areas in which British interests lay.

Geneva had been a disaster for France, which was also facing independence campaigns in Tunisia and Morocco. The result was in turn a disaster for E.D.C. This had by now secured the ratification or assurance of ratification of the other five powers, but the French Premier, M. Mendès France, whose willingness to face facts had ensured the success of the Geneva Conference, could not promise French ratification of E.D.C. without further concessions to French interests. These the other five felt bound to reject, and the French Assembly refused ratification on 30 August 1954. Molotov no doubt rejoiced, but was not allowed to enjoy the prospect of Western disunity for long. Eden found an acceptable alternative in a plan to bring Western Germany into NATO and the Brussels Treaty, which would have the advantage of providing Europe with a mutual defence pact shorn of the supranational features of the E.D.C. Britain would be a member, and Germany would rearm. In spite of his dis-appointment at this setback to the unity of Europe Dr Adenauer accepted the plan and promised voluntarily not to manufacture atomic weapons. At the decisive moment in the London Conference at the end of September Eden promised to maintain four divisions and a tactical air force in Europe, and the plan took final form in the Paris Agreements of 23 October 1954. The Brussels Treaty Organization was known henceforth as Western European Union.

At almost exactly the same time negotiations, mainly in Washington, led to the conclusion of the South-East Asia Collective Defence Treaty, which was signed in Manila, together with the so-called Pacific Charter, on 8 September 1954. Lord Reading represented Great Britain. It satisfied the American desire for an anti-Communist front in South-east Asia, and if there was an embarrassing absence of South-east Asian powers (although Pakistan, the Philippines, and Thailand, together with Australia and New Zealand, took part) it promised British, French, and American support to any power needing it in the area, thus guaranteeing the Geneva decisions. Eden had gone to great lengths to keep the Commonwealth countries in touch with the Geneva negotiations, although he was not able to persuade India, Burma, and Ceylon to abandon 'non-alignment'.

Thus SEATO (South-East Asia Treaty Organization) was added to NATO and in a somewhat less systematic fashion a Middle Eastern defence system was built up. The Americans havered a good deal over this; Dulles approved of a pact but would not join in September 1954. The Iraqi Prime Minister, Nuri es-Said, had begun canvassing a plan for a defence pact which would strengthen the Arab League by adding Turkey and bringing in Britain and the United States. Egypt was violently opposed, but Turkey and Irak signed what became known as the Baghdad Pact on 24 February 1955, and Britain joined on 4 April. Pakistan joined in September and Iran in October. The pact had the unusual distinction of being distrusted by both the Israelis and the Egyptians.

Taking Stock: The Middle Fifties

The period of almost exactly ten years since the war had thus seen a remarkable transformation in the basic assumptions governing British foreign policy and its related treaty structure. Before the war Britain's world-wide responsibilities had been greater than she could adequately defend; her armament capacity and limited hopes of allied support had necessitated a system of priorities in defence and the avoidance of simultaneous clashes with her three potential enemies, Germany, Italy, and Japan. She had been, with France, a leader without many followers, and collective security had proved to be a much canvassed delusion. Now, with the substitution of an almost universal Communist bugbear for the dispersed Fascist movements of the pre-war years, the range of her responsibilities had not perhaps greatly increased; but in the three security groupings of NATO, SEATO, and CENTO it was shared and buttressed by a varying range of partners with more precise obligations than had ever been achieved under the League Covenant before the war. The power and authority of the United States, conspicuously lacking before, was now supporting each combination.

The surviving weaknesses in Britain's position as a world power were due less to any deficiency in the material or economic strength of these groupings than to a continued scepticism abroad as to her single-minded loyalty to their aims. British foreign policy was to a far greater extent a development of earlier policies than was the case with any of the other strong powers of the day. France in her abandonment of empire in Asia (less so in North Africa) and her friendship with Germany, West Germany and Japan in their new peaceable and liberal roles, the United States in her change from isolationism to world power, and the Soviet Union in a similar advance from the 'socialism in one country' neutralism of pre-war days, had all made more clear-cut and perhaps more fundamental changes of course. It could certainly be argued that as the only active world power before 1939 Britain had less need to change her basic policies than to develop and modify them to suit the new conditions of the post-war world. But the other powers were remarkably quick to suspect and dissociate themselves from any British activity which seemed likely to involve the security groupings in the defence of her individual interests.

No British Government could readily accept the view that its exertions in its own defence were not *ipso facto* a contribution to the common good, and no doubt other Governments, including the United States, thought the same of themselves. Nevertheless this situation cast a certain doubt on Britain's ability to pursue indefinitely the traditional objectives of foreign policy as they had been redefined in the Attlee–Bevin era, and although the authority of the United Nations Organization and the basic deadlock in East–West relations remained unchanged there was a growing uncertainty as to whether Britain's role might not have to be again defined.

Doubts on this point were partly due to the power of the liberal conscience in British politics; the sense of guilt felt by all left-wing opposition parties over the somewhat apologetic self-assertion of Conservative Governments had a remarkable outing in the Suez crisis of 1956 but did not stop there. Doubts were also partly due to the changing character of the Communist offensive which had originally brought the Western powers together. The United States during the Dulles era was alive to Communist manifestations throughout the globe from Berlin to Guatemala and almost anywhere in the Pacific, but with no very clear theory as to how to handle the troublemakers of the uncommitted world. When the Communist-inclined Government of President Arbenz in Guatemala began to import arms the United States Navy was instructed in May 1954 to blockade the Guatemalan coast, and Eden at once protested that the British Government could not acquiesce in forcible action against British ships on the high seas in peacetime. Dulles replied that rules applicable in the past must be revised or flexibly applied to suit cold war conditions. Arbenz's régime was overthrown with American help shortly afterwards. On 24 January 1955 President

Eisenhower gave a public warning (in the form of a request for authority from Congress) that the United States would fight to protect the Nationalist régime in Formosa and the Pescadores from Chinese Communist attack, and Eden's attitude was reserved; he was anxious not to embarrass Washington, but the smaller off-shore islands at least were regarded in the Foreign Office as legally belonging to the Chinese People's Republic. Episodes such as these, which caused criticism in England and doubts as to the wisdom of following the American lead too blindly, were increased by the agility with which the new leaders in Moscow extended the cold war to the non-committed world, while talking a good deal about East–West reconciliation.

After replacing Malenkov in February 1955 the Bulganin-Khrushchev régime made further gestures of reasonableness. It is true that they found it necessary to reply to the Paris Agreements with a defence treaty between the Soviet Union and seven European satellites (the Warsaw Treaty of 14 May 1955), but they followed this with the proposal of a summit conference of heads of state which met at Geneva from 18 to 23 July. Eden, who had become Prime Minister in April, and Mr Harold Macmillan, the new Foreign Secretary, represented Great Britain. There was much amiability and the Foreign Ministers were directed to study measures for disarmament, European security, and the progressive elimination of East–West tension. The ensuing Foreign Ministers' Conference at Geneva in November provided the inevitable disappointment; it turned out that the Soviet Government, while demanding the dissolution of NATO, was not, after all, prepared to offer anything much in exchange. Mr Macmillan said, perhaps a little too neatly, 'the terrible thing is that the Russian Government fears our friendship more than our enmity'. All the same, the Soviet initiatives were not without their effect on world opinion. Bulganin and Khrushchev, abandoning talk of East–West reconciliation for awhile, began to woo the Afro-Asian powers whose pretensions had been advertised by the Bandung conference of the previous May. They visited India,

Burma, and Afghanistan (November–December 1955), denounced colonialism, averred their support for Indian claims
to Goa and Kashmir, and promised lavish aid. Earlier in
bilateral talks in London they had sought to drive a wedge
between Japan and the West. Dulles seemed disconcerted by
these moves. He tended to seek the favour of Afro-Asian
states by criticizing both colonialism and communism. They
were only half convinced: being ostentatiously neutral in the
East–West struggle they found it more natural to equate anti-
Communism with various forms of finance imperialism.[1]

Suez and After

This situation supplied much of the background of the
Hungarian and Suez crises in the autumn of 1956. There was a
certain parallelism between the two cases, for both Russia and
Great Britain, after a conciliatory phase of policy, were
disconcerted by challenges which seemed to threaten their
vital interests, and which convinced them that concessions had
gone too far. The fact that each condemned the other's conduct
was due to differences of ideology rather than of circumstance.
The working-class rising in Berlin and other East German
cities in June 1953 revealed early hopes of some alleviation of
conditions following Stalin's death; they were suppressed by
Russian troops but subsequent measures were not vindictive.
The Soviet Government signed a peace treaty with Austria in
May 1955. When Khrushchev on 25 February 1956 proclaimed
the end of Stalinism, Poland responded with her own repudiation of Stalinism, after which a modified Communist régime
under the former deviationist, M. Wladislaw Gomulka,
established a successful *modus vivendi* with Moscow. In Hungary,
on the other hand, the process of de-Stalinization proceeded
with little change in the governing personnel, and with
mounting and increasingly vocal criticism of Russia, whose ex-
actions were considered to be the cause of the country's economic depression. When on 23 October 1956 a revolutionary

[1] Avon, III, pp. 291–311.

movement commenced in Budapest and led rapidly to the overthrow of the governing elements throughout the country there were demands for the withdrawal of Soviet troops and for a genuinely democratic régime, and the Soviet leaders decided that they must intervene. Soviet troops at once began to be moved into Hungary in large numbers. British relations with Egypt were on a different footing in that the British Government believed that it had settled all outstanding differences by 1954; but similar in the conviction that an actively hostile opponent had been revealed.

Dulles came to the conclusion in the summer of 1956 that Colonel Nasser should be 'cut down to size', and then left the task to the British and French Governments.[1] They accordingly found his subsequent censure of 'colonialism' more than a little exasperating. Dulles and Eden had both sought to keep on friendly terms with the new Egyptian régime, although Nasser showed himself increasingly inclined after his attendance at the Bandung conference in April 1955 to follow a dynamic, anti-Western policy, helped but not dominated by Communist military and financial aid. In the autumn of 1955 an arms deal with Czechoslovakia foreshadowed an attack on Israel, although the promise of American and British finance for the building of the Aswan Dam on the Nile preserved relations of ostensible friendship with the Western powers for a time. But the earmarking of the Egyptian cotton crop to pay for Soviet–Czech arms and Nasser's hopes of a Soviet loan apparently convinced Dulles that the United States and the World Bank would be left to bear the main burden of paying for the Dam, and on 19 July he withdrew the American offer of aid. Britain did the same. Neither Government appears to have anticipated or discussed the possible consequences. A week later, on 26 July, when Nasser announced the nationalization of the Suez Canal Company, he talked of compensation, but nullified this by earmarking the Canal revenues for the building of the Dam.

[1] The Suez crisis has already produced a substantial literature. Lord Avon's story is given in *Full Circle*, pp. 419–584. *Survey of International Affairs, 1956–1958* (1962) avoids taking sides: A. Nutting, T. Robertson, are critical of Anglo-French policy, H. Finer of Dulles (see bibliography).

The company's balance of 5 million Egyptian pounds in the Ottoman Bank was seized, and he declared that he was fighting British and American imperialism, that America had refused the loan in order to force him to join the Baghdad Pact, and that Britain had refused arms for the fight against Israel, itself the vanguard of imperialism.[1]

All this meant at the very least that Nasser was exploiting the well-known sensitiveness of the British over the Canal to give himself a popular triumph while at the same time securing increased revenue. Behind this loomed more serious possibilities: if he were not challenged he might interfere with the Canal traffic for blackmail to secure political ends, emboldened by the fact that for four years Egypt had been able to ignore with impunity the Security Council's resolution condemning the closing of the Canal to Israeli commerce. Building up his power by the exploitation of nationalist grievances he might well be poised for a Hitlerite or Mussolini-like career.

Three-quarters of the 14,666 ships which passed through the Canal in 1955 belonged to NATO and nearly one-third were British. A great part of the oil supplies of Western Europe flowed through the Canal. In his memoirs, Eden quoted his comment that a man with Colonel Nasser's record could not be allowed 'to have his thumb on our windpipe'. France had similar reactions, and a separate grudge against Nasser because of his encouragement of resistance in Algeria. In the House of Commons on 27 July Gaitskell deplored the Egyptian Government's 'high-handed and totally unjustifiable step'.

If by the following November Egypt's thumb had proved irremovable the reason was not that the suffering victims – the Canal users – lacked material strength to free themselves but that they had not the moral unity to exert it to the full. This is true of the British Government, which was more susceptible to domestic criticism than the French. Nasser's action, however exasperating, was economic, not military; the Canal flowed through Egyptian territory; Nasser might not be a budding Hitler but he might by the same argument be an ambitious,

[1] Kilmuir, op. cit., p. 267.

violent, reckless man who would prefer the risks of world war to surrender. Fear of war and fear of the stigma of colonialism, together with the political advantages of discrediting a British Conservative Government, brought together the Soviet Union and the United States, most of the Afro-Asian countries, and the British Labour Party, in shocked condemnation of the use of force, although it was evident that the Soviet veto would prevent effective action by the Security Council. It was announced on 30 July that British forces were being assembled in the eastern Mediterranean, and French forces were brought to Cyprus. The signatories of the 1888 Suez Canal Convention were invited to meet in London, and in mid-August eighteen states accepted an American proposal for a Suez Canal board to take over the international operation of the Canal. But Nasser rejected this plan flatly on 7 September, and Dulles was not prepared to insist on it or recommend it to the Security Council. It seems evident that from this point he was prepared to accept almost any Egyptian assurances at their face value.

Dulles now proposed a 'users' club' which would control the Canal traffic in conjunction with Egypt. He was not willing to enforce it and so the majority of the eighteen also held back. Nasser again refused to co-operate. Referring to the Canal issue, Dulles told a Press conference on 2 October that matters encroaching in some form or other 'on the problem of so-called colonialism' found the United States 'playing a somewhat independent role'. However, he told Selwyn Lloyd soon after that he was with Britain on every point and did not even rule out the use of force as an ultimate resort.

The Labour Party meanwhile was demanding reference to the Security Council with increasing passion. Dulles had for a time opposed this, but the problem did come before the Council early in October, and all that emerged was a list of six principles which affirmed Egypt's sovereignty while promising 'free and open' transit of the Canal. The British and French attempt to strengthen these proposals by securing the Security Council's affirmation of the mid-August proposals was defeated by the

Soviet veto. It is important to notice that, in spite of the way in which Eden had become fixed in the public mind as the most uncompromising opponent of the Egyptian President, he was not initiating policy; the decisive turn to events at each stage was given by others, Dulles and Nasser and now the Soviet Government. In the last stage the initiative was seized by the Israeli and French Prime Ministers, Ben-Gurion and Mollet. The extent to which they had agreed in advance on concerted action against Egypt is still not fully known, and if Eden and Selwyn Lloyd were wholly or partly uninformed they may be freed of the charge of 'collusion' while laying themselves open almost to the charge of incompetence: it was their business to know what was going on.[1] But after the Anglo-French intervention on 30 October it was Eden who at last took a completely independent decision when he ordered the cease-fire on 6 November. The French would have preferred to continue.

It was an odd affair in every respect, a six-days blunder which emphasized once again the unresolved conflicts of principle and interest in the Western world. There was some rather confused talk about the present-day futility of gun-boat diplomacy. It was asserted that Great Britain or France had no longer the power to undertake independent military operations as they had done in the nineteenth century. This was evidently not true; since 1945 the French had fought single-handed – unsuccessfully it is true – in Vietnam and Algeria, and the British had operated successfully in Malaya, Kuwait, and elsewhere; they still had ample military resources for dealing with smaller opponents. They had the strength to seize and hold the Canal. It might be argued that they could not ignore the opinion of other powers, or of the General Assembly of the United Nations, but there had been similar problems in the nineteenth century; Britain had to secure the tacit agreement of other European powers before intervening in Egypt in 1882, and even so French jealousy embarrassed her continually thereafter until the Anglo-French Agreement of 1904, when she bought

[1] Cf. Avon, III, pp. 522–9; Kilmuir, p. 278.

relief only with concessions over Morocco. France in 1840, Russia in 1853, Austria–Hungary in 1914, the United States after the Bay of Pigs fiasco in 1961, were powerful states which discovered that for one reason or another they could not coerce weaker neighbours with impunity. Thus the Suez crisis did not provide any new fact or evidence about Britain's power in the world.

Egypt was one of the key-points along the international frontiers between the world's great blocs at which no Government, however powerful, can intervene unilaterally. The reasons are partly strategical, partly emotional and ideological. Some curious consequences follow: the small power in these circumstances can act more irresponsibly than the great power, thumbing its nose at the Security Council and enjoying much local credit for dangerous living. It is in fact reasonably safe: it is the greater power whose action is paralysed, and the degree of paralysis almost becomes an indication of its international standing. Suez was a blunder in diplomatic tactics, for these considerations were largely ignored. The whole course of the negotiations from late July to mid-October served to advertise the issue in its widest ideological terms, and to demonstrate the fact that the Canal users could not re-establish their rights by argument alone. Recognizing this, and facing a Presidential election, Dulles had soon drawn back. If, as may well be the case, the Israeli intervention was regarded by the British Government as introducing a genuinely new element into the situation, the fact remains that it was not staged in circumstances which were likely to bring about any sympathetic re-action of world opinion. The embarrassing consequences for Great Britain of a continued Israeli offensive which might have brought about the intervention of Jordan (which Britain was pledged by treaty to defend) were also not much advertised.

The crisis, by pinpointing the existing difficulties of effective action by the Western powers, did produce some remedies, after which the basic deadlock in international relations was restored. As a condition of Anglo-French withdrawal, an international police force was hastily assembled and dispatched, and in spite of his cries of triumph Nasser accepted the patrolling of the main trouble spot, the Gaza strip, and the opening of the port of Eilat. On 5 January 1957 President Eisenhower, safely re-elected, announced a new doctrine for the Middle East in the form of an undertaking to protect any Middle Eastern state against Communist aggression up to a figure of $200 million. This decision to supplement the ineffectual machinery of the United Nations was followed by Anglo-American talks in Bermuda in March 1957 which re-established the personal links between the two Governments, gave Dulles an opportunity for some moralizing about the misdemeanours of lesser men, and reaffirmed the Security Council's resolution of October 1956 as to the freedom of the Suez Canal. In January Eden had resigned owing to illness, but the new Prime Minister, Mr Harold Macmillan, maintained the continuity of foreign policy by retaining Mr Selwyn Lloyd as Foreign Secretary.[1]

Winds of Change

The Macmillan era (1957–63) as it affected foreign policy was remarkable at the personal level for the studied urbanity of the Prime Minister and his two unflappable Foreign Secretaries, Selwyn Lloyd and the Earl of Home. The result was probably to conceal in some measure a major attempt to adjust British policy to the realities of existing world relations; it was further concealed by the limited success of the attempt. On the whole it must be concluded that this was no more than an attempt to play an effective role in terms of the established policy of interdependence, and this was perhaps the main reason for failure. But the result was at any rate a nimble and at times a bold effort to solve a range of outstanding problems.

For a time it looked as if Macmillan's diplomacy would achieve a substantial *détente* between the Soviet and Western blocs. The degree of success and failure seems to have been directly dependent on Khrushchev's calculations and growing

[1] Avon, III, pp. 581–4.

self-confidence: from July 1957, when his dominant position in Moscow was finally established, until the Cuban crisis in October 1962, he acted on the assumption that Soviet armed strength and technological achievement would enable him to secure some major political triumphs, although he had no desire for war. The launching of the *Sputnik* on 4 October 1957 was certainly a blow to America's industrial morale. Soviet relations with Communist China were still publicly amicable. The assassination of King Feisal and Nuri-es-Said in Iraq on 14–15 July 1958 threatened the Baghdad pact; British and American forces were sent to Jordan. The rebellion of French settlers in Algeria brought General de Gaulle back to office in France. To these embarrassments of the Western Alliance could be added a fresh dialectical duel between Peking and Washington shortly after Khrushchev's visit to China in August 1958; this died down only after Communist honour had been satisfied by a prolonged bombardment of Quemoy. Then on 27 November 1958 the Soviet Government demanded the withdrawal of all occupation forces from Berlin within six months. Soviet spokesmen kept up the pressure during the following weeks, and on 5 February 1959, following a visit by Dulles to London on the 4th, Macmillan announced that he proposed to visit Moscow to return the visit of Bulganin and Khrushchev in 1956.

Dulles was a dying man; for the moment Macmillan was the peripatetic spokesman of the West. Bonn feared that Britain was weakening; so too did journalists in London and the States. In fact Macmillan had come merely to inquire and propose a Foreign Ministers' Conference, and Khrushchev reacted irritably; but later he became more agreeable, and on 2 March Macmillan was even allowed to make an uncensored broadcast. On the 19th Khrushchev recognized at a Press conference the validity of Western rights of occupation in Berlin. Perhaps the visit did no more than demonstrate to the Russians that the Western powers did not intend to budge, but for Macmillan it was a successful turning of a difficult corner, for he was convinced that some degree of agreement was possible at the top level. It was soon noticed that the six-months' Soviet ultimatum had been quietly forgotten. The Foreign Ministers' Conference took place in the summer of 1959 without progress on the question of a German peace treaty; in September Khrushchev visited the United States, and perhaps was impressed by what he saw. He found Eisenhower ready for a summit conference. This met in May 1960, and Macmillan could look forward to the success of his hopes. But the result was a much-dramatized fiasco. The shooting down of an American U-2 reconnaissance plane over Russia on 1 May led Khrushchev to a violent attack across the table on Eisenhower and ultimately to a refusal to continue the summit conference while Eisenhower remained in office. It is generally thought that Khrushchev was compelled to act in this way by his more intransigent followers. Macmillan appealed sadly for the proceedings to begin, in vain. Ultimately the Russians (starting in August 1961), built the Berlin Wall, thus solving their own most urgent problem of the unending flight of East German refugees; the allied occupation continued. Khrushchev's war of nerves against the United States ended when President Kennedy stood firm in the Cuban crisis of 1962.

In this last decisive episode Macmillan was an onlooker, although the personal relationship with President Kennedy and his entourage was intimate and trusting. But apart from the rapid extension of independence within the Commonwealth to a succession of African states, starting with Ghana in 1957 and Nigeria in 1960, the last great adventure that we shall record in this volume was the belated attempt to enter the European Common Market. Because it failed the final question as to the Cabinet's motivation remained unsolved. It had yet to be seen whether close ties with Europe were compatible with the traditional Commonwealth links; and whether the wind of change had blown away the reality of interdependence.

Certainly the failure during the fifties to keep in step with the movement towards European integration was not due to unqualified aversion to the idea of a European Economic Community (E.E.C.), but rather to some scepticism as to its feasibility and some mental sluggishness amid the distractions of contemporary politics in thinking realistically about the difficulties. The programme involved high tariffs and a threat to Commonwealth suppliers; the supranational ideal, warmly advocated by M. Schuman in and after 1950, needed thinking out and getting used to. When the treaty between the 'Six' (France, Germany, Italy, and the Benelux countries) creating the European Coal and Steel Community, was signed on 18 April 1951, Britain merely asked to be kept informed. By August 1954 the failure of the E.D.C. proposals, partly because of Britain's unwillingness to join, perhaps strengthened scepticism in London about the economic programme. However, the Six elaborated their plans for E.E.C. and Euratom (European Atomic Energy Community) and embodied them in the treaty of Rome of 25 March 1957. Macmillan at the Treasury in 1956 had initiated discussions in O.E.E.C. for a European free-trade area, with a common internal tariff system, but this was rejected by the French Government in November 1958. States outside the Rome Treaty formed EFTA, the European Free Trade Association (Norway, Denmark, and Sweden, Austria, Portugal, Switzerland, and the United Kingdom) on 21 July 1959. The Six and the Seven were not easy at finding themselves in potential rivalry, but the key to reconciliation clearly rested primarily with the British Government.

In the Common Market, it has been said, it is all Cartesian; everything comes down to matters of principle. The pragmatic British step-by-step approach to great decisions was never in accord with the dedicated labours of the authors of the Treaty of Rome, and after Macmillan's re-election in 1959 the Government again took time for a good look round the world before its next step. On 3 February 1960 Macmillan referred in Cape Town to the winds of change that were blowing through Africa, but it seems that this was a memorable example of political phrase-making rather than the announcement of a new Commonwealth policy. And yet, as Mr Duncan Sandys told the Conservative Party Conference in October 1961, the

political and economic nationalism of new Commonwealth
countries as well as of the older Dominions was unsympathetic
towards the creation of a Commonwealth customs union or
huge internal market. Certainly the growing industrial self-
sufficiency of a country like Australia was rapidly eroding the
case for the older economic relationship with the United
Kingdom. It was thus natural to ask whether the Government's
application for membership of the Common Market on 10
August 1961 meant that it was turning its back on the
Commonwealth, but this the Government's spokesman
strenuously denied. EFTA was being built up by easy, give-
and-take methods of negotiation without any undue preoccupation with theory, and it was no doubt felt in London
that by reasonable compromises a profitable relationship with
both Commonwealth and Common Market could also be
worked out. It would be necessary to ensure that the suppliers
of wheat and other temperate-zone products from the
Commonwealth should not be too hard hit by high tariffs,
and that the subsidies on British farm produce should be reduced gradually. New Zealand would have to be allowed a
special relationship, which the Six were willing to concede.
They also agreed, after much British pressure, to 'Associated'
status for the new African Commonwealth countries, who all,
except Sierra Leone, declined the offer. The negotiations took
time, for the Six had to agree about each move among themselves and to reconcile innovations with the principles of their
general programme. But the affair seemed to advance.

It ended abruptly when General de Gaulle refused on 14
January 1963 to allow the talks to continue; he told a Press
conference that Britain must abandon all Commonwealth
preferences, agricultural exemptions, and commitments to
EFTA. He accused Britain of wanting the best of both worlds.
It seemed very clear that he did too, if with different ends. The
remaining five members were thought to be shocked. But were
the French's objections partly or even mainly political?
Undoubtedly de Gaulle intended to raise the status and
influence of his country by exploiting the East–West deadlock

and by building up a Western European system independent of American control, although dependent on her strength. The significant event was probably the meeting at Rambouillet on 15–16 December 1962, when Macmillan failed to offer him a share in nuclear development; shortly afterwards Macmillan and Kennedy met at Nassau in the Bahamas from 18 to 21 December and after some difficult negotiations agreed that Britain should receive Polaris missiles to compensate for America's abandonment of the Skybolt missile. De Gaulle appeared unperturbed by Macmillan's blunt statement on 30 January 1963 that the Common Market failure was 'bad for us, bad for Europe, bad for the whole free world'.

In fact no great upheaval or world disaster followed, and inter-dependence remained the basis of British foreign policy, if with a growing sense of its inadequacy. The need for new definitions was accepted by the three major parties, although with little practical result during the next few years.

Epilogue

Looking back over the period of forty years or more covered by this volume it is easy to over-emphasize the embarrassments and hesitations of British Foreign Secretaries. Writing in April 1964 Lord Franks described the period as that of 'the Great Retreat', which was, however, he thought, nearly over. Britain had retreated from a position of eminence unchallenged in the nineteenth-century world. The milestones were the surrender of naval primacy in 1921; the fall of Singapore in 1942, proof that Britain could no longer wage full-scale war on two fronts on opposite sides of the world; the dissolution of the Indian Empire in 1947; the evacuation of Suez and loss of control over the Canal. He conceded that on the whole the long movement of disengagement had been amazingly well conducted. But he thought that 'as the years have become decades the process has increasingly been felt as a weariness of the flesh, with no adventure, no inspiration in it, nothing positive, only an endless negative'.[1]

This view is in many ways unconvincing. It is certainly possible, at the end of our period, to detect some sense of frustration among individuals in governing and professional circles who favoured a bolder role for Great Britain in world affairs; but the country at large had had a surfeit of action and achievement in two world wars, and the public mood had hardly been one of impatience for fresh adventures in the two post-war eras. In any case, Britain's 'unchallenged eminence' in the world before 1914 is something of a myth. Contemporaries

[1] Lord Franks, 'The Great Retreat is Nearly Over' (*Sunday Times*, 26 April 1964).

spoke of it as a time of 'splendid if dangerous isolation', and were not so sure that it was splendid.[1] The peculiar quality of her world authority had lain in the fact that it was dominant only where it encountered no serious great-power competition. Where it did she was more inclined to buy herself out of trouble by colonial bargains than to seek support by alliances which would entangle her irrevocably in the rivalries of continental Europe. It had already been clear long before 1914 that she could not fight major wars single-handed in both Europe and the Pacific, a conclusion implicit in the signature of the Anglo-Japanese Alliance in 1902. She had long since abandoned competitiveness with the United States. If the Cabinets of the inter-war years were cautious it was partly because they were guided by Foreign Office professionals who were steeped in the nineteenth-century tradition of mediation and non-involvement as the ideal attitude towards other people's affairs. But in fact the country's commitments in the inter-war years were much greater than they had been in the nineteenth century; power, influence, and responsibility were greatly extended in the Middle East and Africa, and the Government had to live up to the wider responsibilties implicit and explicit in the Versailles Treaty, League Covenant, Locarno Agreements and the like.

Thus it is, to say the least of it, an over-simplification to view the broad sweep of British foreign policy solely in terms of an overall retreat from world power. The notion of retreat was partly due to the fierce and contemptuous tone of opposition criticism in the thirties, which was demanding ever greater activity on the world stage, while deprecating the conventional basis of strength in the form of national armaments. Perhaps the one thing really new in British foreign policy in the inter-war years was the advent of the Labour Party, critical and idealistic, completely innocent of pre-1914 experience of office and its problems, always tending to assume that what was ideologically and morally desirable was practicable to men of faith and goodwill. The Tory dissidents, more down to earth in

[1] There is an illuminating discussion of this point in Christopher Howard's essay, *Splendid Isolation* (1967), especially pp. 14–29.

some respects, assumed that desired ends were attainable by courage and political flair. Faced with a highly articulate opposition, the Government in the thirties certainly seemed bumbling and indecisive at times, but with the guarantees to Central and East European states in 1938 and 1939 it extended still further the range of the country's commitments, as compared with the pre-1914 era.

Again, if the Bevinite–Eden decade after 1945 is to be thought of in terms of retreat, it was a retreat from the preeminent position held by Great Britain at the end of the Second World War rather than from the limited obligations of the late nineteenth century. Russia and the United States, recognized as potential giants even in the nineteenth century, had forcibly organized themselves in response to the do-or-die challenges of the war into super-powers of tremendous potency. Great Britain had shown in the war that she still possessed the military aptitude, the industrial power and expertise, the political grasp and capacity for leadership of a greater world power; but her economic base made it impossible for her to maintain in peacetime the vast military establishments and enormously costly weapon systems of the other two. Nevertheless, the Bevinite revolution in British foreign policy in the late forties was, at least in intention, anything but a graceful retreat from greatness; it involved a readjustment but also an overall extension of peacetime commitments (as compared with the nineteenthirties) made possible by the more active role that others were prepared to play, and including now a permanent military presence on the continent of Europe.

Eden followed Bevin down to the mid-fifties in a very active policy in the three interdependent spheres of British diplomatic activity; he was evidently well satisfied as to the importance of Britain's central position and the continued weight of her influence. There is again no sign of a consciousness of overstrained resources, and even the Suez episode, although disastrous for Eden's reputation as a political realist and skilled negotiator, is from this point of view evidence of overconfidence in Britain's power to command events and to defend her interests. Under his adroit and imperturbable successor, Harold Macmillan, there was a revival for a time of the high mediatory role within the Western system which the Bevin–Eden era seemed to have established.

It is only at the beginning of the nineteen-sixties that signs begin to multiply of a rather sudden loss of confidence in the adequacy of the policy of interdependence, followed by moves to concentrate the main weight of British political and economic influence in Europe. The decision to seek entry into the European Common Market in 1961 was certainly an abrupt reversal of course in the economic field, but it has yet to be known how far it involved a planned relaxation of political ties with the Commonwealth and the United States, in short, whether it was anything more than a reapplication of policy based on multiple obligations. It might well be asked whether the Great Retreat ends or begins in the early sixties. Speaking as late as July 1967 Sir Robert Menzies, until recently Prime Minister of Australia, claimed to be still unable to understand the change in Britain's attitude to the Common Market. He pointed out that ten years before, when Britain had the chance to be a founder member, France had been economically distressed and favourable terms could have been made with the Commonwealth; but Britain had then found conclusive arguments against membership. Now, facing an unwelcoming and strongly revived France, an overwhelming majority of all the British political parties found these objections insubstantial.

These comments are apt, for something was undoubtedly lacking or unconvincing in governmental explanations of the change of course. It may be that Mr Macmillan at any rate saw no incompatibility between Common Market and Commonwealth, and we have seen that Tory spokesmen strongly denied that there would be any abandonment of the essential Commonwealth commitments. But in that case President de Gaulle's cold and very explicit appraisal in January 1963 of the difficulties of Britain's entry could hardly be said to have distorted the facts.

The question arises as to how far it is possible for Great Britain at the present time to accept a truly common tariff, as the Continent does, for this would involve giving up all Commonwealth preferences, renouncing all claims for privileges for her agriculture, and treating as null and void obligations entered into with countries forming part of the Free Trade Area. Can she do this? That is the question. It cannot be claimed that this question has been answered.

The British negotiators professed to have no doubt in 1962, and in 1967 when the application was renewed, that the necessary reconciliation (although at some disadvantage to the Commonwealth) could be worked out by give-and-take bargaining in the economic sphere, although the French continued to ask for prior evidence on this point. But the argument was continually shifting to the political and spiritual case for entry. It was in this direction that Lord Franks hoped for advance and regretted de Gaulle's decision in 1963. Britain, he argued, could have gone forward, helping in the creation of something new, a new framework of life in Europe, political, economic, and social, with so many of her neighbours. 'It would have given a different savour to life, a relish we should have enjoyed.'

But it is possible to find a rather different explanation of the malaise that seemed to be affecting British foreign policy. It was not so much that Great Britain had ceased to play a major part in world politics as that world politics themselves had largely ceased. Foreign policy is not the deployment of power but the exercise of influence based on power. It cannot function without a purpose, without problems, aspirations, and challenges, and these in the traditional world of competing states had always been abundant, taking the form either of the seizure of national advantage or the organization of defence against attack, real or anticipated. But by the end of the fifties the nuclear deadlock meant that the organization of defence against any form of military and political aggression between the two great power blocs had become so complete as virtually to paralyse all major initiatives in world affairs. Even in the mounting Vietnam crisis both sides professed to be acting defensively. The fading out of the conventional sense of crisis – which had been acute for so many centuries in the past, and was

still very much alive in the decade after 1945 – meant that no
major power had any foreign 'policy' worthy of the name,
apart from the effort to keep everyone else as quiet as possible.
An adamantine refusal to budge from any position of advantage had become almost the criterion of great-power status,
and there was little call for constructive goodwill.

It is true, as M. Raymond Aron has recently remarked, that
although weapons have never been so terrifying, they have
never inspired so little terror in those not equipped with them.
The two warring brothers, Russia and America, were united,
in spite of their conflicting interests and ideologies, against a
total war in which they would be the first victims; but if they
could not dominate each other they could also not impose
pressure proportionate to their strength on other powers.[1] And
yet the signs of independence within the two blocs so recently
dominated by the two giants were not due to any shifting of
sides or desire for dangerous living on the part of the lesser
members. The two super-states would neither abuse their
power nor share it; their superior airs were irritating, and there
was some kudos and not much danger in harassing them.
Accordingly there was much restlessness and even open defiance of the leaders within the two blocs, and competition
between the leaders themselves to buy influence and esteem in
the non-committed Afro-Asian countries and even within the
rival camps. In spite of these competitive gestures the policies
of all governments remained basically defensive and quiescent.

In these circumstances Great Britain found herself in a
curious, intermediate position. She was as dedicated as the
United States to the maintenance of a peaceful world in terms
of the damming of Communism, and she can be seen to share
the outlook of the two super-powers in such actions as the
signing with them of the Nuclear Test-Ban Treaty of 5 August
1963, with the evident aim of preventing the acquisition of
nuclear weapons by other states. But she was not, in fact, one
of the super-states; in Commonwealth matters she had felt at
times the hostility of both, and she shared in some measure the

[1] R. Aron, *Peace and War* (1967), pp. xiv, 651–3.

French inclination to take a line of her own. There was in consequence much talk now of the need for her to find a new role in the world, a new purpose in international life, a reinvigorated sense of mission – it apparently did not much matter what it was.

No doubt the habits of thought in a liberal-democratic society make it difficult for Englishmen to be content with a circumspect defence of existing national interests as the sole standard of statesmanship. Hardest to accept was the view that there simply were no major alternatives to the existing policies, and little for the country to do except to be content with its not hard lot. There were no more empires to win, no more Fascist of even Communist dictatorships to be fought; and the realistic recasting of the defence budget was soon to establish the case for a staged reduction of the country's remaining obligations east of Suez. It was admitted that the advantages and disadvantages of entry into the Common Market were rather finely balanced and if the renewed application for entry in 1967 was greeted with some enthusiasm it was mainly perhaps with a sigh of relief that something was going on.

If we can detect a genuine sense of guilt or inadequacy among commentators on this position it was mainly in connexion with the Commonwealth, and it would seem that before coming to office in 1964 the Labour Party was still looking more to the Commonwealth and the undeveloped world than to Europe for its distinctive sphere of action. Mr George Brown, speaking to the Foreign Press Association in May 1963, called on the British (and no doubt the Government) to be less selfish, 'to think rather less of ourselves, rather more of the kind of society that we want the world to be, rather more of what we can give than what we can take'. And in March 1964 Mr Harold Wilson said that Britain had always been a world power, and should 'not be corralled in Europe'; her role in the Commonwealth was to put out brush fires everywhere. 'Britain does wish for radical changes,' wrote a sympathetic commentator a few months later, 'not changes in frontiers or in national spheres of influence, but in the global organization both of military security and of the war against backwardness and poverty.'[1]

But during the next two or three years it could hardly have appeared to a New Zealander or Australian or even a sympathetic American observer that these vaguely altruistic aspirations were much compensation for the disintegrating effect of Britain's progressive abandonment of her commitments as a world power. The intra-structure of the Commonwealth, the social, educational, linguistic, professional, and scientific relationships generally, were probably not much affected and could be expected to continue. But the directing and co-ordinating forces, let alone the military and economic support which she had in the past supplied, were now largely gone, and would be still further reduced if Britain entered the Common Market. Many of the new members of the Commonwealth were small, weak, isolated countries, struggling to survive; all that could be hoped was that some help and direction might come to them through United Europe and those parts of the Commonwealth in close alliance with the United States, and the Commonwealth might perhaps live on in this new shape.

Yet it would be quite wrong to speak as if this situation was one which could have been substantially arrested or reversed by isolated British action; the withdrawal of the imperial authority had been a steady process of adaptation and response to internal and external pressures for a century or more, and the Commonwealth was now what its members and not the Mother Country had made of it. Her obligations and commitments throughout the world were still enormous, wider than those of any power except the United States. Her capacity to deal with them remained formidable. There was perhaps no particular disadvantage in allowing international affairs to follow their own course for the time being, and no particular evidence that any initiative on her part at this stage would usefully divert the tide of events.

[1] Kenneth Younger, *Changing Perspectives in British Foreign Policy* (1967), pp. 70, 138.

Some Key Statements on British Foreign Policy

LORD ROBERT CECIL
House of Commons, 21 July 1919, on the League of Nations

The great weapon we rely upon is public opinion. . . . If you do not rely upon public opinion the decision of the assembly ceases to be of the first importance. If you have a decision in the assembly of overwhelming opinion on one side or the other it matters very little whether it is unanimous or not, because the whole course of public opinion will fasten round the great mass of the overwhelming majority. I believe that is the way it will work, if it works at all . . . you will get the whole weight of public opinion behind the one side and you will find, I think, that the nation that is in the wrong will not persist in the course which has been publicly and over-whelmingly condemned. That is my view.

D. LLOYD GEORGE
House of Commons, 21 July 1919

I knew what Europe had suffered from the setting up of one Alsace-Lorraine, and I knew that if we set up another it would simply repeat the same crime, the same blunder, and the same disaster. I know of no Alsace-Lorraines that were set up in this Treaty [of Versailles].

LORD CURZON
Speaking to Commonwealth representatives, 22 *June* 1921

> We have, as I read the lesson of the time, to keep what we
> have obtained, sometimes against our will; not to seize any-
> thing else; to reconcile, not defy; to pacify, not to conquer.

AUSTEN CHAMBERLAIN
Speech to League Council on 12 *March* 1925, *rejecting Geneva Protocol*

> His Majesty's Government cannot believe that the Protocol
> as it stands provides the most suitable method [of clarifying
> the meaning of the Covenant or strengthening its provi-
> sions]. As all the world is aware, the League of Nations, in
> its present shape, is not the League designed by the framers
> of the Covenant. . . . To them [the economic sanction]
> appeared to be not only bloodless, but cheap, effective and
> easy to use, in the most improbable event of its being neces-
> sary. But all this is changed by the existence of powerful
> economic communities outside the limits of the League. It
> might force trade into unaccustomed channels, but it could
> hardly stop it. . . . Since the general provisions of the
> Covenant cannot be stiffened with advantage, and since the
> 'extreme cases' with which the League may have to deal will
> probably affect certain nations or groups of nations more
> nearly than others, His Majesty's Government conclude that
> the best way of dealing with the situation is, with the co-
> operation of the League, to supplement the Covenant by
> making special arrangements in order to meet special needs.

AUSTEN CHAMBERLAIN
Speech at Birmingham, 29 *January* 1927

> In the Far East, at any rate, we are a nation of shopkeepers.
> All we want is to keep our shops open, and to be on good
> terms with our customers. We realize, no less than the most
> patriotic Chinese nationalist, that the old treaties are out of

date, and we desire to put our relations with China on a basis suitable to the times in which we live. . . . There is no [central] Government in China at this moment, but the demand for treaty revision has become so insistent, and is fundamentally so reasonable that, in spite of the difficulties involved by the prevailing dissensions among the Chinese, we must try to negotiate this change with the contending Governments in the vortex of a civil war.

SIR JOHN SIMON
Speech to League Assembly, 7 December 1932

I would wish to point out that, contrary to the impression which exists in many quarters, this [Lytton] report does not give a one-sided account, painting everything black on the one side and presenting it in spotless raiments of white on the other. It makes a measured criticism of both the side of China and that of Japan. Japan does not accept every statement in the report; neither does China. For example, we have heard on behalf of China the existence of an antiforeign feeling warmly challenged, and yet this report draws the conclusion on that matter that such a movement undoubtedly exists. . . . I take leave to say that no fair account of the contents of this report can be given which does not include the description of the deplorable condition of Manchuria in Chapter II and the objective account of the antiforeign boycott in Chapter VII. For my part and on behalf of my Government I associate myself entirely with what was so well said yesterday by M. Benes, when he observed that he did not desire to be the judge on either side.

SIR JOHN SIMON
House of Commons, 13 June 1934

Belgium is no less vital to the interests and safety of this country today than it has been in times past. That is a geographical fact which nothing can change. Indeed changed conditions, especially in connection with the air, have not altered that historic fact at all; they have served to emphasize it.

STANLEY BALDWIN
House of Commons, 30 *July* 1934

Let us never forget this. Since the day of the air the old frontiers are gone. When you think of the defence of England, you no longer think of the chalk cliffs of Dover; you think of the Rhine. That is where our frontier lies.

STANLEY BALDWIN
House of Commons, 28 *November* 1934

His Majesty's Government are determined, in no conditions, to accept any position of inferiority with regard to what air force may be raised in Germany in the future.

GEORGE LANSBURY
House of Commons, 21 *March* 1935

I want our country to take the lead in saying to the world: 'We will lay on the altar of disarmament this business of aerial warfare. We are willing to give up for good and for all, with other nations. . . . It is said very often, and it has been said here before, that other people will not do this. I repeat that we want that our country shall make the challenge. If we are not successful, we cannot help it. At least, we shall have tried. . . .'

SIR JOHN SIMON
House of Commons, 21 *March* 1935

We are not going to bear the reproach – the British people I am sure would never willingly do so – of leaving anything undone which might help to make peace more secure by the better means. The object of British policy has been – and this is the better means – to help to bring this great State [Germany] back into the councils and comity of Europe on terms which are just to her and which are fair and secure for all of us.

ANTHONY EDEN
House of Commons, 9 March 1936, following German reoccupation of the Rhineland

In case there should be any misunderstanding about our position as a signatory of the Locarno Treaty, His Majesty's Government think it necessary to say that, should there take place, during the period which will be necessary for the consideration of the new situation which has arisen, any actual attack upon France or Belgium, which would constitute a violation of Article 2 of Locarno, His Majesty's Government in the United Kingdom, notwithstanding the German repudiation of the treaty, would regard themselves as in honour bound to come, in the manner provided in the treaty, to the assistance of the country attacked.

STANLEY BALDWIN
House of Commons, 12 November 1936

You will remember the election at Fulham in the autumn of 1933, when a seat which the National Government held was lost by about 7,000 votes on no issue but the pacifist. . . . My position as the leader of a great party was not altogether a comfortable one. I asked myself what chance was there – when that feeling that was given expression to in Fulham was common throughout the country – what chance was there that within the next year or two of that feeling being so changed that the country would give a mandate for rearmament? Supposing I had gone to the country and said that Germany was rearming and that we must rearm, does anybody think that this pacific democracy would have rallied to that cry at that moment? I cannot think of anything that would have made the loss of the election from my point of view more certain.

ANTHONY EDEN
House of Commons, 1 *November* 1937

There are those who are convinced that supposing the insurgent forces are victorious the result will be a Spain in active alliance in a foreign policy directed against this country. I do not accept that. . . . This country is still, and will continue to be, I trust, the greatest naval Power in Europe. This is not without its effect when it is known that we have no intention, no kind of after-thought, either direct or indirect, about the territorial integrity and the political independence of Spain. Spaniards know that very well. They know very well, too, that no British war material has killed any Spaniard on either side. These factors will, I believe, be important in the future.

NEVILLE CHAMBERLAIN
Broadcast speech, 27 *September* 1938

How horrible, fantastic, incredible it is that we should be digging trenches and trying on gas-masks here because of a quarrel in a far-away country between people of whom we know nothing. . . . I am myself a man of peace to the depths of my soul. Armed conflict between nations is a nightmare to me; but if I were convinced that any nation had made up its mind to dominate the world by fear of its force, I should feel that it must be resisted. Under such a domination life for people who believe in liberty would not be worth living; but war is a fearful thing, and we must be very clear, before we embark on it, that it is really the great issues that are at stake.

NEVILLE CHAMBERLAIN
Speech at Birmingham, 17 *March* 1939

We need not be downhearted. This is a great and powerful
nation – far more powerful than we were even six months
ago, and acts of violence and injustice bring with them
sooner or later their own reward. Every one of the incursions
raises up fresh dangers for Germany in the future, and I ven-
ture to prophesy that in the end she will bitterly regret what
her Government has done.

LORD HALIFAX
At Chatham House Dinner, 29 *June* 1939

Our first resolve is to stop aggression. I need not recapitulate
the acts of aggression which have taken place, or the effect
which they have had upon the general trust that European
nations feel able to place in words and undertakings. For
that reason and for that reason alone we have joined with
other nations to meet a common danger. These arrangements
we all know, and the world knows, have no purpose other
than defence. They mean what they say – no more and no
less. But they have been denounced as aiming at the isolation
– or as it is called the encirclement – of Germany and Italy,
and as designed to prevent them from acquiring the living
space necessary for their national existence. . . . What are the
facts? They are very simple and everybody knows them.
Germany is isolating herself, and is doing so most successfully and most completely.

NEVILLE CHAMBERLAIN
House of Commons, 12 *October* 1939

Past experience has shown that no reliance can be placed
upon the promises of the present German Government.
Accordingly acts – not words alone – must be forthcoming
before we, the British people, and France, our gallant and

trusted Ally, would be justified in ceasing to wage war to the utmost of our strength. . . . Either the German Government must give convincing proof of the sincerity of their desire for peace by definite acts and by the provision of effective guarantees of their intention to fulfil their undertakings, or we must persevere in our duty to the end. It is for Germany to make her choice.

LORD HALIFAX
Broadcast speech, 22 *July* 1940

Many of you will have read two days ago the speech in which Herr Hitler summoned Great Britain to capitulate to his will. . . . The peoples of the British Commonwealth, along with those who love truth and justice and freedom, will never accept this new world of Hitler's. Free men, not slaves; free nations, not German vassals; a community of nations, freely co-operating for the good of all – these are the pillars of the new and better order that the British people wish to see.

WINSTON CHURCHILL
Broadcast speech, 22 *June* 1941

No one has been a more persistent opponent of Communism than I have been for the last twenty-five years. I will unsay no word that I have spoken about it, but all this fades away before the spectacle that is now unfolding. . . . Any man or State who fights against Naziism will have our aid. Any man or State who marches with Hitler is our foe. This applies not only to organized States, but to all representatives of that vile race of quislings who made themselves the tools and agents of the Nazi régime. . . . It follows, therefore, that we shall give whatever help we can to Russia and to the Russian people.

WINSTON CHURCHILL
House of Commons, 27 *February* 1945

Most solemn declarations have been made by Marshal Stalin and the Soviet Union that the sovereign independence of Poland is to be maintained, and this decision is now joined in both by Great Britain and the United States. Here also the World Organization will in due course assume a measure of responsibility. The Poles will have their future in their own hands, with the single limitation that they must honestly follow, in harmony with their Allies, a policy friendly to Russia. That is surely reasonable.

WINSTON CHURCHILL
Victory broadcast, 13 *May* 1945

There would be little use in punishing the Hitlerites for their crimes if law and justice did not rule, and if totalitarian or police Governments were to take the place of the German invaders. We seek nothing for ourselves. But we must make sure that those causes which we fought for find recognition at the peace table in facts as well as words, and above all we must labour that the World Organization which the United Nations are creating at San Francisco does not become an idle name, does not become a shield for the strong and a mockery for the weak. It is the victors who must search their hearts in their glowing hours, and be worthy by their nobility of the immense forces that they wield.

WINSTON CHURCHILL
Speech at Fulton, Missouri, 5 *March* 1946

Neither the sure prevention of war nor the continuous rise of the World Organization will be gained without what I have called the fraternal association of the English-speaking peoples. This means a special relationship between the British Commonwealth and Empire and the United States.

... Nobody knows what Soviet Russia and its Communist international organization intends to do in the immediate future, or what are the limits, if any, to their expansive and proselytizing tendencies. ... From Stettin, in the Baltic, to Trieste, in the Adriatic, an iron curtain has descended across the Continent.

ERNEST BEVIN
House of Commons, 22 January 1948

While I do not wish to discourage the work done by voluntary political organizations in advocating ambitious schemes of European unity, I must say that it is a much slower and harder job to carry out a practical programme which takes into account the realities which face it, and I am afraid that it will have to be done a step at a time. But surely all these [Communist] developments which I have been describing point to the conclusion that the free nations of Western Europe must now draw closely together. I believe the time is ripe for a consolidation of Western Europe. First in this context we think of the people of France. ... I hope treaties will be signed with our near neighbours, the Benelux countries, making, with our treaty with France, an important nucleus in Western Europe. We have then to go beyond the circle of our immediate neighbours. ... There is no political motive behind the Marshall offer other than the overriding human motive to help Europe to help herself, and so restore the economic and political health of the world.

ANTHONY EDEN
Speech at the Nine-Power Conference, London, 29 September 1954

The United Kingdom will continue to maintain on the mainland of Europe, including Germany, the effective strength of the United Kingdom forces which are now assigned to SACEUR[1] – four divisions and the tactical Air Force – or what-

---

[1] Supreme Allied Commander, Europe.

ever SACEUR regards as equivalent fighting capacity. The United Kingdom undertakes not to withdraw those forces against the wishes of the majority of the Brussels Treaty Powers. . . . This undertaking would be subject to the understanding that an acute overseas emergency might oblige her Majesty's Government to omit this procedure. If maintenance of the United Kingdom forces on the mainland of Europe throws at any time too heavy a strain on the external finances of the United Kingdom then we would invite the North Atlantic Council to review the financial conditions on which the formations are maintained.

SELWYN LLOYD
Speech to United Nations General Assembly, 17 *September* 1959

In those territories where different races or tribes live side by side, the task is to ensure that all the people may enjoy security and freedom and the chance to contribute as individuals to the progress and well being of these countries. We reject the idea of any inherent superiority of one race over another. Our policy therefore is non-racial. It offers a future in which Africans, Europeans, Asians, the peoples of the Pacific, and others with whom we are concerned, will all play their full part as citizens in the countries where they live and in which feelings of race will be submerged in loyalty to the new nations.

HAROLD MACMILLAN
Speech to the South African Parliament, 3 *February* 1960

The most striking of all the impressions I have formed since I left London a month ago is of the strength of this African national consciousness. In different places it may take different forms, but it is happening everywhere. The wind of change is blowing through the continent. . . . As a fellow member of the Commonwealth, it is our earnest desire to give South Africa our support and encouragement, but I hope you won't mind my saying frankly that there are some aspects of your policies which make it impossible for us to do this without being false to our own deep convictions about the political destinies of free men, in which in our own territories we are trying to give effect.

HAROLD MACMILLAN
House of Commons, 31 *July* 1961

The Commonwealth is a great source of stability and strength, both to Western Europe and to the world as a whole, and I am sure that its value is fully appreciated by the member Governments of the E.E.C. I do not think that Britain's contribution to the Commonwealth will be reduced if Europe unites. On the contrary I think it will be enhanced. . . . No British Government could join the E.E.C. without prior negotiation with a view to meeting the needs of the Commonwealth countries, of our European Free Trade partners, and of British agriculture consistently with the broad principles and purposes which have inspired the concept of European unity and which are embodied in the Rome Treaty.

Bibliography

This list of books and documents is limited as far as possible to titles bearing directly on British foreign policy. It is obvious, however, that there is much of interest in general histories of international relations for this period. These include the *Survey of International Affairs* (Royal Institute of International Affairs, more or less annual volumes since 1927); P. E. G. Renouvin, *Histoire des relations internationales*, vols 7 and 8 (Paris, 1957–8); *The Annual Register*; the annual volumes of *The United States in World Affairs* (New York: Council on Foreign Relations); and the *History of the Peace Conference at Paris* (1920–4, edited by H. W. V. Temperley). The first section below includes collections of documents and books covering the whole or large parts of the period; after this the arrangement is by topics.

General

M. BAUMONT, *La Faillite de la Paix (1918–1939)* (1951)

E. H. CARR, *Ambassadors at Large: Britain* (1939); *The Twenty Years Crisis, 1919–1939* (1939)

G. M. CARTER, *The British Commonwealth and International Security* (1947)

IAN COLVIN, *Vansittart in Office* (1965)

G. A. CRAIG and F. GILBERT (eds.), *The Diplomats, 1919–1939* (1953)

J. DEGRAS (ed.), *Soviet Documents on Foreign Policy, 1917–1941* (3 vols, 1951–3)

B.D.: *Documents on British Foreign Policy, 1919–1939* (ed. by E. L. Woodward, Rohan Butler, W. N. Medlicott, and others, H.M.S.O., 1947, continuing)

F.D.: *Documents Diplomatiques Français, 1932–1939* (1965, continuing)

G.D.: *Documents on German Foreign Policy, 1918–1945* (ed. by Hon. Margaret Lambert and others, H.M.S.O., Ser. C & D, 1949, continuing)

Documents on International Affairs (Royal Institute of International Affairs, 1948, continuing)

J. C. R. DOW, *The Management of the British Economy* (1965)

M. R. D. FOOT, *British Foreign Policy since 1898* (1956)

Foreign Relations of the United States (State Department, Washington, continuing)

History of the Times, 1921–1948 (2 vols, 1952)

H. V. HODSON, *Slump and Recovery, 1929–1937* (1938)

P. N. S. MANSERGH, *Survey of British Commonwealth Affairs*, vol. 3, *Problems of External Policy, 1931–39* (1952)

W. N. MEDLICOTT, *Contemporary England, 1914–1964* (1967)

C. L. MOWAT, *Britain between the Wars 1918–1940* (1955)

F. S. NORTHEDGE, *The Troubled Giant* (1966)

P. A. REYNOLDS, *British Foreign Policy in the Inter-War Years* (1954)

R. W. SETON-WATSON, *Britain and the Dictators* (1938)

LORD STRANG, *Britain in World Affairs* (1961); *Home and Abroad* (1956)

A. J. P. TAYLOR, *English History, 1914–1945* (1965); *The Trouble-makers* (1957)

D. C. WATT, *Personalities and Policies* (1965)

E. WINDRICH, *British Labour's Foreign Policy* (1952)

A. WOLFERS, *Britain and France between Two Wars* (1940)

A. J. YOUNGSON, *The British Economy, 1920–1957* (1960)

The Peace Settlements

R. ALBRECHT-CARRIÉ, *Italy at the Paris Peace Conference* (1938)

H. H. CUMMING, *Franco-British Rivalry in the Post-War Near East* (1938)

LORD D'ABERNON, *An Ambassador of Peace* (3 vols, 1929–30)

M. GILBERT, *The Roots of Appeasement* (1966)

G. GLASGOW, *MacDonald as Diplomatist* (1924)

G. A. GRÜN, 'Locarno, Idea and Reality' (*International Affairs*, October 1955)

LORD HANKEY, *The Supreme Council at the Paris Peace Conference 1919* (1963)

F. W. HIRST, *The Consequences of the War to Great Britain* (1934)

H. N. HOWARD, *The Partition of Turkey* (1931)

W. M. JORDAN, *Great Britain, France, and the German Problem* (1943)

E. KEDOURIE, *England and the Middle East* (1956)

T. KOMARNICKI, *Rebirth of the Polish Republic* (1957)

D. LLOYD GEORGE, *The Truth about the Peace Treaties* (2 vols, 1938); *The Truth about Reparations and War Debts* (1932)

P. MANTOUX (ed.), *Les Délibérations du Conseil des Quatre* (2 vols, 1955)

F. S. MARSTON, *The Peace Conference of 1919* (1944)

R. B. MCCALLUM, *Public Opinion and the Last Peace* (1944)

I. F. D. MORROW, *The Peace Settlement in the German–Polish Borderlands* (1936)

H. I. NELSON, *Land and Power* (1963)

H. NICOLSON, *Peacemaking, 1919* (1933); *Curzon, the Last Phase* (1934)

J. P. SELSAM, *The Attempts to Form an Anglo-French Alliance, 1919–1924* (1936)

S. P. TILLMAN, *Anglo-American Relations at the Peace Conference of Paris* (1961)

A. J. TOYNBEE, *The Conduct of British Empire Foreign Relations since the Peace Settlement* (1928)

LORD VANSITTART, *The Mist Procession* (1958)

W. W. WHITE, *The Process of Change in the Ottoman Empire* (1937)

H. R. WINKLER, 'The Emergence of a Labor Foreign Policy in Great Britain, 1918–1929' (*Journal of Modern History*, September 1956)

United States, Japan, and The Far East (*to* 1939)

R. BASSETT, *Democracy and Foreign Policy* (1952)

J. M. BLUM, *From the Morgenthau Diaries* (vol. 1, 1959)

R. L. BUELL, *The Washington Conference* (1922)

Correspondence with the Self-governing Dominions and India regarding the Development of the Singapore Naval Base (Cmd. 2083, 1924)

R. L. CRAIGIE, *Behind the Japanese Mask* (1946)

H. FEIS, *The Road to Pearl Harbor* (1950)

R. H. FERRELL, *American Diplomacy in the Great Depression* (1957)

I. S. FRIEDMAN, *British Relations with China: 1931–1939* (1940)

J. K. GALBRAITH, 'The Imperial Conference of 1921 and the Washington Conference' (*Canadian Historical Review*, 1948)

J. C. GREW, *Ten Years in Japan* (1944)

E. M. GULL, *British Economic Interests in the Far East* (1943)

G. F. HUDSON, *The Far East in World Politics* (1938)

Y. ICHIHASHI, *The Washington Conference and After* (1928)

T. ISHIMARU, *Japan Must Fight Britain* (1936)

F. C. JONES, *Japan's New Order in East Asia* (1954)

D. E. T. LUARD, *Britain and China* (1962)

I. H. NISH, 'Japan and the Ending of the Anglo-Japanese Alliance' (in *Studies in International History*, eds. K. Bourne and D. C. Watt, 1967)

J. T. PRATT, *War and Politics in China* (1943)

S. R. SMITH, *The Manchurian Crisis, 1931–32* (1948)

E. SNOW, *Red Star over China* (1937)

H. L. STIMSON, *The Far Eastern Crisis* (1936)

H. L. STIMSON, and M. and G. BUNDY, *On Active Service in Peace and War* (1948)

R. W. STORRY, *The Double Patriots* (1957)

T. TAKEUCHI, *War and Diplomacy in the Japanese Empire* (1936)

E. TEICHMAN, *Affairs of China* (1939)

W. W. WILLOUGHBY, *Foreign Rights and Interests in China* (2 vols, 1927); *The Sino-Japanese Controversy and the League of Nations* (1935)

F. UTLEY, *Japan's Feet of Clay* (1937); *China at War* (1939)

Britain, The League, and Disarmament

J. BARDOUX, *'L'Ile et l'Europe: La Politique anglaise (1930–1932)* (1933)

VISCOUNT CECIL, *A Great Experiment* (1941)

R. A. CHAPUT, *Disarmament in British Foreign Policy* (1935)

J. F. CHARVAT, *L'influence Britannique dans la Société des Nations* (1938)

DAVID DAVIES, *The Problem of the Twentieth Century* (1930)

R. H. FERRELL, *Peace in Their Time, the Origins of the Kellogg–Briand Pact* (1952)

M. GILBERT, *Plough My Own Furrow: the story of Lord Allen of Hurtwood* (1965)

M. A. HAMILTON, *Arthur Henderson* (1938)

W. P. MADDON, *Foreign Relations in British Labour Politics* (1934)

A. MARWICK, *Clifford Allen* (1964)

P. J. NOEL-BAKER, *The Geneva Protocol* (1925); *The Private Manufacture of Armaments* (vol. I, 1936)

R. G. O'CONNOR, *Perilous Equilibrium: The United States and the London Naval Conference of 1930* (1962)

J. SCHWOEBEL, *L'Angleterre et la sécurité collective* (1938)

A. C. TEMPERLEY, *The Whispering Gallery of Europe* (1939)

F. P. WALTERS, *A History of the League of Nations* (2 vols, 1952)

C. K. WEBSTER and S. HERBERT, *The League of Nations in Theory and Practice* (1933)

J. W. WHEELER-BENNETT, *The Disarmament Conference* (1934)

A. ZIMMERN, *The League of Nations and the Rule of Law* (1939)

Mussolini, Spain, and the Mediterranean

DUCHESS OF ATHOLL, *Searchlight on Spain* (1938)

EARL OF AVON, *The Eden Memoirs: Facing the Dictators* (1962)

E. DE BONO, *Anno XIII, The Conquest of an Empire* (1937)

F. BORKENAU, *The Spanish Cockpit* (1937)

M. BOVERI, *Mediterranean Cross-Currents* (1938)

F. W. D. DEAKIN, *The Brutal Friendship* (1962)

A. FAHMI, *La Conférence de Montreux, 1937: L'Abolition des Capitulations en Egypte* (1938)

H. FEIS, *Seen from E.A. Three International Episodes* (1947)

H. FINER, *Mussolini's Italy* (1935)

G. T. GARRETT, *Mussolini's Roman Empire* (1938)

W. L. KLEINE-AHLBRANDT, *The Policy of Simmering* (1962)

M. H. H. MACARTNEY and P. CREMONA, *Italy's Foreign and Colonial Policy, 1914–37* (1938)

E. MONROE, *The Mediterranean in Politics* (1938); *Britain's Moment in the Middle East, 1914–1956* (1963)

E. ALLISON PEERS, *The Spanish Tragedy, 1930–1936* (1936); *Catalonia Infelix* (1937)

VISCOUNT TEMPLEWOOD, *Nine Troubled Years* (1954)

H. THOMAS, *The Spanish Civil War* (1961)

M. TOSCANO, *Le Origini del Patto d'Acciaio* (1948)

E. WISKEMANN, *The Rome–Berlin Axis* (1949)

Central and Eastern Europe (to 1938)

M. BELOFF, *The Foreign Policy of Soviet Russia, 1929–41* (2 vols, 1947)

F. BORKENAU, *The Communist International* (1938)

G. BROOK-SHEPHERD, *Anschluss: the Rape of Austria* (1963)

A. L. C. BULLOCK, *Hitler: a Study in Tyranny* (1952)

E. H. CARR, *A History of Soviet Russia* (1950, continuing)

W. P. and Z. K. COATES, *A History of Anglo-Soviet Relations* (2 vols, 1943, 1958)

I. DEUTSCHER, *Stalin* (1949)

U. EICHSTÄDT, *Geschichte des Anschlusses Österreichs, 1933–1938* (1955)

L. FISCHER, *The Soviets in World Affairs* (2 vols, 1951)

G. E. R. GEYDE, *Fallen Bastions* (1939)

J. GEHL, *Austria, Germany, and the Anschluss* (1963)

G. HILGER and A. G. MEYER, *The Incompatible Allies* (1953)

A. HITLER, *Mein Kampf* (unexpurgated English translation, 1939)

W. LAQUEUR, *Russia and Germany* (1965)

M. LITVINOV, *Against Aggression: Speeches* (1939)

MARQUESS OF LONDONDERRY, *Ourselves and Germany* (1938)

C. A. MACARTNEY, *Hungary and her Successors: the Treaty of Trianon and its Consequences* (1937)

H. NICOLSON, N. ANGELL, MARQUESS OF LOTHIAN, *Germany and the Rhineland* (addresses at Chatham House, March–April 1936)

S. H. ROBERTS, *The House that Hitler Built* (1938)

H. SCHACHT, *The End of Reparations* (1931)

W. SELBY, *Diplomatic Twilight 1930–1940* (1953)

G. STRESEMANN, *His Diaries, Letters, and Papers* (1935, 1937)

J. W. WHEELER-BENNETT, *Hindenburg the Wooden Titan* (1936); *The Nemesis of Power, the German Army in Politics, 1918–1945* (1953)

E. WISKEMANN, *Czechs and Germans* (1938)

The Coming of War, 1939

FRANCE: *Ministère des Affaires Étrangères: Pièces relatives aux événements et aux négociations qui ont précédé l'ouverture des hostilités . . .* (1939)

GERMANY: *Auswärtiges Amt: Urkunden zur letzten Phase der deutsch-polnischen Krise* (1939); *Dokumente zur Vorgeschichte Krieges* (1939)

GREAT BRITAIN: *Final Report of Sir Nevile Henderson on the Circumstances leading to the Termination of his Mission to Berlin* (20 September 1939: Cmd. 6115); *Correspondence between H.M. Government in the United Kingdom and the German Government, August 1939* (Cmd. 6102); *Documents concerning German–Polish Relations and the Outbreak of Hostilities between Great Britain and Germany on September 3, 1939* (Cmd. 6106)

POLAND: *Official Documents concerning Polish–German and Polish–Soviet Relations 1933–1939* (published by the Authority of the Polish Government: London, 1939)

LORD BIRKENHEAD, *Halifax* (1965)

G. BONNET, *Quai d'Orsay* (1965)

B. CELOVSKY, *Das Münchener Abkommen von 1938* (1951)

W. S. CHURCHILL, *Step by Step, 1936–9* (1939)

B. DAHLERUS, *Der Letzte Versuch, London/Berlin, Sommer 1939* (1948)

D. J. DALLIN, *Soviet Russia's Foreign Policy, 1939–42* (1944)

H. DALTON, *Memoirs 1931–1945: The Fateful Years* (1957)

A. DUFF COOPER, *Old Men Forget* (1953)

K. EUBANK, *Munich* (1963)

K. FEILING, *Life of Neville Chamberlain* (1946)

A. H. FURNIA, *The Diplomacy of Appeasement* (1960)

M. GILBERT and R. GOTT, *The Appeasers* (1963)

N. HENDERSON, *Failure of a Mission, Berlin 1937–1939* (1940)

E. L. HENSON, 'Britain, America, and the month of Munich' (*International Relations*, April 1962)

W. HOFER, *War Premeditated – 1939* (1955)

D. L. HOGGAN, *Der erzwungene Krieg: Die Ursachen und Urheber des 2. Weltkriegs* (1964)

I. A. KIRKPATRICK, *The Inner Circle* (1959)

W. L. LANGER and S. E. GLEASON, *The Challenge to Isolation, 1937–1940* (1952)

I. N. MACLEOD, *Neville Chamberlain* (1961)

I. M. MAISKY, *Who Helped Hitler?* (1964)

W. N. MEDLICOTT, *The Coming of War in 1939* (1963)

R. J. MINNEY, *The Private Papers of Hore-Belisha* (1960)

L. B. NAMIER, *Diplomatic Prelude* (1948)

E. M. ROBERTSON, *Hitler's Pre-War Policy and Military Plans 1933–1939* (1963)

W. R. ROCK, *Appeasement on Trial* (1966)

R. W. SETON-WATSON, *From Munich to Danzig* (1939)

E. SPIER, *Focus: A Footnote to the History of the Thirties* (1963)

A. J. P. TAYLOR, *The Origins of the Second World War* (1961)

C. K. WEBSTER, 'Munich reconsidered: a survey of British policy' (*International Affairs*, April 1961)

T. DESMOND WILLIAMS, 'Negotiations leading to the Anglo-Polish agreement of 31 March 1939' (*Irish Historical Studies*, 1957)

J. W. WHEELER-BENNETT, *Munich, Prologue to Tragedy* (1948)

Diplomacy at War, 1939–45

EARL OF AVON, *The Eden Memoirs: Facing the Dictators* (1965)

XAVIER DE BOURBON, PRINCE, *Les Accords Secrets Franco-Anglais de décembre 1940* (1949)

J. R. M. BUTLER, J. EHRMAN, and OTHERS, *Grand Strategy* (1956, continuing)

W. S. CHURCHILL, *The Second World War* (6 vols, 1948–54)

J. EHRMAN, 'Lloyd George and Churchill as War Ministers' (*Transactions, Royal Historical Society*, 1961)

E. ESTORICK, *Sir Stafford Cripps: a Biography* (1949)

H. FEIS, *Churchill–Roosevelt–Stalin* (1957)

D. L. GORDON and R. DANGERFIELD, *The Hidden Weapon* (1947)

H. DUNCAN HALL, *North American Supply* (1955); with C. G. WRIGLEY, *Studies of Overseas Supply* (1956)

T. HIGGINS, *Winston Churchill and the Second Front* (1957)

S. HOARE, *Ambassador on Special Mission* (1946)

H. KNATCHBULL-HUGESSON, *Diplomat in Peace and War* (1949)

W. L. LANGER, *Our Vichy Gamble* (1947); with S. E. GLEASON, *The Undeclared War* (1953)

W. N. MEDLICOTT, *The Economic Blockade* (2 vols, 1952, 1959)

A. S. MILWARD, *The German Economy at War* (1965)

NILS ØRVIK, *Norge i Brennpunktet* (1953)

R. J. SONTAG and J. S. BEDDIE, *Nazi-Soviet Relations 1939–1941* (1948)

E. L. WOODWARD, *British Foreign Policy in the Second World War* (1962); 'Some Reflections on British Policy, 1939–45' (*International Affairs*, July 1955)

British Foreign Policy since 1945

H. C. ALLEN, *The Anglo-American Predicament* (1960)

C. R. ATTLEE, *As It Happened* (1954)

EARL OF AVON, *The Eden Memoirs: Full Circle* (1960)

M. BELOFF, *New Dimensions in Foreign Policy* (1961)

M. and S. BROMBERGER, *Secrets of Suez* (1957)

M. B. BROWN, *After Imperialism* (1963)

J. F. BYRNES, *Speaking Frankly* (1947)

MIRIAM CAMPS, *Britain and the European Community, 1955–1963* (1963)

R. CROSSMAN, *A Nation Reborn* (1960)

H. DALTON, *Memoirs, 1945–60; High Tide and After* (1962)

L. D. EPSTEIN, *Britain – Uneasy Ally* (1954); *British Politics in the Suez Crisis* (1964)

H. FINER, *Dulles Over Suez* (1964)

A. G. B. FISHER, *International Implications of Full Employment in Great Britain* (1946)

M. A. FITZSIMONS, 'British Labour in search of a Socialist foreign policy' (*Review of Politics*, April 1950); *The Foreign Policy of the British Labour Government, 1945–1951* (1953)

R. W. GARDNER, *Sterling–Dollar Diplomacy* (1956)

G. GOODWIN, *Britain and the United Nations* (1957)

ROY E. JONES, 'Reflections upon an eventful period in Britain's foreign relations' (*International Relations*, October 1963)

J. B. KELLY, *Eastern Arabian Frontiers* (1964)

EARL OF KILMUIR, *Political Adventure* (1964)

W. C. MALLALIEU, *British Reconstruction and American Policy, 1945–1955* (1956); 'The origins of the Marshall Plan; A study in policy formulation and national leadership' (*Political Science Quarterly*, December 1958)

J. MARLOWE, *The Seat of Pilate: an Account of the Palestine Mandate* (1959)

F. V. MEYER, *The Seven* (1960)

F. S. NORTHEDGE, *British Foreign Policy: The Process of Readjustment, 1945–1961* (1962)

A. NUTTING, *Disarmament: an Outline of the Negotiations* (1959)

H. B. PRICE, *The Marshall Plan and its Meaning* (1955)

T. ROBERTSON, *Crisis, the Inside Story of the Suez Conspiracy* (1965)

H. SETON-WATSON, *Neither War nor Peace* (1960)

J. STRACHEY, *The End of Empire* (1959)

H. S. TRUMAN, *Year of Decisions 1945* (1955); *Years of Trial and Hope, 1946–53* (1956)

H. M. VINACKE, *The United States and the Far East, 1945–51* (1952)

P. WINDSOR, *City on Leave* (1963)

E. WISKEMANN, *Germany's Eastern Neighbours* (1956)

C. M. WOODHOUSE, *British Foreign Policy since the Second World War* (1961)

K. YOUNGER, *Changing Perspectives in British Foreign Policy* (1964)

Index